Jeanne McCarthy
621-3248

Families, Professionals, and Exceptionality

A Special Partnership

Ann P. Turnbull
University of Kansas
and
H. Rutherford Turnbull, III
University of Kansas
with
Jean Ann Summers
Mary Jane Brotherson
Holly Anne Benson

MERRILL PUBLISHING COMPANY
A Bell & Howell Company
Columbus Toronto London Sydney

Published by Merrill Publishing Company
A Bell & Howell Company
Columbus, Ohio 43216

This book was set in Souvenir.
Administrative Editor: Vicki Knight
Copyeditor: Fred Marcus
Cover Designer: Cathy Watterson
Production Coordinator: Anne Daly

Photo credits: Peter Sandrian, p. 1; Robbin Loomis Kern, pp. 23, 47, 67; the
Behr family, p. 85; Dutchie S. Riggsby, p. 113; Dave Lutz, pp. 137, 225, 253;
Democratic National Congressional Committee, p. 165; Renée Johnson, pp.
199, 277, 303; Darrell Sampson, p. 325.

The excerpt on pp. 260–261 is from *Selecting a Preschool: A Guide for Parents
of Handicapped Children* (Austin, Texas: Pro-Ed, 1984), pp. 102–103.
Reprinted by permission.

The excerpt on pp. 282–283 is from an essay by Martha Bernal, "Consumer
Issues in Parent Training," in *Parent Training: Foundations of Research and
Practice*, ed. by R. F. Danzel and R. A. Polster, pp. 487–488, copyright © 1984
by the Guilford Press. Reprinted by permission.

The Code of Ethics and Standards of Professional Practice on pp. 379–390 is
reprinted by permission of the Council for Exceptional Children.

Table 7–1 (pp. 142–143), Table 10–2 (pp. 242–244), the Family Assessment
Interview Guide (pp. 359–362), and the Family Information Preference
Inventory (pp. 368–373) may be reproduced for noncommercial purposes
without the publisher's prior written permission.

Library of Congress Catalog Card Number: 85-63033
International Standard Book Number: 0-675-20484-4
Printed in the United States of America
5 6 7 8 9 — 91 90 89

To Jay, Amy, and Kate—
each exceptional, each our family, and each our teacher,
enriching our personal and professional lives,

and

To Elizabeth M. Boggs—
family advocate and our mentor, whose shoes are too large for
us to fill but whose footprints are our landmarks

Preface

Families, Professionals, and Exceptionality: A Special Partnership concerns families, people who are exceptional, professionals, and how they can work together more effectively. Although this is not an original topic, the focus of this book is unique and the book itself is different from previous works in several important ways.

First, we deal with exceptionality in broad terms, addressing all types of disability (mental, emotional, physical, language, and sensory) and giftedness. We regard people with exceptionality as having essentially similar characteristics with respect to how they affect and are affected by their families and professionals. Accordingly, when we refer to people with exceptionalities, we include people who have disabilities as well as people who are gifted. But we recognize that there are distinctions that make a difference. People are different because of the type and extent of their exceptionality. We address their differences as well as their similarities.

Second, we do not keep our discussion within a particular age range. We address the needs of families and people with exceptionalities throughout their life cycles, from the earliest years, through childhood and school years, into adulthood. Although the subject matter requires that some aspects of the book have a deliberate school-years focus, for the most part, we deal with families at all life stages.

Third, we take into account the enormous variety in families and guide professionals through a systematic and scholarly analysis of families. We apply the family systems approach in the context of exceptionality accross the life cycle. In doing so, we present state-of-the art knowledge and reality-tested practice in family-professional relationships. We combine theory and application, not just in the four chapters that specifically address the family systems concept, but also throughout the book, showing in many chapters how professionals may work with families within that conceptual framework.

Fourth, we address the family in all of its diversity: in size, cultural background, geographic location, values, interaction styles, met and unmet needs and the changing characteristics of a given family over time. Moreover, by addressing the family as a system, we are not bounded by a focus on one member of a family, typically the person with an exceptionality. Indeed, we seek to show the complex inter-relatedness of all members of a family and the importance of adopting a comprehensive view of professional interventions. We stress that each family has its own critical balance, its peculiar center of gravity, to maintain if any professional intervention is to be beneficial to any family member or to the entire family. We encourage professional support of families.

Fifth, in using a broad approach to exceptionality and families, our aim is to make this book useful to a wide range of professionals—to people working in special education, social welfare, psychology, counseling, health and allied health, and even in seemingly tangential professions as the ministry and gerontology. Our orientation is consciously interdisciplinary, relying on the most recent comprehensive research in such fields as education, social work, counseling, law, and ethics, and providing relevant illustrations, suggestions, and organization.

Sixth, we draw heavily on the published and unpublished stories of families, with the option of using this book along with *Parents Speak Out: Then and Now,* a book edited by ourselves and published by Charles E. Merrill. Accordingly, we have seasoned this book with a compelling real-life flavor. We undergird its theories and concepts with the reality of the living laboratory, the reality of family life. Our own experience has added to this combination of theory and reality—the fact that our three children are exceptional, each in a different way. Our son Jay, who is mentally retarded, has been our catalyst for special personal insights that augment our decade-old professional research and service in human services and exceptionalities. Our contributing authors have highly respectable credentials in adult services, early childhood services, social welfare, and counseling.

Seventh, we have synthesized wide-ranging subjects. We emphasize, first, the history of parental roles in exceptionalities, then family systems concepts. After tying those concepts to family-professional communication skills and strategies, we present the dominant legal framework within which families and professionals work, and we conclude with a discussion and analysis of moral issues in family and professional relationships.

Finally, we convey optimism, hopefulness, and enthusiasm about families, people with exceptionalities, and family-professional relationships. In this respect, we emphasize the positive contributions that people with exceptionalities, their families, and professionals make to each other, and we reject the focus of so much other literature on pathologies and negative stereotypes related to exceptionality.

Our goal has been to organize knowledge so that it is understandable, holistic, and relevant. Above all else, our hope is that the information we present makes a positive difference in the lives of families and professionals.

We urge you to communicate with us at any time about ways we can enhance the relevance of the content in future editions.

A.P.T.
H.R.T.III
Lawrence, Kansas

Acknowledgements

In producing this book, we have been assisted immeasurably by staff of the University of Kansas at Lawrence. This book is the product of a *team effort*—typical of the Bureau of Child Research and Department of Special Education. The team members have cheerfully and conscientiously given their best efforts, and each has played a vital role in this book's production. They are Mary Beth Johnston, Dorothy Johanning, Marilyn Fischer, Connie Roeder-Gordon, Harriet Schaffer, Thelma Dillon, Lori Llewellyn, Joni Randel, Barbara Bartz, Lisa Wilshire, Jon Gaines, and Kiesa Harris. Numerous colleagues and students at this university and throughout the country have given us much help in making the book useful and relevant. We owe a special bouquet to Vicki Knight, our patient but persistent editor at Charles E. Merrill Publishing Company who has been supportive and helpful and with whom it has been a privilege to work. We also are indebted to the constructive criticism of Cindy Bernheimer (University of California at Los Angeles), Pam Winton (University of North Carolina at Chapel Hill), Joan Safran (Youngstown State University), George Sugai (University of Oregon), and Jane Morse during the review of the completed manuscript. We have had the pleasure to collaborate with our colleagues and friends, Jean Ann Summers, Mary Jane Brotherson, and Holly Benson; we value and appreciate their vital contributions. Finally, to the contributors to *Parents Speak Out* and other families who generously shared their experiences, we express deep gratitude.

Ann P. Turnbull
H. Rutherford Turnbull, III

Contents

CHAPTER 9
REFERRAL AND EVALUATION 199

CHAPTER 10
PARENT PARTICIPATION IN DEVELOPING THE IEP 225

Chapter 1

Historical and Current Roles of Parents

We begin by discussing the history of parent roles in the care and education of children with exceptionalities, for several reasons. First, history helps us understand current issues and approaches; indeed, many current issues relating to family adjustment and family-professional interactions are legacies from the past. Second, many of the challenges that families and professionals currently face can be aided by the lessons of history. Third, history provides insight into the fickle nature of seemingly entrenched approaches, for the pendulum has swung numerous times on family issues. Current approaches may seem as improbable to the 21st century as previous approaches seem now.

Parents have assumed or have been expected by professionals to assume eight major roles: parents as (a) the source of their child's problems, (b) organization members, (c) service developers, (d) recipients of professionals' decisions, (e) learners and teachers, (f) political advocates, (g) educational decision-makers, and (h) family members. These roles did not develop during, and do not represent, discrete time periods, each with a clear demarcation of beginning and end. Rather, there is significant overlapping of roles and eras. There is, however, a general and approximate chronological order of their respective beginning, peak period of emphasis, and decline. With this general background in mind, we will describe each of these 8 roles.

PARENTS AS THE PROBLEM SOURCE

The eugenics movement (1880-1930) contributed greatly to the view that parents are the source of a child's disability. The intent of the eugenics movement was to "improve" the human race through selective breeding. According to Scheerenberger (1983), it was based on (a) genealogical investigations such as Goddard's (1912) study of the Kallikak family, (b) rediscovery of Mendel's heredity laws, and (c) studies indicating that delinquent behaviors were strongly associated with "feeble-mindedness" (MacMurphy, 1916; Terman, 1916). Indeed, the eugenics movement asserted that heredity is the cause of mental retardation. Barr (1913), a leading physician during the eugenics movement, linked heredity with mental retardation:

> Heredity is herein proven law, as inexorable in the descending as it is beneficent in the ascending scale; heredity—whether it be direct from parent to child, collateral as from other relatives, or reversional reappearing ever and anon through generations—which none may escape.
>
> Again, a knowledge of causation and the assurance that many pathways lead to one condition of ill, idiocy—a condition which may be doubled and quadrupled through inheritance—should surely have its influence in induc-

ing the adoption of means of prevention, wiser and more humane than those practised by older nations to preserve the integrity of society. Not by destroying the life of the weakling but by refusing to allow him to perpetuate a maimed existence; next by a simplification of all life, be it the pursuit of wealth or learning, of occupation or amusement—a conservation in lieu of a dissipation of energy; then, after this elimination of harmful influences, such selection in mating, as shall insure only the survival of the fittest. (p. 123)

The eugenics movement resulted in laws restricting the marriage of persons with intellectual disabilities, requiring compulsory sterilization, and causing a sharp increase in institutionalization. Based on U.S. Department of Commerce (1923, 1934) data, Scheerenberger (1983) reported that 9,334 persons with mental retardation were institutionalized in 1900 and 68,035 in 1930.

The policies and practices of state institutions and hospitals further reinforced the view that parents have negative influences on their children. In *Parents Speak Out: Then and Now,* Tot Avis (1985), a social worker with extensive experience in institutional settings, described standard practices that existed even through the early 1970s:

Practices within institutions seemed to separate parents from their children. Visiting hours were limited, and sometimes visits were supervised. Permissions were required. It is not too hard to interpret that the child needs protection from the parents—or the reverse.

If, in the past, parents requested a home visit for their child, a social worker made a home study—another test of measuring up that parents had to weather. Old records show refusals of requests for visits because of housekeeping standards and other value judgments. Often the reasons given for refusal were that the child needed further training and time for adjustment. I am still not entirely sure what that meant, and in some instances we might wonder what training was being considered. However, if one had accepted the rationale that only professional people could care for the child, then there must be something (beyond a mere parent's understanding) that was going on that shouldn't be interrupted.

As if these elements weren't formidable enough, there was also the process of getting a question answered by mail. In some institutions responses to letters always were signed by the director or superintendent. This person was usually a physician and obviously a very important person since he was responsible for such a lot of people. Some people hesitated to ask or apologized for taking his time when what they wanted was news of their child's progress. When they did ask, responses were often terse and impersonal, lacking in warmth. Letters spontaneously sent from an institution to families indicated serious illness or an accident—or a Christmas appeal, hardly welcoming although understandable within the context of the time and the size of institutions. (pp. 188–189)

In other areas of exceptionality, parents were scorned for maladaptive personality traits and child-rearing practices. Often they were viewed as the source of their children's problems, particularly when the children had autism, asthma, and emotional disturbance. It was typical in the 1940s and 1950s for professionals to describe parents of autistic and psychotic children as rigid, perfectionistic, emotionally impoverished, and depressed (Kanner, 1949; Marcus, 1977). A leading professional, Dr. Bruno Bettleheim (1950; 1967), contended that the autistic child's severe withdrawal was a response to the stress created by parental attitudes and feelings. He even advocated "parentectomy," institutionalizing the child to replace parents with institutional staff and professionals considered more competent and caring. By contrast, a current definition of autism states that "no known factors in the psychological environment of a child have been shown to cause autism" (National Society for Autistic Children, 1977). In light of that definition, Frank Warren (1985), whose son has autism, discusses his reaction to Bettleheim's theory of causation:

> That means we didn't do it, Bruno. We've known that all along. It means that careful, objective, scientific people have carried out study after study, test after test, interview after interview, and have written paper after paper in journal after journal which show that we, the parents of autistic children, are just ordinary people. Not any crazier than others. Not "refrigerator parents" any more than others. Not cold intellectuals any more than others. Not neurotic or psychopathic or sociopathic or any of those words that have been made up. It means, Dr. Bettleheim, that you, and all those others like you who have been laying this incredible guilt trip on us for over 20 years, you are wrong and ought to be ashamed of yourselves. (p. 217)

Of course, some disabilities in children may be traced to the parents. For example, some conditions (e.g., cystic fibrosis) are clearly genetic in nature. Others (e.g., fetal alcohol syndrome) can be caused by a mother's excessive use of alcohol or drugs during pregnancy. Mild mental retardation can be caused by poor nourishment during pregnancy or in early life, or by the absence of parental stimulation during preschool years. In these cases, it may help in diagnosis to attribute the cause to parents, but will not if professionals who work with the child or family instill guilt in the parent or are unable to work effectively with the parent or child. The impact during this century of causation theories has sent many parents on a tremendous "guilt trip" and, in turn, has produced barriers to constructive parent-professional relationships—resentment, low self-esteem, lack of trust, and defensiveness.

Although causation theories have declined over the last 20 years, each of us can help eradicate erroneous accusations wherever they occur—whether in professional literature, teachers' lounges, or parent-professional conferences. Through our professional and personal experiences, we have come to the conclusion that parents do the best they can in the difficult circumstances they are facing, and that it is impossible to judge another person until we have "walked a mile in his moccasins."

PARENTS AS ORGANIZATION MEMBERS

Largely because of inadequate public and professional responses to their children's educational and other needs, and as a result of their own needs for emotional support, parents began to organize on a local level in the 1930s and on a national level in the late 1940s and 1950s. In 1933, 5 mothers of children with mental retardation in Cuyahoga County, Ohio organized a group to protest the public schools' exclusion of their children. Their efforts led to a special class that they themselves sponsored. In 1950, 42 parents and other concerned individuals from 13 states met in Minneapolis to establish the National Association of Parents and Friends of Mentally Retarded Children (now, ARC/USA—The Association for Retarded Citizens). Alan Sampson, the Chairman of the Steering Committee, set forth their mission when he gave the keynote address at their first convention:

> To me, this is a thrilling and auspicious occasion; another milestone, carved from travail and tears, and indomitable purpose, in the progress against intolerance, for understanding.
>
> Each of us present are here because originally we were selfish, we were hurt, chagrined, and bitter, and in trying to solve our own individual problems, we have, quite without knowing it, contributed to our own growth, and sensible acknowledgment as well as broadening the community acceptance of mental subnormality.
>
> First of all, why we do need a national organization: A fair question. One answer is that mental retardation is a national problem—an international one. Another reason is that other organizations to ameliorate health problems have grown to national stature. Anti-tuberculosis, Poliomyelitis, Crippled Children and Adults, Multiple Sclerosis, and others. Why do you immediately recognize these names, and this I'll answer, because they are national. They have a legitimacy, and standing, and recognition.
>
> It seems to me that we can stand up straight and throw our shoulders back and say, "now it's time to do something for the mentally deficient child," and unified in spirit and in purpose, as we hope to be now, our powerful voice will be heard.
>
> True, there are now and have been, professional organizations interested in this field, but their approach has been mostly scientific; they are small in

Table 1–1
MILEPOST ACCOMPLISHMENTS OF THE ASSOCIATION FOR
RETARDED CITIZENS

Mileposts

The Association for Retarded Citizens has worked for three decades to make a difference in the lives of mentally retarded people. A great deal has been accomplished. But none of it happened by chance. Change has occurred because as an Association we believe that retarded people can grow, can develop, can learn, and can be contributing members of society. Here are some of the ARC's major accomplishments.

1952   The Research Advisory Board was established; *Children Unlimited,* a newspaper, was produced by a volunteer editor.

1954   The first national headquarters opened in New York City; President Dwight Eisenhower declared the first National Retarded Children's Week.

1955   The Association's first film, "Tuesday's Child," was produced; membership rose to 29,000 with 412 local units.

1956   "Federal Program of Action for America's Retarded Children and Adults" was presented to Congress; testimony was provided on bills to expand teaching and research in the education of mentally retarded children.

1957   We supported social security coverage for adults disabled in childhood, funding for medical facilities for retarded persons through the Hill-Burton Act, and increased appropriations for vocational rehabilitation programs.

1958   *Mental Subnormality,* an important cornerstone in research literature in the field of mental retardation, reported findings of a three-year Association survey. Concurrently, support began for research projects and policies formulated for comprehensive programming and institutions.

1959   We published a landmark report, *Decade of Decision,* describing the Association's accomplishments and prospects for meeting service needs of retarded persons.

1960   *Decade of Decision* was presented to The White House Conference on Children and Youth; membership totaled 62,000; Association approved as one of 10 voluntary health organizations by the President's Committee on Fund Raising in the Federal Service.

1961   Under an Association grant, new screening test for phenylketonuria discovered by Dr. Robert Guthrie.

1956–   Federal support for mental retardation services and research increased
1961   from $14 million to $94 million.

1962   The Association received the Joseph P. Kennedy Foundation International Award.

1963   The President's Panel on Mental Retardation recommended the Mental Retardation Construction Act, maternity and child care projects, expansion of the Vocational Rehabilitation Act, and establishment of special education programs.

1964	Membership totaled 100,000; the first interorganization conference on mental retardation convened with representatives from 28 national organizations.
1965	Association On-the-Job Training Project was established.
1967	Youth NARC, now ARC Youth, founded at the National Convention in Portland, Oregon.
1968	ARC stepped up insistence on immediate eradication of inhumane treatment and improvement of institutional care.
1969	We co-sponsored Project Star, a national demonstration of minority and poverty outreach approaches. We initiated the annual Christmas card fundraising program.
1970's	National headquarters and state associations began assistance in the preparation of court suits to defend the rights of mentally retarded citizens in state institutions and to ensure their right to an education. We also became strong advocates of normalization, developmental approaches to retarded people, and community-based residential services.

The Association played a major role in the formation of the Developmental Disabilities Services and Facilities Construction Act and spearheaded the formation of the national Consortium Concerned with the Developmentally Disabled. We significantly expanded our involvement with the federal government. This included such diverse issues as immigration, benefits for dependents of service people, civil aeronautics authority regulations, fair labor standards as applied to mentally retarded workers, lead paint poisoning and immunization programs. |
1973–1976	We emphasized the complex issues surrounding the use of human subjects in research, both bio-medical and behavioral. We made one of the major presentations to the National Commission on Research on Human Subjects.
mid-1970s	The Association worked for two major programs which significantly impacted on the lives of retarded people—Supplemental Security Income and Title XX Social Services.
1975	The Association's Research and Demonstration Institute was founded.
1977	We announced the search for cures for conditions and disorders involved in mental retardation.
1978	Our activities concentrated on the extension of two acts, the Rehabilitation Act and the Developmental Disabilities Act. Included in the Developmental Disabilities Act was a refocusing of the entire program developed by the Association.
1979	We addressed the issue of meeting the mental health needs of retarded individuals and focused attention on legislation to ensure funding for community housing.
1980s	Emerging issues will require our energetic involvement on behalf of mentally retarded people. Service issues will require our continuing help so people can achieve a meaningful role in American society. We will also focus on prevention and cure related issues so we can give hope to the yet unborn generations.

Note: From Association for Retarded Citizens brochure, Association for Retarded Citizens. Adapted by permission.

members, and low in funds, and have had little encouragement from the public, or from state officials or actually from anyone. Now, we, the parents, joined in one unified body, with guidance and conviction, can support and expand the work. (National Association of Parents and Friends of Mentally Retarded Children, 1950, pp. 2–3)

Over the years the ARC has exerted a powerful influence at the national, state, and local level to represent the interests of persons with mental retardation and their families. Table 1–1 highlights ARC's major accomplishments.

United Cerebral Palsy Associations, Inc. (UCP) has a similar history. It was founded in 1949 largely through the efforts of Leonard H. Goldenson, the father of a child with cerebral palsy. Here is what he related about UPC's beginnings:

One day, realizing the cost of driving our child into New York City from Westchester, my wife said to me, "Leonard, I know we can afford to do this but what about the poor people? How can they afford to do it?" And she added "Why don't we look into the possibility of trying to help others in this field?"

It was on that basis that I started to investigate the whole field of cerebral palsy.

Actually, cerebral palsy are words that at that time generally were not in use. The word *spastic* was used, which really was not an all-inclusive title because, as you know, that's only one form of cerebral palsy.

Upon investigation, I found there were probably only twenty-some-odd doctors in the entire United States who knew anything about cerebral palsy. I found there were only a few local parents groups in the country that were trying to do something about it. But the parents were so involved with their own children and had to take so much time with them, they could not get out to raise money and inform the public about the subject. (Goldenson, 1965, pp. 1–2)

The original UCP purposes were

1. To further by publication and education the knowledge of the causes and treatment of cerebral palsy and to promote the application of such knowledge to provide better and more adequate techniques and facilities for the diagnosis and treatment of sufferers of cerebral palsy.
2. To promote a normal outlook for the cerebral palsied.
3. To promote the employment of the cerebral palsied.
4. To provide scholarships, endowments for the care, rehabilitation, education, and employment of the cerebral palsied.
5. To cooperate with governmental and private agencies concerned with the welfare of the physically handicapped.

6. To promote research and circulate information valuable to all persons concerned in the care of, rehabilitation, education, and employment of cerebral palsied.
7. To solicit, collect, and otherwise raise money for the above purposes and for the purpose of endowing facilities for the care, treatment, and study of sufferers of cerebral palsy.
8. To establish local chapters and to cooperate with them for the above purposes. (The United Cerebral Palsy Association, 1950, p. 3)

By 1983 UCP had grown to 228 local affiliate organizations with a total financial income exceeding $184 million. Its current program priorities include advocacy, family life skills, respite care (child-care services to allow parents a respite from child rearing responsibilities), independent living, and least restrictive alternative. (The last term refers to opportunities for people with disabilities to live, attend school, work, and recreate in settings with persons who are not disabled.)

Other parent groups have been organized—the National Society for Autistic Children in 1961, the National Association for Down Syndrome in 1961, and the Association for Children with Learning Disabilities in 1964. During the early 1960s when other parent groups were forming or flourishing, Lucito (1963) shared his views of barriers facing parents of students with giftedness:

> Another value high in most societies is that a person is not supposed to publicize his own virtues—society insists upon modesty from its members. This makes it difficult for parents of the gifted child to acknowledge publicly that their child is gifted. A typical statement from parents of a gifted child is: "Something should be done for the gifted, but my child is not gifted. He is just a *good, average* student." One of the common mechanisms used by other areas of exceptionality and regular education is to organize support from the parents of the students. As long as modesty hinders a large number of parents from admitting their child is gifted, they are not able to identify with any parent group working toward a betterment of educational practices for the gifted. Parents of gifted children are probably the most unorganized of all parent groups. (p. 225)

In 1981, there were 123 local and state parent groups for students with giftedness in 37 states (Grossi, 1981).

Undoubtedly, parent groups have exerted a profound influence by creating opportunities for children and providing hope and support to families. (Two major areas of impact are in service delivery and political advocacy, which will be discussed separately in two later sections.) Parent organizations, however, do not meet the needs of every parent. For instance, one mother is very satisfied with her role in a parent organization:

I am proud to be the only person who has been continuously active in some volunteer capacity within the National Association for Retarded Citizens since I participated in its founding in 1950. I believe that NARC has a unique role to play, and that the existence of a strong lay advocacy group which continues to recognize and respond to the great diversity of need among persons called retarded is the single most essential element in securing their future. I have jealously guarded my amateur status within the association even when positions as a consultant and lecture fees have come my way on the outside. In the early days I carried out many unbudgeted assignments which are now executed by paid staff. In recent years I have been able to accentuate multiple linkages with other agencies and movements that no one with ties to a paid position could have made. The cause has taken me to 44 states, plus Puerto Rico and 10 foreign countries. It is hard to put a job title on the role I've played. One could say that I've been a social synergist with a predisposition toward communication and collaboration rather than confrontation. (Boggs, 1985, pp. 39–40)

By contrast, another mother is not satisfied at all:

My first phone call to my local unit produced a pleasant enough response from the office secretary and a promise of some information to be mailed. This material consisted of a short summary of the unit's programs and services and a long questionnaire on which I could indicate areas in which I would be delighted to volunteer. There were numberless areas where I would be useful to the unit; there seemed little they had to offer me. The meetings sounded dull and preoccupied with large and small bureaucratic issues; nothing seemed to have a bearing on Kathryn's development until she could attend a nursery class three years hence. The message was clear: a parent in my circumstances, trying to cope with a trauma of uncertain dimensions, should marshal her forces, muster her energies, and get out and work for the cause. . . .

If I had had an unretarded baby, I'd never in a million years have thought of volunteering for anything during that period. Now that I had Kathryn, why in the world would I be expected to do anything of the kind? Yet in the face of minimal help from the organization, it was telling me I should help it. And numb from shock and diminished self-confidence, I did my best to comply. (Bennett, 1985, p. 163, 164)

Moreover, a government committee's findings indicated that parent organizations tend to consist primarily of white, middle-class parents, and that minority parents and parents who are very rich or very poor tend not to join (President's Committee on Mental Retardation, 1977). Another trend is the "graying of parent organizations" described by Alice Scrogin, the President of the Association for Children with Learning Disabilities (ACLD) in the ACLD *Newsbriefs* in 1979:

The older parents are now tired veterans who had expected the younger parents to replace them, to refresh the troops in the struggle. They find that many younger parents with learning disabled children take special education for granted. (Serf, 1979, p. 53)

Please note this phenomenon is not unique to ACLD; rather, it is occurring in parent organizations representing the range of exceptionalities. Thus, you should keep in mind that some parents, but not others, are helped by parent organizations. The "parent movement" is helpful to many parents, but it is not for everyone.

PARENTS AS SERVICE DEVELOPERS

Another parental role, developed largely through the concerted effort of parent organizations, is to help develop services for persons with exceptionalities. To begin with, the emphasis in the 1950s and 1960s was on creating education programs for children who had moderate and severe disabilities and who were excluded from public schools. Local parent groups organized classes in community buildings or church basements and solicited financial support from charitable organizations. Over the years, parent organizations initiated services in education, recreation, residential living (group homes), and vocational alternatives. Some parent organizations started the necessary services and have devoted a substantial portion of their time to operate them. Other organizations adopted the role of a catalyst for services, and they work with other community organizations such as public and private schools, recreation agencies, and social service agencies (President's Committee on Mental Retardation, 1977). Still others combine the two roles, serving as advocates and watchdog agencies while providing services to satisfy unmet needs.

It is important to recognize the profound impact of parents in developing special education services, an impact described by Kirk (1984), a distinguished special educator over the last five decades:

It has been a source of satisfaction to participate and help the parent movements—first, for children with cerebral palsy, then for the mentally retarded, and lastly, for the learning disabled. I found a satisfaction in associating with many intelligent and knowledgeable parents in these organizations. I found that through association with other parents they learned what the best programs were for their children. If I were to give credit to one group in this country for the advancements that have been made in the education of exceptional children, I would place the parent organizations and parent movement in the forefront as the leading force. (p. 41)

Although the role of service developer and provider interests some parents, professionals should not expect parents to start services within the professionals' own realm of responsibility. Parents for example, should not be expected to start a vocational training program for students with disabilities, just as parents of other children would not be expected to start a college preparatory curriculum in their local high schools. Parents have full rights to collaborate with professionals in making educational decisions (see Chapter 8), but they should not have to assume full responsibility as did Elizabeth Boggs and her fellow parents in the early 1950s.

Currently, many parents within and outside of parent organizations devote substantial efforts to the development of services other than education—scouting, religious education programs in churches, community recreation, and adult services. In these areas, their children usually do not have the same right to services as they do in education. This fact requires professionals to be especially aware of the time binds caused by innumerable family and work responsibilities that constrict many parents (Turnbull & Winton, 1984).

PARENTS AS RECIPIENTS OF PROFESSIONALS' DECISIONS

During the 1950s through 1970s, a primary role of parents was to enroll their children in programs and comply with the professionals' decisions. This role applied particularly to parents whose children were mildly disabled and served by the public school system. Many professionals expected that parents should defer decision-making to them, as in a leading methods textbook of this period:

> Should it be judged that special class placement will probably be of most benefit to the child, then placement should be made without delay. . . . The entire program should be explained so the parents will understand what lies ahead for the child and so they can support the efforts of the teachers with the child. The special class should be described as an opportunity, not a punishment for poor accomplishment or bad behavior. (Kolstoe, 1970, p. 42)

Another example from the 1960s addresses the alternative roles of educators and parents of gifted students in making placement decisions:

> Frank discussions between lay groups, local educators, and representatives of state and federal offices of education are needed to clarify the roles each can play most effectively. Some "guts" to speak straight from the shoulder would be helpful to the educators in this situation. Then the lay groups probably would realize they must delegate some of their authority to the educators to make necessary decisions for improving the education of students. For example, an overwhelming majority of parents do not have the

sophistication in educational matters to decide whether or not their young-ster would be better off educationally if placed in a differential program for the gifted. The decision of placing or retaining a student in first, second, or third grade is of the same technical order as placing students in other educational groupings. Parents could better spend their time: (a) supporting parent organizations for raising funds and influencing state and federal legislation, and (b) learning techniques to aid their own youngsters toward high achievement. (Lucito, 1963, pp. 227–228)

These passages indicate a tenor of the times—first, professionals were expected to make educational decisions and then interpret these decisions to parents, and, second, parents were expected not to question profes-sionals and to be appreciative recipients of services.

This expectation of a passive role for parents definitely has decreased during the last 10 to 15 years; however, it still pervasively exists in practice. Professionals who believe that parents should be seen but not heard convey this message both directly and indirectly. Moreover, they create an important psychological barrier to effective parent-professional relation-ships. (Turnbull, 1983)

PARENTS AS LEARNERS AND TEACHERS

The role of parents as learners and teachers emerged in the late 1960s, peaked in the 1970s, and appears to be somewhat declining in the 1980s. Several factors have contributed to the development of this role. In education and psychology, the influence of the environment on intelli-gence was receiving increased recognition (Hunt, 1972). And, in political debates, the New Frontier and the Great Society of the Kennedy and Johnson administrations were initiating compensatory education pro-grams, such as Head Start.

A premise of these programs was that the cultural deficits of parents from minority backgrounds resulted in inadequate child-rearing skills. Thus, programs such as Head Start offered parent training programs, directed at teaching parents how to be better teachers of their children, so their children would, in turn, make more progress.

This approach was generalized to parents of children with exceptionali-ties. Parents were viewed as agents for increasing children's progress and achievement; the professional view was that parents must first learn before they can teach. Parent training programs taught behavioral principles to parents, who then were expected to work with their children at home. Enthusiasm was sparked by encouraging results that documented the effectiveness of parents as teachers of their children (Bricker & Bricker, 1976; Shearer & Shearer, 1977). Professionals, more emphatically than parents, served as proponents of the parent-as-teacher role.

Because parents *could* be effective teachers, many professionals believed that parents *should* be teachers. They also believed that "good" parents taught their children frequently (Benson & Turnbull, in press).

The use of the term *parent* is actually a misnomer in this context. It is more correct to say that "good" *mothers* taught their children frequently. The professional emphasis was on the mother being her child's teacher. The literature of this period contains almost no reference to the role of fathers in their children's development.

Early childhood education programs have stressed parent training. Consider the following passage describing the type of parent involvement expected in the Handicapped Children's Early Education Program Network (early childhood projects), funded by the U.S. Department of Education:

> It thus becomes mandatory that projects develop training programs for parents with the objective of teaching parents to be effective in working with and teaching their own child. (Shearer & Shearer, 1977, p. 213)

Given the strong emphasis on the parent-as-teacher role, Karnes and Teska (1980) identified the competencies that parents need to acquire to carry out this role:

> The parental competencies required for direct teaching of the handicapped child at home involve interacting with the child in ways that promote positive behavior; reinforcing desired behavior; establishing an environment that is conducive to learning; setting up and maintaining a routine for direct teaching; using procedures appropriate for teaching concepts and skills; adapting lesson plans to the child's interests and needs; determining whether the child has mastered knowledge and skills; keeping meaningful records, including notes on child progress; participating in a staffing of the child; communicating effectively with others; and assessing the child's stage of development. (p. 99)

It is important to note that these are less than half of the parental skills they identified as essential to the home-teaching role. You may be interested in comparing these competencies to the ones in your professional training programs. However, we question whether it is realistic to expect parents to engage in this role to such a substantial degree.

The impact of the parent-as-teacher role on parent-child relationships has received negligible professional attention. Anecdotal accounts from some parents indicate the occurrence of unintended consequences, such as guilt and anxiety if they are not constantly working with their child. Other parents have found their role as their child's teacher to be very satisfying. As we repeatedly point out, different roles have different impacts on different parents.

One reason that the role of parents as learners and teachers has declined recently is the relatively low attendance rate at training sessions (Chilman, 1973; Rosenberg, Reppucci, & Linney, 1983). It appears that many parents have increasingly less time to carry out the learning and teaching roles—particularly in cases of single parents, or where both parents are employed outside the home. Yet many parents would like to have more information (not necessarily formal classes) on various topics.

The almost exclusive emphasis on behavioral training programs in the 1970s has changed so that today training opportunities are available on topics such as educational advocacy, teaching academic and preacademic skills, and future planning. Chapter 12 addresses the information needs of families and strategies for providing information.

PARENTS AS POLITICAL ADVOCATES

Parents were tremendously successful as advocates in the political process, but they had to work for many years and in many different forums of advocacy to obtain services. For example, during the decade from 1949-1959 the number of states providing special education for students with mild retardation (educable) rose from 24 to 46 and for students with moderate mental retardation (trainable) from very few to 37 (President's Committee on Mental Retardation, 1977). Still, services for students with severe and profound disabilities lagged behind during this period.

An advocacy landmark occurred in the late 1960s when parents of students with mild to severe mental retardation, in collaboration with the Pennsylvania Association for Retarded Children, sued the state to obtain a free appropriate education for all children with disabilities (*Pennsylvania Association for Retarded Citizens v. Commonwealth of Pennsylvania,* 1972). They won their lawsuit, and the court held that all children with mental retardation must be provided with a free public program of education and training.

Right-to-education suits were brought thereafter in almost every state, usually successfully. The time thus was right to establish by federal legislation what had been decreed in the courts as a matter of state law and federal constitutional right (Turnbull, 1986). Parent organizations from all areas of exceptionality, particularly the ARC-USA, joined forces with parents who were not organization members and with professionals, particularly the Council for Exceptional Children, to seek comprehensive federal legislation mandating that all students with disabilities be provided a free and appropriate public education. They were immensely successful, and Congress passed the Education of the Handicapped Act in 1970, an amendment in 1973, the Education for All Handicapped Children Act (P.L. 94–142) in 1975, and two amendments since then (1978 and 1983). We discuss this law in detail in Chapter 8. It is a tribute to parent advocacy—greatly aided by and sometimes led by professional organizations—that these laws have been passed and improved, that the parent organizations were able to form coalitions with each other and with professional groups, and that all of this has been accomplished over such an extended period of time in a continuous and consistent manner.

In addition to an education focus, parent advocacy has targeted the standards of treatment in institutions, the development of community-based living facilities, personnel training, research in prevention and amelioration, Social Security entitlements, architectural accessibility, and anti-discrimination legislation.

The role of parents as political advocates continues in the 1980s with a strong and powerful constituency. Lowell Weicker (1985), a United States senator from Connecticut and a father of a son with Down syndrome, described the impact of political advocacy on the Reagan administration's attempts to de-emphasize the federal role in special education:

> The administration did not get its way. Why? Because the disabled people in this country and their advocates repudiated a long-held cliché that they were not a political constituency, or at least not a coherent one. It was assumed that in the rough and tumble world of politics they would not hold their own as a voting block or as advocates for their cause. But that assumption was blown to smithereens in the budget and policy deliberations of 1981, 1982, and again in 1983. In fact, I would be hard-pressed to name another group within the human service spectrum that has not only survived the policies of this administration but has also defeated them as consistently and as convincingly as the disabled community has. Indeed, it has set an example for others, who were believed to be better organized. (p. 284)

Senator Weicker sums up the role of parents as political advocates in these words:

> To say for our children what they would say if they had access to power— that is our responsibility as parents. We have an obligation to repair and strengthen the bridges Congress has built to bring disabled Americans into the mainstream of life. Those who would bomb those bridges must be stopped by astute political organizing and grassroots action at the local and national level. (p. 286)

PARENTS AS EDUCATIONAL DECISION-MAKERS

The role of parents as educational decision-makers was established in 1975 when Congress enacted the Education of the Handicapped Act

(EHA). This law is revolutionary because it contains numerous requirements granting active decision-making rights to parents of children, and youth with disabilities. But the law also is very traditional, because it recognizes the very important role that parents play in their children's development and the necessity for subjecting schools to parental oversight. Parents have traditionally had oversight opportunities through mechanisms such as local school boards. (Although children with giftedness are not included in the federal laws for children having disabilities, they do receive aid under other federal laws and some state laws.)

An analysis of the testimony recorded in the Congressional Record prior to the passage of the EHA revealed the intentions of Congress in granting these pervasive parent rights (Turnbull, Turnbull, & Wheat, 1982). Congress's basic premise was that parents of children with disabilities could make no assumptions that schools would educate their children—that schools would even allow parents to enroll their children, much less that schools would educate the children appropriately. Thus, Congress viewed parents as agents for accountability, as persons who should or could ensure that professionals provide an appropriate education. This view, promoted by the political advocacy of some parents, reflected a major switch in expectations about parents' roles. No longer were parents to be passive recipients of professionals' decisions concerning services to their children. Now, they were to be educational decision-makers.

Many parents are keenly aware of this change. Prior to the EHA, they were simply told by school administrators whether and how their children were to be educated. They knew that their children's education depended on the discretion of the administrators. But now, given their children's right to an education and their rights as parents, parent-professional relationships have become more equal, and parents by and large are justified in believing that they can help shape their children's present and future capabilities (see Chapter 8).

Similarly, federal laws dealing with the training, habilitation, and rehabilitation of adults with disabilities also give parents—and, of course, the people with disabilities themselves—a right to participate in the development and implementation of individualized habilitation programs. Again, these laws stress the role of parents as partners with service professionals.

Just as all parents are not eager to be teachers of their children or political advocates, neither have all parents embraced the role of educational decision-maker (Turnbull & Turnbull, 1982). Research over the last 10 years indicates that the majority of parents participate in educational decision-making in a passive rather than active style (Goldstein, Strickland, Turnbull, & Curry, 1980; Lusthaus, Lusthaus, & Gibbs, 1981; Lynch & Stein, 1982).

Moreover, there are significant barriers to active decision-making by parents (see Chapter 10). Carol Michaelis, a mother of five children, one of whom is disabled, identified some of the problems associated with this role:

> Since funding for Special Education was tenuous, it also meant that to keep (my son) Jim in the class, I had to be involved. I lobbied at the school board and in the legislature. Keeping Jim in school also meant leaving housework and babies to attend parent conferences across town. No wonder I didn't have time to even try to mainstream myself into the coffee-cup conversation in the neighborhood kitchens. . . . Although sophisticated services are being implemented in many places, the Individualized Education Program conferences, the school visits, and the parent groups take more time for already busy parents. Early intervention means all of this starts sooner and it is possible that the parent and the child are labelled and out of the mainstream even sooner. (Michaelis, 1981, p. 15)

The role of parents as educational decision-makers, in addition to the roles as learners/teachers and political advocates, has focused primarily on the needs of the child or youth with a disability. Parental expectations have been defined in relation to that one individual. The parent perspective revealed by Michaelis indicates that parents have needs in addition to those associated with any of their children.

PARENTS AS FAMILY MEMBERS

Currently, professionals and parents alike are recognizing and emphasizing the role of parents as family members. This role is based on the premise that successful family life requires that the needs of all family members, including parents, be identified and addressed. This premise is consistent with family systems theory, which views the family as a social system with unique characteristics and needs. A basic premise is that the individual members of a family are so interrelated that any experience affecting one member will affect all (Carter & McGoldrick, 1980; Goldenberg & Goldenberg, 1980; Minuchin, 1974). For example, a mother might be so heavily involved in teaching her child and participating in educational decision-making that she neglected to spend adequate time with her husband and other children, and she ignored her own personal needs. Whereas an earlier focus was almost exclusively on the parents (or mother) and their involvement with their child with an exceptionality, now more attention is being given to the diverse needs of each family member and the competing time and responsibility demands placed on parents. Ann Turnbull (1985) illustrates the importance of this perspective:

After Jay returned home (from a private institution for preschoolers, there being none available locally), Rud and I found ourselves overwhelmed with advocacy responsibilities which we felt were our duty as parents of a retarded child. We had meetings on an average of four or five nights a week. We were actively involved with the Association for Retarded Citizens, the group home and sheltered workshop boards of directors, a day-care coalition, a special education task force for the local schools, and a coalition aimed at legislative impact. We were constantly on the go and had little time for family relaxation. It occurred to us that we had brought Jay home from an institution only to leave him with a baby sitter while we went out and advocated for him. I could not help wondering why I saw so few of my professional colleagues at these evening meetings. Rud and I began to question whether the concept of normalization applies to families of handicapped individuals as well as to handicapped persons themselves. There was nothing normal about our schedules. We were not just consumers; rather we were consumed by the need to establish programs and services for Jay. When we reached the point of exhaustion and frustration, we realized that family priorities had to take precedence over advocacy needs. (p. 134)

This example demonstrates the essence of a family systems perspective—that it is responsive to family priorities related to every member of the family, not just the facet with an exceptionality.

The role of parents as family members is manifold. There is increased emphasis on deinstitutionalization—preventing institutionalization by helping families to stay intact, and returning persons who have been institutionalized to home and community environments (Conroy, 1985; Willer & Intagliata, 1984). Parents are viewed as capable of providing a nurturing home environment rather than as needing to abdicate their parental responsibilities to the professional staff of institutions. Further, interventions such as respite care provision of financial subsidies to families with members who have a severe disability, and sibling support groups are examples of interventions that support the role of parents as family members.

Over the last several years, we and our colleagues have synthesized the literature in sociology on family systems theory with the literature in special education on the impact of children and youth with exceptionalities on their families (Benson & Turnbull, in press; Turnbull, Summers, & Brotherson, 1984; Turnbull, Brotherson, & Summers, 1985). We have proposed a framework, depicted in Figure 1-1, to organize family systems concepts. Here are the four major components of this framework:

1. *Family resources* consists of the descriptive elements of the family, including characteristics of the exceptionality (e.g., type, level of severity); characteristic of the family (e.g., sizes and forms, cultural

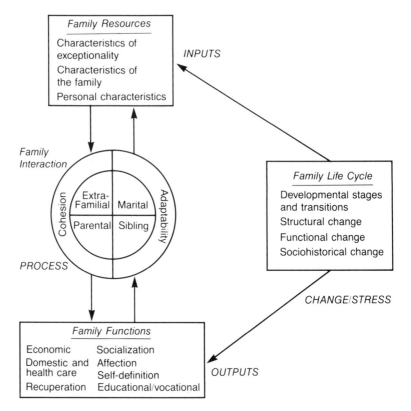

Figure 1–1
FAMILY SYSTEMS CONCEPTUAL FRAMEWORK

Note: From Working with Families with Disabled Members: A Family Systems Approach (p. 60) by A. P. Turnbull, J. A. Summers, and M. J. Brotherson, 1984, Lawrence, KS, Kansas University Affiliated Facility, University of Kansas.

backgrounds, socioeconomic status, geographic locations); and personal characteristics (e.g., health, intellectual capacity, and coping styles). From a systems perspective, resources can be thought of as the *input* into family interaction.

2. *Family interaction* refers to the relationships that occur among subgroups of family members on a daily and weekly basis. These relationships, the *process* of interaction, are responsive to individual and collective family needs.

3. *Family functions* represent the different categories of needs the family is responsible for addressing. The purpose or *output* of family interaction is to produce responses to fulfill the needs associated with family functions.

4. *Family life* cycle represents the sequence of developmental and nondevelopmental *changes* that affect families. These changes alter family resources (e.g., a child is born) and family functions (e.g., mother stops working outside the home, which provides more time for child-rearing but less family income). These changes, in turn, influence how the family interacts.

Chapters 2–5 discuss these four components of the family systems framework. These chapters emphasize family system concepts and the application of concepts to professionals working with families.

Recognizing that parents are family members with myriad responsibilities and individual needs and preferences has a profound influence on parent-professional relationships in special education settings. The same concept of individualization embraced by the field of special education as pertinent to children and youth also applies to parents and other family members. A family systems philosophy suggests that an understanding of family resources, interaction, functions, and life-cycle can serve as the basis of meaningfully individualizing parent-professional relationships for the benefit of all concerned—the child, parents, other family members, and professionals. Furthermore, we can begin to consider family-professional relationships rather than merely parent-professional relationships.

SUMMARY

Many different parent roles have existed during this century. These include parents as the sources of their child's problems, organization members, service organizers, recipients of professionals' decisions, learners and teachers, political advocates, educational decision-makers, and family members. No role can characterize all parents. Parents vary in the roles they assume, and professionals vary in the roles they consider appropriate and, in turn, recommend to and expect from parents.

The pendulum has swung in many ways: from viewing parents as part of the problem to viewing them as a primary solution to the problem, from expecting passive roles to expecting active roles, from viewing families as a mother-child dyad to recognizing the presence and needs of all members and from assigning generalized expectations from the professionals' perspective to allowing for individualized priorities defined from each family's perspective. Parents and professionals alike may feel caught up in time-zone changes, much like world travellers. Avis (1985) has described the concept of "deinstitutionalization jet lag," referring to parents who were told years ago the state institution was best for their child, and who currently are told the community is preferable. But professionals also experience "parent-role jet lag." Expectations and philosophies have drastically changed since the eugenics movement and the initial formation of parent organizations. Understanding the distance that has been travelled in this chapter provides a foundation for the forthcoming journey into the family systems orientation. This journey starts by considering the vast diversity in resources characterizing family life.

Chapter 2
Family Resources

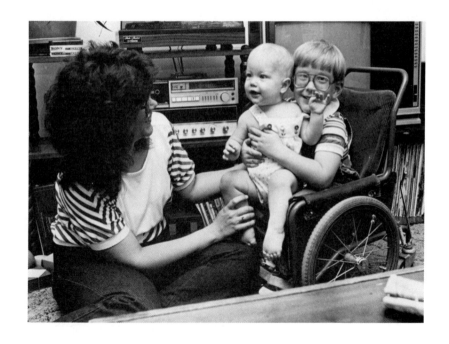

The word *family* brings to mind the nostalgic picture of a mother, father, and two or three children living together at home. The father works during the week and spends evenings and weekends repairing things, mowing the yard, and playing with the children. The mother keeps house and nourishes body and soul with home-cooked meals and plenty of love. Grandparents are nearby ready to take the kids fishing, bake cookies, and dole out wise counsel. And on Thanksgiving all the aunts, uncles, and cousins gather for a day of family solidarity and joyous feasting.

The truth is, however, that few American families fit this nostalgic picture. People are delaying marriage longer and choosing to live alone more often. Couples who do marry are increasingly likely to choose not to have children or to have only one (Masnick & Bane, undated). In 1980, 43% of adult women in the United States were in the workforce (Hobbs, Dokecki, Hoover-Dempsey, Moroney, Shayze, & Weeks, 1984). In 1978, that figure included over half of all mothers with children under 18 (Masnick & Bane, n.d.). In addition to the increase in the number of two-worker households is the equally familiar increase in the divorce rate. Today about 40% of marriages end in divorce; one in five children of school age are living in single-parent households (Drake & Shellenberger, 1981).

Historians tell us that the concern these statistics raise is nothing new. People in this country have decried the "decline" of the idealized nuclear family since the American Revolution, and it is doubtful that a "typical" American family ever existed (Hareven, 1982). But whether or not we are witnessing fundamental changes in family structure, the point is that few people live in a "traditional" nuclear family.

Beyond their demographic characteristics, families vary in a multitude of other ways. They differ in religion, ethnic background, education, and wealth. They differ in their location—rural, urban, suburban. They differ in their values—what they think is important in life—and in their beliefs about how people should and should not behave. They differ in the number of friends and extended family members. They differ in their personal idiosyncracies and orientations toward daily living. It is probably safe to say, given all the different ways families can vary, that *every family is idiosyncratic, if not unique.*

Yet despite the fact that statistics about divorce and working mothers are familiar features in the media, and despite the fact that all of us were raised since grade school with stories of the American melting-pot and its rich cultural diversity, the nostalgic image of the "traditional" family continues to cloud professional-family relationships. Family support and parent involvement programs for families with children with exceptionalities often are best suited for nuclear two-parent, one-worker, middle-class families— a minority in today's society. The first step in working with families, then, is to understand their diversities. The idea of diversity leads to the firm belief that you need to individualize your approach to families.

Understanding that you should individualize, however, how do you accomplish this? First consider more specifically how families differ and how those differences shape the impact of the child's exceptionality on that family. The range of reactions to an exceptionality in turn shapes the varying needs of families for different kinds of support and involvement.

There are three important considerations in the way an exceptionality affects a given family. First, *the characteristics of the exceptionality itself shape the family's reaction.* Exceptionality, a broad term, includes students who are gifted as well as those with severe and multiple disabilities. Exceptionality includes non-normative conditions of a person's senses (hearing and sight), health (heart, lungs, or other internal organs), body (limbs), mind (mental capacity or learning ability), psyche (emotional disturbance), and language (speech). We will explore how the nature of the exceptionality may create different effects on families in the first section of this chapter.

Second, *the characteristics of families shape their reaction to the exceptionality.* The family's cultural background, socioeconomic status, size, and other characteristics can be potential resources to enable the family to cope with their child's exceptionality. Some of these characteristics, such as membership in a minority culture or single-parenthood, also create special issues for school professionals. The possible differences in any family member's reaction to exceptionalities, and special considerations for professional-family relationships as a result of these family characteristics, will be the topic of the second section.

Finally, *every family is composed of individuals, each of whom has personal resources and problems.* In some cases these personal characteristics (for example, parents with disabilities or families involved in abuse and neglect) present special issues. In other cases the individual styles of coping with an exceptionality serve as resources that professionals can help strengthen. The third section of this chapter will explore some of these issues.

CHARACTERISTICS OF THE EXCEPTIONALITY

The nature of the exceptionality is closely related to the family's reaction to it. An uninsured condition requiring frequent medical attention may be a severe drain on the family's finances. A child with a terminal illness poses issues of grief and loss. A child with a hearing impairment presents a communication problem that pervades everyday existence—how to understand what the child wants and how to make sure the child is understanding the rest of the family. One father expressed his frustration when his daughter with profound deafness had to be hospitalized with meningitis:

> Right now, when we needed to communicate with her the most, we could not. Our own daughter—and we hardly knew her! What if she never recovered? She could lip-read several hundred isolated words, but she couldn't speak her own name. She had never said "I'm tired," "I'm hungry" or "My tummy hurts." She had never said "I love you." She had never asked for a doll or a stuffed teddy bear. She had never told us what she liked or wanted or who she played with.
>
> Communication! That's what we had been denied. An uncontrollable anger welled up within me. We had been cheated—it wasn't fair! Why? Why? Why? (Spradley & Spradley, 1978, p. 189)

In addition to the type of exceptionality, the severity of the exceptionality creates differences in families. One is tempted to assume that a more severe exceptionality will mean a more intense family impact, but such a formula does not always work in practice. The effects may be qualitatively, but not quantitatively, different. If a child has a severe disability, it may be apparent at birth and parents must deal immediately with the shock (Fortier & Wanlass, 1984). When the disability appears later, the parents may not feel so much shock as a sense of relief that their nagging doubts have been resolved (Lonsdale, 1978). On the other hand, when the exceptionality is discovered later, parents may have to cope with a complex set of emotions. With a learning disability, for example, there may be no identification of a problem until a child enters school, or parents may react with anger to the hyperactivity or "willfulness" that may often characterize a young child with a learning disability (Faerstein, 1981). After the child's problem is identified, the parents may feel a sense of guilt because they "pushed" the child or were angry (Faerstein, 1981).

Also, severe exceptionalities are often more visible. On the one hand, this fact may excuse a child's inappropriate public behavior. On the other hand, the family may experience more stigma and rejection from the public. Milder exceptionalities may be invisible, leading siblings to worry whether something is wrong with them, also (Powell & Ogle, 1985). With a severe disability, the family's adjustment to the idea of future dependency can be made fairly early (Turnbull, Summers, & Brotherson, 1984). But with a milder disability, the family may find itself on a roller coaster of expectations, with hopes for the future alternately raised and dashed as the child makes progress or falls back (Wadsworth & Wadsworth, 1971).

Nor is stress precluded for a family with a child who is gifted. Parents may be concerned about just how much they can or should sacrifice the needs of other family members in order to develop a child's musical or artistic talent. The family may be exhausted by a young child's continual questions and explorations. Or, if the family has traditional values about sex roles, there may be a concern about a gifted daughter's career ambitions and her potential to attract a husband (Perino & Perino, 1981). The demands of a child's exceptionality are another factor affecting its impact on the family. Beckman (1983) found that 66% of the variance in mothers' stress could be accounted for by unusual caretaking demands of infants with disabilities, including fussiness, irritability, and a lack of responsiveness. An older child with a physical disability may require feeding, toileting, catheterization, medication, lifting, bathing, dressing, or other physical care that most children of the same age provide themselves.

Of all the caretaking demands, however, none seems to have more impact than the demands of coping with a child who has a behavior problem. Frank Warren (1985) describes this effect graphically.

> A harried mother, her face drawn with fatigue, large blue circles under her eyes from sleepless nights, her hair unkempt, her clothes disheveled, struggles to keep a beautiful, curly-haired child of eighteen months or so on her lap. The child is moving constantly, crawling, reaching, pulling, never still, fretting, making funny noises, going over her shoulder, leaning backward off her lap, pulling at her dress, going, going. . . .
>
> "He won't sleep. He jumps in his crib all the time, up and down, up and down. He has already torn one crib apart jumping. And he has these tantrums. I don't know what starts them. I can't seem to do anything about them. He screams. I know the neighbors think I'm killing him. And it goes on, sometimes all night and all day." (Warren, 1985, p. 208)

As the child grows older, the issue of behavior control becomes more crucial. For a youth with autism, episodes of tantrums or aggression may be less frequent, but are often more devastating because of his or her size (Neulicht, 1984). Families may go out in public less often because they fear one of these episodes (Bristol & Schopler, 1983).

Aside from its effects on their own quality of life, many parents are concerned about the impact of behavior problems on their child's opportunities for independence and acceptance in the community. Lyn Isbell (1983) describes her efforts to control the behavior of her son with Down syndrome:

> Walter's way of admiring a man's tie is to say "TIE!" and give it a strong yank. When he does so, the inevitable sequence of events is this:
>
> 1. The man turns purple.
> 2. The man quickly loosens his necktie knot and turns normal color again.
> 3. Walter's parent-in-charge-right-then says, "Walter, don't do that. That's rude!"

4. The man says, "Oh no, that's all right. I don't mind."
5. Walter smirks.
6. Parents feel helpless. Man feels embarrassed. Walter wins . . . and loses
    . . . and loses. . . .

It *hurts* people to see you spanking that poor little handicapped child, and
people don't like to be hurt. These same people, however, don't live with the
vision of the poor little handicapped child growing into a poor large
handicapped adult with no idea in the world why he hasn't got much of a fan
club. (Isbell, 1983, pp. 48–49)

You need to be aware of some of the family implications of a child's
particular exceptionality. Instructional objectives that could help the child
and family (e.g., improved communication, social skills, or behavior
control) perhaps should be given high priority. Some families might be
interested in educational programs for behavior management at home;
Chapter 12 includes a discussion of the types of programs available for this
purpose. Other families might welcome information about services in the
community, such as respite care or personal care attendant services. The
nature and extent of each child's exceptionality and the particular other
characteristics of each child carry special implications for the family.
Services should be designed and delivered and instructional objectives
tailored to mitigate negative and enhance positive effects of the exceptionality on the family.

CHARACTERISTICS OF THE FAMILY

By family characteristics, we mean characteristics of the family as a
whole: its size and form, cultural background, socioeconomic status, and
geographic location. Each shapes the family's responses to an exceptionality, and each serves as a potential resource to help the family cope. We
will consider each of these characteristics in turn.

Family Size and Form

Much of the research on families with members with exceptionalities
suggests that larger families tend to be less distressed by the presence of a
child with an exceptionality. Why this is so, however, is unclear. It may be
that in large families there are more people available to help with chores
and special adaptations related to the exceptionality. Or it may be that with
a large number of children there is a greater atmosphere of normalcy
(Trevino, 1979). A larger number of siblings may be able to absorb
parents' expectations for achievement that, in two-child families, often

seem to fall on the shoulders of the only child without an exceptionality (Powell & Ogle, 1985). Parents may be more philosophically accepting of the exceptionality if the presence of other children without exceptionalities serves as evidence that they are capable of producing "normal" children. Other children may also give parents a frame of reference from which they learn that their child with an exceptionality is actually more like than unlike the brothers and sisters in the family (Turnbull, Summers, & Brotherson, 1984). One parent noted that the problems of disability were no greater, or perhaps even less difficult, than problems of adolescent rebellion, drug involvement, or pregnancy (Turnbull, Blue-Banning, Behr, & Kerns, 1985). Finally, especially when the child with an exceptionality is one of the younger children, the experience of parenting in general may give parents the skills to cope. One mother, whose premature child was blinded at birth by an overdose of oxygen, noted:

> It was fortunate that she was not our first child. As parents of four, we had had experience; and perhaps I had developed a kind of knack with children. . . . Two premature babies before Elizabeth had taught me that they may, at first, resist cuddling. They are stiff and unrelaxed because they have had weeks of lying on the hard surface of an isolette where they are handled as little as possible to avoid infections. If a mother doesn't realize this, she may feel disappointed when her baby seems to prefer the crib to her arms. . . . Elizabeth was like that at first. . . . But I was determined not to give up. (Ulrich, 1972, pp. 22–23)

In addition to the number of children, the number of parents in the household may cause a difference in a family's reaction to the exceptionality. The presence of a supportive husband—even when he does not participate in child care—seems to be an important predictor of a mother's ability to cope with an exceptionality (Friedrich, 1979; Kazak & Marvin, 1984). But, given the high general divorce rate, you are almost certain to encounter single–parent families in the course of your work with students having an exceptionality.

A majority of single parents with custody of children are women, although a small but increasing percentage of fathers are maintaining custody (Simpson, 1982). Due to their lower earning power, single mothers often face financial problems. (Masnick & Bane, undated). Single mothers may be stressed by unrelieved child-raising plus work responsibilities (Simpson, 1982), and may become isolated from friends, neighbors, and relatives (Frieze, Parsons, Johnson, Ruble, & Zellman, 1978). Given these pressures, single parents may have neither the time nor the emotional energy to be heavily involved in their child's education. We encourage you to take these factors into consideration; for example, switching from a home-based to a center-based early intervention program might relieve some of the pressure. Respite care and involvement in support groups might be important sources of help for some parents who feel isolated (see Chapter 13). Finally, time-efficient communication, such as notes or phone calls, might take the place of more traditional parent-teacher conferences for parents whose responsibilities mean severely constrained schedules (see Chapters 6 and 7).

An opposite situation—more than two parents—exists in families in which one or both of the parents in the original family have remarried. Since 80% of people who divorce do remarry (Visher & Visher, 1982), the likelihood of encountering a remarried or blended family is also very high. In such situations, a bewildering array of family variations and touchy emotional situations are possible. The blended family may have children from two or more previous marriages. Children may see acceptance of a step-parent as disloyal to their biological one (Sager, Brown, Crohn, Engel, Rodstein, & Walker, 1983). They may have to adopt rules and lifestyles in two different households, or give up adult roles they may have assumed while the custodial parent was single (Visher & Visher, 1982). Parents may be uncertain about their authority over their spouse's children or, with a "ready-made" family from the first day of marriage, may not have the privacy and time to establish their new relationship (Sager, et. al., 1983). Issues of financial obligations regarding the previous mate(s) may surface causing jealousy or resentment (Sager et al., 1983). The resentments among all the adults—both former and current spouses—may surface in conflicts over the children, including visitation schedules, discipline, lifestyle, and so on (Sager, et al., 1983).

You need to be sensitive to possible tensions in a remarried family and make accommodations both for the academic and behavioral performance of the children, and for the implications for involvement of the parents (Simpson, 1982). If both parents and a step-parent are involved in educational decision-making, for example, an Individualized Education Program (IEP) conference may be an experience ranging from an amiable discussion about the child's best interests to a family power struggle with professionals inadvertently thrust in the middle.

Because of the variations of remarried families in the possible configurations, issues being faced, and ranges of emotional tension or comfort, it is difficult to develop any general rules for working with them. It is important, of course, to avoid taking sides with one parent or another in any conflicts. But, should the noncustodial parent be allowed to pick up the child after school, or have access to the child's records? Probably such a decision should only be made by the custodial parent (see Chapter 14 for a possible ethical dilemma surrounding this question). In general, you should encourage involvement by everyone, including step-parents (Simpson, 1982), whenever that is possible and agreeable to all parties. The positive side of a remarried family is that a wide circle of interested family members can potentially offer greater support both to each other and to the person with the exceptionality.

Cultural Background

Individual family members usually have a sense of belonging to a family group; in turn, the family as a whole may have a sense of identity with a larger group within society (McGoldrick, 1982). Ethnic background and religion influence a family's daily life in foods eaten, rituals and traditions celebrated, and so on. Cultural background lays a foundation of values and perspectives of the world that help the family define "who we are." These values and perspectives play an important role in shaping a family's reaction to an exceptionality.

The problem in any attempt to understand cultural differences is treading a thin line between glossing over differences and promoting stereotypes. For example, the fact that some ethnic groups, like Italians and Mexican-Americans, value total family well-being over individual achievement (Rotunno & McGoldrick, 1982; Falicov, 1982) will obviously not be true in all cases. In fact, some cultural stereotypes, e.g., that Black Americans do not value education, are not only untrue but also hinder good school-family relationships (Deiner, 1983). It is important to understand the *potential* for differences in values that may create a very different set of expectations and goals from those held by school professionals. It is also important to consider how some cultural lifestyles may serve as strengths in the family's attempt to cope with the implications of an exceptionality.

In the 1800s and early decades of this century, the Americanization of newcomers to this country was an important task of public schools (Sarason & Doris, 1979). Recently, however, the metaphor of the cultural mosaic has begun to replace the image of the melting pot (Pepper, 1976), and people are more often encouraged to celebrate their ethnic heritage. Even so, schools and other human service agencies still tend to mirror the dominant Anglo culture. Agencies' policy-makers are often White, middle-class community leaders, and a large proportion of professionals also come from White, middle-class backgrounds.

Some of the values of the Anglo culture include an achievement orientation, competition, a belief in individual autonomy and independence, an orientation toward the future, and a belief in controlling the environment and one's self through a rational, scientific approach (McGill & Pearce, 1982). These values permeate special education curriculum and other professional interventions from large issues, such as selecting instructional goals to enhance independence, to daily learning activities, such as competitive learning games.

Values that differ from these, or from those held by a given professional, have a number of implications for both curriculum and for relationships with families. For example, many traditional Mexican-American families value cooperation over competition; thus, a student from that family background may be more frustrated than motivated by a competitive learning situation (Castaneda, 1976). Similarly, Native American children may prefer a quiet or private type of recognition to public praise of their accomplishments (Pepper, 1976). Urging a family to think about the future, or about goals for independence for their child with an exceptionality, may be either difficult or meaningless for non-Anglo families who neither think much about the future nor attach any particular value to independence. Finally, families from, for example, Asian cultures, may have difficulty assuming control of family-professional decision-making, because they may see professionals as authority figures to be respected and obeyed (Deiner, 1983).

Especially with families from minority cultures, it is important for professionals to recognize that parents may approach the school or another service agency with caution based on a very real history of past discrimination. Over-representation of minority students in special education programs has been well-documented (e.g., Mercer, 1973). One study found that school psychologists tended to refer minority students to special education programs more often than non-minority students and to contact minority parents less often than other parents (Tomlinson, Acker, Canter, & Lindborg, 1977). It is for these reasons that the Education of the Handicapped Act requires nondiscriminatory evaluation and specifies parents must be notified in their own language of evaluations and educational planning conferences. (See Chapter 8 for a discussion of these legal issues and Chapter 9 for evaluation practices designed to avoid discrimination.)

Overcoming the effects of discrimination requires more than laws, however. It requires you to cultivate rapport and trust with parents who have a different ethnic background than your own, to be aware of your own cultural biases, and to learn many of the verbal or nonverbal styles of the cultures represented in your school or agency. Respect, for example, may begin by taking care to address parents as "Mr." or "Mrs.," and avoiding patronizing tones and educational jargon (Deiner, 1983). Simpson (1982) provides a Minority Self-Assessment Survey designed to help professionals uncover any underlying biases or discomfort they may hold about minorities. He notes that even if one cannot erase these biases, knowing they are there may help mitigate their effects. Finally, it is important for you to learn more about particular traits common to cultural groups in the local area. For example, Native Americans may avoid eye contact and speak very little (Simpson, 1982). Without knowledge of such customs, a school professional may see these parents as uncooperative, and the parents, on their part, might see the professional as intrusive and garrulous.

Family values and lifestyles in some cultural groups may also serve as sources of strength in coping with an exceptionality. For example, the stereotype that Black families are typically matriarchies (i.e., the major power figure is a strong mother or grandmother) is generally untrue. But this faulty perception may have arisen from the fact that Black families do often have flexible role structures and seem to be able to adopt a wide variety of family arrangements as situations demand (Williams & Stockton, 1973). The implication of these variations for educational involvement is that other family members (e.g., an aunt or grandmother) might be included in educational decision-making, especially if they are the ones with actual responsibility for the child. Also, Black families tend to have strong kin networks into which a child or adult with an exceptionality can be enfolded to provide support for such needs as financial management, child care, and emotional support (Utley & Marion, 1984). Families with these resources may not have such great need for formal community services such as respite care. They may be better served by help that strengthens their own natural support system, for example, teaching positioning or motor therapy exercises to extended family members who may care for the child. Again, however, they may not.

In summary, successful relationships with families requires a great deal of self-awareness on your part. Your own values and communication styles may not be shared by others, and it is important to realize that "different" does not necessarily mean "bad." In fact, a close look at the values and customs of other cultures reveals many strengths—such as cooperation or supportive extended family networks—that may make these groups more resilient in the face of an exceptionality than the dominant culture. The realization that you can learn helpful lessons from all persons with whom you interact is the beginning of respect that should characterize all family-professional relationships.

Socioeconomic Status

A family's socioeconomic status (SES) includes its income, the level of education of the family members, and the social status implied by the occupations of its wage-earners. Such a definition implies that a higher SES family might have more resources available to cope with an exceptionality. Indeed, the ability to pay for services and a higher level of education (leading to knowledge about the exceptionality) are definite resources. But once again, the equation is not that simple; higher SES does not automatically guarantee better coping. Lower SES families have resources, also—they may have large families and extensive support networks, and values come into play and shape the family's reaction to exceptionality.

Because higher SES families are often more achievement-oriented, they may consider an exceptionality involving a mental or physical disability as a severe disappointment of their aspirations for their child's future. This is what Farber and Ryckman (1965) called the "tragic crisis." Lower SES families tend to value achievement less than other values such as family solidarity or happiness (Lee, 1982; Rubin, 1976). Therefore, they may not experience a "tragic crisis" so much as they must face the problem of how to care for the child: a "role organization crisis" (Farber & Ryckman, 1965). Conversely, giftedness may be more stressful to a lower SES family with few resources to help a child develop his or her talents.

Another difference between higher and lower SES groups may be a sense of control of the environment and of the future which higher SES families may have. Consider the reaction of one father, a professional, to his son's diagnosis of Down syndrome:

> In those first days, my initial reaction was to control. I wanted to understand. I wanted to control the situation by the intellectual processes with which I was familiar. But what I learned was not very helpful. . . . While every child's future is uncertain, my son's future seemed hopeless. I could not imagine for him a life so very different from my own. (H. M. Isbell, 1983, p. 22)

In contrast, many working-class families may not believe in the possibility of controlling their environment, with the corollary that very few may plan for any child's future, let alone for the future of a child with an exceptionality (Rubin, 1976). For example, Rubin (1976) asked one 36-year-old refinery worker if he recalled thinking as a boy about what he would do when he grew up. He replied:

> I didn't think much about it. I just kind of took things as they came. I figured I knew I'd work; I worked most of my life. I started working at real jobs when I was fourteen. . . . There wasn't much point in dreaming. I guess you could say in my family we didn't—maybe I should say couldn't—plan our lives; things just happened. (Rubin, 1976, p. 39)

On the one hand, therefore, higher-SES families may be more stressed by an event, such as an exceptionality, that contradicts their belief that they are in control of their lives. On the other hand, lower-SES families may have difficulty considering future options for their child and might be caught unprepared when it is time for their child to enter new programs— finding a long waiting list at an adult service program, for example.

Furthermore, a belief that there is "no point in" trying to control a situation or plan ahead might make lower-SES families less active participants in educational decision-making.

Beyond value differences in families of different SES groups, there are the harsh survival problems of families who live in poverty. For these families, a child with an exceptionality may seem to be the least of their worries. Indeed, human service providers are hard-pressed to attract families in poverty into educational programs. For example, Rosenberg, Reppucci, and Linney (1983) reported the efforts of a program designed to provide parent education to low-income families whose children were at risk for developmental delay, abuse, or emotional disturbance. The program had a capacity to serve 130 families. But even though professionals widely agreed that there was a great need for the program, only 25 parents attended one or more group meetings in the first year. Rosenberg, et al. (1983) speculated that immediate problems were too overwhelming to allow parents to attend to more long-term needs. They note:

> We met several parents who were struggling to provide their children with the most basic needs (food, shelter, health care) and joining a group would do nothing to meet those needs. . . . For example, one woman, a mother of seven, four of whom were under five years of age, had a series of unfortunate incidents during the time that the groups were in progress. Each child became sick, her son became involved with the juvenile court, she had thyroid trouble and then surgery, her house was condemned, her husband returned suddenly after leaving her many years ago, and because of her husband's previous reputation, the protective service unit of the welfare department increased their interest in the family. Although she may have derived support from being a group member, the group was perceived as one additional drain on her energies, regardless of possible future benefits. (Rosenberg, et al., 1983, pp. 218–219)

As with families with different cultural backgrounds, it is important [in the case of working-class or poverty families] to keep a tight rein on your own values and judgments. Parents who do not participate in educational programs do not necessarily care less about their children than those who do. A more likely explanation is that the daily responsibilities of sheer survival must take precedence over education. Witness the comments of a mother with 14 children, a mother who had recently entered a job training program:

> I can get as much on Welfare. You get fifty dollars pay an you have to pay the baby-sitter an you end up with nothin. You have to have carfare. You have nothin. Am I right? So you may as well stay home.
>
> But I don't have that attitude. You know, if I make fifteen dollars profit, it's mine. I feel worthful. It's a feelin I have like God bless me for helpin friends.

> I like to go out there while I got the courage . . . go out there an earn a little somethin.
>
> I love these little children. I love bein with them, but still, it would feel good to work. . . . I've always been with them, but to go out an work, I think it's a healthy thing. (Sirkis, 1970, p. 71)

Given the complexities facing impoverished families, it seems a discouraging question to ask what, if anything, professionals can do. On an individual level, a beginning may be to build rapport and trust. On the school level, support and related services staff should be available for nonthreatening home visits, counseling, and nutrition consultation that is realistic within the family's budget. On the community level, especially families with multiple problems underscore the need for workable interagency collaboration. Social services, health agencies, and schools need to cooperate to serve these families more effectively. See Chapter 13 for a description of types of interagency cooperation.

Geographic Location

With today's electronic media and increased mobility, regional differences in family values and forms are becoming less and less apparent. Yet traces of regional stereotypes remain: Southern hospitality, Yankee stoicism, Midwestern conformity, and Western independence are values still discussed by family therapists and sociologists (McGill & Pearce, 1982). The same influences of modern society can be seen on homogenizing values of rural and urban families. For example, while farm families once tended to value having many children partially because of their usefulness in working on the farm, modern farm technology has reduced the need to produce large numbers of children (Miller, Bigner, Jacobson, & Turner, 1982). Furthermore, the image of rural life as a peaceful existence is fast disappearing; farming is now considered to be in the top ten percent of high-stress occupations, as farmers struggle with complex machinery, computerized operations, huge debts, and new definitions of the role of farm wives in the farm business (Wiegel, 1982).

Although families themselves may be more similar in values and form than they once were, there are some very different problems associated with providing special education services in rural areas. Most of these problems have their roots in scarce services and the distances between families who have children with exceptionalities. While isolation may be a problem for many families, a rural family may experience even greater isolation if there are no other families in their immediate community whose children have similar situations. Cole, Smith, and Ranken (1981) suggest that one possible solution might be for parent advocacy groups (e.g.,

Association for Children with Learning Disabilities, Association for Retarded Citizens, United Cerebral Palsy) to offer memberships at large in
rural areas, rather than the more traditional local chapters with a minimum
membership size.

Providing services over great distances to a few families requires some
creative approaches. Latham (1981) points out that parents in rural areas
may literally be the only resource available to provide therapy or
instruction during the early childhood period. He describes a model in
place in Utah using a combination of in-home video instruction tapes,
self-instructional manuals, a WATS line, and a family newsletter. The
problem with rural service models is that rural families may be as busy—
if not more so—than most other families (see Chapter 4 for a discussion of
the many responsibilities families have), and taking on major responsibility
for their child's instruction may be too much without extensive support.

One of the reasons for diminishing differences [in family characteristics]
among geographic locations is the increased mobility of families. Some
families move in order to find services. One mother, who had two children
with hearing impairments, remarked:

> We lived in a small town in . . . , where they had almost nothing for
> handicapped children in the schools. We decided that if our children were to
> get an education, we would have to move; so we started looking at programs
> all over the country. . . . Finally we settled on Starr King because it had a
> first-rate oral program. My husband had to quit a good job; we moved to
> . . . , he had to search for another job and take a cut in pay. But it was
> worth it! (Spradley & Spradley, 1978, pp. 214–215)

When a family does relocate, the stress of finding a new home and
settling into a new community may be compounded by the problem of
finding new services for the child with an exceptionality. Military families,
migrant farm workers, and others whose jobs require frequent moves face
this problem. For example, the Knighton family's military career (1985)
required six major moves during Denise's childhood. Each move meant a
search for a new program; each move was a gamble that Denise, who had
aphasia, could continue the progress she was making. Aside from the
possible interruptions in the child's instructional program, parents may find
themselves starting over at ground zero, repeating the same family and
medical histories to new people, learning the personalities and support
potential of new staff. Yockey (1983) described an unfortunate encounter
with an uncaring professional in his daughter's new school, and commented:

> As I write this today, certain descriptive adjectives and a few phrases of street
> vernacular come to mind, but none of them really do justice to the man.
> Why, you might ask, did we not respond to this unmitigated arrogance by

simply telling the "good doctor" to go straight to hell? Because we were in a strange city, in a strange part of the country, in a new school, meeting with a group of people we didn't know, Barb with all the worries of a new house, me with a new job, both of us trying to get off on the right foot. That's not an apology, merely an explanation. (Yockey, 1983, p. 85)

It is helpful to be aware of the anxiety that often accompanies a family's relocation. Communication with and receipt of records from the child's previous school is essential. The interdisciplinary team should avoid reiterating routine family and medical history questions except in cases where information is missing from the file. Every attempt should be made to provide the new family with tours of facilities, descriptions of programs, and introductions to staff and other families in the program. The process of "settling in" a new child and his or her family should be as painless and smooth as possible.

The description of family characteristics emphasizes some of the many ways families can vary, as well as issues for your consideration. Large or small families, single parent or blended families, different cultural backgrounds, and the family's geographic location (or re–location) each present unique sets of needs and values. The underlying themes in individualizing your approach are respect for divergent values, an understanding of some of the many other issues—in addition to their child's exceptionality—the family may be facing, and a creative willingness to capitalize on some of the unique strengths and resources which can usually be found in even the most problem-bound of families.

PERSONAL CHARACTERISTICS

The diversity of family units resulting from variations in cultural and other characteristics increases many times because each family member has idiosyncratic characteristics. These personal characteristics can be strengths or drawbacks for the family as a whole. Each family member has a state of mental and physical health that affects his or her tolerance to stress, an intellectual capacity to understand what is happening, and styles of coping with pressure. All of these affect the family's reaction to an exceptionality, as well as professional approaches to the family.

Family Health

People who do not feel well have a more difficult time coping with stressful situations. Conversely, stress produces physiological responses that can make people sick. Parents of children with exceptionalities often report suffering from headaches, lower back pain, depression, and other stress-related problems (Bristol & Schopler, 1983; McAndrew, 1976). Whether the physical problem is caused by worry about the exceptionality or whether it has another source, the result is the same: reduced ability to cope. You might recommend family support programs such as relaxation training and respite care (see Chapter 13) to help stop the escalating spiral of stress build-up.

Another issue related to the family's mental health is the problem of the abusing family. It is not a small problem. Estimates of the incidence of abuse vary, but it is likely that about 20% of all children may be neglected or physically, sexually, or emotionally abused by their parents (Harrison & Edwards, 1983). The causes of abuse are complex. Often abusing parents were themselves abused as children (Meier & Sloan, 1984). Consider the comments of a mother who had herself been physically and sexually abused by both her parents as a child:

> He was a very fussy child. His screaming drove me crazy. I can remember screaming back at him. I tried so hard, but it was just like being a kid again. Trying so hard to make somebody like me, and he just hated me. . . . His screams reminded me of my own screams as a kid. I wanted so much to do the right thing, but I was failing just like I did when I was a kid. Failing to make my parents love me, be proud of me, or even like me. . . . I remember throwing a Melmac dish against the wall in his general direction and watching it break against the wall. I was holding myself in the corner and thinking, "Oh God! I am just like her." (Harrison & Edwards, 1983, p. 43)

Frequently, abusing parents are younger and have fewer friends (Embry, 1980). Other than that, however, there are few demographic characteristics that might indicate a family at-risk for abuse. Data show that abuse occurs at all socioeconomic levels and within all cultural groups (Embry, 1980).

Various research studies have found that the percentage of abused children who show some sort of physical or intellectual problem (some type of exceptionality) ranges from 8 to 55% (Frodi, 1981). Johnson and Morse (1968) suggested that the most likely targets of abuse are children who are hyperactive or difficult to control. Even giftedness may mark a child as different enough to single him or her out for abuse. Here are the comments of a woman who was abused as a child:

> The summer after my ninth grade year, I went to a community college. I had to do something to keep out of the house, and college classes were much cheaper than trying to go to summer camp. I loved it there! Mom didn't think I could pass my college classes. I was taking three sections on earth science. I did pass. She nicknamed me "smartass" that year. I decided that I didn't want to go to high school; I wanted to stay in college. I applied for a grant which I received. Mom said that I couldn't go. . . . "Who do you think you

---

Table 2–1
CHARACTERISTICS OF ABUSED AND NEGLECTED CHILDREN

Abused or neglected children are likely to share some of the following characteristics:

1. They appear to be different from other children in physical and emotional makeup, or their parents' describe them as being different or bad.
2. They seem afraid of their parents.
3. They may bear bruises, welts, sores, or other skin injuries which seem to be untreated.
4. They are given inappropriate food, drink, or medication.
5. They are left alone with inadequate supervision.
6. They are chronically unclean.
7. They exhibit extremes in behavior: cry often or cry very little and show no real expectation of being comforted; they are excessively fearful or seem fearless of adult authority; they are unusually aggressive or extremely passive or withdrawn.
8. They are wary of physical contact, especially with an adult. They may be hungry for affection yet have difficulty relating to children and adults. Based on their experiences, they feel they cannot risk getting close to others.
9. They exhibit a sudden change in behavior, exhibit regressive behavior, such as wetting their pants or bed, thumb-sucking, whining, or becoming uncommonly shy or passive.
10. They have learning problems that cannot be diagnosed. Their attention wanders and they easily become self-absorbed.
11. They are habitually truant or late to school. Frequent or prolonged absences from school may result from the parent's keeping an injured child at home until the evidence of abuse disappears. Or they may arrive at school early and remain after classes instead of going home.
12. They are tired and often sleep in class.
13. They are not dressed appropriately for the weather. Children who wear long sleeves on hot days may be dressed to hide bruises or burns or other marks of abuse, or they may be dressed inadequately and suffer frostbite or illness from exposure to the weather.

Note. From Child Abuse *(p. 65) by R. Harrison and J. Edwards, 1983, Portland, OR: Ednick Publications. Copyright 1983 by Ednick Communications. Reprinted by permission.*

are?'' she would yell at me when I pleaded with her. . . . (Harrison & Edwards, 1983, pp. 32–33)

Researchers suggest that abuse may arise when children with exceptionalities are slow to respond to parental instructions (Meier & Sloan, 1984), when parent and child have had the bonding process interrupted due to temporary separation at birth (Blacher & Meyers, 1983), or because some infants—particularly premature babies—do not have a cuddly appearance and often have a high-pitched and aversive cry (Frodi, 1981). Other researchers, however, point out that abuse and neglect themselves may cause developmental delay due to brain damage, emotional trauma, or lack of early stimulation (Meier & Sloan, 1984). The most probable explanation is that both dynamics are at work: some exceptionalities may arouse aggressive responses in parents who are predisposed to violent reactions, and some exceptionalities may be the result of abuse.

It is important, however, not to make an erroneous twist of reasoning. It is statistically true that a large percentage of children who experience abuse also have exceptionalities. The reverse conclusion—that a large percentage of children with exceptionalities are abused—does not follow. The vast majority of parents whose children have exceptionalities do not abuse them (Embry, 1980).

Whether exceptionality is the cause or the result of abuse is of vital interest to researchers who are attempting to find ways to prevent it. But, in dealing with the end result—people who are both battered and have exceptionalities—the cause makes little difference. The issue is: what to do?

First, most states have laws requiring school and health professionals to report cases of suspected abuse. But what constitutes "suspicion"? Table 2–1 lists some of the physical and behavioral indicators of different types of abuse.

It is important to remember that many children who are not abused can and do show any one of these signs. But the presence of many of these indicators, over time, should trigger further inquiry. Most schools have written policies and procedures on this issue, and each state has different laws on when, how, to whom, and under what circumstances, to report suspected abuse. You should be familiar with these policies and laws. If children confide in someone at school, they should be taken at their word. A school professional who has been so entrusted should be straightforward with the child about what will happen next, and how long it will take. Referral to a social service agency does not automatically mean the child will be removed from the home, but rather that the agency will look into the question. While school counselors and social workers should be involved, it is important for school policy to be flexible enough to allow the continued involvement of the specific professional the child trusts most (Harrison & Edwards, 1983).

Second, when it does become necessary to report suspected abuse or neglect, the question arises as to how—and whether—to tell the parents a report has been made. Schools have different policies about this issue. Although, in most states, the source of the report is kept confidential, it is often not difficult for parents to guess who made the report. As a result, many advisors recommend telling the parents (Harrison & Edwards, 1983). Such an interview should stick to facts and remain nonjudgmental and sympathetic. The professional should explain the school's legal obligation without casting blame, and offer the school's concern and support (Harrison & Edwards, 1983).

Third, there are curricula available to teach children about abuse, to help students distinguish between discipline and abuse, to assure them that abuse is not their fault, and to point out that the adult who is doing the abusing needs help too and can get it if the child confides his or her problem to someone in authority. The book *Child Abuse* (Harrison & Edwards, 1983) provides some examples of curricula and lists a number of films and other resources. If you do undertake such a curriculum, you should invite parents to attend class and/or give them a description of the course.

Abuse and neglect is one of the most difficult dimensions of family-professional relationships. It is important to remain nonjudgmental and respectful. Abusing parents are as much victims of the cycle of violence as their children are. They may suffer from learned helplessness and low self-esteem arising from their own abused childhoods (Embry, 1980). One must make the assumption that they do not *want* to abuse their children. They need your support as much as their children do.

Parents with Disabilities

While much of this book considers issues surrounding a child with an exceptionality whose parents are "normal," professionals frequently must deal with the opposite question. That is, how should they approach families in which the parents are disabled, whether or not the children have an exceptionality? When a parent has a physical disability, the problems of professional-family relationships are no more (or less) those of logistics: providing accessible meeting rooms and communicating through alternate means, such as the telephone. But when parents have sensory or intellectual deficits, there are special issues to consider.

Parents with visual or hearing impairments rely on their children in many situations. For example, parents with visual impairments may ask their children to read prices in grocery stores and otherwise guide them through daily transactions. They may depend on an older child to provide care for younger siblings. Such children may be brought into the parental subsystem (see Chapter 3) and expected to act as "little adults." Whether this is detrimental, of course, depends on the individual family, and whether parents can also allow the child on whom they depend the time to be "just a kid." The child's role as the parent's assistant does have some implications for your consideration. The child may not have the time to participate in school extracurricular activities, for example. Another example is illustrated by a teacher who told of a parent-teacher conference with a mother who had a hearing impairment:

> We didn't have anybody who had sign language because our district's deaf education teacher was strictly from the oral school. So I asked Jeannie to interpret at our conference, since I knew she was very good at sign language. Unfortunately, what I needed to tell Jeannie's mother was that I had some concerns about her behavior in class. . . . The mother just nodded and smiled. I thought she must be either stupid or just as perverse as her daughter. . . . It was only later that I discovered that Jeannie had not, to say the least, translated accurately what I was saying!

A more difficult set of problems is posed when the parents have mental disabilities. Partially, the difficulty centers around the problem of separating prejudice about parents who have been labeled mentally retarded from the real difficulties they may experience. As discussed in Chapter 1, there are long-standing taboos and discriminations against parenthood for people with mental retardation. Persons with mental retardation have been barred by law in many states from having children, even though parents with other problems, such as alcoholism or a tendency to abuse, may have problems caring for their children (Haavik & Menninger, 1981). It is also very difficult to separate difficulties in parenting due solely to mental disability from other factors—such as low income status, a lack of experience with children, or inadequate models of parenting—which people with low IQs tend also to experience (Haavik & Menninger, 1981). Neglectful mothers in general have been found to have below average IQs (Sheridan, 1956), and other researchers have expressed the opinion that "incompetence" in child-rearing is more a product of poverty than intelligence (Budd & Greenspan, 1984). Despite this fact, child protection workers and other professionals seem to operate from a prejudgment that parents with mental retardation will not be "fit" (Budd & Greenspan, 1984). In fact, in some areas, proof that a parent has a mental disability is adequate grounds for removal of a child from the home (Budd & Greenspan, 1984).

However, a low IQ is not necessarily an indicator of poor parenting skills. Rosenberg and McTate (1982) note that "concern and willingness" to place a child's need ahead of one's immediate wants are often more important predictors of the ability to improve child care skills than is intelligence (p. 24). Budd and Greenspan (1984) note that the problems experienced by parents with mental retardation are more often due to low IQ. For example, poor social skills may make it difficult for a parent to negotiate successfully with a professional. Poor practical skills resulting from lack of experience or inability to foresee consequences may lead parents with mental retardation to feed or clothe their children improperly or to leave them in hazardous situations. In one example, a mother punished her child by standing him in a corner for many hours, because this was how she had been punished when she was in an institution (Rosenberg & McTate, 1982). Budd and Greenspan (1984) noted:

> We have learned of mothers who had difficulty meeting their children's physical needs, who didn't realize how serious the situation seemed to outsiders, and who didn't act contrite when told of their errors. This chain of events, a product of poor judgment rather than ill will, can lead to removal of a child from the retarded mother's care. (p. 487)

Programs designed to teach parenting skills to adults with mental retardation are fairly scarce but increasing. Some authors advocate developing screening programs to identify at-risk parents before they have children in order to provide training (Haavik, in press). Training for parents with mental retardation should involve very concrete instructions, demonstrations, and feedback. In many cases, parent education programs originally designed for parents in general can be successfully used for parents with mental retardation with only a few modifications (Budd & Greenspan, 1984) to make more concrete instructions and follow-through with role-playing, modeling, and feedback.

It is clear that support for parents with mental retardation should be an integral part of general services for adults with developmental disabilities. The social, self-advocacy, and other independent living skills taught for adult life will also serve the adult well when he or she becomes a parent. It is important for schools serving the children of parents with mental retardation to work closely with community programs serving adults.

Coping Styles

Individual family members may also vary in the particular strategies they adopt to deal with stress. Stress is highly prevalent in our society, and the presence of a child with an exceptionality may be only one of many pressures impinging on a family. Coping is defined as any strategy a person may choose to reduce feelings of stress (Pearlin & Schooler, 1978). It may consist of taking some sort of positive action to solve a problem, or it may include changing the way one thinks about a situation to make it seem less stressful.

There are, therefore, many ways to cope. Categories of coping styles developed by Olson and associates (Olson, McCubbin, Barnes, Larsen, Muxen, & Wilson, 1983) include

1. Passive appraisal (ignoring a problem in the hope it will go away)

2. Reframing (changing the way one thinks about a problem, in order to solve it and/or to make it seem less stressful)

3. Spiritual support (deriving comfort and guidance from one's spiritual beliefs)

4. Social support (receiving practical and emotional assistance from friends and family)

5. Professional support (receiving assistance from professionals and human service agencies).

These coping styles have many implications for developing family support programs. We will explore these coping strategies, and consider ways they can be strengthened, in detail in Chapter 13. Here the main point is that not everyone has the same favorite coping strategies. For example, one person might think that talking over one's troubles with friends is too burdensome and intrusive on the friends. This person might instead use another coping strategy, such as reframing or spiritual support. It matters little what the preferred strategy is as long as the result is the same: *reduced stress*.

We encourage you to be sensitive to the variety of ways people can cope, and to work to enhance preferred styles rather than focus on support that may not be useful to the family. Chapter 13 will suggest many ways to do that.

SUMMARY

The main point of this chapter is that every family requires an individualized approach. Families have diverse resources arising from different exceptionalities, family sizes and forms, cultural backgrounds, socioeconomic status, geographic locations, and individual characteristics such as health, intellectual capacity, and coping styles. The multitude of possible combinations and permutations of all these factors create infinite variations that make each family literally as unique as a snowflake or a fingerprint.

The concept of individualizing is a very familiar one when working with special students. Individualized instruction is not only a value for maximizing each student's potential, but is also a legal requirement. If students benefit from individualized approaches, why not also individualize approaches to their families? Doing so requires an appreciation of the unique situations of each family. It also requires a respect for diverse values, lifestyles, and cultures. Beginning from a base of self-awareness about your own values and backgrounds, it is possible to forge family-school relationships that are truly rewarding for everyone involved.

Understanding families' unique resources is necessary but does not provide the complete understanding of how a family system operates. Family resources shape how a family interacts with its own members and with persons outside the family, such as yourself. We will discuss family interaction in the next chapter.

Chapter 3

Family Interaction

The family is a unit of many interactions—an interactional system. Events affecting any one member can have an impact upon all family members (Carter & McGoldrick, 1980; Minuchin, 1974). Why is knowledge about a family's interaction important to professionals who work with children and youth having exceptionalities? Because, as professionals, it is important to focus not exclusively on the child with an exceptionality, but to examine the child within the context of the family. This is so because the child does not function in isolation, but as part of a family that is impacted by and impacts the child. You therefore should consider that every point of contact and intervention with families might have an impact on a family and its interactions.

Consider the example of a mother who has agreed to implement a home-based toilet training program for her child. She has agreed to use the same procedures and schedule as in the classroom. She places her child on the toilet every two hours for ten minutes during the day and every four hours during the night, each morning and evening. Carrying out this home program interrupts her and her husband's sleep. Lack of sleep adversely affects both parents' efficiency at work, their time and patience for their other children, and their time and energy for their own personal needs.

A typical focus in special education has been on changes in the child or on mother-child interaction. But, as this example points out, there can be effects on other family members as well, such as on the marital relationship and siblings. You must be aware that interventions affect all family members, and you should therefore seek to aid the entire family.

This chapter will examine family subsystems (the component parts of the family's interactional system) and discuss the different ways that members of that interactional system interact.

FAMILY SUBSYSTEMS

A family consists of four major subsystems within the traditional nuclear family (Turnbull, Summers, & Brotherson, 1984):

1. marital subsystem—husband and wife interactions
2. parental subsystem—parent and child interactions
3. sibling subsystem—child and child interactions
4. extrafamilial subsystem—whole family or individual member interactions with extended family, friends, neighbors, and professionals.

The configuration of a family's subsystems will depend upon its idiosyncratic family structure. For example, in single-parent families there is no marital subsystem; in a family with only one child, there is no sibling subsystem. The following sections will discuss some of the impacts of exceptionality on the interactions of each of these subsystems.

Husband and Wife Interactions

The marital subsystem consists of interactions between husbands and wives. Both husband and wife have needs and roles as marital partners. The presence of a child with an exceptionality, however, can have an impact on their relationship and interactions. Many studies have indicated that having a child with an exceptionality can have a *negative impact* on the parents' marriage. Featherstone (1980) noted:

> A child's handicap attacks the fabric of a marriage in four ways. It excites powerful emotions in both parents. It acts as a dispiriting symbol of shared failure. It reshapes the organization of the family. It creates fertile ground for conflict (p. 91).

Divorce, marital disharmony, and husbands' desertion have been reported to be disproportionately high in marriages where there is a child with an exceptionality (Gath, 1977; Murphy, 1982, Reed & Reed, 1965). One study assessed marital harmony in 59 couples soon after the birth of a child with spina bifida and nearly a decade later (Tew, Payne, & Lawrence, 1974). Contact was maintained with these couples as well as with 58 control couples. The couples with a child with spina bifida had lower marital harmony and twice the divorce rate as the control group couples. It appeared that the birth of a child with spina bifida presented a serious challenge to marital stability, with many marital needs and activities being subordinated to the child's needs.

Couples with exceptional children can also experience difficulty in marital communication (Murphy, 1982). A father of a daughter with cerebral palsy described how his daughter had affected the communication in his marriage:

> There have been no raised voices from the time she was very young. We couldn't raise our voices in front of her or she would cry. She felt her security rested between both of us—if we would argue, she felt insecure. We've never been able to get into some good hard arguments because it would upset her. You need a good hard argument every once in awhile in a marriage.

Although some studies indicate that having a child with an exceptionality can have a negative impact on marriage, other studies indicate that having a child with an exceptionality can have a *positive impact* on marriage. Some husbands and wives feel their marriage is closer and stronger as a result.

Gath (1977) compared 30 couples with infants with Down syndrome and 30 couples of infants without exceptionality. Although she did find marital disharmony in nine of the couples with infants with Down syndrome and in none of the control couples, she also found positive effects in the couples with children having exceptionalities. Almost half of these couples with children with exceptionalities reported that they had been drawn closer together and that their marriage was strengthened rather than weakened by their shared experience.

A more recent study (Kazak & Marvin, 1984) compared marital stress in 56 couples with children with spina bifida and 53 couples with children without exceptionality. The results indicated no significant difference between the groups in total marital satisfaction. Analysis of the subscales, however, indicated that the couples with children having spina bifida actually experienced somewhat higher levels of marital satisfaction. These results are in direct contrast to the study discussed earlier (Tew, Payne & Lawrence, 1974). Kazak and Marvin (1984) state that the present findings lend support to the idea that having a child with an exceptionality may actually function in some cases to strengthen marital relationships.

These mixed research results highlight a very important point for professionals—you should not automatically assume that couples necessarily experience a negative impact on their marriage as a result of their child. Many marriages are strengthened by a child with special needs. It is also important to recognize that spouses have specific needs and roles to fulfill (e.g., affection, socialization, and self-definition) as marriage partners. Interventions with families should demonstrate respect for the needs and roles of a husband and wife, regardless of the fact that they are parents of a child with an exceptionality. Table 3–1 provides some suggestions for recognizing these needs.

Parent and Child Interactions

The parental subsystem is composed of interactions between parents and their child or children. In each family parents assume certain roles as a mother or as a father or as both. These roles are either explicit or implicit, and they can change with time (Minuchin, 1974). The presence of a child with an exceptionality has impact on parent roles, and fathers and mothers can be affected in different ways.

Parents can be affected in different ways in their interactions with their child depending on whether their child is *a son or a daughter*. Some fathers, regardless of social class, have shown a greater initial impact if their child is a boy, and mothers a greater impact if their child is a girl (Farber,

Table 3–1

SUGGESTIONS FOR RECOGNIZING THE NEEDS OF THE MARITAL SUBSYSTEM

1. If couples indicate to you that they don't have any time alone, encourage them to consider activities that they may wish to engage in separate from their child or children.
2. Make information available to couples on community respite care or baby-sitting services in the event they would choose to spend time separate from their child or children. Possibly you may know two or more couples who would be interested in trading off child care evenings.
3. Consider the time and energy implications of home interventions on the needs of the marital subsystem. If you are unsure, ask, "Will this home program interfere with your evening time with your husband or wife?" "Are there some alternatives that might work better?"
4. Seek ways to offer flexible scheduling or alternatives if a planned school activity conflicts with an activity that a couple has planned. Maybe a couple participates in a gourmet club the first Tuesday of every month, but this is the time they are scheduled for a parent-teacher conference. What are some alternatives to that scheduled meeting?

Jenne, & Toigo, 1960). Tallman (1965) found fathers to be more adversely affected by a son than a daughter, and cope less skillfully than mothers in raising either a son or a daughter.

Fathers, more than mothers, have also been found to be more concerned about the community stigma that their family may face (Gumz & Gubrium, 1972; Tallman, 1965). This stigma may be accentuated by the sex of the child. For example, some children with developmental delays may develop skills traditionally associated with a female role (e.g., nonassertiveness or domestic abilities) and develop less skills traditionally associated with a male role (e.g., prowess in athletics or leadership). A father may feel greater stigma over a sixteen-year-old son just learning how to throw a ball than a sixteen-year-old daughter. One father of a son having a physical disability expressed disappointment that he was not able to share what he considered male hobbies with his son:

> I would have liked to have taken him fishing and hunting. I try not to think about it. It is one of the things you put up with. (Turnbull, Summers, & Brotherson, 1982)

Rud Turnbull shared his disappointment in not being able to look forward to a usual father-son relationship:

> He is my boy and my child, but he will never be fully my son. The pleasures and disruptions that my parents and I experienced will not be ours; because

of his retardation he cannot be my companion in much of life. His disability is not just his; it is mine, too. It twice curses—it debilitates him and me alike—as it deprives us both of normalcy. (Turnbull, 1985, p. 120)

Past research with mothers and fathers suggests that the presence of a child with exceptionalities tends to highlight differences in traditional *parent roles* (Gallagher, Cross & Scharfman, 1981; Gumz & Gubrium, 1972). Historically, parent roles have been characterized as expressive or instrumental (Parsons & Bales, 1955). The expressive roles, often filled by mothers, include those activities that relate to the internal affairs of the family (e.g., affection, physical care, and self-definition). The instrumental roles, often filled by fathers, include those activities that relate to the external affairs of the family (e.g., financial, educational, and vocational).

One study (Gumz & Gubrium, 1972) compared the attitude of 50 mothers and 50 fathers of children with mental retardation. They found that mothers were significantly more concerned than fathers with emotional family strain, additional child-care time, and ability to maintain family harmony and integration. Fathers showed a higher degree of concern about their child in activities outside the family than within the family.

Gallagher et al. (1981) compared 50 mothers and 50 fathers of preschool children with exceptionalities and found similar parent role differences. Fathers predominantly were the providers, protectors, and maintainers of outside-home equipment. Mothers predominantly kept books, shopped for and prepared food, maintained the inside of the home, served as social hostess and nurse, provided transportation, and selected clothing.

The results of both studies parallel the traditional parent role differences of mother-expressive and father-instrumental. However, these traditional parent and child interaction patterns may be changing. In the Gallagher study (Gallagher et al., 1981), when parents were asked to state their "ideal" parent role allocation, both mothers and fathers agreed that fathers should take a more active expressive role.

In addition, a recent study with 23 fathers and 25 mothers of young adults with exceptionalities found no significant difference between mothers and fathers when addressing the adult needs of their child (Brotherson, 1985). Mothers and fathers were addressing both instrumental and expressive needs when planning for the future of their son or daughter with an exceptionality.

Fathers of children with exceptionalities, similar to fathers in general (Eversoll, 1979), may be assuming a role that increasingly focuses on the expressive needs of their child. Mothers of children with exceptionalities may be assuming a role that increasingly focuses on the instrumental needs of their child (Brotherson, 1985). Parents may be beginning to share more of the same roles when caring for their child with an exceptionality.

Couples approach parenthood with expectations of mother and father roles within the family context (Carter & McGoldrick, 1980). Some of the parenting skills and roles that couples learned from their own parents may not be effective or relevant with a child with an exceptionality, either because of differences in the child or changes in our society. As Gallagher et al. (1981) note, "the traditional father roles of physical playmate and model for the male child are largely diminished or not present at all with moderately to severely handicapped children" (p. 13). Carol Michaelis (1980) writes:

> For some fathers, the lack of interaction with the child may be the result of a perceived inability to meet the child's needs. Since the mother receives most of the instruction about the child and attends most of the conferences, the father may not have the information that would allow him to be comfortable interacting with a child who has a handicapping condition. Although this inability may be a perceived inability rather than a lack of skill, it may actually make the father feel like an outsider in the mother-child and mother-child-school interactions. (p. 92)

Professionals therefore should plan services and programs that respond to both parents' needs, not approaching parents as a homogeneous pair. Their needs, roles, and interactions as a mother or as a father can be quite different. Fathers may share many of the same concerns as mothers, but they may also have concerns and challenges that are quite different from mothers (Cummings, 1976; Cummings, Bayley, & Rie, 1966; Gumz & Gubrium, 1972). Both parents may experience stress in their roles as a parent or just not know alternative roles of interaction. Suggestions to help mothers and fathers develop and maintain successful interactions both with their child and with their child's school are included in Table 3–2 (p. 54).

Child and Child Interactions

The sibling subsystem is composed of sibling interactions—the interactions between brothers and/or sisters in the family and the child with an exceptionality. The child's impact upon siblings often has not been understood or recognized by professionals who work with families (Vadasy, Fewell, Meyer, & Schell, 1984). Possibly siblings find it difficult to discuss their feelings, or possibly parents are less sensitive to the needs of other children when focusing on the needs of the child with an exceptionality. As one young woman of a sister with Down syndrome wrote:

> My parents never sat me down and said, "This is the problem, this is what's wrong with her. Do you understand? Do you have any questions?" My

attempts to communicate with my parents were all in vain. I remember several times trying to tell my Mom how I felt and she would say, "Your feelings are wrong and you'd better change them."

It was devastating to always be told that my feelings were wrong, and yet still not be able to get rid of them. Besides feeling guilty about having angry feelings, I began to think there was something definitely wrong with me. (Ellifritt, 1984, p. 19)

Although siblings may not always reveal their needs, the research on siblings suggests that they may have some special concerns as a result of their brother's or sister's exceptionality. In addition to an increased risk for emotional problems and increased demands for caretaking, however,

---

Table 3–2
SUGGESTIONS FOR RECOGNIZING THE NEEDS OF THE PARENTAL SUBSYSTEM

---

1. Assist mothers and fathers in identifying alternative roles that they can fulfill when the parental roles with which they are most familiar are diminished or inappropriate in light of the needs of their child with an exceptionality. For example, a father may not be able to play softball with his son with a physical disability, but they could collect sport facts about their favorite players. A mother may not have a daughter who can follow in her footsteps as a good pianist, but she could give her daughter opportunities to choose records from some of the great artists.
2. Provide and encourage visiting opportunities at school for both mothers and fathers. Seeing their child at school can help both parents have a better understanding of: their child's capabilities and needs, the activities and methods you use, and the overall school program. You might send a letter home at the beginning of the year (with quarterly reminders) of your visiting policy. For example, your letter might inform parents that they are always welcome, but Thursday afternoons—a language and sharing time—is a particularly good time to visit. Ask them to stop by the office when they arrive and tell them that when they enter the room (or observation booth) you will continue doing the present lesson or activity. Inform them they are free to come and go on their own schedule. Possibly the entire school may want to schedule a regular or rotating visiting day, and a member of the PTA could keep a pot of coffee in the lounge, ready for all visiting parents.
3. Develop more flexible scheduling to accommodate both working fathers and mothers for IEP, evaluation, or parent-teacher conferences. School policy may dictate the times for some conferences, but discuss in school staff meetings the possibility of professionals choosing to work from 12 to 8 o'clock as opposed to 8 to 4 o'clock on scheduled parent-teacher conference days. When only one parent can attend, it is often unfair or unrealistic for that parent to be responsible for explaining all the results or discussions to the other parent. If it is a single-parent family, flexible scheduling may increase the opportunities for the single parent to attend with a friend, relative, or other advocate.

4. Aid both fathers and mothers in locating information to provide them with necessary knowledge. Both parents may have a great need for a variety of information pertaining to their child's exceptionality; information on aspects of a particular exceptionality (e.g., spina bifida, giftedness, cerebral palsy); information on legal issues and policies relating to rights and benefits; and information on estate planning, guardianship or consent issues. In addition to professional literature, parents may benefit from reading the personal experiences of other parents. (See Chapter 12 for more discussion on providing information to families). If there is a library containing this information at the school, parents should be given access to check these materials out. If no library exists, possibly one member of the school team would agree to start a parent library specifically for this purpose.

5. Provide parents with the opportunity to discuss with other parents their concerns, successes, and experiences in raising a child with an exceptionality. One strategy is to set up father, mother, or parent support groups. Another strategy is to arrange "mentor" relationships between "experienced" parents who would agree to spend time with parents having younger children. Within the school setting, the most appropriate person to conduct these strategies might be the school social worker, counselor, or psychologist. One program that conducted father support groups (i.e., Supporting Extended Family Members Father's Program) at the University of Washington, found positive effects of the support group on both parents. Parents reported lower levels of stress and depression, and higher levels of satisfaction with social support as a result of professional and peer support (Vadasy, Fewell, Meyer, & Greenberg, 1984).

---

siblings also can experience some very positive outcomes as a result of their brother's or sister's exceptionality.

Grossman (1972) conducted one of the most well-known sibling studies with 83 college-age siblings of brothers and sisters with exceptionalities. Grossman found that approximately 45% of the siblings reported that they had benefited from having a sibling with an exceptionality. The benefits included more tolerance and compassion, greater understanding of other people, increased awareness of prejudice and its consequences, and greater appreciation of their own health and intelligence. In addition, 45% of the siblings reported negative experiences from having a sibling with an exceptionality. These negative experiences included resentment and guilt, fear that they too might be exceptional, shame, and a sense of being neglected by their parents. Sometimes the time, energy, affection, money, and other family resources that are given to the child with an exceptionality can create resentful feelings for siblings. In other situations, siblings can develop an understanding and appreciation of life that is far above their years. Cleveland and Miller (1977) found that having a brother or sister with an exceptionality affected the life goals of siblings. Brothers and sisters who interacted daily with their sibling with an exceptionality ranked learning to accept hardships and devotion to a worthwhile cause as higher life goals than siblings who had less frequent interactions.

Siblings also often are expected to take responsibility to help with physical and care-taking needs of their brother or sister. Older sisters of the child with an exceptionality seem to be most vulnerable for increased responsibility (Cleveland & Miller, 1977; Farber, 1960; Gath, 1974). In some instances siblings experience a need to overachieve in an effort to compensate for their brother's or sister's disability (Cleveland & Miller, 1977; Grossman, 1972). Grossman (1972) found that siblings in a two-child family experienced special pressure, particularly when the sibling is a son.

As previously mentioned, some siblings become more tolerant and accepting of differences. This can affect their socializations in a positive way. Some siblings, however, feel a great deal of stigma at school and a reluctance to bring friends into their home (Lonsdale, 1978). As one sister wrote:

Table 3–3
SUGGESTIONS FOR RECOGNIZING THE NEEDS OF THE SIBLING SUBSYSTEM

---

1. For some siblings, it may be very important to include them in interventions and/or ask them to attend the IEP conference. Indeed research has indicated that siblings can be very effective in training programs, and several reports suggest that when siblings of children with exceptionalities are included in training and therapeutic programs, the entire family may benefit (Miller & Cantwell, 1976; Weinrott, 1974). But it is important to recognize that involving siblings may not be advantageous for either child. Michaelis (1980) describes an example.

    > Each afternoon Jane drops by the classroom to see if her brother, Tom, has any homework to take home. It would be easy just to explain the assignment to Jane and have her see that Tom completes it, but part of what Tom needs to learn is to complete assignments independently. So if Jane takes the materials and responsibility home, it may not be good for either Jane or Tom. (p. 103)

    If a sibling chooses to assume an active part in the education and training of the child with an exceptionality, and it is advantageous to both, make opportunities available for siblings to have a role. Allow opportunities to participate in a variety of ways and to the extent that the sibling chooses.

2. Provide information or resources to siblings who would like more information about exceptionality. This could be part of the parent resource library and could be coordinated by a special education teacher, social worker, school psychologist, or counselor. Part of providing information could just be making yourself available if a sibling would like someone to talk to. Two helpful sources of information for siblings are the newsletter, *Sibling Information Network*, at the Department of Educational Psychology, University of Connecticut, Storrs, CT 06268 and a recent book by T. H. Powell and P. A. Ogle (1985) entitled *Brothers and Sisters—A Special Part of Exceptional Families*.

3.   Arrange a time for siblings to observe their brother or sister in the special classroom. This could give siblings an opportunity to observe the successes of their brother and sister, as well as to observe the methods and procedures that are used. One special educator (and mother of a child with an exceptionality) notes that an open-room visiting policy for siblings may give the sibling status in having "another room" at school (Michaelis, 1980). It is important to remember, however, that for those siblings who indicate a personal need not to be associated with their brother or sister with an exceptionality, this choice of separateness at school should be respected.

4.   A sibling support group is a strategy to allow siblings to get information and discuss their feelings and fears in a safe environment. They will also have an opportunity to share positive aspects of having a sibling with an exceptionality with others who have had similar experiences. As one sibling writes:

> They (siblings) should be given a concise explanation of the disability (i.e., what it is, why it happened, what the prognosis is), be permitted the opportunity to explore their feelings about their sibling, and be given some guidance in problem-solving and coping skills to help them deal with their feeling in a constructive manner (p. 95).

She adds:

> They need to know that it's all right to feel resentful, embarrassed, uncomfortable and inadequate. They also need to be told about the joy, love, challenge and opportunities for growth and fulfillment that such a situation can offer (p. 97). (Helsel Family, 1985)

A sibling support group could be conducted by a teacher, principal, social worker, psychologist, counselor, or a PTA member who might be a sibling of a brother or sister with an exceptionality.

> My friends would come over to play, take one look at her, and some would actually turn around and leave. I felt like everything I did, Bonnie had to do, also. I could not get away from her. If I took piano lessons, she had to take piano lessons. When I was in Girl Scouts, she was in Girl Scouts . . . And finally, the last straw—she was mainstreamed into my junior high school. (Ellifritt, 1984, p. 17)

Siblings may encounter some socialization difficulties. Especially at adolescence, they may need an opportunity to develop their own identity separate from their brother or sister.

Siblings have expressed concern and worry regarding their future responsibilities for their brother or sister with an exceptionality. Even at the age of seven, one young sister shared her worries about whether her brother would have a job, nice clothes and a good place to live. She added, "He won't have to worry because I'll give him my money. I don't want him to be a bum" (Turnbull, 1985, p. 123). McCullough (1981) administered questionnaires to parents and siblings in 23 families with a child with an exceptionality to examine the families' future plans. Only 41% of the parents thought siblings would assume at least partial care for the child with an exceptionality, while 68% of the siblings thought they would assume some responsibility of care. Chapter 5 discusses in detail some of the future concerns of siblings.

Siblings can experience an impact in many different ways. To plan effective interventions for them, you should recognize their variety of feelings and needs. Addressing siblings' needs is one important way of enabling the entire family to help the child with an exceptionality grow and develop. Table 3–3 provides some suggestions for addressing the variety of special needs of siblings.

EXTRAFAMILIAL INTERACTIONS

The extrafamilial subsystem is composed of family or individual inter-actions with extended family, friends, neighbors, and professionals. Each family will vary in the size and degree of dependence on its extrafamilial subsystem. Extrafamilial interactions can make a major contribution to the progress of the child with an exceptionality, as well as provide parents with a network of support. Strategies to help families build and maintain social support, both informal and formal, are discussed in more detail in Chapter 13.

This section will focus on the interactions of family members with relatives, close friends, and neighbors. These persons may have many of the same problems that people in general have toward exceptionality. Misinformation or lack of information and experience may create attitudes of fear, mistrust, dislike, or condescension. These persons may also have to deal with their own feelings of grief, shock, anger, or disappointment at the same time they support the family (Vadasy, Fewell, & Meyer, in press).

Think of the roles that extended family members, close friends, and neighbors play in your life and the lives of many families. Often, these are the persons who provide care and supervision for the children if parents need to go out for a while. Cousins can be the persons at picnics who start the ball games or nature walks. Grandparents can be the persons who stay for the weekend so the parents can take a short vacation or shopping trip.

These persons can be the source of various kinds of support in many families. In families with children with exceptionalities, however, they often do not know how to fill many of the same roles. In one program that provides a support group for grandparents (Vadasy, Fewell, & Meyer, 1985), about half of the grandparents reported they had never visited a medical professional (52%) or an educational professional (48%) with their grandchild. Fifty-seven percent said they had doubts that they were doing the right things for their grandchild. Sixty-seven percent understood some of their grandchild's needs, but they wanted many questions answered. Some of their questions for professionals, as reported by Vadasy, Fewell and Meyer (1985), included:

> How can we help him in therapy? What is the earliest program we can find? What kinds of programs are most effective? What is his potential? What can we do to develop her talents? How can we avoid sheltering the child too much? (pp. 14–15)

An additional challenge for family members is introducing new family members to exceptionality. Margery Helsel DeWert shared her concern about how to introduce her fiance to her brother:

> . . . I made a conscientious effort to teach my archaeologist fiance about developmental disabilities in general and Robin in particular.
>
> John proved to be an enthusiastic pupil, bombarding me with questions: "How can I communicate with him if he can't talk?" "Will he be able to understand what I say to him?" "What should I do if he has a seizure?" "Is it OK to touch him?" After a crash course in charades *a la* Helsels, our family's special method of communicating with Robin, I took John to my parents' house, introduced him to Robin, and crossed my fingers. (DeWert & Helsel, 1985, p. 101)

Many extended family members, close friends, or neighbors will not be able to provide support to the child and the family unless some of their needs for knowledge, experience, and skills can be met. Addressing some of the needs of the family's extrafamilial subsystem is a strategy for helping children and for supporting families. The failure to address some of these needs can have a devastating effect on the entire family. Jennifer Ackerman (1985) shares the negative impact on her mother as a result of lack of interaction with friends and relatives:

> In raising Beckie, Peg (Mom) was determined to do everything to help her reach her potential. Since she had no access to respite care and few offers of reprieve from family and friends, she had little energy left over for normal life, for other needs. She had no healing time—no time to lounge or to go to a friend's house for lunch, to weed the garden or rearrange the linen closet. More important, she had no time and little energy to cultivate friends and interests outside the world of handicapped children. (p. 151)

She continued:

> When Peg was ill with cancer, friends and relatives responded well. They arrived at the door with meals, flowers, and books, and stayed only a short time, considerate of her need for privacy and sleep. They ran errands, returned library books, picked up prescriptions, drove her to the hospital. Their gestures were imaginative. One relative, having heard that Peg

---

Table 3–4
SUGGESTIONS FOR RECOGNIZING THE NEEDS OF THE
EXTRAFAMILIAL SUBSYSTEM

---

1. Ask the parents if there are any friends or relatives who would like more information about exceptionality. What type of information do they want? The same check-out resource library made available to parents and siblings could also be made available to others.
2. Consider conducting a grandparent or other extended family member support group. This could give relatives an opportunity to share their concerns and successes with others in similar situations. This could be organized by the school social worker, psychologist, counselor, or possibly a PTA volunteer who is a grandparent or an extended family member of a child with an exceptionality.
3. As suggested with siblings, opportunities could be made available for relatives or close friends to visit the child in the classroom or therapy sessions. Also, the invitation could be extended to friends and relatives who wish to take part in training or intervention to attend the IEP conference.

---

needed certain vitamins to counteract the effects of the chemotherapy, brought health foods—molasses bread, nuts, raisins—loaded with the appropriate nutrients; another brought rich almond tortes and pastries, lovely soaps and salt baths—part of a philosophy that holds life is full of good rich things to enjoy; one friend suggested that she and Peg take a class in quilt-making—an ambitious project, a lifetime undertaking. Some of these gestures were more appropriate, some less, but they all said, "We care; we want to get you involved with life." This went on for months; and as I loaded the chicken casseroles and quiches into the freezer, I wondered why people found it so easy to approach Peg in her illness, and so difficult to reach out to her when she was raising Beckie. (Ackerman, 1985, pp. 151–152)

Table 3–4 includes some suggestions to provide extended family, friends, and neighbors with the information and skills that can enable them to support the child and family.

COHESION AND ADAPTABILITY

We have just described the subsystems—the people who interact in the family. Now we will discuss *how* they interact. We will explain two elements of interaction—cohesion and adaptability—and discuss implications for professionals. The degrees of cohesion and adaptability in a family describe the ways the subsystems interact (Olson, Russell, & Sprenkle, 180).

Cohesion

Family cohesion is both the close emotional bonding that members have toward each other and the independence of an individual within the family system (Olson et al., 1980). It can be visualized on a continuum, with high disengagement on one end and high enmeshment on the other. One author describes cohesion in the family by the physical metaphor of "the touching of hands" (Carnes, 1981):

> The dilemma is how to be close yet separate. When the fingers are intertwined, it at first feels secure and warm. Yet when one partner (or family member) tries to move, it is difficult at best. The squeezing pressure may even be painful. . . . The paradox of every relationship is how to touch and yet not hold on. (pp. 70–71)

Some families end up not touching enough—disengagement. Some families end up becoming too intertwined—enmeshment. And many families are in the wide swath in the center.

Enmeshment. In a family that is highly enmeshed, the boundaries between subsystems are blurred or weak (Minuchin, 1974). For example, consider a family situation where a mother with many physical care demands for the child gives many of the responsibilities to an older female daughter. The sibling may have less parent-child and other sibling interactions and is drawn into the parental subsystem. Her own needs as a child and a sibling may be overlooked or subordinated.

Interactions in families that are highly enmeshed are often characterized by overinvolvement and overprotection. Family members are allowed little privacy, and all decisions and activities must be family-focused. In such situations family members often have difficulty developing a sense of self or individuality. Many professionals encounter families they describe as overprotective. Overprotection occurs when the family protects or isolates the child from demands and situations that require independence or risk-taking by the child (Fotheringham & Creal, 1974).

Risk-taking can be frightening, but everyone is a risk-taker in varying degrees. For those families that are overprotective and have difficulty with risk-taking for the child, you may want to consider risk-taking in smaller steps. For example, a teacher may want to encourage motor development for a child (with developmental delays) in a family that fears injury. The teacher may therefore suggest trials in which the child holds on to a chinning bar before he or she suggests a climb on the jungle gym. With risk comes the element of unpleasant consequences—the child may fall. Teachers cannot abdicate responsible supervision and goal-setting, but everyone learns through failures and successes. It is part of encouraging autonomy and independence.

Highly enmeshed families also may organize interactions around the exceptionality as though it were the focal characteristic of the family. This may be true in part because the effort to locate, organize, and implement services can be time-consuming for some or all family members. Also, certain types of exceptionality can be stigmatizing for a family, disconnecting it from contact with others. When working with an enmeshed family, we suggest helping parents to identify others in their extrafamilial subsystem (friends or extended family members) who could help meet some family needs. In addition, consider helping family members to identify friends and activities that they may want to pursue both individually and as a family. Not all non-family activities need be centered around the exceptionality (e.g., advocacy work, parent support group, or only friends who are parents of children with exceptionalities).

Disengagement. A high degree of disengagement also can have a negative impact on family interactions. Highly disengaged families have very rigid subsystem boundaries (Minuchin, 1974). For example, consider a family where the child with an exceptionality is considered separate from other family members. Limited interaction leaves the child without support, closeness, and assistance in developing independence. A poem by Fritz Perls (1969), "Gestalt Prayer," characterizes family disengagement:

> I do my thing you do your thing
> I am not in this world to live up to your expectations
> And you are not in this world to live up to mine
> You are you and I am I
> And if by chance we meet, it's beautiful
> If not, it can't be helped.

Interactions in families that are highly disengaged often are characterized by under-involvement, few interests or friends in common, and excessive privacy and time apart. Few decisions require family input. For all family members, particularly the member with an exceptionality, this can be a lonely and difficult situation.

Disengagement can be both within and between subsystems. Disengagement within a subsystem exists, for example, when a father denies the exceptionality and withdraws both from parental and marital interactions. Disengagement between subsystems exists when the maternal or paternal grandparents reject the child with an exceptionality, even to the point of not wanting the child to be a part of holiday dinners. As suggested earlier, information, skills, or greater opportunities to observe and share may help parents or extended family members increase their positive interactions with the child.

Implications of cohesion. There are two reasons it is valuable to understand cohesion in families with children with exceptionalities. First, it is important to recognize the levels of cohesion both between and within subsystems in order to help the family as a whole to meet its needs as well as the child's needs. A balance between the extremes of enmeshment and disengagement characterizes well-functioning families (Olson et al., 1980). In well-functioning families, boundaries between subsystems are clearly defined, and family members experience both a close bonding and a sense of autonomy.

Jane Schulz describes how she felt giving both autonomy and closeness to her adult son with an exceptionality. It is a balance that is not always easy to achieve:

> Is anything comparable to the anguish parents feel when their children leave home? . . . Handicapped children and their parents don't know what to expect from separation . . . My definition of anguish is seeing Billy, suitcase in hand, climb the steps of the group home and then receiving this phone call:
>
> "Mom, I had a dream about you last night and cried a lot."
>
> "I'm sorry, Billy, what's wrong?"
>
> "A little bit homesick. Have to stay here. Fred said."
>
> "Oh . . . "
>
> "I love you, Mom."
>
> "I love you too, Billy."
>
> Although I look upon the two years' separation with all its problems and uncertainties as the most painful experience of my life, I now see it as a vital part of Billy's growth and of mine. (Schulz, 1985, pp. 16–17)

Remember that most families fall somewhere within a wide to normal range on the continuum of cohesion (Olson et al., 1980). The family's values and cultural background influence its individual degree of cohesion. For example, some Italian-American families may value close family ties and family-centered activities more than families from other ethnic backgrounds (Rotunno & McGoldrick, 1982).

A second important reason for understanding cohesion in families with children having exceptionalities is to enable you to examine your interventions. Does a particular intervention or program encourage enmeshment or disengagement in a family? Mothers involved in early childhood programs often receive reinforcment for establishing enmeshed relationships with their young child. They are encouraged to spend time in the classroom, attend mothers' groups, provide home interventions, and transport children to numerous services. When they spend this much time with the child, what happens to their needs and the needs of other family members? Oftentimes, if they do not perform all these tasks, they run the risk of being labeled uninterested in their child. These are often the same mothers who are criticized later for being overprotective or not letting go.

Adaptability

Family adaptability is the ability of the family to change in response to situational and developmental stress (Olson et al., 1980). Family adaptability is the ability of the family to plan and to work out differences when they occur (Carnes, 1981). Adaptability, similar to cohesion, is influenced by family values and cultural background.

Adaptability, also similar to cohesion, can be viewed on a continuum. Some families are unable or unwilling to change in response to situational or developmental stress—rigidity. Some families are characterized by inconsistent change and family instability—chaotic. And many families are in the wide swath of balance in the center.

Rigid Families.   Rigid families demonstrate a high degree of control and structure. Their interactions often are characterized by many strictly enforced rules. The power hierarchy in the family is rigidly delineated and negotiations are seldom tolerated. Roles are also very rigid and there is little role-sharing.

Consider the example of a son who becomes physically disabled by a diving accident. This change in the family requires new and demanding energies for meeting many physical and emotional needs. If, in the past, meeting these needs was primarily the role of the mother, these added demands may be more than she can handle. If the family is highly rigid, it will have difficulty changing or sharing these roles with the mother, thereby creating stress and difficulty for her and other family members.

The rigidity of the family power hierarchy is an important consideration for many professionals when working with families with children having exceptionalities. One issue is that families must be able to adapt their power hierarchies over time. For example, an adolescent would have a greater voice in family decision-making than a young child. As persons with exceptionality enter adolescence or adulthood, you need to consider their abilities to choose and make decisions for themselves. Often family members and professionals tend to keep the child low on the hierarchy of power even into adulthood, treating persons with exceptionality like children long after they have ceased to be children.

A second issue is identifying the person or persons (e.g., parent, parents, grandmother, or uncle) who maintain(s) strict control over family decisions and rules. For example, a teacher might have a mother work on procedures to implement a home-based language program. If her husband, who maintains strict leadership in the family, rejects the program, chances may be nonexistent that it will be effective. Indeed, if the mother carries out the intervention against her husband's wishes, he may withdraw from interactions with both the mother and the child. As suggested earlier, it is important to examine the impact of an intervention on each parent and the parents as a couple. It may help to talk with the father to understand his values and goals and to discuss how an alternative intervention may be more consistent with them. As lead decision-maker in the family, his support of a program is vital to the family and the program's success.

Chaotic Families. Chaotic families demonstrate a low degree of control and structure. Their interactions often are characterized by few rules, which in turn are seldom enforced and often changing. Promises and commitments are often unkept, and family members cannot depend upon one another. Frequently, there is no family leader, there are endless negotiations, and unsure and often changing roles. One of the signs of a chaotic family is that it does not plan together for the future (Carnes, 1981).

All families can have periods of chaos during stressful life events. But, for a family where chaos is a consistent life-style, the consequences can have a negative impact on the family and the child with an exceptionality. Consider the example of a mother with three children, one with a severe developmental delay. The mother also has a live-in boyfriend who is the family's primary source of financial support. In the last two years the live-in boyfriend has become alcoholic and abusive to family members. When the boyfriend begins fights, there is harsh interpretation of the rules for children. When the fighting escalates, the rules change—survival being the main rule. Later, the remorseful boyfriend becomes extremely indulgent—creating a third set of rules. And the instability and chaos continues (Carnes, 1981).

Implications of Adaptability. A balance between the two extremes of rigidity and chaos characterize well-functioning families (Olson et al., 1980). It is important to remember that most families fall within a wide to normal range on the continuum of adaptability. But for those families whose interactions are extremely rigid or chaotic, there are several actions you may take. One is referral for counselling. Another is to help families plan for change. If possible, discuss change and transitions well in advance of the time they will occur. Ask yourself, "Is a change too sudden or radical for a given family's level of adaptability?" If so, some children and families may benefit from gradual transitions. When a child will be changing classrooms or school buildings, start with a gradual transition, one day a week, before making the complete transition. If a child needs to begin to learn how to ride the bus, and the family cannot adapt to this change, identify intermediate steps: riding only part of the way or riding with a friend or family member.

You also may encourage families to learn how to examine alternatives. Many families that lack adaptability may demonstrate only a few alternatives (Walsh, 1982). Families might benefit from assistance in brainstorming alternatives, a step of the problem-solving process (See Chapter 13). For example, one mother was experiencing a very frustrating morning routine with her child, who refused to dress. After generating several alternatives, the mother and teacher agreed to send the child to preschool in the morning in her pajamas. This improved interactions between the mother and child, and after a period of time, the dressing procedures learned at preschool were put into practice at home.

SUMMARY

This chapter has described many of the issues and concepts of family interaction. It has described who interacts in the family (family subsystems) and how they interact (cohesion and adaptability). Both of these elements of family interaction will vary greatly depending upon each family, its values, resources, cultural background, and family membership. Remember that cohesion and adaptability change as the family moves through the life cycle. For example, the needs, roles, and interactions of families raising young children usually are different than those for families in the process of launching adult children from the home. Also remember that balance is essential. Well functioning families are those that are able to maintain a balance of cohesion and adaptability in the family's interaction (Olson et al., 1980). Most of all, remember that the family consists of interactions— i.e., it is an interactional system. The child cannot be approached in isolation, for the child is part of an interacting system that must function as a whole to meet the many needs of each member. Each of these many needs of the family as a whole will be discussed in more detail in Chapter 4. Nevertheless, addressing some needs of parents, siblings, grandparents, close friends, and other extended family members ultimately nurtures and assists the child.

Chapter 4

Family Functions

Families exist to meet the individual and collective needs of their members (Caplan, 1976; Leslie, 1979). The tasks that families perform to meet those needs are family functions. Functions exist generally in seven areas: (a) economic, (b) domestic and health care, (c) recreation, (d) socialization, (e) self-definition, (f) affection, and (g) educational/vocational (Turnbull, Summers, & Brotherson, 1984). In each of these areas family activity generally has two purposes: (a) to meet current family and individual needs at a reasonable level, (b) and to transfer responsibility for meeting those needs from the older to the younger generation (Brotherson, Backus, Summers, & Turnbull, in press). Table 4–1 provides examples of tasks associated with each function.

It is important to examine families' functions because a professional focus on only the educational/vocational needs of a child tends to obscure the many other responsibilities of families. For example, parents carrying

Table 4–1
TASKS ASSOCIATED WITH FAMILY FUNCTIONS

Economic	*Domestic/Health Care*	*Recreation*

Generating income
Paying bills and banking
Handling investments
Overseeing insurance
   benefit programs
Earning allowance
Dispensing allowance
	Food purchasing and food
	   preparation
	Clothes purchasing and
	   preparation
	Health care and maintenance
	Safety and protection
	Transportation
	Home maintenance
		Individual and family oriented
		   recreation
		Setting aside demands
		Developing and enjoying hobbies

Socialization	*Self-identity*	*Affection*

Interpersonal relationships
Developing social skills
Engaging in social activities
	Establishing self-identity and
	   self-image
	Recognizing strengths and
	   weaknesses
	Sense of belonging
		Nurturing and love
		Companionship
		Intimacy
		Expressing emotions

Educational/Vocational	
Continuing education for parents School work Homework Cultural appreciation	Career choice Development of work ethic Support of career interests and problems

Note. *From* Working with Families with Disabled Members: A Family System Perspective *(p. 36) by A. P. Turnbull, J. A. Summers and M. J. Brotherson, 1984, Lawrence, KS: University of Kansas. Adapted by persmission.*

out evening and weekend home teaching programs to increase their child's language or cognitive skills may have less time and energy to address the functions of affection, self-definition, or recreation. By recognizing the needs of the family and the individual with an exceptionality in total context, you can help the family meet its needs in a balanced fashion. Accordingly, this chapter discusses the ways that a family member with an exceptionality can influence how families attend to functions and suggests how you may help meet family needs.

IMPACT ON FAMILY FUNCTIONS

Each area of family functions can be impacted negatively, positively, or neutrally by the presence of a family member with an exceptionality. Consider the following examples of differential impact and suggestions of ways professionals can respond.

Economic Needs

Most families need to earn a living and decide how money will be spent for family needs. The presence of a member with an exceptionality can create special economic needs by increasing the family's consumptive demands and decreasing its productive capacity (Turnbull et al., 1984). In one study, 29% of the families reported that their child's physical disability had created a financial hardship (McAndrew, 1976). For some families, the child's special needs can include costly medical bills, expensive equipment, or structural adaptations to the home. When one father of a son with a physical disability was asked to name the most stressful factor in planning his son's future, he answered:

> Finding finances. I don't know where the money is going to come from. We've had to have help over the years. I quit counting when Ron's hospital bill topped $600,000. (Brotherson, 1985)

Just as the presence of a family member with an exceptionality can negatively affect the amount of money the family has to spend on other needs, so it can also negatively affect the amount of money a family can produce. Some families have reported sacrificing careers to care for the child or to relocate in a geographic area with appropriate services (Turnbull, Summers, and Brotherson, 1984). One study found 27% of the families believed their work performance was affected by having an exceptional child (Lonsdale, 1978). This study included children with a variety of disabling conditions and levels of severity. Parents mentioned such factors as "lack of concentration, needing to take a lot of time off work, needing to take a less well-paid job . . . " as affecting their work (Lonsdale, 1978, p. 117).

Not all children or youth necessarily cost a family more or affect its ability to generate income. In fact, in some situations the child may even cost the family less because the child may not be requesting such expensive items as a new video recorder, personal computer, or car.

Professionals usually cannot directly reduce the economic impact of exceptionality, but they can make information on financial sources available to families who request it. Some families may need information about social security disability benefits or other sources of governmental assistance. Others may need advice on wills, trusts, and estate planning. Others may live in states where family subsidy programs are available. Following are suggestions to provide information to families:

1. Collect and include resources on financial information and planning as part of the family resource library. For example, *Alternatives: A Family Guide to Legal and Financial Planning for the Disabled* (Russell, 1983) includes chapters on wills, guardianship, trusts, government benefits, taxes, insurance, and financial planning.
2. Identify appropriate community contacts, and provide parents with names and telephone numbers of persons to contact, e.g., an attorney experienced in estate planning or an employee of the state social services agency who can tell parents how to apply for disability benefits or family subsidies. The school could serve as a referral source to other agencies if personnel are not available to address this topic directly.
3. Invite guest speakers to a PTA or parent support group to discuss financial planning issues.
4. Ask a panel of parents who have been successful in obtaining financial sources or who have completed financial planning to speak with other parents.
5. Serve as a referral source to help families investigate scholarships and financial aid.

Domestic and Health Care Needs

A basic function of families is to meet the physical and health needs of their members. This includes the day-to-day tasks of living: cooking, cleaning, laundry, transportation, obtaining medical care when needed, and so forth. For some parents, the child's domestic and health care needs create stress, which often increases over the life cycle as the child's needs increase. One study found that the physical caregiving of a child with a disability required an average of two hours a day (McAndrew, 1976). Leah Ziskin describes the stress of meeting these needs in her family.

As Jennie grew older and bigger, it became increasingly more difficult for her caregivers to bathe, dress, toilet, and generally take care of her at home. In addition, because she was more active (and we encouraged her activity), she could also get into more things around the house, thus increasing her potential for harm. One Sunday morning, for example, I set out on the table three Styrofoam cups, two of which were to be filled with cocoa for Jennie's brothers; the remaining one was filled with hot coffee for Jennie's dad. In the short time that it took to carry the cocoa from the kitchen counter to the table, Jennie (who was then nine) had pulled the cup of coffee down on herself. The hot coffee soaked through her shirt and burned her chest. Most of her skin suffered first-degree burns and healed rapidly. But one area, about the size of a quarter, suffered a third-degree burn and remains heavily scarred to this day. (Ziskin, 1985, p. 75)

When parents are busy meeting a child's domestic and health care needs, they sometimes may overlook their own needs. One mother describes the exhaustion she experienced when she finally submitted to her physical need for rest:

I can remember having to restrain my child at 5:00 in the morning because he had paced all night. I was exhausted and there was nothing left to do except restrain him. In his bed he finally drifted off to sleep. (Blue-Banning, 1985, p. 6)

Families' domestic and health care needs vary depending on the type, degree, and severity of exceptionality. For example, a child or youth with a sensory loss probably will not create the same extent of domestic and health care demands as one with severe mental retardation. But just because children can create greater stress in this family function does not mean they always do so. In fact, there are many positive contributions that children can offer to this family function. They can help with housekeeping, yard work, laundry, or the needs of younger siblings. The following suggestions may help those families that are experiencing stress in meeting this family function.

1. When selecting self-help or personal care goals at schools, discuss priorities with family members. Encourage families to bring their priority goals and objectives to the IEP conference. For example, you may be teaching a student to appropriately blow her nose and keep her fingernails clean, but at home, exceedingly more important, is the need to learn wheel chair transfer skills.

2. Work with family members to identify those skills needed by the student to contribute to the domestic and health care functions (e.g., taking out the trash, vacuuming or dusting, assisting with laundry, driving other family members, diapering or feeding a younger sibling).

3. Provide practical suggestions and information on meeting domestic and health care needs through the family resource library. One recent helpful book addressing these needs is *Managing Physical Handicaps* by B.A. Fraser and R.N. Hensinger (1983). This book offers suggestions on such things as wheel chair travel, lifting methods, positioning techniques and other day-to-day care suggestions.

4. Many parents of children with exceptionality find creative ways to meet the domestic and health care needs of all family members. Arrange for experienced parents to share their successes at parent groups or through mentorships between sets of parents. Consider sending a notebook back and forth from school to homes and let family members (e.g., parents, siblings, grandparents) share their successes and suggestions with other families in a collective classroom notebook that would travel between families.

5. Remind parents that all family members have physical and health care needs. Parent needs are legitimate, too. If you see parents looking tired and run-down, let them know the teaching program, parent group, new recipe for dinner, or the laundry can wait.

6. Select one member of the professional team to seek out and become familiar with respite and child care options in the community through social service agencies, volunteer groups, or church groups. Let parents know these groups are available if they would like a reprieve from physical and health care demands.

Recreation Needs

The family serves an important function as an outlet where members can relax and be themselves. Sometimes this function is curtailed by a family member with an exceptionality. Some families have reported that they had difficulty enjoying family outings such as trips to the beach, picnics, or trips to the swimming pool or cinema (Dunlap & Hollingsworth, 1977; Lonsdale, 1978). While this function may be curtailed for some families, for others, these aspects of exceptionality can enhance their ability to rest and recreate.

Leah Ziskin, whose daughter has mental retardation, describes how her daughter's initial limitations on the family's recreational opportunities resulted in a very positive contribution to the family as a whole:

> One example that comes to mind is our acquisition of a cabin or summer house, as we call it. Our favorite vacations used to be finding a cabin in the wooded area away from civilization. It was always difficult to take Jennie because we had to cart cribs and other paraphernalia, not knowing what we would find wherever we settled ourselves. We therefore decided that it

would be much easier for us if we had our own cabin already stocked with the equipment we all wanted. After diligent searching, we found a cabin in a woods an hour from our home. It is now one of the main forces that keeps us a united family and is a great source of inspiration and joy to all of us. In a sense, we have to thank Jennie for making it more difficult to travel and for prompting us to find our own cabin. (Ziskin, 1985, p. 72)

Educational objectives for leisure and recreation often have been accorded low priority in the educational process, yet this is a very important function of family life (Ball, Chasey, Hawkins, & Verhoven, 1976). The following may help the students with exceptionalities work towards meeting their own recreational needs in life, as well as help the family as a whole perform the function of recreation for its members.

1. As part of your educational assessment, identify skills in the natural environment that the student with exceptionality could use to meet his or her own recreation needs in the future. For example, as part of your curriculum on leisure and recreation skills, offer students 20 minutes a day to play board games such as checkers. If, however, in assessing the child at home, you find the child's greatest leisure interest is listening to music, you could support this natural interest by teaching the student to handle and store records and to use a stereo independently.

2. Students who are gifted usually have a wide, versatile range of interests but may have problems concentrating in one area for a period of time (Stewart, 1978). Encourage the gifted student to follow through on recreation and leisure activities for real mastery rather than going through a lot of hobbies or sports activities in a short time.

3. Opportunities for hobbies, vacations and recreational pursuits outside the home are growing for persons with an exceptionality and their families. One member of the school team could obtain and share community offerings with parents for such activities as horseback riding, canoeing, dancing, camping, and tour packages, as the school and families may not be aware of all community recreational opportunities.

4. Be sure to consider mainstreamed recreational options such as scouts, 4–H clubs, arts programs, and dance lessons, and so forth for children and youth with exceptionalities. These options sometimes may be overlooked by families and professionals alike. Janet Bennett states:

A long time ago I stopped looking at newspaper listings of special programs for retarded children. Now I just notice what Kathryn might like. All kinds of courses are given by community schools, YMCA's, or churches   .   .   . Grandparents and teenagers, beginners, or those with some familiarity with the subject—all take the same course. Though there may be beginning, intermediate, or advanced levels, nobody would notice or care if someone took the same level course several times. For most of us, and especially for retarded children, taking enough time is more important than special techniques. (Bennett, 1985, p. 171)

5. Remember to include as part of your family resource library information on recreation and leisure. One resource that describes a lifelong leisure skills curriculum based upon the personal preferences and needs of students and their families is *Longitudinal Leisure Skills for Severely Handicapped Learners* (Wuerch & Voeltz, 1982).

Socialization Needs

Socialization is vital in determining the overall quality of life for most individuals. Families are the bases from which individuals learn to interact with others. They are keys in the achievement of socialization for all members (Skrtic, Summers, Brotherson & Turnbull, 1984).

Many families experience stress in attempting to meet socialization needs. A review of the literature on social development of children having exceptionalities concluded that "almost all exceptional children, regardless of their disability, have significant social handicaps" (Strain, 1982, p. 2). Another study recently found that, after residential options, socialization options were the greatest need identified by parents for young adults with mental retardation (Brotherson, 1985). As one mother said: "People with disabilities are lonesome, lonesome people" (Brotherson, 1985).

Lack of socialization options can be caused by specific skill deficits (e.g., lack of mobility or verbal skills) or be attributed to the fact that community members, neighbors, and relatives have negative attitudes toward persons with an exceptionality. In one study of 116 mothers, one-third of those mothers felt their relationships with friends were adversely affected. Friends were reported to be "frightened, embarrassed, and don't know how to approach us" (McAndrew, 1976, p. 229). Overcoming these barriers can be difficult for families. In addition to the negative reactions parents often experience when they take their child into the community, they also find it difficult to meet their own socialization needs. One-third of the mothers in McAndrew's study (1976) also reported that their child had put restrictions on their socialization opportunities, primarily because of the difficulty of finding someone to stay with their child. One mother states: "There are simply times we don't do things because of our son. He requires so much, it's exhausting to just sit down and explain to a babysitter what has to be done. It's just easier not to do it" (Blue-Banning, 1985, p. 1).

There also can be positive effects of exceptionality on socialization for family members. Many parents have reported that parent programs were the catalyst for friendships that have lasted long after their children left the programs. Parent organizations also offer many parents an avenue to build friendships and reduce isolation.

All members of the family need an opportunity to socialize. Socialization opportunities may be few and hard to find for some families. Janet Bennett describes the importance of a friendship between her older adolescent daughter and a friend.

> Her close friends have been two: the girl next door, who, sad to say, has moved to Long Island, and a girl we met in a drugstore downtown when a chance conversation revealed that they both knew some sign language and had the same first and middle names. This second Kathryn has been my Kathryn's best friend for five years now. She has problems with some academic subjects, but she's smarter and wiser than most adults I know. She can explain situations and events and emotions to Kathryn in simpler, clearer language than I can produce, and her patience, understanding, and loyalty are nothing short of phenomenal. And because this girl is generally so able, they can go bowling or to movies or the mall by themselves, without me. Kathy is regularly here overnight on weekends; they work out dance routines or watch "Love Boat" and "Fantasy Island." What Kathy draws from Kathryn is warmth, affection, and an easy, relaxed, noncompetitive enjoyment that I suspect is not so readily available among her public school classmates. (Bennett, 1985b, p. 182)

How can you help all family members meet their social needs? Here are a few suggestions:

1. As suggested earlier, knowledge about possible respite care can be made available to those parents who choose to use it. This may give them the opportunity to meet some of their own socialization needs. Also, suggest to parents that providing training or information to a relative may help them to be more comfortable in either providing care for their child or asking their child out for a social occasion. If there is an interested relative, invite him or her to the classroom to observe some of the techniques you use.
2. Some children or youth may have inappropriate behavior problems that make it very difficult for family members to take them into the community. Make available to parents (or other family members) behavior management techniques (See Chapter 12) that would make it easier to take their child into social situations.
3. A member of the school team may be willing to conduct a family support group so that families may exchange ideas about how they handled uncomfortable social situations. This group could share suggestions for coping with stares and rude comments made by persons in public.

Family members may benefit from role-playing embarrassing situations and exploring different ways to handle these types of situations. One mother, for example, handles impudent stares of strangers by saying, "You seem interested in my son; would you like to meet him?" (Schulz, 1985, p. 6)

Affection Needs

Families provide a very important environment for meeting the needs of physical intimacy (e.g., touching, hugging, and kissing) as well as feelings of unconditional love and esteem by others. A child with an exceptionality can have both a positive and negative impact on a family's ability to be affectionate (Turnbull, Summers, and Brotherson, 1984). For example, a family can be drawn together and experience a close sense of bonding as a result of the exceptionality. As one sibling put it:

> I always felt that there was something very different about our family. Of course, you know, Cathy is that difference. Because of her difference there was a degree of specialness or closeness . . . it was sort of a bond that made us all very, very close. We all pitched in and helped each other out and Cathy was the one thing in difficult times that we could focus on. (Klein, 1972, p. 25)

A negative impact can also occur in families with members who are exceptional. For example, some families may fail to establish affectional bonds with the child who is exceptional either because of fear the child will die or leave the family, or because the child is physically deformed (Featherstone, 1980). Leah Ziskin wrote about her difficulty in developing affectional bonds with her daughter:

> There was a time when I was haunted: if Jennie was to be dependent all her life and eventually might be put in an institution, why was I waiting for this time? Why was I allowing myself to grow to love her, to care for her? Why shouldn't I give up now before these ties of love develop? (Ziskin, 1985, p. 70)

As youth with exceptionalities grow older, their needs and means of expressing affection are often complicated by emerging sexuality. Sexuality can be a difficult topic for many families, but in families with children who are exceptional it can be even more difficult. As Ann Turnbull comments about her son, who is moderately mentally retarded:

> He is physically mature, even more so than most sixteen-year-olds. Puberty has created tumultuous emotions for him, partially because he does not understand what is happening. His rapid physical changes stand in stark contrast to his slow cognitive growth, and the imbalance has been difficult for me to adjust to. (Turnbull, 1985a, p. 139)

Other parents may refuse to acknowledge the needs and changes of affection and sexuality that accompany aging. As one mother of an adolescent son with a disability said:

> He has no needs along this line. I don't see any sexual desires expressed. He asked, "Will I ever get married?" and I said, "No." Besides, it is against the church. (Brotherson, 1985)

The following are some suggestions that may help families meet the affectional needs of their members:

1. Encourage families to recognize the needs all members have for affection. If carrying out a home teaching program each night means omitting the family's opportunities for just sitting close on the couch and eating popcorn together, then reconsider a balance towards meeting all needs, not just educational needs.
2. Provide materials in the resource library or discussion groups that could help both parents and students with an exceptionality gain a better understanding of sexuality. Young adults or adolescents with exceptionality, depending on age, type, and severity of exceptionality, benefit from accurate and sensitive information about sexuality.
3. Identify resource persons that could help families deal with difficult issues of affection and sexuality. One mother describes how a referral to one professional addressed her family's concerns:

> One psychologist at the university helped a lot with the sexual things. He showed Rick what things he could do and should do in what places. He used slides and models and things like that. (Brotherson, 1985)

4. Many parents and other family members have reported the positive contributions that their family member with an exceptionality has made to the family function of affection (e.g., closeness, understanding differences, patience, and love). Often, however, family members and professionals alike focus more on the stresses and less on the positive contributions of the child with an exceptionality. Help parents to identify the positive contributions of their child to affection as well as other family functions. One possible strategy might include a positive contributions discussion at a family group.

Self-Identity Needs

Persons perceive their own competence and worth by self-identity. Family membership plays an important role to help individuals establish who they are and their worth as people. Exceptionality can have an impact on the self-identity of all family members. Parents of children and youth with an exceptionality can often experience difficulty with their own self-esteem. Parents of infants, for example, may be at-risk for developing a self-identity as competent parents, possibly because infants with exceptionality are sometimes less responsive to soothing or stimulation, and their cues are often difficult for parents to read. Janet Bennett states the importance of an identity not based on exceptionality:

> Early on, I decided that I would not be a parent of a retarded child. I would resist the tendency to alter my fundamental identity in response to the twist in the road that had come with retardation. The road might have twisted, but it was still the same *I* who walked the road. Kathryn was not "a mongoloid," nor was she later on that equally invasive "child with Down syndrome." She was a child, she was Kathryn, and she had mongolism by whatever name anyone cared to use. An ARC unit or any other kind of group could offer me services or information or moral support or advice but it would not provide me—or Kathryn—with an identity. (Bennett, 1985, p. 165)

Even parents with gifted children may experience difficulty with self-identity. Most parents anticipate raising "normal" children; if they are confronted with raising a child with giftedness, they may feel uncertain and even threatened (Dettmann & Colangelo, 1980). Parents' inability to accept an exceptionality may also greatly affect the ability of the child or youth with an exceptionality to develop a healthy self-identity. If parents have difficulty showing pride and pleasure in the uniqueness of their child, then their child will grow to view their exceptionality or "differentness" as a defect and societal deviance (Rousso, 1984). A young woman with cerebral palsy makes this point quite clear:

> My mother was quite concerned about the awkwardness of my walk—not only did it periodically cause me to fall but it made me stand out, appear conspicuously different—which she feared would subject me to endless teasing and rejection. To some extent it did. She made numerous attempts over the years of my childhood to have me go for physical therapy and to practice walking more "normally" at home. I vehemently refused all her efforts. She could not understand why I would not walk straight. Now I realize why. My disability, with my different walk and talk and my involuntary movements, having been with me all of my life, was part of me, part of my identity. With these disability features, I felt complete and whole. My mother's attempt to change my walk, strange as it may seem, felt like an assault on myself, and incomplete acceptance of all of me, an attempt to make me over. I fought it because I wanted to be accepted and appreciated as I was. Teasing was painful, but not nearly as painful as losing a part of myself. I suspect that my mother then and perhaps even now has difficulty understanding my perspective, and not because she was uncaring. (Rousso, 1984, p. 9)

Assisting children and youth with exceptionalities, as well as all family members, to develop a positive self-identity is critical to enduring quality of life. The following suggestions may help families meet their self-identity needs.

1. Help family members to develop self-identity in areas other than exceptionality by pursuing their own interests, hobbies, or personal goals. If all or most family activities (e.g., parent groups, other friends of children with exceptionality, advocacy efforts, home programs) revolve around exceptionality, it may become the major identifying characteristic of the family. If the family's identity remains tied to the person with exceptionality, the family may have difficulty in encouraging the young adult to exercise greater independence (Turnbull, Summers, and Brotherson, 1984). Siblings may also be at-risk for healthy self-identity if family activities revolve solely around exceptionality.

2. Encourage children and youth with exceptionalities to identify and develop interests that give them pride and self-esteem. One strategy might be to place children with an exceptionality in the role of helper rather than recipient of help. Children with exceptionalities are often placed in the position of being helped by various people including their classmates without an exceptionality (e.g., peer tutoring), but they are infrequently placed in a position in which someone needs their help. Most of us enjoy the feelings of value from being needed. The National Center for Citizen Involvement has recently published a book, *Involving the Handicapped as Volunteers: A Guidebook* (1984). This book was developed on the premise that community service is one way that persons with an exceptionality can develop independence and self-esteem and become productive and empowered participants in community life. This pilot project found persons with an exceptionality providing friendship to isolated elderly persons, teaching preschoolers fire prevention and motor skills, and organizing bingo nights for the local church group. Persons with exceptionalities can make many positive contributions in the lives of people. Their sense of self-worth and self-identity can grow at the same time they become contributing members of their community.

3. Encourage children and youth with exceptionalities to express their own choices as a strategy to enhance self-identity. Often we professionals have visions of what all persons with an exceptionality *should* have, to constitute a quality of life. Quality of life, however, is different for different people. Allowing children and youth to choose what is important to them allows them greater control and independence in their lives.

Educational/Vocational Needs

Educational/vocational needs is the area that professionals often emphasize more than families (Turnbull, Summers, & Brotherson, 1984). This is appropriate if this emphasis is consistent with the family's values and cultural priorities (see Chapter 2). If not, the difference between the focus of school, other service agencies, and home can cause strain or possible conflict in the home and school relationship. As stated earlier, educational/vocational needs are only one function of many the family must address. Parents or the child can respond negatively to a perceived over-emphasis on educational/vocational needs. Maddux and Cummings (1983) warn:

> If academic learning is required in both the home and the school, a child who has difficulty learning gets very little relief. The home ceases to be a haven from scholastic pressures. Imagine how most of us would feel if the most frustrating, least enjoyable, and most difficult thing about our work were waiting for us when we came home each day. (p. 30)

Most school professionals are trained in this function and are most familiar with it in helping children and families. The following, however, are some suggestions to consider:

1. Think about the time, energy and emotional investment that is required for each educational/vocational intervention. Families are very busy and one more educational or vocational task or expectation may be more than the family can handle. Ask family members if they have the time and the desire to teach their child at home or come to a family support group. If they do not, help to generate other alternatives to address family needs. If lack of time is a problem, possibly one member of the school team or PTA might be willing to conduct a time management workshop. Table 4–2 provides some time management suggestions for families.
2. For families who choose greater involvement in educational/vocational planning, provide a variety of strategies for involvement. Many strategies for involving families in IEP conferences are included in Chapter 10 and for providing educational and vocational information to families in Chapter 12.
3. Sometimes professionals in education assume that parents of children who are gifted are also gifted themselves. This often leads to the assumption that parents will know the most appropriate educational and vocational strategies for encouraging their children. This assumption and conclusion is often false (Callahan & Kauffman, 1982). These parents might benefit from assistance by directing their child's energies and interest, selecting mentors, and setting limits. One strategy for selecting a mentor for a child who is very interested in astrology might

---

Table 4–2
TIME MANAGEMENT TIPS

---

1. Recognize that inevitably some of your time will be spent on activities outside of your control.
2. Don't waste time regretting your failures; concentrate on action steps to further your goals.
3. Don't waste time feeling guilty about what you don't do; concentrate on things which yield the greatest long-term benefit.
4. Allow yourself to relax and "do nothing" for brief periods.
5. Try to enjoy whatever you are doing. Don't short-change yourself during relaxation or work.
6. Before you start a task, ask yourself why you're doing it. If your answer is not convincing, do something else.
7. Schedule a regular 5–15 minute daily planning time to make a "to do" list of specific items.
8. Arrange "to do" items in order of priority.
9. Do first things first; teach yourself to go down your "to do" list without skipping over difficult items.
10. Have confidence in your judgment of priorities and stick to them in spite of difficulties.
11. Set *reasonable* timelines for yourself and others.
12. Try not to run only one errand at a time or go to the store for only one item; save up tasks to do once a week.
13. Take along some small tasks you can do if you need to be someplace where you'll have to wait (for example, the doctor's office).
14. If you can, delegate some responsibilities if they become too great. A little give and take with your support systems can go a long way.

Note. *From* Meeting the Challenge of Disability and Chronic Illness—A Family Guide *by L. Goldfarb, M. J. Brotherson, J. A. Summers, and A. P. Turnbull, in press, Baltimore, Paul H. Brookes Publishing Co. Copyright applied for. Adapted by permission.*

be to post a notice in the local newspaper or community buildings (e.g., museums, churches) asking if persons with this expertise are interested. Another strategy might be to contact a local university.

4. Helping students plan their own vocational needs is a curriculum area sometimes slighted in special education programming. Students often need help in vocational planning and awareness of employment opportunities. Expose students to a variety of possible future jobs through books, field trips, class projects, classroom visits by different professionals or craftspersons, and so forth, so that students have an opportunity to choose a vocation of interest to them. Do not wait until a student is ready to graduate to identify skills that will be needed for specific jobs. To enhance the vocational success of students, these skills should be incorporated into the IEP process over several years.

Table 4–3 provides a summary of each family function and the suggestions that have been discussed.

Table 4–3
ADDRESSING FAMILY NEEDS

Family Need	*How Professionals Can Help*
Economic	Provide information on sources of governmental assistance (resource library).
	Provide information on wills, trusts, and estate planning (resource library).
	Provide the names of contact persons in the community who can provide assistance (e.g., attorneys, social security service staff).
	Provide information on available family subsidy programs.
Physical and Health Care	Provide practical information on meeting physical and health care needs (resource library).
	Encourage ways for parents who are innovative in meeting these needs to share with other parents (e.g., parent group, mentorships).
	Share with family members community respite care options to give them a break from caregiver responsibilities.
	Remind other family members that their physical and health care needs are important, too.
	Identify ways in which the child can contribute to helping the family with this function.
Recreation	Identify recreational interests and skills that the child with an exceptionality could pursue on into adulthood.
	Identify and share with families all available community recreational options (e.g., recreation newsletter or PTA presentation).
	Include as part of the resource library information on airlines, hotels, buses or trains that make special adaptations for travelers with exceptionality
Socialization	Help families identify friends or relatives who might be interested in either child care at home or taking the child with exceptionality out into the community.
	Make information (e.g., resource library) or visits to the classroom available to anyone who chooses to take a greater role in helping to meet the child's socialization needs.
	Provide behavior management training to those parents who are interested in reducing inappropriate social behavior.
	Encourage family members to share with other families how they handle uncomfortable social situations (e.g., mentorship, parent group, coping with stigma highlights in newsletter).

Three important points have been interwoven throughout these suggestions:

1. the importance of balancing *every* family member's needs,
2. the importance of using a social support network to help whenever possible,
3. the importance of identifying the positive contributions of children and youth having an exceptionality to each function.

Table 4–3
Continued

Family Need	How Professionals Can Help
Affection	Provide materials (e.g., resource library) that would help families gain a better understanding of issues of affection and sexuality.
	Examine whether home teaching programs or other educational goals might be interfering with the time families have available to meet affection needs.
	Identify community or school resource personnel who could help families deal with issues of sexuality.
	Provide opportunities for interested parents to share their concerns and successes of meeting affection needs with other families (e.g., family groups, mentorships).
	Provide opportunities for parents and other family members to share the positive contributions their child makes to the family's affection needs.
Self-Identity	Encourage children and youth with an exceptionality to choose hobbies and interests that give them pride in accomplishment.
	Provide opportunities for children and youth with an exceptionality to help other persons, either at school or in the community, so that they are not always the ones receiving help.
	Encourage other family members to pursue their interests and hobbies that are separate from issues of exceptionality.
Educational/ Vocational	Allow parents to choose the level of involvement that is consistent with their time and energy level.
	For parents who choose greater involvement provide a variety of strategies for involvement in educational and vocational planning and implementation (e.g., school visits, home visits, visits to possible future work sites, information prior to IEP conferences).
	Expose students to a variety of possible future employment options and allow students to choose a vocation consistent with their interests and skills.
	Include skills needed for success in specific jobs or sites into the IEP several years before graduation.

SUMMARY

Just as families vary in their resources, size, values, and interaction patterns, so they also vary in meeting family functions. Families with exceptional children may focus more intensely on certain functions and may have more difficulty attending to some functions than others. Families vary in the functions they consider most important as well as in the intensity with which they experience stress associated with these functions.

Parents may assume that professionals do not have the resources to help meet their family needs (Vincent, Laten, Salisbury, Brown, & Baumgart, 1981). But professionals have a responsibility, as one of many systems serving children and families, to be familiar with the referral resources in their own or surrounding communities. Professionals have a responsibility to acknowledge that families have many needs to fulfill both collectively and individually for all members. Remember that each time you intervene with families and children, you potentially enhance or hinder their ability to meet family functions. Helen Featherstone (1980) describes a situation where she felt the school asked too much:

> I remember the day when the occupational therapist at Jody's school called with some suggestions from a visiting nurse. Jody has a seizure problem which is controlled with the drug Dilantin. Dilantin can cause the gums to grow over the teeth . . . The nurse had noticed . . . this overgrowth, and recommended, innocently enough, that (his) teeth be brushed four times a day, for five minutes, with an electric toothbrush. The school suggested that they could do this once on school days, and that I should try to do it the other three times a day . . . This new demand appalled me . . . Jody . . . is blind, cerebral palsied, and retarded. We do his physical therapy daily and work with him on sounds and communication. We feed him each meal on our laps, bottle him, bathe him, dry him, put him in a body cast to sleep, launder his bed linens daily, and go through a variety of routines designed to minimize his miseries and enhance his joys and his development. (All this in addition to trying to care for and enjoy our other young children and making time for each other and our careers.) Now you tell me that I should spend fifteen minutes every day on something that Jody will hate, an activity that will not help him to walk or even defecate, but one that is directed at the health of his gums. This activity is not for a finite time, but forever. It is not guaranteed to help, but "it can't hurt." And it won't make the overgrowth go away but may retard it. Well, it's too much. Where is that fifteen minutes going to come from? What am I supposed to give up? Taking the kids to the park? Reading a bedtime story to my eldest? Washing the breakfast dishes? Sorting the laundry? Grading students' papers? Sleeping? Because there is not time in my life that hasn't been spoken for, and for every fifteen-minute activity that is added one had to be taken away. (pp. 77–78)

As Featherstone shows, professionals must recognize the impact they can have on a family's abilities to meet all of their functions. They need to ask, "Are we asking too much or giving too little to aid the family in the many needs they must fulfill? Are our suggestions consistent with their priorities? Are those priorities changing?" In the next chapter, we examine the last part of that question—change over the life-cycle.

Chapter 5
Family Life Cycle

The last three chapters presented a portrait of the family system and how it is affected by exceptionality. The predominant image is one of complexity. First, the many ways in which families can differ—in size, membership, ethnicity, values, personal idiosyncracies, to name a few—create such a wide range of diversity that we can truly say every family is unique. Second, every family is an interactive system, which means that anything happening to one person reverberates in one way or another throughout the system. Third, every family is busily engaged in a variety of activities designed to fulfill a number of tangible and intangible needs of all its members.

However, there is yet another layer of complexity in the family system: change. The portrait of diversity, interaction and wide-ranging functions is only a snapshot in what should more accurately be portrayed as a motion picture. All families experience change as their members are born, grow up, leave home, bring in new members through marriage or other permanent relationships, retire, and die. In addition, families may experience unexpected or sudden changes that drastically alter their lives. Couples may divorce. Families may be separated by war, immigration, or job transfers. Unemployment, natural catastrophes, or a windfall inheritance may suddenly decrease or increase a family's resources. Religious conversions, political movements, or an unusual education (for a given family) may cause shifts in family values and attitudes. In this context, exceptionality is in itself an event that may profoundly change the family experiencing it.

Exceptionality is more than a change event, however; it cannot be considered by itself. Exceptionality both affects and is affected by the other changes that occur in the family. The needs of a family with a young child are not the same as the needs of a family with a young adult with an exceptionality. Nor, most likely, can a family's attitudes and values about the exceptionality—and educational involvement—remain the same over time.

It is important for professionals to understand how families change over time and how those changes affect their needs and attitudes toward an exceptionality. This chapter will explore some of those changing needs and perspectives at different times in a family's life.

An understanding of families and change lies within the domain of family life cycle theorists. The chronicle of a family's movement through time is its *life cycle*. Life cycle theorists usually begin with a consideration of the particular life cycle stages of each member in a family, most typically in three generations (Terkelson, 1980). For example, the oldest members of a family might be entering old age and facing the task of preparing for their own death and that of their peers; their children may be facing mid-career shifts and the prospect of an "empty nest"; their grandchildren may be leaving home and experiencing the first travails of independent adulthood. But the family life cycle involves more than the sum of each person's own life cycle. It involves the *interactions* among all these changes (Carter & McGoldrick, 1980). In the example of the three generations, the "middle" generation may face the need to take responsibility for increasingly dependent parents while they must also begin to "let go" of their own responsibility for their children. As responsibility shifts, so are values and approaches to life transmitted down the generations. Thus the basic identity of the family is preserved while the main characters change (Terkelson, 1980).

The family life cycle may be considered a series of *developmental stages*. These are periods of time when the family's lifestyle is relatively stable, and each member is engaged in a series of developmental tasks related to that period of life (Duvall, 1957). For example, in a family whose children are preschoolers, the parents are learning how to care for their offspring and what it means to be a parent. Typically, children are learning how to walk and talk, to dress themselves, and to explore their environment within the safe parameters established by their parents. The family's style of interaction may be best suited to accomplish the developmental tasks of a given stage. For example, on measures of adaptability and cohesion, Olson et al. (1983) found that families with young children tend toward extremes (either highly adaptable and enmeshed or rigid and disengaged), perhaps in order to meet children's needs for protection and close supervision. Families with adolescents tend to be more balanced on both measures, perhaps to accommodate the children's growing needs for autonomy without losing a sense of identity with the family Olson et al., (1983).

The exact number and character of life cycle stages is more or less arbitrary. Theorists have identified as many as 24 and as few as 6 (Carter & McGoldrick, 1980). It is important also to realize that life cycle stages are culturally and historically specific. A hundred years ago, when people tended to have very large families and shorter lifespans, a "post-parental" life stage—when there were no dependent children in the household—was very rare (Hareven, 1982). Also, in ethnic groups placing a strong emphasis on close extended families and less value on independence, children may not leave home (Falicov, 1982). Further, in blended or remarried families, particularly when there are older children from a previous marriage, there may be several life cycle stages occurring at the same time (Sager, et al., 1983).

There is, in short, nothing magical about the particular life cycle stages identified by family theorists. Every one is necessarily a generalization drawn to help understand the process of change. With this caution in mind, we will present our own generalizations about life cycle stages and the possible demands of exceptionality on each one. We will concentrate on four major life cycle stages when the family is most likely to experience contact with schools: birth and early childhood, elementary school years, adolescence, and young adulthood. Following these sections, we will consider the general issues of transition from one stage to another and how exceptionality affects, and is affected by, the family's ability to adjust smoothly to change.

BIRTH AND EARLY CHILDHOOD

For most families, the early childhood years are a period of intense absorption with the inner workings of the family (Olson, et al., 1983). If the family is not a blended family, the childless couple has (we hope) explored the parameters of their relationship, welded the norms of two families of origin into one new unit, and learned how to respond to each other's needs (Duvall, 1957). Now, suddenly, one or more small newcomers arrive on the scene, each dependent on the parents for their physical and emotional well-being. While the children are engaged in the task of learning to master their bodies and their immediate environment, the parents are faced with the task of nurturing their children and meeting their needs without, somehow, forgetting their own.

In addition to these expected developmental tasks, a family member having an exceptionality faces two major issues. First, early childhood is often the time that the exceptionality is discovered and the time the family needs to come to terms with the fact. Second, the exceptionality may bring the family into contact with the bewildering world of medical, educational, and social services for the first time. These issues are interrelated, but each has implications for the family's ability to face the lifelong tasks of living with the impact of an exceptionality.

Discovering the Exceptionality

Early Diagnosis: The Grief Cycle.   For some children, the exceptionality may be apparent at birth or soon after. The reactions of parents to the news of their child's exceptionality has been likened to the experiences of people who lose a loved one through death or some other separation (O'Hara & Levy, 1984). The loss in the case of an infant with an exceptionality is, presumably, the fantasized mental image of the perfect child—the baby who will be cute and adorable, excel in school or sports, and otherwise exceed his or her parents' own achievements (Bristol, 1984). It is this perfect child who has "died" and in its place is a baby with apparent and frightening problems and unknown prospects for the future. The feelings of grief may be complicated by guilt as parents mourn the lost perfect child, while the child with the exceptionality is very much alive and making his or her demands for affection and care (Trout, 1983). It is important then for professionals to help parents see that their feelings of grief are natural and that expressing those feelings is a healthy step toward resolution. One mother described her feelings:

> Shock, grief, bitter disappointment, fury, horror—my feelings were a mixture of all these after my doctor told me that our new little son, Peter, was born with Down syndrome. I was afraid to have him brought from the nursery . . . I didn't want to see this monster. But when the nurse brought in this tiny, black-haired baby with up-tilted, almond-shaped eyes, my heart melted . . . But the grief and fear didn't go away just because we fell in love with our son. They came in great, overwhelming waves. I felt a deep need to cry it out—to cry and cry until I had worked this immense sorrow up from the center of my being and out into the open . . . I think we should give honest and full expression to our grief. I suspect that when, in our attempts to be brave and face the future we repress our feelings, these feelings of pain and sorrow last longer. All I'm trying to say is that there's a time for weeping and then a time for pushing ahead, and I don't think you can do the second without going through the first. (Vyas, 1983a, p. 17)

The various "grief models" applied in cases of loss hypothesize an orderly sequence of stages, leading from initial shock to the final acceptance of reality. Clinicians utilizing one of these models have identified from three to seven stages through which parents must pass on their way to acceptance (see Blacher, 1984, for a review). In general, these stages include: (a) feelings of shock, denial, and disbelief; (b) feelings of anger, guilt, and/or depression; and (c) a reorganization of thoughts from self to others (i.e., the child with the exceptionality) and constructive attempts to seek services and otherwise incorporate the exceptionality into the reality of daily life (Blacher, 1984a).

Whether or not these stages are real and experienced in a similar sequence by all parents is open to controversy. Some commentators point out that, as in any effort to classify events, families are not so simple (Trout, 1983). Others note the phenomenon of chronic sorrow that stays with parents throughout life (Olshansky, 1962).

At the point of diagnosis, however, this professional controversy is irrelevant. What parents need at this time is permission to express their feelings. They also need full and honest information about the condition of their child. Attempts to spare feelings are often misguided, and many parents wish, in retrospect, that they had been told about their child's exceptionality earlier, more fully, and with greater empathy (Lonsdale, 1978). There is some evidence that frank and specific communication about the diagnosis is related to parents' faster and fuller acceptance of the diagnosis (Lipton & Svarstad, 1977). Also, most parents will not hear much of the information the first time it is presented. It is important to repeat the information in many different ways and at different times. Parents should be encouraged to call with questions or to ask for additional meetings while they are in the process of absorbing the news about the exceptionality.Some parents have also pointed out the importance of presenting a balanced perspective when explaining the meaning of the exceptionality to new parents:

> One father commented that "when normal children are born, the doctors do not recount for parents all of the problems that could happen to their child like drug involvement, flunking out of college, sexual promiscuity, or teen-age suicide; however, when a child with Down syndrome is born, the doctors only point out the negatives." Another parent said that "when you go into something expecting it to be bad, it naturally is going to influence your adjustment." (Turnbull, Blue-Banning, Behr, & Kerns, 1985, pp. 7–8)

Professionals may withhold information because they feel the parents cannot cope with it emotionally (Donnellan & Mirenda, 1984), or because they themselves cannot admit to a problem they cannot "cure" (Sarason & Doris, 1979). They may paint an overly bleak picture of the nature of the exceptionality based on out-dated research, their own prejudices, or lack of knowledge of services available (Sarason & Doris, 1979). They may tend to be more vague when the exceptionality is milder, perhaps because with severe exceptionalities the parents may already be aware a problem exists (Lipton & Svarstad, 1977). Whatever the reason, an unbalanced first contact with the exceptionality leaves parents at a distinct disadvantage in their ability to cope with their own and their child's needs in the future. It is an area for research and professional education that requires much more attention.

Later Discovery: Gradual Awareness   While the discovery of an exceptionality at birth is dramatic and has received much attention in the literature, many families notice their child's exceptionality much more gradually. Often accumulated evidence is not confirmed for several years—perhaps not until the child enters school or even upper elementary grades. In the case of gifted children, for example, a father might be startled by his son's walking at eight months, or a mother might be badgered with incisive "why" questions from her three-year-old daughter. Grandparents might be astounded by a four-year-old's advanced vocabulary and liberal use of adjectives. Mothers might be irritated by a preschooler's incessant proclivity to collect things (Perino & Perino, 1981).

But the label "gifted" may not enter the minds of family members until it is placed there by school personnel.

For other exceptionalities, also, there may be no evidence at birth. Autism is one example of an exceptionality in which a child may appear to be developing normally for the first year or two of life. In some cases of learning disability the only evidence in the preschool years might be irritability or clumsiness; in other cases there might be no evidence at all until the child experiences difficulty in school. In still other exceptionalities, the problem becomes gradually more noticeable as children increasingly fall behind their age peers in development of motor skills or language (Donnellan & Mirenda, 1984).

When awareness of an exceptionality dawns gradually, a model of grief parallel to the loss of an imagined child may not fit. For some parents the diagnosis, when it finally comes, is less a blow than a relief. The nagging doubts have a name. They weren't crazy after all. This was the experience of Rud Turnbull:

> Another early warning sign was [Jay's] plain dullness—not that he wasn't a beautiful child with an abundance of blond curls; it is just that he didn't turn over, move about, push himself up on his elbows, or do the other things that my friend's children of his age had done. His pediatrician . . . seemed to pooh pooh my concerns . . . Had it not been for Dr. Neal Aronson, the neurologist who leveled with me, the entire staff of Johns Hopkins Hospital might have kept me in eternal ignorance . . . He let me know so gently that all I felt was absolution, the soft vanishing of my present and past anxiety— not the pain of the future. (H.R. Turnbull, 1985, pp. 109–110)

Parent narratives are rife with stories about professionals who discounted the parents' concerns or labeled them as "overanxious." Time and again, they are told "he'll grow out of it," or "all babies develop at their own rate," yet the nagging doubts do not go away. One mother expressed her feelings about such treatment:

> A mother is supposed to be behind her child 100 percent of the way. I wanted to believe my kid was the brightest, smartest, fastest, the one who could do no wrong in my eyes. Yet I was the one who was constantly pointing out the negatives to professionals who just couldn't see anything wrong. I resented very much being put in that position.

When a diagnosis does finally arrive, it may be incomplete. The professional may deliberately suppress part of the information on the assumption that he or she knows how much parents can handle, or, conversely, the diagnosis may be elusive because the exceptionality is complex or rare or slow to unfold (Donnellan & Mirenda, 1984). Parents may react to this ambiguity by taking their child to another specialist and then another, in a search for answers to their questions. Such parents may be labelled "shoppers," people who have failed to accept their child's exceptionality (Blacher, 1984a).

There are undoubtedly cases of "shoppers" who are unwilling to face the reality of exceptionality and are engaged in a fruitless odyssey for a cure. But it is likely that at least an equal number of "shoppers" seek other opinions not because they reject their child but because they are simply seeking clarity about the problem (O'Hara & Levy, 1984). It is important that professionals who want a true partnership with parents must be prepared to accept—and respect—parents who disagree with them. When a parent disagrees with you, ask yourself honestly whether there is room for doubt about your conclusions. Did you present the information clearly and without euphemisms that might be interpreted in more than one way (e.g., "slow")? If parents want a second opinion, encourage them to obtain one, and ask to have copies of the reports. Compare the results of the second assessment with the first and discuss similarities and differences with the parent. Avoid defensiveness and work constructively with the parents; after all, the main objective is not to see which professional's label is more accurate, but how to get appropriate services for the child.

Accessing Early Childhood Services

Learning about the exceptionality is only the first of a lifelong series of interactions with professionals. Families with young children whose exceptionalities have been identified are likely to be plunged almost immediately into the world of infant stimulation, early intervention, preschools, respite services, medical services, and so on. With more and more mothers remaining in the workforce after their children are born (Masnick & Bane, undated), the involvement of families in general with preschools and day-care centers is not unusual. But in the case of a young child with an exceptionality, that involvement is much more systematic. Parents learn to think of their child's development less as natural growth and more as a sequence of skills that must be deliberately taught. Therefore, the preschool must be selected with an eye toward its ability to meet those developmental needs. Parents must consider such issues as mainstreaming or special programs, availability of support services, class size, opportunities for individualized instruction, and teacher qualifications and attitudes (Winton, Turnbull, & Blacher, 1984).

Further, because parent involvement is rapidly becoming the *sine qua non* of early childhood services, families are likely to find themselves quickly and intensively involved once they have selected a program. Service providers look to families on theoretical grounds because parents are "the single most important educational influence on the lives of children" (Latham, 1981, p. 26). Parents have been found to be effective teachers of their own children and have successfully taught a wide variety of academic, social, and motor skills (Altman & Mira, 1983).

Some parents, especially those with young children, may gladly embrace the role of intensive involvement. It is something concrete to do, and may provide a feeling that they are not entirely helpless. The involvement, however, is not an unmixed blessing. One mother expressed her ambivalence this way:

> I found the infant stimulation program to be very helpful in providing an opportunity to learn parenting skills (Peter was our first child). It also helped our morale in that it gave us specific things to teach Peter, and so we could see steady progress in his development. This created strong feelings of guilt in me because I felt that if I wasn't working with him at every opportunity, then I wasn't doing enough. If his progress was slow, I felt it was my fault. (Vyas, 1983b, p. 51)

From the point of view of parents—even those who are eager to be involved—parent involvement is neither cheap nor convenient (Turnbull, et al., 1985c). Chapter 4 has amply illustrated the many responsibilities that families pack into their daily lives. Yet many service providers continue to expect families to sacrifice their other needs to become involved with their children's program. One single mother explained her reluctance to participate:

> I work full-time. When I get home in the afternoon, I'm tired and I have to fix dinner. Sally has been in a situation all day where she's had someone telling her she has to work on this and that. I don't feel like she's ready for more education at night. I think it's time for fun and enjoying Mommy for awhile. Plus, I don't think children learn as well from their parents on some tasks that are particularly difficult. Parents tend to want to do the work for their children rather than watch them suffer. (Winton, et al., 1984, p. 6)

The importance of early intervention to prevent or reduce the impacts of exceptionality is well-documented and undeniable (see, e.g., Hayden, 1983). But early childhood professionals, in their zeal to attain those all-important early developmental gains, should not push parents to the point of burn-out. Early childhood professionals will pass the child on to new programs; their task will be finished when the child reaches school age. But the family will only be beginning a lifetime of responsibility. For early childhood programs, an equally important task to achieve developmental gains is to prepare families for the long haul. Families must learn to pace themselves, to relax and take time to meet everyone's needs. They must learn that the responsibility of meeting an exceptional child's needs is not a 100-yard dash to be completed in one intensive burst of effort. It is more like a marathon, where slow and steady pacing wins the race (Weyhing, 1983).

ELEMENTARY SCHOOL YEARS

Entry into school often marks a widening of horizons for a child. Unless he or she has had preschool experience, a child may be spending a major portion of the day away from home for the first time. Where learning had been an incidental part of the child's daily experience, it now becomes a more structured responsibility. The elementary years also mark the beginning of the development of a peer group. From the parents' point of view, these years are the beginning of a long "letting go" process, in which parents must turn over responsibility for their child to others, and begin giving more and more responsibilities to the child.

For families with exceptionality, entry into school may mark their first encounter with many of the issues to which we have devoted whole chapters of this book. The elementary years are a time when parents learn to participate in their child's individualized education plan (see Chapter 10), to select a placement (mainstream versus special class), and to understand their legal rights (see Chapter 8). The experiences of parents in the early elementary years will shape their expectations about their relationship to the school for many years.

The specific issues families face when a child with an exceptionality enters school are tied closely to the nature of the exceptionality itself. If the child has been involved in an early intervention program, the family may need to adjust to a program in which parent involvement is much less intense. Busy elementary teachers may not have the time to exchange daily communication at the classroom door. In fact, school bus transportation may result in rare face-to-face encounters between teachers and parents. Also, parents may need to shift from a noncategorical early intervention program to the idea of labels used in special education. There may no longer be systematic home visits. The parent support group the family attended may have been attached to the preschool program and is no longer available to the family whose child is in elementary school.

When the exceptionality is not identified until the child enters school, the parents may experience all the same reactions at this time that other families experienced in the preschool years. As a child slips farther behind his or her classmates, the parents and teachers may come into increasing conflict over a solution. If a child has not yet been identified as gifted, the parents may become concerned at their child's apparent boredom and restlessness (Perino & Perino, 1981).

A mild exceptionality brings ambiguity. The family's hopes may be raised and then dashed as the child makes progress and slips back (Wadsworth & Wadsworth, 1971). There is a reluctance for the child to be labelled, while there is also a recognition for a need for special services (Wadsworth & Wadsworth, 1971). With learning disabilities, the difficulty in achieving an accurate diagnosis may place parents at odds with professionals (Willner & Crane, 1979).

The elementary school years may also be the first time that siblings encounter social stigma, especially when the child with an exceptionality rides the same school bus or attends the same school as a brother or sister. Many siblings then may feel a strong need to defend their brother or sister from teasing or ridicule (Skrtic, Summers, Brotherson, & Turnbull, 1984). They may be asked to carry medication, relay messages to parents, and serve as a classroom aide to the sibling with an exceptionality. Such "singling out" can be acutely embarrassing to the sibling (Powell & Ogle, 1985). School professionals should take care to allow the sibling to make his or her own choices about their extent of involvement with a brother or sister with an exceptionality. Any interactions that are necessary should be handled with discretion.

The perceptions school professionals have about families may be another source of strain. Professionals may judge parents as "good" or "bad" according to the degree to which they involve themselves with their child's education (Turnbull & Summers, 1985). If parents' expectations for the child's achievement are higher than the professionals', the parents are perceived to have failed to accept the reality of their child's exceptionality. If their expectations are lower than the professionals, they are perceived to be overprotective. There may indeed be parents who are overprotective or unaccepting or uncaring. But it is important for professionals to begin by giving parents the benefit of the doubt. The fact that responsibilities other than education may have a higher priority does not make them "bad" parents. The parents' perceptions about the child's potential is not necessarily inaccurate, nor is it necessarily an indication of an emotional disturbance on the part of the parent. It should be viewed as different—not necessarily wrong—and the efforts of communication should be bent toward narrowing the gap through increased awareness on both sides.

ADOLESCENCE

Adolescence is the next life cycle stage in the individual's growth. This period of the life cycle can create some difficult changes, not only rapid physical changes, but also many psychological changes. Puberty, the beginning of sexual maturity, usually marks the start of adolescence, which is accompanied by a host of developmental tasks including: development of self-identity, development of a positive body image, adjustment to sexual maturation, emotional independence from parents, and development of mature relationships with peers of both sexes.

Adolescence in general can be a very challenging time for both the individual and his or her family. Parents may find their authority challenged as adolescents experiment with new-found sexuality or begin to assert their independence. Also, the parents may be facing problems of their own as they enter mid-life. They see their children becoming attractive adults as their own perceived attractiveness and youthfulness begins to decline (Figley & McCubbin, 1983). In a national study that was conducted with over 1,000 families in the general population (Olson, et al., 1983) parents reported that the life cycle stages of adolescence and launching young adults were the two stages with the highest amount of stresses and strains.

An exceptionality may either compound or mitigate some of the storms of adolescence. For example, with some exceptionalities, parents might not be confronted with rebellion and conflict because the youth may have fewer peers to model such behaviors (Turnbull, Summers, & Brotherson, 1984). In other cases, adolescence may bring greater isolation, a growing sense of "differentness," and confusion and fear about emerging sexuality. Some of the issues families might face in the adolescent years surround the problems of sexuality, developing peer groups, growing stigma, and a growing need for physical care.

Sexuality

Emerging sexuality may be a difficult problem in any family. When the adolescent has an exceptionality, however, the issues may be compounded. Some parents may not even recognize that it is possible for their child to have sexual needs (Brotherson, 1985). Even for those who do recognize their child's sexuality, there may be difficulty for both parent and child in reconciling an adult body with a less rapidly developing mind. Ann Turnbull (1985) noted:

> [Jay] is physically mature, even more so than most sixteen-year-olds. Puberty has created tumultuous emotions for him, partially because he does not understand what is happening. His rapid physical changes stand in stark contrast to his slow cognitive growth, and the imbalance has been difficult for me to adjust to. (p. 139)

For girls with exceptionalities, families may fear that their vulnerability arising from their need for acceptance may lead to sexual exploitation (Gardner, in press). For boys, parents may fear their sons will exhibit inappropriate sexual behavior such as masturbating in public or making public affectionate advances on women (Haavik & Menninger, 1981).

All of these issues, of course, require programs in sex education, both for the youth and the family. While sex education is important for everyone, for adolescents with exceptionalities it is doubly so, since parents may need help in teaching their sons or daughters about sexuality. There are a number of good sex education programs available (see Resource Section). But if the school is contemplating providing a sex education program, it is important to involve parents in the curriculum planning and implementation at every step (Haavik & Menninger, 1981).

Developing a Peer Group

At this point, the peer group often begins to replace the family in importance for the adolescent. This is essential for those adolescents who are going to separate from their families and assume responsibility for their own lives. Developing a peer group can be difficult for many adolescents and can present special problems for adolescents who are exceptional. One consequence of the drive to be accepted by the peer group is the often-noted tendency for many adolescents to conform with the group. They want to be seen as "in step with" their peers, and they are highly critical of any developmental or physical discrepancies. Exceptionality is a difference that often makes adolescents feel ostracized from their peer group.

Adjusting to "differentness" at a developmental stage when "sameness" is so important can be complicated further if family members are not sensitive to this issue. One young woman shares how her family assumed that she would not develop relationships with peers of the opposite sex.

> "Oh, you're not different from anyone else" my younger sister always told me. "You're just shorter." One day, soon after my 13th birthday, I realized that wasn't true. I wasn't just short—my *proportions* were different. I am what they call a dwarf . . . From that day on I was convinced I'd never go out on a date, would never have a boy friend, would never marry. I began to notice that my family treated my sister and me differently. They'd talk about "when Gloria goes to the prom," "When Gloria gets a boy friend," "When Gloria gets married." Nothing about me, Ann. (Carrillo, Corbett, & Lewis, 1982, p. 61)

This quote was excerpted from a book called *No More Stares* by Carrillo, Corbett and Lewis (1982). This and other personal accounts from persons with an exceptionality could be very useful to young adolescents struggling with "differentness." The book discusses such issues as how to deal with stares, how to develop a positive self-image, and how to gain autonomy from parents.

The degree to which an adolescent experiences a sense of difference from his or her peers will depend partially on the type and degree of exceptionality. For students who have severe mental retardation, their differentness may be from their awareness. For students who have more visible exceptionalities (e.g., cerebral palsy, blindness, spina bifida), their differentness from their peer group is more obvious both to themselves and to their peers. The exceptionality of a learning disability is an example of a more invisible exceptionality, yet one which presents problems for adolescents. O'Hara and Levy (1984) state that:

> The invisibility of their handicap continues to be a source of difficulty and misunderstanding for learning-disabled teenagers in establishing peer relationships. As difficult as it is for adults to understand the diagnosis of learning disability it is that much more difficult for peers. (p. 72)

For some exceptionalities, the responsibility of finding a peer group and developing social interactions may fall upon the family. Parents are frequently concerned about their child's growing isolation (Brotherson, 1985). One mother, whose daughter has cerebral palsy, expressed her anger about thoughtless friends:

> I wish people wouldn't make promises to Sharon if they don't intend to carry them out. They talk to her at school and say, "I might drop by sometime." To them it's just a polite thing to say, but to Sharon it's a promise. For days after that she sits by the window in the evening, waiting. She won't go anywhere with us because she doesn't want to miss them in case they drop by. The disappointment on her face when she finally realizes they aren't coming is almost too much for me to take.

Gifted students can also experience difficulties in developing peer relationships. Many students are fearful of being singled out as a "brain." This "differentness" can alienate them from their peers and be very difficult to cope with (Perino & Perino, 1981). "Many gifted and talented adolescents feel more comfortable pursuing academic and related areas than competing in the social arena. Even when they are involved in activities such as music, they experience social difficulties" (p. 113). In particular, gifted girls may face problems arising from the need for conformity with traditional sex roles. A gifted girl may fear that aggressiveness or achievement orientation may make her seem unfeminine. Often outshining one's boy friend in achievement could lead to an abrupt loss of the relationship (Perino & Perino, 1981). Professionals may need to devote special time to help gifted students develop both social and academic skills, particularly at this stage of the life cycle.

Growing Stigma

While adolescents themselves may be more aware of their growing differences at this time of the life cycle, family members are also becoming more aware of these differences. For many family members the stigma of exceptionality grows as the child grows. It may be more difficult to use community services, both because of inaccessibility and because of fear of community members. Some family members have reported that their communities are more understanding when their children are younger (Suelzle & Keenan, 1981). One mother cites a specific example of this growing stigma:

> The community accepts our children much more easily when they are small and cute. The problems we face with Lindsay today are partially the result of his growing up and not being "cute" anymore. People are apt to be fearful around him. Doctors and dentists are fearful. It's very hard to give a shot to a six-foot, two-hundred-pound man who doesn't want one. Babyish mannerisms are no longer acceptable. Lind has had real problems with his social relationships. He simply does not know how to initiate a friendship. He has difficulty maintaining a sensible conversation with his peers. He doesn't handle teasing well, so he is teased unmercifully. (Anderson, 1983, p. 90)

One strategy to help reduce stigma for both the individual with an exceptionality and family members is to provide age-appropriate activities and materials. For example, the adolescent should have clothing that is socially acceptable for someone in his or her age group. Likewise, an adolescent should be given opportunities to participate in leisure time games or activities that are consistent with his or her peers.

The issue of age-appropriateness, however, may conflict with the choices of some adolescents with exceptionalities. If autonomy is the real goal, then choices should be respected, even when they are not age-appropriate. Elizabeth Boggs (1985) makes this point about her son, David's, preference for a rubber duck:

> Making sure that each retarded person has opportunities to make choices for himself and to take care of himself within an appropriate range is one important way of respecting basic rights. The importance of small consider-ations in David's life may be illustrated by tracking his rubber duck. . . . Shortly after the first ICF/MR survey, David's rubber duck disappeared. I was advised that the duck was not "age-appropriate." . . . As it turned out, a programmatic purpose for the duck was soon discovered by the direct care staff, who observed that, in the absence of the duck, David found other things to do with his hands such as untying his shoes. The duck . . . reappeared. . . . Now that David senses his autonomy in the matter of the duck is being respected, his behavior has changed in subtle ways. (Boggs, 1985, pp. 58–59)

The main point is that age-appropriateness is not a criterion to be applied to all individuals in all situations. The preferences and needs of both the child and the family must be considered in the selection of materials and activities.

The stigma surrounding an exceptionality attaches not only to the individual but to the family as well. Kathryn Morton (1985) describes this effect:

> Each day presents us with the challenge of figuring out how to do everything that would be done if we didn't have a handicapped child, while managing the handicapped child we clearly do have. That might entail, for instance, grocery shopping with the retarded child in tow. When Beckie was little, such an excursion required only the extra energy needed to carry her on my hip and choose groceries one-handed, or the skill to maneuver her special stroller with one hand and the grocery cart with the other. But when she hit her teens, a completely new ingredient was added to the challenge. I took her shopping with me only if I felt up to looking groomed, cheerful, competent, and in command of any situation, so that when she bellowed and stamped with joy as she always did when we walked through the supermarket door, people who stared could quickly surmise that I would handle the situation, quiet my strange child, and get on with my shopping. To look as tired and preoccupied with surviving as I so often felt would have turned both of us into objects of pity, and that I clearly did not need. If I could not play the role of the coping, competent mother, I did better to stay at home and grocery shop after she went to bed, or ask one of the other children to come home early and sit for me, or leave the big shopping until another day and ask a neighbor to pick up a necessity or two for me, or make do with what I had until I felt more energetic, though chances were excellent that I wouldn't. (Morton, 1985, pp. 143–144)

Growing Physical Care Needs

This shopping account points to another concern of adolescence—growing physical care needs. As children with severe exceptionalities become older, larger, and heavier, it can take increasingly more physical energy to provide care and to meet their needs. Family members may experience greater fatigue with such day-to-day tasks as bathing, dressing, and leaving the house. Kathryn Morton also describes the toll of physical and psychic demands over the years:

> The sapping of energy occurs gradually. The isolation it imposes does, too. As I work professionally with young mothers, I see them coping energetically with the demands of everyday life. They are good parents, caring ones, doing everything possible to help their retarded child reach full potential, sometimes doing more than they have to; and if they have other children,

they are doing the same for them. Most of these young mothers even get out, see friends, attend meetings, volunteer in the community, and do all the things their friends and families expect them to do. All this is at least possible when one's child is little, though it demands enormous energy. But to look at the mothers of children who have turned into teenagers is to see the beginnings of the ravages. Their life-style is changing. They go out less, see fewer people, do less for their children. They are stripping their living to the essentials. And to look at parents of retarded adults still living at home is to see lives that are far removed from those of their peers. The physical and psychic effects of 20 or more years of extraordinary demands on their energies are visible, and they have given up the struggle to be normal. (Morton, 1985, p. 144)

For adolescents who have a severe disability, the physical care needs will probably increase over time. For some families, part of the stress of increasing care needs is accentuated by the realization of continued dependency by the child at a time when many parents would be launching their children "out of the nest." When working with these families, it is important to help them build their coping strategies, particularly the use of a social support network. Coping strategies are described in more detail in Chapter 14.

All adolescents with an exceptionality, however, do not have greater physical needs as they mature. For many adolescents, this stage of the life cycle is a time of growing independence, as they assume more responsibility for meeting their own needs. It is a time when many adolescents begin to strike out on their own and seek "less interference" from their parents. As discussed in Chapter 4, greater independence can also mean greater risk for failure. But risk-taking is part of independence, and possible consequences of failure are something that all adolescents experience.

To help family members prepare for the risk-taking and independence that adolescents will experience, opportunities for both should be given prior to adolescence. A 14-year-old girl with a physical disability may want to go to summer camp for two weeks, but her parents find this too frightening. Possibly other experiences could build up to this young girl's expression of independence. These experiences might include: spending the night with friends, going camping for the weekend with friends or neighbors, or spending several days with an aunt in a near-by city. These are ways the adolescent could experience independence in small increments before spending two weeks away from her family in a strange environment. Successive approximation is a strategy to build confidence as well as to support families in learning to cope with change during the life cycle.

ADULTHOOD

Adulthood is the next life cycle stage in the individual's growth. Adulthood can be culturally attained in many ways (e.g., getting married, becoming a parent, entering the armed services), but we will define adulthood as the age of 21. This is also the end of school eligibility for learners with exceptionality.

For most adults in our majority culture, moving into adulthood means finding employment and moving away from home. For the young adult this is a process of attaining greater independence and responsibility. For the parents this is a process of "letting go" of their son or daughter. This process can be difficult in any family, but is especially challenging in families with young adults who are exceptional. Following are some challenges the individual and his or her family might face:

The Right to Grow Up

The right to grow up—to attain the status of adulthood—is an opportunity that is taken for granted by most adults in our society. With the move into adulthood comes the responsibility for meeting one's own needs to the greatest extent possible. Also, with the move into adulthood comes the opportunity for greater choice and control in one's life. Granted, the decisions regarding how independence and responsibility will be divided among the young adult, the family, and other support systems can be difficult. But some families (and professionals) fail to reach this point because they continue to view the young adult as a child. George Harris, the father of a deaf girl discusses this issue of adulthood for persons who are exceptional:

> [I] think many parents extend their responsibility far beyond what is reasonably expected of them. Failure to anticipate this eventual separation of parent and child may, in fact, impede the child's progress toward whatever self-sufficiency is attainable. If parents believe they will always take care of their child, then what does it really matter whether tasks of daily living taught in school are reinforced at home? Many people automatically assume, as I did, that parents of handicapped children have a lifelong legal obligation to provide care for the child. This attitude probably originated years ago when handicapped children lived in their parents' attics and spare bedrooms throughout their adult lives. However, such thinking impedes the development of humane sheltered living programs. Our society is only now beginning to accept that handicapped children have a right to an education; it may take some time before it accepts that handicapped adults have the right to live apart from their parents, as independently as their abilities allow. In a normal developmental sequence a child establishes an identity separate from that of the parents, who move on to activities appropriate for their own

stages in life. This progression is healthy for all children and all parents. (Harris, 1985, pp. 266–267)

Planning for adulthood to involve possible separation of parents and child must begin early, not when the young adult reaches age 21. Several parents have reported it was important, in the early years of their child's life, to observe other persons with exceptionalities living and working independently in the community. Parent visits to adult programs at times when their child is still in school could be a helpful future-planning strategy.

Creating Adult Opportunities

No matter how much planning for adulthood takes place, the fact remains that current services available for adults with exceptionalities are inadequate to meet needs. Families report much stress as they search for appropriate services to meet their young adult's needs (Brotherson, 1985). The reality of less adequate services as the child enters adulthood strikes many families. Research has indicated that parents at later stages of the life-cycle experience greater parent burn-out, less support, less community acceptance, fewer services, and more isolation (Bristol & Schopler, 1983; Suelzle & Keenan, 1981).

The individual and his or her family face many barriers and questions. One of the authors (Rud Turnbull) shares some of the concerns he feels:

> Jay will pass too soon from public school to adult services. He will move from a school system that must serve everyone to a nonsystem of multiple programs with usually inconsistent goals, functions, eligibility criteria, funding and governing authorities, and accountability—programs that need not serve him but must merely practice nondiscrimination. He will go from a relatively protective system to one that may impose responsibilities on him that he cannot meet. And he will graduate from a system in which I can legally and functionally command services and accountability to a system that is far less amenable to my importunings. Will there be a group home for him, a job, entitlement benefits, recreation, and other opportunities for growth and protection? Frankly, the answer is unclear, and the pending transition from some certainty to great uncertainty is profoundly disquieting to me. (Turnbull, 1985, p. 119)

As parents take on the task of creating adult opportunities they may be faced with inadequate public funds, sluggish bureaucracies, and social stigma. One woman described her battle at a zoning hearing, attended by people who were opposed to the development of a group home in their neighborhood. She describes the bigoted statements and hurtful remarks parents must endure as they advocate for services:

We have come to this room to beg. All of us are proud men and women, and it is hard for us to beg. We have done it many times before . . . We have come once more to be told, "I read in the paper that 'these people' can't tell right from wrong." We have come to listen to the old lie, "Everybody knows 'those kids' have superhuman strength and may get violent." . . . I look at the members of the commission. I look at the flag. I cannot look at these angry neighbors. I cannot speak. My mouth is dry. Finally I look across the room at my friend. Her retarded child is only 4; mine is 14. She is weeping. It is her first time. . . . (Isbell, 1983, pp. 179–181)

For some exceptionalities the issue of creating adult opportunities blends with plans for post-secondary education. Career development and planning for gifted students should begin early, with explorations of a variety of career options. Perino and Perino (1981) advocate helping students to think about swiftly developing technology and to prepare for flexible careers that will allow them to adapt to change. Others have noted the need to provide students who are gifted with a sensitivity to the needs of humanity, moral courage, and a sense of responsibility to others (Bruch, 1984).

Beyond making decisions about future careers, planning for a post-secondary education implies selecting a program and finding financial resources. Such planning cannot begin in the last year of high school. Students planning to attend post-secondary programs require guidance in weighing the programs at different colleges and universities; such a process might require careful study over a period of several years. Parents and students alike need to receive advice about scholarship opportunities, loans, and work-study programs.

Students with learning disabilities, sensory impairments, or physical disabilities need to consider a variety of other special needs in selecting a post-secondary institution. Is the campus accessible for wheel chair users? Does the college provide special assistance such as tutoring programs for students with learning disabilities or interpreters for students with hearing impairments? Does the vocational rehabilitation program provide financial assistance for personal care attendants while the student is attending college? High school counselors should have this type of information available about area colleges, universities, and technical schools.

Sibling Issues

As members of the family age, siblings may experience some unique issues and challenges. They often assume responsibility for the needs of their sibling, particularly as they see their parents aging. Powell and Ogle (1985) have divided adult sibling concerns into three broad areas:

1. genetics.
2. long-term care of the sibling who is exceptional.
3. help to the sibling to enjoy quality of life.

Some siblings may not have had the implications of their brother or sister's exceptionality fully explained to them. They may become concerned about the genetic implications of having children of their own. Often these issues reach the forefront when a sibling considers marriage.

The long-term care of the dependent sibling is another major concern. Siblings may be unsure of what their guardianship, financial, and advocacy roles should be. They may be unsure of their options in these areas. If there is more than one sibling, they may be unsure how the roles and responsibilities will be divided. One sibling shares the mayhem that resulted in their family when the death of her mother, the primary advocate and case manager, resulted in unclear roles and responsibilities:

> At first we responded to calls from the school in a haphazard fashion. Family visits were sporadic. Six months would pass without anyone's arranging to see Beckie, and then suddenly everyone would show up at the school's Christmas play. Or one of us would mention to a staff member that we thought Beckie should come home for Christmas and then never follow up on the suggestion, leaving the staff to question our commitment. (Ackerman, 1985, p. 153)

Siblings also have concerns regarding the quality of adult life for their brother or sister. They may want their sibling to live nearby in the community, but they have no information about possible residential or work options. Or, if there are no options in their community, they may be unsure of the role they should or can take in regard to developing options.

Obviously, there are many challenges for the child with an exceptionality, his or her siblings, and parents to face. Table 5–1 provides a summary of many of these issues faced by the family at the four life cycle stages discussed in this chapter (see p. 106).

LIFE CYCLE TRANSITIONS

Beyond the developmental tasks that the family and individual members must accomplish at each stage, an important life cycle concept is the transition from one stage to another. Transitions are the periods of time between stages when the family is adjusting its interactional style and roles to meet the needs of the new developmental stage (Terkelson, 1980). They are usually, but not always, briefer periods than the stages they interface. Because these shifts may result in confusion and conflict, the transition period is almost always a time of greater stress (Neugarten, 1976; Olson, et al., 1983).

Two factors tend to reduce the amount of stress most families feel during a transition from one developmental stage to another. First, the roles of the new stage are fairly well defined in every culture. The transition may be marked by some kind of ritual, such as a wedding, bar mitzvah, graduation, or funeral. These serve as signals to the family that their relationships following the ceremony will be changed (Friedman, 1980). The interactions and roles for the new stage are modeled by other families with the same previous or present experiences. Thus, the future is not entirely unknown. Second, the timing of transitions is also fairly well expected. In our culture, children are often expected to leave home after they graduate from high school. Death may be expected and psychologically prepared for in old age. Life cycle transitions seem to be much more traumatic and stressful when they occur at other than the expected times (Neugarten, 1976).

Table 5–1
POSSIBLE ISSUES ENCOUNTERED AT LIFE CYCLE STATES

Life Cycle Stage	Parents	Siblings
Early Childhood, ages 0–5	Obtaining an accurate diagnosis Informing sibling and relatives Locating services Seeking to find meaning in the exceptionality Clarifying a personal ideology to guide decision making Addressing issues of stigma Identifying positive contributions of exceptionality	Less parental time and energy for sibling needs Feelings of jealousy over less attention Fears associated with misunderstandings of exceptionality

Life Cycle Stage	Parents	Siblings
School Age, ages 6–12	Establishing routines to carry out family functions Adjusting emotionally to educational implications Clarifying issues of mainstreaming v. special class placement Participating in IEP conferences Locating community resources Arranging for extracurricular activities	Division of responsibility for any physical care needs Oldest female sibling may be at risk Limited family resources for recreation and leisure Informing friends and teachers Possible concern over surpassing younger sibling Issues of "mainstreaming" into same school Need for basic information on exceptionality

Life Cycle Stage	Parents	Siblings
Adolescence, ages 13–21	Adjusting emotionally to possible chronicity of exceptionality Identifying issues of emerging sexuality Addressing possible peer isolation and rejection Planning for career/vocational development Arranging for leisure time activities Dealing with physical and emotional change of puberty Planning for postsecondary education	Overidentification with sibling Greater understanding of differences in people Influence of exceptionality on career choice Dealing with possible stigma and embarrassment Participation in sibling training programs Opportunity for sibling support groups

Life Cycle Stage	Parents	Siblings
Adulthood, ages 21–	Planning for possible need for guardianship Addressing the need for appropriate adult residence Adjusting emotionally to any adult implications of dependency Addressing the need for socialization opportunities outside the family for individual with exceptionality Initiating career choice or vocational program	Possible issues of responsibility for financial support Addressing concerns regarding genetic implications Introducing new in-laws to exceptionality Need for information on career/living options Clarify role of sibling advocacy Possible issues of guardianship

Both these points have implications for families with exceptionalities. The expected roles as well as the future of a person with an exceptionality may not be as clear, and a ritual to mark the change may be absent. Nor may the transition itself, if it does occur, happen at the expected time. We will consider the implications of uncertain futures and off-time transitions for families with exceptionalities.

Uncertainty About the Future

For many exceptionalities, the future is a frightening unknown. There may be few norms and models of expected behavior for either the child or his or her family. The common admonition to "take things one day at a time" arises not only because there are more than enough responsibilities for the family in the present, but also because the future is simply too ambiguous (Featherstone, 1980). One father shares his perceptions about the reasons parents may fail to address the future:

> Most parents anticipate their children's future with enthusiasm, expecting such happy events as scholastic achievement, success in sports, graduation, marriage, birth of grandchildren, and promising careers. In contrast parents of a retarded child usually view their child's future with apprehension, anticipating scholastic failure, exclusion from services (educational, social, recreational), inability to work or else menial employment, problems in sexual adjustment, inability to live independently, and a life of loneliness and

Table 5–2
TIPS TO EASE TRANSITION

Early Childhood	Begin preparing for the separation of preschool children by periodically leaving the child in the hands of others. Gather information and visit preschool options in the community. Arrange for "mentorships" between veteran parents and parents who are just beginning this transition process. Familiarize parents with possible career options or adult programs so parents have an idea of future opportunities.
School Age	Provide parents with the opportunity to view a variety of school placement options (e.g., mainstreaming, resource room, self-contained classroom). If parents know another family already involved in IEP conference, they may ask to attend as guests to see what an IEP conference is like. Arrange opportunities for family support groups or mentorships so that family members have an opportunity to discuss transition with others who have completed transition.
Adolescence	Arrange for family support groups so that adolescents and their families can prepare for the physical and emotional changes of puberty. Help families and adolescents identify community leisure time activities. Identify skills that will be needed in future career and vocational programs so that these can be incorporated early into the IEP. Visit or become familiar with a variety of career and living options.
Adulthood	Ask families if they need information regarding guardianship, estate planning, wills, and trusts. Assist family members in transferring responsibilities to the individual, or other family members, or service providers. Assist the young adult or family members in embarking on career or vocational choices. Address the issues and responsibilities of marriage and family for the young adult.

isolation. Realistically, services tend to become less adequate as the retarded person ages, increasing the parents' frustrations. Hence, while most normal people are future-oriented, parents of a retarded child tend to retreat from the future as a source of pain and shift toward past orientation. (Roos, 1985, p. 252)

Further, the rituals that serve as "punctuation marks" for transitions may be blurred or nonexistent. A time when a transition occurs—or should occur—may not be marked with a celebration but with a fresh bout with feelings of chronic sorrow (Wikler, Wasow, & Hatfield, 1981). There may be no movement to a new classroom each year. There may be no graduation, no wedding, no moving away from home. Thus, not only is the family uncertain as to exactly how their interactions might change, they may also have no cues that the interactions *should* change.

Some of these problems can be mitigated by helping families plan ahead for transitions. School personnel can help families think ahead to next year or 5 years from now by discussing instructional objectives in terms of the child's future needs. Visits to new classrooms or community programs such as group homes, meetings with future teachers, talks with parents of older children with similar exceptionalities, can all help to reduce the fear of the future by making it less unknown. Table 5–2 provides some tips to ease the transitions into and out of each of the life cycle stages discussed in this chapter.

Off-Time Transitions

Families with a member having an exceptionality are especially likely to experience a life cycle transition that occurs at other than its expected time. Transitions that are delayed or fail to occur at all occur often. For example, a young adult might remain at home with his or her parents for years. Bob Helsel (1985) describes how continued dependency becomes more of a problem as a child with an exceptionality becomes older:

> In the past [Robin] didn't present any special problems with respect to limiting my life . . . But he was a member of the family. We had other children, so taking care of Robin didn't place any special burden on us.
>
> But it seems to me as I approach retirement age and would like lots of personal freedom, he will present a problem in limiting my ability to go where I want when I want. I am aware of the possible limitations or freedom to leave home . . . [For parents of normal children] if they aren't out of the nest, they are at least old enough so that the parents can say to them, "Take care of yourselves; I'll see you next month!" But with Robin, we can't do that. (p. 91)

In addition to transitions that are delayed or do not occur, for some exceptionalities a transition may occur earlier than the expected time. For instance, researchers have found that placing a child in a living situation outside the home does not generally reduce the overall stress the family feels (Fotheringham, Shelton, & Hoddinott, 1972). When a child leaves home at nineteen, it may not be easy for his or her parents, but at least it is expected and seen by our society as desirable. But when a young child leaves home for an alternative living placement, the parents may feel a sense of guilt and inadequacy. There may be an implication from professionals that parents who cannot keep their children with exceptionalities are failures (Kupfer, 1982). Additionally, there is a sense of abandonment and loss. Rud Turnbull (1985) described his feelings when he was forced to place his young son in a residential facility:

> It was at Pine Harbor that, in the most wrenching moment of my life, I performed the most difficult act of my life, and handed Jay to Katie, a teen-age volunteer and an utter stranger; crying, burbling, stammering, I managed only to say, "Take him, he's yours now." Jay's screams and his look ["Again? You are leaving me again!"] remain with me today—vivid, poignant, immediate. (p. 112)

Another off-time transition is the illness or death of a young child. Illness and death may be an expected (though perhaps not accepted) part of life for an older person, but when it happens to a child it seems like a strange and cruel twist of fate. Helen Featherstone (1980) described her conversation with a mother whose three-year-old child with an exceptionality had died:

> I asked how things had gone since the spring.
>
> "Last summer was very hard, but when fall came, things started to get good."
>
> "You missed Ellie a lot?"
>
> "Well, no. I felt tremendous relief and then tremendous guilt about the relief."
>
> Catherine went on to say that Peter had been miserable, too, because he really did miss Ellie very much. His grief intensified her self-reproach. . . . (p. 132)

The mixed feelings of relief, guilt, and grief are common. They may require, as in the case Featherstone (1980) described above, counseling or therapy to allow parents to resolve their feelings both about the child's death and toward each other. It is important for professionals to understand the tremendous pressures in a family with a child who is terminally ill. The key to successful adjustment both before and after the death seems to be an atmosphere that allows open communication of feelings, and permission to grieve or to express anger. Professionals should be prepared to allow time for parents and siblings of a dying student to express themselves. Frank Deford (1983) offers a poignant account of his daughter's life and death in *Alex: The Life of a Child,* a book that celebrates and grieves.

Beyond the immediate family, a child's death may have emotional consequences for his or her classmates. Children and adolescents seldom think about death, and, in particular, seldom think it possible that one of their peers could die. When death comes to someone their own age, it can be a real shock. When a child with a terminal illness is in the classroom, it is important not to gloss over or ignore the feelings of the other students. A special presentation on death and dying, along with individual talks with teachers and counselors for those who seem especially concerned, might be helpful. Many community mental health centers or hospice programs provide information and/or make such presentations.

SUMMARY

The process of change in a family is a complex phenomenon. As family members enter and leave the system, and as they grow and change, so too must the family's interactional style and approach to life. The needs of a family with a young child with an exceptionality are very different from the needs of a family with an older child or young adult. At each developmental stage the family must accomplish a number of tasks and face a number of issues associated with the exceptionality. Transitions, too, are difficult to negotiate under the best of circumstances. But when the family has a member with an exceptionality, those transitions may be even more difficult from the uncertainty of the future and the off-schedule nature of change.

School personnel can help mitigate some of the stresses families experience as they cope with change. The school professional may be able to help families anticipate change by describing what the future holds, inviting parents to visit future classrooms or adult programs, and encouraging planning. Chapter 12 describes the future planning process in greater detail.

But perhaps the most important aid school professionals can offer is understanding. The professional should recognize when families are in transition, or when the transition is delayed or premature, think about the needs they may have to cope with new or changing roles, and realize that, in the face of uncertainty and change, perhaps what families could use is a little firm reassurance that help will always be available.

in the face of uncertainty and change, perhaps what families could use is a little firm reassurance that help will always be available.

The concepts of change and the life cycle complete the portrait of the family system. Briefly, the major assumptions of family systems and their implications for educators are:

1. Every family has a different set of resources, values and styles to bring to their experience with exceptionality; thus professionals should individualize their approach to working with families.
2. Families have an interactional style that dictates the way the members are arranged into subsystems and their preferred levels of cohesion and adaptability; professionals should encourage balance and adapt interventions to accommodate families' ability to adapt.
3. Families have a variety of functions to meet a range of tangible and intangible needs for all their members; professionals should respect each family's priorities and encourage the family to attend to the needs of all its members.
4. Families change over time; professionals should provide services that meet the needs of the different developmental stages and also ease the stress of transition from one stage to another.

Because of the importance of these elements of the family system for professionals, an assessment of each family's characteristics is critical to the professional's ability to individualize his or her approach to each family. As we will note in Chapter 9, a family assessment should be an integral part of the overall evaluation process for the child. A suggested format for family assessment is included in Appendix A.

In assessment as well as day-to-day interaction with families, one critical key to success is communication. Good communication skills are a resource for families as they seek to meet their needs among themselves and in interaction with those outside the family. For professionals, good communication is also critical to successful relationships with families. The next two chapters will first consider some of the skills necessary for open and meaningful communication and then some strategies for maintaining good communication between families and professionals.

Chapter 6
Communication Skills

The challenge of the 1980s for both parents and professionals will be to find ways to carry out the legislative mandates for collaborative efforts to help children. Legislation alone cannot achieve this process. It is a human, psychological, and educational process that must begin with people learning about one another. We must learn to appreciate the perspectives of others, learn to share with one another, and learn how to learn from one another. (Klein & Schleifer, 1980, p.3)

This chapter covers communicating and working with others. It concerns communication in open, genuine, and meaningful ways with families of children with exceptionalities. The ability to engage in such communication is not easily acquired; on the contrary, many go through life seeking to develop this quality in themselves. It requires hard work to awaken this quality in ourselves and inspire it in others.

Communication is a process by which people exchange and transmit information. It has been said that, when people are gathered together, it is impossible for them not to communicate on some level (Gilmore & Fraleigh, 1980; Miller, Nunnally, & Wackman, 1978). Because of the special needs of children with exceptionalities, many families and professionals have frequent opportunities to communicate with each other. Unfortunately, communication among families and professionals is frequently perceived as less than adequate (Sonnenschein, 1984). Research conducted with special education and regular teachers has indicated that teachers rank communications with parents as a major source of job stress (Bensky, Shaw, Gouse, Bates, Dixon, & Beane, 1980). Interestingly, parents report the same feelings of stress when working with teachers and other professionals (Turnbull, 1983):

> I was fortunate in having established myself as a professional in the field of mental retardation before I became a parent of a retarded child. Things did not go smoothly, though. Surprisingly, my wife and I embarked on a long series of catastrophic interactions with professionals which echoed the complaints I had heard so often from other parents. (Roos, 1985, p. 13)

If we are to meet the challenge of the law and education, then we must find ways to transform inadequate communication among parents and professionals into communication that is open, genuine, and meaningful.

PREREQUISITES TO POSITIVE COMMUNICATION

There are a number of prerequisites to the development of positive communication among families and professionals. In the next section, we will address these prerequisites as well as the benefits that result when parents and professionals work together as partners.

Knowing Ourselves

The first step in learning to communicate effectively and work with others is learning to know and work with ourselves. The more we know about and appreciate ourselves and our behaviors, the better we can understand and appreciate the personalities and behaviors of other people (Benjamin, 1969; Traux & Mitchell, 1971; Trungpa, 1976; Webster, 1977). In Benjamin's words:

> As we become more familiar with ourselves, we may feel less threatened by what we find. We may even get to the point that we genuinely like some of the things about us and, therefore, become more tolerant of the things we like less or do not like at all. And, then as long as we keep on examining and wanting to find out, it is possible we shall go on changing and growing. Oriented to ourselves, we may become comfortable with ourselves and thus be able to help others become comfortable with themselves and with us. In addition, because we are at ease with our own self, there will be less of a tendency for it to get in the way of our understanding another self. . . . (p. 7)

The development of self-awareness and self-acceptance can be a difficult and painful task requiring commitment and perseverance. It is a task that most of us will never complete in our lifetimes. Fortunately, according to Rogers (1961) and Benjamin (1969), *complete* self-awareness and acceptance is not a necessary prerequisite for persons who are in positions of helping others. What is important is a willingness to engage in the dual process of understanding and accepting ourselves while simultaneously attempting to make attitudinal changes (Webster, 1977). An attitude that favors understanding of ourselves favors understanding of others. Without such an attitude, we cannot expect to have effective and meaningful exchanges with others. The sequence of exchange begins with ourselves.

Developing Respect and Trust

Becoming familiar with, working with, and appreciating who we are forms the basis not only for effective communication with others but also for the development of mutual trust and respect (Traux & Mitchell, 1971). Trust and respect are essential to the development of effective and meaningful communication among parents and professionals. In Turnbull's (1985) words:

> When professionals interact with parents, respect is a necessary ingredient. . . . One of the most meaningful interactions I have had as a parent with a professional since Jay has been home was with a psychologist. As I shared some very personal concerns with her related to planning for Jay's future,

tears came down her cheeks. We sat in silence for a long time, both considering the course of action that would be in Jay's best interest. The silence was beautiful. It confirmed that she was hearing what I was saying and was sharing my feelings on the subject. There was no easy answer. An immediate response, telling me not to worry about things, would have insulted my sensibilities. I knew she respected me when she poignantly shared my feelings. The result of that interaction was that my respect for her as a professional grew one hundredfold. (p. 133)

Without mutual trust and respect, the probability for the development of meaningful and productive communication among families and professionals is severely compromised (Simpson, 1982). Moreover, lack of trust and respect affects not only the family and professional, but the child as well. In Rutherford and Edgar's (1979) words: "when teachers and parents find themselves in adversary roles, distrusting each other, children suffer" (p. 20).

The establishment of effective and meaningful communication among families and professionals requires a willingness to work with others as well as ourselves. It also requires a certain amount of skill. Later in this chapter we will describe a variety of specific communication skills that we feel are important for effective interactions with families. First, however, let us turn to the benefits of effective communication.

Forming a Family-Professional Partnership

When family and professionals respect, trust, and communicate openly with one another, a partnership is formed. Both families and professionals have unique contributions to bring to a partnership. Such partnerships can be beneficial not only for the child, but for parents and professionals as well. Heward, Dardig, and Rossett (1979) have described the multiple benefits of parent-professional partnerships:

A productive parent-professional relationship provides professionals with:

- Greater understanding of the overall needs of the child and the needs and desires of the parent.
- Data for more meaningful selection of target behaviors that are important to the child in his or her world outside the school.
- Access to a wider range of social and activity reinforcers provided by parents.
- Increased opportunities to reinforce appropriate behaviors in both school and home settings.
- Feedback from parents as to changes in behavior that can be used to improve programs being implemented by professionals and parents.

- The ability to comply with legislation mandating continuing parental input to the educational process.

A productive parent-professional relationship provides parents with:

- Greater understanding of the needs of their child and the objectives of the teacher.
- Information on their rights and responsibilities as parents of an exceptional child.
- Specific information about their child's school program and how they can become involved.
- Specific ways to extend the positive effects of school programming into the home.
- Increased skills in helping their child learn functional behaviors that are appropriate for the home environment.
- Access to additional important resources (current and future) for their child.

And, of most importance, a productive parent-professional relationship provides the child with:

- Greater consistency in her two most important environments.
- Increased opportunities for learning and growth.
- Access to expanded resources and services. (p. 226)

In addition, family-professional partnerships provide professionals with the opportunity to gain greater insight into the strengths and needs of families with members with exceptionalities, as well as the opportunity to develop and refine skills for working with families. Last, family-professional partnerships provide both parties with the satisfaction of cooperatively working with one another for the benefit of the child in a relationship that can prevent or minimize conflict.

A SYSTEMS PERSPECTIVE ON COMMUNICATION

When families and professionals interact, a whole host of variables come together. In Barsch's (1969) words: "What would at first glance appear to be a relatively mechanical, simple encounter is in truth a very complex situation" (p. 12). Families and professionals come from varied social, economic, educational, ethnic, racial, and religious backgrounds as discussed in Chapter 2. Although these differences alone can sometimes preclude effective partnerships, there are other issues to consider: the parent's past experience in dealing with professionals, the professional's past experience in dealing with parents, the level of interpersonal communication skill possessed by parents and professionals, their personalities and values, and the expectations and stereotypes that parents and professionals hold for one another all play a role in determining the nature of their relationships (Seligman, 1979). When family-professional relationships become problematic, there often is a tendency to place the blame on one or the other party, to define the problem as existing in either the professional or the family:

> Making appointments and not showing up, playing professionals against one another, presenting oneself as less capable than one really is, playing "yes, but . . . " as a way to close down communication, holding grudges while never confronting the "accused professional offender," etc., are some examples of parental behavior that are devastating to parent-professional relationships. (Mulick & Pueschel, 1983, p. 28)

How a problem is defined will determine to a large extent what people do about it (Germain & Gitterman, 1980). If professionals take the position that it is families who are responsible for the problems that arise in interactions, then chances are that they also believe that it is families' responsibility for ameliorating the problems. It is probably safe to assume that the same is true when families see professionals as the cause of the conflict. When this happens, it is usual for conflicts to not only remain but also to become larger and ultimately more difficult to solve. The systems perspective provides an alternative method for viewing problems and problem resolution.

From the systems perspective, communication breakdowns are representative of a faulty system rather than faulty people. The locus of communication problems is viewed as residing in the interactions between people, not within people. This is not to say that individuals cannot, and do not need to, improve their interactions with others; on the contrary, much can be done. That is, from a systems perspective, when problems arise between people, the emphasis is on changing their interactional patterns rather than changing one individual or the other. The systems perspective leaves no room for placing blame when communication is less than optimal. In fact, the act of attempting to place blame for the problem on one person or another is viewed as counterproductive to problem resolution. Instead of focusing on the issue of blame, one is free to explore the variables that may contribute to the breakdown in communication. This provides professionals and families with the opportunity to see how the problem appears to themselves and each other.

Sometimes it may be easy to identify the variables that contribute to the problem, such as when parents cannot participate regularly in school meetings because they have no telephone or transportation. In other cases, the variables may be less obvious and more difficult to identify and address, such as in situations where there is a personality clash between the parent and professional. From the systems perspective, the important point is that the parties involved work together to explore and resolve the problem. By engaging in the process of mutual problem-solving, both parties have the opportunity to express and try to fulfill their needs. Furthermore, a willingness to share responsibility for breakdowns in communication maximizes the probability that families and professionals can work toward mutual solutions in a non-threatening and non-defensive manner.

The process of confronting and solving problems is difficult and painful. It is precisely because of the pain events generate in us that we call them problems. Yet, according to Peck (1978), "it is in this whole process of meeting and solving problems that life has its meaning" (p. 116). When we solve problems, we learn and grow. When we solve problems together with others, we learn and grow together. Mutual problem-solving among families and professionals is ideal but does not always occur. We can take responsibility for confronting and working on our communication problems with others; however, we have little direct influence over whether or not those persons are willing to do the same. Professionals who endeavor to establish good communication with families must be willing to work zealously in situations in which there appears to be resistance. This requires demonstration of a willingness and openness to accept mutual responsibility for both the problem and its resolution. Evidence of this willingness alone can often do much to influence the behavior of others. In addition, it is helpful for professionals to have some degree of insight into the barriers that typically influence family-professional interactions. Identification of barriers is an important first step to overcome them.

BARRIERS TO EFFECTIVE FAMILY-PROFESSIONAL INTERACTIONS

Barriers to productive family-professional interaction can be grouped into four general categories: (a) psychological, (b) attitudinal, (c) cultural/ideological, and (d) logistical. In Chapter 2, we discussed the many ways cultural and ideological differences among families and professionals can contribute to difficulties in their interactions, and we suggested strategies and methods for minimizing these differences. Later, in Chapter 10, we will describe many of the logistical barriers perceived by both parents and professionals which sometimes affect the degree to which they can work together effectively. In this chapter we focus on some common psychological and attitudinal phenomenon that frequently contribute to the development and maintenance of barriers. Remember that, although barriers to effective family-professional partnerships can be broken down into neat, distinct categories for our discussion, in actuality these barriers are comprised typically of a combination of factors, all of which may interrelate at some level. This complexity of issues can sometimes make it difficult for families and professionals to address and find solutions to their communication problems.

Psychological Barriers

One of the psychological barriers that often underlies family-professional interactions deals with perception, that is, how one views the world. The way in which people view the world can vary widely according to a complex interaction of internal and external forces (Webster, 1977). This interaction of forces is so complex that it is safe to theorize that no two people perceive the world in exactly the same way. First , we perceive our world through our sensory receptors. Although this fact alone accounts for much consistency in perception among people, it is possible that differences exist even at this very basic level. It is obvious that these differences exist when we interact with deaf or blind persons; these differences may be less obvious in persons who experience other more subtle disorders of perception such as hyperesthesia (an abnormal increase in sensitivity of a sensor process, e.g., exaggerated sensitivity to heat, cold, pain . . .) or acroparesthesia (a recurrent numbness of the extremities).

A second factor that contributes to the variability in perception among people has to do with the meaning one attaches to perception. As information about our world comes to us, we filter and edit it to make sense of what we hear, feel, see, and smell. This process can be referred to as "interpretation" and characteristically takes the form of impressions, conclusions, assumptions, expectations, and/or prejudices. It is important to recognize that interpretations are different from observations; two people may observe the same event but interpret it quite differently. For example, a professional may interpret a child's crying as attention-getting behavior, but the parent may see it as an expression of pain and frustration. When we acknowledge our tendency to interpret sensory data, we also may become aware of the fact that our interpretations may not always be accurate.

Many of us seldom question our perceptions of the world around us. We generally accept our perceptions and interpretations as a true representation of reality. This can and does lead to problems when we interact with other people who do not share our view of reality. It becomes even more problematic when we insist that others agree with our projected images. In order to set the stage for the development of productive communication with others, we must be willing to admit that our perceptions and interpretations, by nature, may be inaccurate, or at least incomplete, as well as different from others. Because we all perceive reality differently, it is likely that families and professionals will continue sometimes to disagree.

It is important to realize that such situations need not take the form of insurmountable barriers to effective interactions. On the contrary, differences in perceptions are a natural outgrowth of the human condition and probably cannot, nor need not, be avoided. What we can do is to alter the approach we take when differences in perception arise. Instead of viewing differences in perception as problems, differences can be viewed as opportunities for both families and professionals to sharpen their perceptual worlds through their interactions with one another. In Webster's (1977) words, professionals can " . . . be grateful that they share bonds with parents in matters of projection and perception, because this sharing makes them much more simply human than otherwise. . . . " (p. 7).

Attitudinal Barriers

In addition to psychological barriers that sometimes underlie family-professional interactions, attitudinal barriers may also exist. Sonnenschein (1984) describes seven categories of attitudes and assumptions sometimes held by professionals that can contribute to the maintenance of inadequate communication patterns between professionals and families. Before we present these seven categories, we wish to make it clear that we by no means wish to imply that *all* professionals hold these attitudes and assumptions, or that professionals are solely to blame for the problems that arise between professionals and families. It is probably safe to state that, in most instances, both families and professionals have a role to play in creating and perpetuating attitudinal barriers that interfere with optimal interactions. The next section is presented, not as a strategy for laying a "guilt trip" on professionals, but as an example of some of the attitudes that have, and can, damage family-professional relationships.

The seven categories as conceptualized by Sonnenschein (1984) are as follows: (a) the parent as vulnerable client; (b) the parent and "professional distance"; (c) the parent as patient; (d) the parent as responsible for the child's condition; (e) the parent as less observant, less perceptive, and less intelligent; (f) the parent as adversary; and (g) parents as "pushy," "angry," "denying," "resistant," or "anxious."

The Situation of Parent as Vulnerable Client. In Sonnenschein's (1984) words, "There seems to be a natural imbalance between the helper and the helped, the powerful and the powerless, the expert and the novice that is difficult to overcome" (p. 130). As a result of this unequal power distribution, parents often feel uncomfortably vulnerable. Professionals need to be aware of the tendency in some parents to feel vulnerable when asking for help. Mary Akerley, the mother of a child with autism, describes her experience of seeking help from professionals:

We were referred to a pediatric neurologist . . . The results, however, were singularly unhelpful. "We can't give you a diagnosis; his symptoms don't fit any known syndrome. We've never seen a child like this." John and I didn't know whether to weep or take a bow. I remember trying to pry something more specific from them. "Is he retarded?" "Autistic?" [I had heard the word about two weeks earlier?] "Disturbed?" Perhaps all of the above although none of the above seemed more like it. At least none of the familiar labels appeared to hit the mark precisely enough for the pros to be comfortable with it; and in their desire to be precise, they overlooked the need to be supportive. We felt totally abandoned. If they didn't know what was wrong who would? And if no one knew what was wrong, then who would know what to do? Eddie was trapped in his misery, and we were trapped right in there with him. (1985, pp. 24–25)

In addition, professionals must be aware their own behaviors may contribute to this reaction. Professionals who exhibit facades of superiority may elicit greater feelings of vulnerability in parents and/or may encourage defensiveness and resistance. According to Benjamin (1969), "The alternative is an atmosphere in which a sense of equality prevails—not equality of knowledge, experience, or professional skill, naturally, but equality of worth and dignity, with each human being fully respecting the other" (p. 94). Professionals who wish to improve the nature of their interactions with parents should strive to create such a climate.

The Parent and "Professional Distance." A second factor that Sonnenschein (1984) identifies as contributing to problems in parent-professional interactions is professional behavior that keeps parents at a distance. According to many parents, this distance typically is accompanied by lack of empathy on the part of the professional. Parents suffer when professionals fail to demonstrate genuine empathy. A mother of three children with muscular dystrophy, two of whom also had mental retardation, writes:

When we are injured, we need nurturance—whatever age we are. I think one of the dilemmas for the professional dealing with parents of handicapped children is that they have to try to help parents, who may also acutely need nurturance themselves, to give extra care and nurturance to the child. Some of the professionals who worked with us let us know that they understood our pain, and that was often all the care we needed. But sometimes the concern for the child became the total focus, and I felt drained and discouraged. (Weyhing, 1983, p. 127)

The fact that professionals sometimes fail to express empathy is not necessarily because they do not experience these feelings. According to Rogers (1961), it is a fear to express attitudes of caring, warmth, and interest that sometimes interferes with its expression:

> We are afraid that if we let ourselves freely experience these positive feelings toward another we may be trapped by them. They may lead to demands on us or we may be disappointed in our trust, and these outcomes we fear. So as a reaction we tend to build up distance between ourselves and others— aloofness, a "professional" attitude, an impersonal relationship. (p. 52)

Parents and professionals need to work together to establish relationships in which it is safe to care and to relate feelings of caring openly.

The Parent as Patient.   From this point of view, parents who have children with exceptionalities need some form of treatment or therapy. Although this may be the case for some parents, it is clearly not the case for the majority. According to Webster (1977), "Counselors learn that, taken as a group, parents of handicapped children are not seriously emotionally disturbed people. Like all other human beings, they struggle with existential anxieties and problems. They also experience joy, satisfaction, and success" (p. 39). In fact, there is evidence that some parents may become emotionally *stronger* as a result (Wikler, Wasow, & Hatfield, 1983). One parent commented: "As a parent of a retarded child, I believe that it has made me stronger. It has made me much more patient than I was. Even emotionally you get an inner strength to deal with everyday care and problems of the child" (Wikler, Wasow, & Hatfield, 1983, p. 112). Turnbull (1985) has noted the paradox that his son's mental retardation impedes as well as accelerates his own growth as a parent and person.

Unfortunately, there are still those professionals who choose to see weakness and pathology in parents with children having exceptionalities. A professional who became a parent of a child with mental retardation writes: "I had suddenly been demoted from the role of a professional to that of the parent as patient: the assumption by some professionals that parents of a retarded child are emotionally maladjusted and are prime candidates for counseling, psychotherapy, or tranquilizers" (Roos, 1985, p. 246).

As professionals we encourage you to develop an awareness in yourselves for any tendencies you may have to view parents as sick or in need of therapy. In Sonnenschein's (1984) words, "If parents sense that they are being perceived as 'troubled' or 'coping badly,' they may do their best to hide any signs of struggle or, perhaps, will feel as helpless and disturbed as they are judged to be" (p. 134). Capitalizing on the family's strengths rather than weaknesses in subtle and obvious ways can do much to change both the family's, and your own perspectives. Inquiring about unique contributions the child makes and asking the family to share ways in which they have coped successfully are two means to accomplish this.

The Parent as Cause. A fourth possible attitudinal barrier to parent-professional interactions is that of the parent as responsible for the child's condition. This view is held not only by some professionals, but by some parents as well. This seems particularly true for parents of children where no organic problem can be found to account for their child's disorder (Doernberg, Bernard, & Lenz, 1976). For example, a mother of an adopted child with a learning disability expressed these feelings during a parent discussion:

> Sometimes I feel so guilty that I have caused Harry's problems; then I stop and think how crazy that is. I didn't even know Harry until he was two years old, and if it's true that these problems start before that, I couldn't be to blame because I didn't have anything to do with him so early. (Webster, 1977, p. 44)

As mentioned in Chapter 1, causation theories have sent many parents on tremendous "guilt trips" and have produced many barriers to constructive parent-professional relationships. (See Chapter 14 for a discussion of the ethics of imposing guilt on parents.) Professionals need to be sensitive to the tendency by some parents to feel guilty that they caused their child's problems. In addition, they must make every effort not to reinforce, nor to invalidate, these feelings. According to Moses (1983), "the temptation on the part of most professionals is to try to take away the guilt. Only the very exceptional person is able to validate the legitimacy of the parent's feeling without seeming to confirm a judgment of fault. To offer such a relationship is to offer a unique opportunity that facilitates growth" (p. 21).

The Parent as Less Observant, Less Perceptive, and Less Intelligent. It is a fact of life that, at some point in their careers, professionals are bound to come into contact with parents who do not appear to be very observant, perceptive, or intelligent. It is important to realize that these persons are no more heavily represented among groups of parents with children with exceptionalities than they are in the general population. Parents of children with exceptionalities are a heterogeneous group drawn from the ranks of normal parents (Boggs, 1969). Unfortunately, some parents have come to believe that they are indeed less observant, perceptive, or intelligent, either based on the fact that they have children with exceptionalities, or based on the treatment and feedback they have received from professionals. One mother shares her reaction:

> I felt like a nobody. Any credits of self-worth that I could give myself from any of my personal endeavors meant nothing. Graduating from college and a first-rate medical school, surviving internship, practicing medicine and

having two beautiful sons and a good marriage counted for nil. All I knew at this point was that I was the mother of an abnormal and most likely retarded child. (Ziskin, 1985, p. 68)

According to Sonnenschein (1984), parents feel that professionals rarely find their opinions and impressions important or useful. It has been demonstrated, however, in study after study that many parents of children and youth with disabilities are *extremely* observant, perceptive, and intelligent. The literature is rife with examples of especially competent parents who have been successful in teaching their children a variety of skills including, but not limited to, walking, talking, and interacting with others (Fredericks, Baldwin, & Grove, 1976; Karnes, Zehrbach, & Teska, 1972; Patterson, 1971; Smith & Smith, 1966; Weikart & Lambie, 1970). In addition, there are examples in the literature of professionals in special education who claim they have learned more by having a child with an exceptionality than from all of their professional training (Turnbull, 1985; Schulz, 1985).

Many parents know much about their children and consequently have much to offer professionals. Professionals who fail to acknowledge and accept this fact not only do a disservice to their job, but also do much to perpetuate barriers to productive family-professional partnerships. A partnership is a relationship in which both parties feel needed, respected, and valued. Professionals who wish to establish such relationships with parents need to let parents know how vitally important and useful their contributions are.

The Parent as Adversary. Sometimes professionals in fields related to exceptionalities view parents as adversaries competing with them in various ways and for various purposes. Sometimes parents view professionals as adversaries. As Sonnenschein (1984) points out, it is possible to understand how adversarial, or competitive, relationships can arise between parents and professionals since both have vested interests in the child's welfare and progress. A father of a child with disabilities comments: "Parents may feel hurt that a stranger is more successful than they are with their child, and professionals may feel threatened that untrained and unsophisticated parents may succeed where they have failed. As a result, parents and professionals may surreptitiously undermine and downgrade each other's efforts" (Roos, 1985, p. 254). Mary Akerley, in her chapter in *Parents Speak Out*, provides an example of the competition that sometimes can arise between parents and professionals:

I remember when Eddie learned to kiss. We had taught him the mechanics and had been getting back a lifeless touch of his lips to our cheeks. Then one night at bedtime it happened—a real kiss. I could hardly wait to report this exciting mark of progress to Doctor Number Two. At our regular session a few days later, he pre-empted me (he had seen Eddie the day before).

"Eddie kissed me," he announced smugly with the most self-satisfied look I had ever seen on a human face.

"Me, too" was all I could say.

"When?" There was actually fear in his voice, and when he heard the answer, he was visibly upset. "That means he kissed you before he kissed me!"

Right, doctor, and that is as it should be. (Akerley, 1985, pp. 28–29)

Roos (1985) warns that parents and professionals need to be constantly cognizant of the tendency to compete with one another, to use one another as scapegoats, and/or to undermine the other's efforts to help the person who experiences the exceptionality. Yielding to the temptation to blame, compete, or undermine can only result in negative effects upon the parent-professional partnership as well as upon the child. When adversarial conditions arise, it sometimes helps parents and professionals to reframe their interpretation of the event by reflecting upon their mutually shared interest, commitment, and dedication to help the child. Often, adoption of this attitude can do much to diffuse the potential for further rivalry and opposition.

Parents as "Pushy," "Angry," "Denying," "Resistant," or "Anxious." The last category of assumptions and attitudes held by professionals toward parents, according to Sonnenschein (1984), is that of parents as "pushy," "angry," "denying," "resistant," or "anxious." This tendency to label parents often results in more harm than good. This is particularly true when labels based on inaccurate interpretations of parents' behaviors are applied. In Sonnenschein's (1984) words:

Parents who disagree with a diagnosis or seek a second opinion are "denying"; those who refuse the kind of treatment that is suggested are "resistant"; and those who are convinced that something is wrong with their child despite inconclusive tests are "anxious." A belief that the parents' perception or suggestion may be the better or more accurate one is rare. (p. 136)

It may well be that parents exhibit these traits. Some parents will exhibit more of them than other parents, and some will exhibit them more often than other parents. Indeed, there sometimes are good reasons rooted in professional behavior for parents to behave in some of these ways. Likewise, there sometimes are no professional causes for such behavior. Where there may be such causes, however, professional candor in acknowledging that fact, apologizing for it, and correcting the cause, can be immensely helpful to parent-professional relationships. Upon learning that his son's neurologist agreed with him that there were professional causes for his anger and having the physician correct those causes by simple, deliberate, humble, and patient discussions, Turnbull noted with relief the "absolution—the soft vanishing of my present and past anxiety—not the pain of the future" (Turnbull, 1985, p. 110).

Whenever possible, professionals must try to resist the temptation to label parents. Labeling does nothing to enhance or improve one's relationships with others, no matter how accurate the label may be. Rather than label, professionals who wish to develop good relationships with parents should seek to cultivate unconditional positive regard. Unconditional positive regard involves acceptance of the parents' expression of positive as well as negative feelings. In Roger's (1961) words: "It [unconditional positive regard] involves an acceptance of and a caring for the [parent] as a *separate* person, with permission for him [her] to have his [her] own feelings and experiences, and to find his [her] own meaning in them" (p. 283).

Interpersonal Communication Skills

Having identified some of the psychological and attitudinal barriers that can sometimes interfere with effective communication among families and professionals, we turn our discussion to the importance of good interpersonal communication skills. We strongly believe that good communication skills are especially important for persons who work in helping professions. The more accurately professionals can communicate thoughts and feelings, the more able they will be to help others. While there are some individuals who seem to have a natural ability to communicate well, most persons must work consciously to develop this ability (Chinn, Winn, & Walters, 1978). Prior to the work of Allen (1967) and Ivey, Normington, Miller, Morrill, and Haase (1968), there were those within the counseling discipline who believed that specific interpersonal communication skills could not be taught or learned (Kroth & Simpson, 1977). Fortunately, it has been experimentally demonstrated often that communication skills can be learned and applied by a variety of professionals and non-professionals alike (Lombana, 1983; Ivey & Authier, 1978; Kasdorf & Gustafson, 1978).

For example, Ivey and Authier (1978) and Kasdorf and Gustafson (1978) cite 150 data-based studies indicating that specific communication skills can be taught to medical students, nurses, social workers, teachers, paraprofessionals, parents, elementary school students, and others in relatively brief periods of time without extensive training. According to Evans, Hearn, Uhlemann, and Ivey (1984), learning and using communication skills is akin to learning another language or playing a sport or musical instrument. The skills must be practiced if they are to be maintained. The advantage of learning communication skills is that they demand no special equipment and can be practiced anywhere—at home, at work, and during leisure time.

There is one last point before discussing specific communication techniques. Although it has been scientifically demonstrated that many communication skills can be taught, many theorists contend that effective communication is an art, not a science (Kroth & Simpson, 1977). The effective use of communication skills as an art relies heavily upon the user's attitudes and personal qualities. According to Rogers (1961), the three most important user-attributes are empathy, genuineness, and unconditional positive regard. Students of interpersonal communication must try to master both the art and the science of communication skills. Furthermore, they must seek to incorporate these techniques and qualities into their personal style so that they become natural and spontaneous rather than stiff and contrived. To integrate these skills successfully into one's personal style requires systematic practice and use of the skills. We strongly urge you to practice and use the communication skills that we will now share with you as much as possible.

Nonverbal Communication Skills

Nonverbal communication includes all communication other than the spoken or written word. Many consider nonverbal communication as an inseparable part of the total communication process. As we communicate verbally, we also communicate nonverbally through the use of gestures, facial expressions, voice volume and intonations, physical proximity to others, and posture (Spiegel & Machotka, 1974). According to Knapp (1972), in a typical conversation between two people, less than 35% of the social meaning is transmitted by words, while 65% is communicated through nonverbal forms of communication. Nonverbal behaviors can strongly influence interactions between people. In fact, according to Hammond, Hepworth, & Smith (1977), most people learn through life experience that nonverbal cues are a more accurate indicator of feelings than spoken words. As a result, when there is a discrepancy between a person's verbal and nonverbal communication, people are more likely to discredit the former (Argyle, 1975; Mehrabian, 1969; Strahan & Zytowski, 1976). Many of the nonverbal cues that we transmit to others are largely beyond our conscious awareness (Hepworth & Larsen, 1982). It is for this reason that professionals who wish to improve the nature of their interactions with parents must deliberately and consciously use nonverbal behaviors consistent with their underlying feelings and intentions.

Mastering *physical attending* is a basic, nonverbal skill that is considered essential to the helping process (Ivey, 1971; Ivey & Authier, 1978). This skill is characterized by such receptive behaviors as leaning forward, facing the other person squarely, maintaining eye contact, and remaining relaxed. Physical attending also requires that listeners give the speakers their fullest and undivided attention at all times throughout the interaction. Some barriers that sometimes interfere with full physical attending can be caused by preoccupation with oneself, preoccupation with judgments about the other person, or inner pressures to find immediate solutions to the other person's problems or complaints (Hepworth & Larsen, 1982).

Professionals who wish to improve their communications with parents need to be aware of both desirable and undesirable nonverbal behaviors. To assist you in evaluating and improving your nonverbal behaviors, we have included an inventory of desirable and undesirable nonverbal communication behaviors (see Table 6–1) developed by Hepworth and Larsen (1982). The developers of this inventory suggest that it be used in the following ways: "(a) to assess your repetitive nonverbal behaviors, (b) to delete nonverbal styles that hinder effective communication, and (c) to sustain and perhaps increase desirable nonverbal behaviors" (Hepworth & Larsen, 1982, p. 76). We encourage you to heed these suggestions as an important first step to achieve mastery of your nonverbal communication skills. (See p. 130.)

Listening is the "language of acceptance" and is considered by many to be one of the most essential ingredients for an effective helping relationship (Gordon, 1970). Unfortunately, true listening rarely occurs naturally or spontaneously. To listen to another person with genuine, undivided attention is a difficult task that requires both diligence and practice. According to Benjamin (1969), genuine listening requires three conditions: (a) that we attend to the other person without preoccupation, (b) that we are aware of the way things are said, the tone in which they are said, and the expressions and gestures used, and (c) that we hear what is not said, that which lies beneath the surface. In Benjamin's (1969) words, "we hear with our ears, but we listen with our eyes and mind and heart and skin and guts as well" (p. 47). Ultimately, the goal of listening is to understand. If professionals wish to have satisfying and productive relationships with parents they need to learn to listen in this manner.

Gordon (1970) and Kroth (1975) have identified two varieties of listeners—active and passive. Although some persons may have a tendency to be one kind of listener or the other, most people unconsciously fluctuate between the two varieties. Truly effective listeners have mastered both listening styles and are able to select the style that is most conducive to a given situation. Passive listeners are the "silent types" who say very little but remain actively involved in the communication exchange through

Table 6–1
INVENTORY OF PRACTITIONER'S NONVERBAL COMMUNICATION

Desirable	*Undesirable*
Facial expressions	
Direct eye contact (except when culturally proscribed)	Avoidance of eye contact
	Eye level higher or lower than client's
Warmth and concern reflected in facial expression	Staring or fixating on person or object
	Lifting eyebrow critically
Eyes at same level as client's	Nodding head excessively
Appropriately varied and animated facial expressions	Yawning
	Frozen or rigid facial expressions
Mouth relaxed; occasional smiles	Inappropriate slight smile
	Pursing or biting lips
Posture	
Arms and hands moderately expressive; appropriate gestures	Rigid body position; arms tightly folded
	Body turned at an angle to client
Body leaning slightly foward; attentive but relaxed	Fidgeting with hands (including clipping nails or cleaning pipe)
	Squirming or rocking in chair
	Slouching or placing feet on desk
	Hand or fingers over mouth
	Pointing finger for emphasis
Voice	
Clearly audible but not loud	Mumbling or speaking inaudibly
Warmth in tone of voice	Monotonic voice
Voice modulated to reflect nuances of feeling and emotional tone of client messages	Halting speech
	Frequent grammatical errors
Moderate speech tempo	Prolonged silences
	Excessively animated speech
	Slow, rapid, or staccato speech
	Nervous laughter
	Consistent clearing of throat
	Speaking loudly
Physical proximity	
Three to five feet between chairs	Excessive closeness or distance
	Talking across desk or other barrier

From Direct social work practice: Theory and skills *(p. 77)* by D. H. Hepworth and J. A. Larsen, 1982, Homewood, IL: The Dorsey Press. Copyright 1982 by The Dorsey Press. Adapted by permission.

the use of nonverbal attending skills, silence, and minimal encouragement. According to Gordon (1970), saying nothing can often communicate acceptance which, in turn, can foster constructive growth and change. Simpson (1982) points out that, while this type of listening style may not be appropriate for all situations, it may offer parents of children and youth with exceptionalities what they need most, " . . . the chance to talk about their attitudes and feelings relative to having an exceptional child to an interested, yet quietly accepting professional person" (p. 94).

Active listeners, on the other hand, take a much more involved and direct role in the process of communication. In contrast to the passive listener, the active listener is animated, makes comments, asks questions, and may even share his or her own personal experiences. According to Gordon (1970), active listening encourages people to accept and express their thoughts and feelings, facilitates problem-solving, promotes friendliness and warmth, and builds constructive and mutually supportive relationships. It is important to realize that active listening is not merely a set of techniques; rather, it is a method to communicate some very basic attitudes that are essential prerequisites for active listening. Gordon (1970) describes these attitudes as follows:

1. You must *want* to hear what the other person has to say.
2. You must sincerely want to help the person with his/her problem.
3. You must genuinely be able to accept the other person's feelings, no matter how different they are from your own.
4. You must trust the other person's capacity to handle, work through, and find solutions to his/her own problems.
5. You must realize and appreciate that feelings are transitory in nature, consequently you need not fear them.
6. You must view the other person as separate from yourself with alternative ways of perceiving the world.

Intimately related to the listening process, and an important aspect of good family-professional relationships, is the ability to experience and express empathy. Empathy requires that we set aside our own internal frame of reference and try to understand and experience the world from the other person's point of view. Benjamin (1969) warns that empathy should not be confused with sympathy or identification. "Sympathy involves sharing common feelings, interests, loyalties and . . . may run the gamut from pity and charity to sincere compassion for another" (p. 51). Neither should empathy be confused with identification. According to Benjamin, when we identify with another, we wish to be him/her at the risk of being ourselves. Empathy differs in that it always involves two distinctly separate selves. Dinkmeyer (1965) provides an excellent description of the experience of empathy:

> If we are to be successful in working with others, it is important to comprehend their subjective view and private logic. It is vital to try to see through his eyes and hear through his ears. . . . It is often helpful as we

either listen, or observe, to ask how we would behave if his physical make-up, relationships, and experiences were ours. Empathy precedes understanding. It will come when you attempt to put yourself in the other's place. (pp. 19–20)

Empathetic listening is completely nonjudgmental and nonevaluative. When one listens empathetically, one does not agree or disagree, but instead attempts to understand what it is like to be in the other person's shoes. When professionals listen empathetically to parents, they convey genuine interest, understanding, and acceptance of the parent's feelings and experiences. This does not mean that professionals must approve of, or agree with, the parent's point of view: only that they try to understand the parent's situation from the parent's point of view, not their own. Listening to understand without judgment or evaluation is a difficult task, but it can be learned. It begins with an awareness of one's own inner states and outer behaviors. Webster (1977) contends that most persons have engaged in empathetic listening at some time, so it is not a new behavior to be learned. It is a behavior that should be used with greater frequency if professionals wish to cultivate and maintain productive and meaningful relationships with families.

Verbal Communication Skills

Although attending skills and listening techniques are both effective and essential means for communicating with families, there are situations which demand other types of responses in order to facilitate communication. Examples of such responses include furthering responses, paraphrasing, response to affect, questioning, and summarization.

Furthering Responses. Furthering responses indicate attentive listening and encourage people to continue to speak and examine their thoughts and feelings. There are two types of furthering responses:

1. *Minimal encouragers,* sometimes referred to as the "grunts and groans" of communication. Minimal encouragers are essentially short but encouraging responses such as "Oh?," "Then?," "Mm-hum," "I see," or "and then?" Minimal encouragers can also be nonverbal and take the form of head nods, facial expressions, and gestures that communicate listening and understanding.

2. *Verbal following* involves restating the main points or emphasizing a word or phrase contained in what the parent has said. When using verbal following, it is important to use the language system of the parent. For example, a parent might say, "I've had a really rough day. Jason woke up with wet sheets and cried all through breakfast. To top

it off the bus came early and I had to send him to school without any lunch." The professional might respond, "You've had a *really* rough day." Verbal following not only encourages the parent to go on speaking but also provides the professional with a means of checking listening accuracy.

Paraphrasing.   Paraphrasing involves using one's own words to restate the parent's message in a clear and succinct manner. In paraphrasing the emphasis is on the cognitive aspects of the parent's message (e.g., ideas, objects) as opposed to the parent's affective state (Cormier & Cormier, 1979). The goal with paraphrasing is to feed back the essence of the parent's statements. Paraphrasing responds to the implicit meaning of what is said as well as the explicit message. Some examples of paraphrasing follow:

Parent:	"I don't know what to do with Jan. One minute she's extremely hyper and the next minute lethargic."
Professional:	"Jan's behaviors are pretty inconsistent."
Parent:	"Everything seems to be a burden these days, doing the housework, taking care of the kids, paying the bills. I just don't know how much longer I can take it."
Professional:	"You're almost at the end of your rope."

Paraphrasing is an extremely useful technique in clarifying content, tying a number of comments together, highlighting issues by stating them more concisely, and checking one's perceptions. Most importantly, paraphrasing communicates interest in, and understanding of, what the parent is saying.

Response to Affect.   To respond to a parent's affect and feelings, professionals must be able to listen empathetically (Carkhuff & Berenson, 1967; Rogers, 1951). When using this technique, professionals verbalize the parent's feelings and attitudes. Attention is not only paid to what the parent has said, but to *how* it is said. Response to affect involves the ability to perceive accurately and sensitively the other person's apparent and underlying feelings, and the ability to communicate understanding of those feelings in language attuned to the parent's experience *at that moment*. As much as possible, professionals should try to use responses that are accurate and match the intensity of the parent's affect. Developing a vocabulary of affective words and phrases can greatly enhance this ability.

The purpose of responding to affect is to provide a mirror in which parents can see their feelings and attitudes. This, in turn, facilitates movement toward greater self-understanding (Benjamin, 1969). In addition, this technique can work to assure parents not only that their feelings have been recognized and understood, but also that their feelings are legitimate and acceptable to the professional. Lastly, response to affect can serve as a tool for professionals to check their perceptions of the parent's feelings. Some examples of response to affect follow:

Parent: "I've been so wound up since Becky went into the hospital. I have all this nervous energy, but there's not one thing I can do to help."

Professional: "You're feeling really anxious and helpless right now."

Parent: "Ever since Elliot was born, my family and friends have become extremely distant. I have no one to turn to and don't know what to do."

Professional: "You're feeling very alone with no one, or no place, to turn to."

Questioning.   There are two general types of questions: closed-ended questions and open-ended questions. Closed-ended questions are generally used to elicit specific factual information. Skillful communicators generally keep their use of closed-ended questions to a minimum, because this type of question limits the parent's response to few words or a simple "yes" or "no." Overuse of closed-ended questions also can make an interaction seem like an interrogation. While closed-ended questions can restrict conversation and elicit limited information, they are appropriate when used sparingly and propitiously. Some examples of appropriately used closed-ended questions are as follows:

"When did Joe first start having seizures?"
"How old is Theresa?"
"Would a ten o'clock meeting be okay for you?"

Unlike closed-ended questions, open-ended questions invite parents to share and to talk more. Some open-ended questions are unstructured and open the door for parents to talk about whatever is on their mind (e.g., "What would you like to talk about?," or "How can I be of assistance?"). Other open-ended questions are more structured in that the professional imposes boundaries on possible responses by focusing the topic (e.g., "What are some of the specific methods you've tried to control Bobby's behaviors?"). According to Hepworth & Larsen (1982), there are three general ways that open-ended questions can be formulated, either by asking a question ("How is Susie getting along with her new wheel chair?"), or by giving a polite command ("Would you please elaborate on your feelings about the new bus route?"), or by using an embedded question ("I'm interested in finding out more about Jack's toileting program at home"). Open-ended questions generally involve use of the words "what" and/or "how". Benjamin (1969) warns that practitioners should stay away from "why" questions as much as possible. Benjamin points out that it is common in our society for the word "why" to connote disapproval, displeasure, blame, or condemnation (e.g., "Why don't you listen to me?" "Why are you late?"). Therefore, the word "why" may well evoke a negative or defensive response from the person with whom we are speaking. Furthermore, "why" questions often imply factual answers, motives, or causes that are either abstruse, readily apparent, or unknown (Cormier & Cormier, 1979). Below are two examples of open-ended questions in response to parent-initiated comments:

Parent: "I just don't know if I'll be able to carry out Sally's feeding program at home."
Professional: "What are you concerned about?"
Parent: "I'm really excited about our new house, we're moving in on Saturday."
Professional: "I'm so pleased for you. Tell me more about your new house."

Summarization.   Summarization is a recapitulation of what the parent has said, with emphasis upon the most salient thoughts and feelings. Summarization is similar to paraphrasing, but different in one important respect—summaries are substantially longer. Summarization serves a number of different purposes. Summaries can be used as a stimulus to further explore a particular topic; they can communicate to parents that the professional is interested in, and listening to, what they are saying; they can serve as a perception check for the professional; and they can synthesize and integrate information that has been shared (Simpson, 1982). There are various situations for appropriate and advantageous use of the skill of summarization. They are: (a) to recall the highlights of a previous meeting, (b) to tie together confusing, lengthy and/or rambling topics, and (c) to acknowledge the point at which a topic has become exhausted.

Improving Communication Skills

We have just summarized specific communication tools that have proven useful and effective in a variety of circumstances. It should be clear now that no *one* skill or approach is appropriate in *every* situation or with *every* individual. Nor is *every* approach comfortable or well-suited for *every* professional. As emphasized earlier in the chapter, it is up to you to incorporate these skills into your unique personal style by combining them with your own experience and knowledge.

One method that has proven helpful to persons seeking to develop their communication skills is to use audio and/or video tapes. While audio tapes are ideal for practicing and evaluating verbal communication skills, video tapes have the additional advantage of providing feedback on both verbal and nonverbal behaviors. Ask a friend or colleague to spend 10–20 minutes talking over an issue or problem with you. Tape your conversation. As you talk, practice using one or two of the skills that we have described. Following your conversation, review the tape critically and take note of the positive contributions that you made as well as those that seemed less positive. Set personal goals for improvement. In addition, ask your friend to provide you with feedback on your performance. As you begin to feel confident with the skills that you have practiced, try adding more skills to your repertoire. Over time, and with enough practice, these skills can become a natural and spontaneous part of your communication style.

SUMMARY

Probably one of the most important attributes that a professional in the human services field can possess is effective interpersonal communication skills. The development of effective interpersonal communication skills is a complex and ongoing process that requires knowledge, experience, practice, and commitment. Effective communication skills are a necessary prerequisite to positive family-professional partnerships. In this chapter we have discussed the multiple benefits of family-professional partnerships, some of the barriers that can interfere with the development and maintenance of positive partnerships, and some specific skills that can help you to communicate more effectively with the families of the students whom you serve. In the next chapter we focus on some specific strategies that have proven effective in establishing and maintaining communication among families and professionals.

Chapter 7
Strategies for Communication

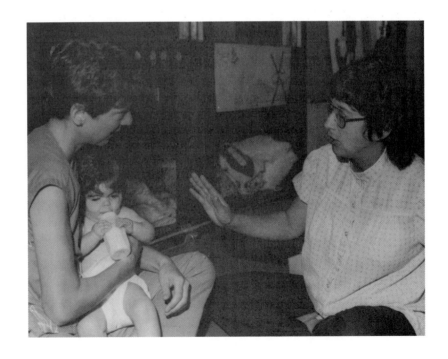

Professionals use a variety of strategies to establish and maintain communication with parents and other family members. Examples of these strategies include school conferences, home visits, weekly telephone calls, daily log books, and occasional newsletters. Some communication strategies can be rather formal in nature and require advanced preparation. Other strategies require comparatively little preparation and are relatively informal. Because families differ in their needs and preferences in communications with the programs that serve their children (Benson & Turnbull, in press; MacMillan & Turnbull, in press), no single approach is appropriate for all families. Neither is a single approach appropriate for all professionals, for they too differ according to preferences, needs, and styles of communication. For these reasons, it is important to have a wide selection of communication alternatives. This chapter presents a variety of useful communication strategies. In addition, we provide guidelines for working cooperatively with families to determine the strategies that best fit their preferences and needs. We begin with a look at the Education for the Handicapped Act (EHA) and its impact on communication among families and professionals.

IMPACT OF THE EDUCATION FOR THE HANDICAPPED ACT (EHA)

The EHA has done much to formalize methods of communication among families and professionals. It grants parents the right to be involved formally in educational decision-making regarding their child. The nature of this involvement can take many forms, including input at IEP conferences, provision of consent for evaluation and placement, the opportunity to review and maintain the confidentiality of pupil records, membership on advisory boards, and initiation of due process hearings (see Chapter 8 for a discussion of the EHA). Although the EHA gives parents authority to participate actively in their child's educational planning and establishes specific requirements for parent participation that public agencies must observe, it also allows parents the freedom to determine the degree and manner in which they will participate. Some parents have welcomed the right and the opportunity for more formal involvement in their child's educational program, while others have chosen to be relatively less involved (Strickland, 1983; Turnbull & Turnbull, 1982). When planning strategies for communication with parents, it is important that professionals be keenly aware that parents differ in their preferences for involvement in their child's educational program. In the next section we will review the literature pertaining to parent preferences for involvement.

CURRENT RESEARCH ON PARENT PREFERENCES FOR INVOLVEMENT

Winton and Turnbull (1981) interviewed 31 mothers of preschool children with mild or moderate disabilities. The children's conditions included hearing impairments, mental retardation, orthopedic handicaps, visual impairments, autism, and significant language delays. Given eight examples of parent activities, parents were asked to perform three tasks: (a) to rate each activity on a scale from 1–5 (indicating degree of like or dislike), (b) to indicate whether opportunities to engage in the activity were currently available, and (c) to select which of the eight activities they most preferred. Results indicated that 100% of the parents favored informal contact with teachers and 65% chose this activity as the most preferred. Interestingly, informal contact was rated substantially higher than the more formal and active roles of volunteering, participating in counseling or training sessions, and serving on policy boards. The two major characteristics of the informal contacts described by parents were that they be frequent and that information shared between parent and professional be exchanged in a "give-and-take" fashion.

Similar results were observed in a follow-up study by Turnbull, Winton, Blacher, and Salkind (1983). They surveyed 100 parents regarding their perspectives on their child's kindergarten program. Fifty of the parents had children with mild disabilities, while the other 50 parents had children who demonstrated no disabilities. The two most important characteristics of kindergartens identified by both groups of parents were informal and frequent communication with teachers and the opportunity to relax each day with the parent knowing that the child's educational needs were being met by the kindergarten program.

In a study conducted in 1983, Ammer and Littleton administered questionnaires to parents of children with exceptional needs to determine their present level of involvement and desired participation in the educational process. The types and percentages of exceptional conditions represented in the survey were as follows: behavior disorders—34%; learning disabilities—24%; educable retarded—15%; speech/language—11%; gifted—8%; trainable retarded—4%; other—4%. The mean age of the children was 10.6 years with a range of 4–24.6 years. Samples were drawn from three types of communities including urban, rural and suburban. Responses were gathered from a total of 217 parents. According to the results, 87% of the parents were not presently involved in their local school program. Seventy-four % indicated that they were satisfied that their child's educational needs were being met. When asked what types of linkages between the home and school they would like to see established to improve communication, the majority of parents (69%) preferred regular communication via letters from the school. The next most preferred activity was school conferences (51%), followed by telephone calls (45%), with home visits (19%) ranking as least preferred. Ninety-seven % of the parents were unwilling, or unable, to suggest alternative methods to establish home-school linkages.

In addition, parents were asked to identify in which of these program activities they would like to be actively involved: (a) curriculum planning, (b) progress review, (c) instructional methods and materials, (d) placement decisions, and (e) other areas of involvement. The majority of parents (60%) indicated that they were most interested in being involved in progress reviews, 54% in placement decisions, and 48% in curriculum planning. Participation in the development of instructional methods and materials was of interest to 40% of the parents, while less than 10% offered suggestions for alternative areas of involvement.

Seeking to determine the actual nature of parent involvement practices, Hocutt and Wiegerink (1983) conducted a survey of third-year Handicapped Children's Early Education Program, or (HCEEP) programs. According to their results, parents tended to be most involved in more passive activities (e.g., receiving information and services) as opposed to more active type activities (e.g., decision making). Similar results were found by Lusthaus, Lusthaus, and Gibbs (1981). These researchers asked 98 parents of children with exceptionalities to specify actual and desired level of participation in making nine different types of educationally related decisions. The results related to actual involvement indicated that most parents find themselves primarily in the role of giving and receiving information. The role of no involvement whatsoever was the second most typical, while the role of having decisional control was third. When asked to select the roles which they would like to assume, parents most frequently indicated a desire to maintain the giving and receiving information role in six of the nine decisional areas, including discipline, class placement, evaluation, instructional grouping, transportation, and special resources. Areas in which parents consistently indicated that they would like to exert actual decisional control pertained to medical services, types of records maintained on the child, and child transfers to other schools.

In summary, these studies indicate that most parents generally prefer informal and frequent communication with their child's educational programs. Activities such as giving and receiving information tend to be preferred over activities that require active decision making. Similar results were found in studies investigating parent preferences for participation in individualized educational program (IEP) conferences (Goldstein, Strickland, Turnbull, & Curry, 1980; Lynch & Stein, 1982). (For a review of these studies see Chapter 10.) Despite current policy requirements for formal and active participation by parents, a more passive role appears to be the dominant practice (Turnbull & Winton, 1984). The need to re-evaluate parent involvement policy and practices is becoming more widely recognized (Foster, Berger, & McLean, 1981; Lynch & Stein, 1982; Morgan, 1982; Turnbull & Turnbull, 1982; Winton & Turnbull, 1981; Yoshida, 1982). In Lynch and Stein's (1982) words:

> Perhaps the next step for educators is to review the definition of active participation as it relates to parent involvement. Can "active" be operationalized to fit all parents, or is active involvement an individually defined phenomenon that varies from parent to parent and family to family? Could the same model of individualization that is used to develop the child's special education program be expanded to provide for some individualization for the family? Instead of measuring and judging parental involvement by the numbers and kinds of comments made at the planning meeting, it may be time to assess the families' present level of involvement, ask them to describe their preferred level of involvement, and mutually develop goals and objectives that will allow them to participate as actively as they choose. This would allow for differences in family preferences and needs while still supporting and encouraging the concept of joint decision making. Despite the mandates and assumptions about the rights and roles of parents in the development and monitoring of their child's educational program, it may be time to recognize that parents, too, have the right to individualization. (p. 62)

Reassessing current parent involvement policy and practice and recognizing the importance of individualizing for families is indeed an important first step in learning to work comparatively and successfully with families. However, knowing that families differ in their preferences for participation is not enough. It is important to know the *specific* ways in which families differ, as well as the specifics relative to the family's needs and preferences. In the next section we discuss methods for gathering this type of information.

ASSESSING FAMILY PREFERENCES

There are a variety of methods to assess family preferences for communication with the service delivery program. Professionals are encouraged to consider these ideas to obtain such information: (a) ask families to complete an inventory such as the one in Table 7–1; (b) initiate an individual, or group, discussion with families regarding their needs and preferences; or (c) seek advice from professionals who have worked successfully with the family in the past. Whatever method is used, the professional should be aware of the fact that family preferences may vary over time and therefore need to be monitored and reassessed on a somewhat regular basis. In addition, professionals who elect to use formal inventories, such as the one in Table 7–1, should avoid including options

Table 7–1
HOME-SCHOOL COMMUNICATION PREFERENCE INVENTORY

To ensure that your child is receiving the best possible educational program, it is important that there be ongoing communication between your family and school professionals. It is our experience that families have different preferences for what kinds of information will be shared. In addition, families have different preferences regarding how and how often such information will be transmitted. The purpose of this inventory is to determine your individual preferences for communicating with the professionals in our program.

Listed below are a number of different examples of types of information that can be shared. There are also a number of different examples of strategies or methods that can be used to share this information.

In the box immediately to the right of each item, please rate your level of interest:

put "0" if it has no interest to you at all
put "1" if the information has a *low* priority for you
put "2" if the information has a *medium* priority for you
put "3" if the information has a *high* priority for you

Next, please tell us how often you would like to share information:

put a (✔) under *never* if you are not interested at all
put a (✔) under *occasionally* if you would like to share the information 3–5 times per year
put a (✔) under *regularly* if you would like to share the information 2–3 times per month
put a (✔) in the appropriate box under *frequently* to indicate whether you would like to share the information weekly or daily

For example, Mr. Christopher filled out the first item this way:

	Priority	Never	Occasionally	Regularly	Frequently Weekly	Daily
Special accomplishments	3	☐	☐	☐	✔	☐

Mr. Christopher's answer tells us that it is very important for school professionals and his family to share his son's special accomplishments and that he would like to communicate on a weekly basis about such accomplishments.

Please indicate your preferences on the following chart.

TYPE OF INFORMATION I WOULD LIKE SHARED BETWEEN HOME AND SCHOOL

	Priority	Never	Occasionally	Regularly	Frequently Weekly	Daily
Special accomplishments	☐	☐	☐	☐	☐	☐
Special activities (e.g., going to the park, going swimming, visiting grandma)	☐	☐	☐	☐	☐	☐

	Priority	Never	Occasionally	Regularly	Frequently Weekly	Daily
Progress toward educational goals/grades	☐	☐	☐	☐	☐	☐
Toileting habits	☐	☐	☐	☐	☐	☐
Eating habits	☐	☐	☐	☐	☐	☐
Sleeping/napping habits	☐	☐	☐	☐	☐	☐
Behaviors	☐	☐	☐	☐	☐	☐
Other (please specify)	☐	☐	☐	☐	☐	☐
_____	☐	☐	☐	☐	☐	☐
_____	☐	☐	☐	☐	☐	☐
_____	☐	☐	☐	☐	☐	☐
_____	☐	☐	☐	☐	☐	☐

HOME-SCHOOL COMMUNICATION STRATEGIES

	Priority	Never	Occasionally	Regularly	Frequently Weekly	Daily
Home visits	☐	☐	☐	☐	☐	☐
Informal school visits	☐	☐	☐	☐	☐	☐
Individual conferences	☐	☐	☐	☐	☐	☐
Group conferences	☐	☐	☐	☐	☐	☐
Telephone calls	☐	☐	☐	☐	☐	☐
Log books, notes	☐	☐	☐	☐	☐	☐
Newsletters	☐	☐	☐	☐	☐	☐
Audio tapes	☐	☐	☐	☐	☐	☐
Report cards	☐	☐	☐	☐	☐	☐
Other (please specify)	☐	☐	☐	☐	☐	☐
_____	☐	☐	☐	☐	☐	☐
_____	☐	☐	☐	☐	☐	☐
_____	☐	☐	☐	☐	☐	☐
_____	☐	☐	☐	☐	☐	☐

that they are unable to deliver, or arrange to deliver. For example, do not give families the option to choose a daily communication strategy if you are unwilling, or unable, to communicate that frequently. When deciding which communication options to offer families, it is important to take into consideration your own, as well as the family's, preferences and needs. We encourage you to modify Table 7–1 to reflect your own preferences and the communication options available to families through your program.

SPECIFIC COMMUNICATION STRATEGIES

Individualizing approaches to communication with families that have diverse preferences and needs requires that professionals be skilled in a variety of communication techniques or strategies. In the next section we present a variety of commonly used formal and informal strategies to establish and maintain effective communication with families. We have divided our discussion into two main sections: (a) strategies for communicating with families via parent-professional conferences, and (b) nonconference strategies for communication.

The strategies that we are about to present are meant to be practical techniques to assist you in your endeavor to work effectively with families. You are the best judge of whether or not these techniques can work for you, and we urge you to evaluate continually the effectiveness and utility of each strategy for your purposes. Whenever possible, modify these strategies to suit your personal style and the unique characteristics of your program. While the development and personalization of these strategies requires an initial investment of time and energy, we believe that use of many of these techniques can actually help you to conserve time and energy in the long run. Communication strategies can be viewed as means of prevention. By providing avenues for sharing concerns between the family and professionals in an ongoing fashion, issues can be aired and dealt with while fresh and before they become more complex.

Parent-Professional Conferences

Conferences are one of the most effective and commonly used methods to facilitate productive partnerships between parents and professionals. In a survey conducted by the *Phi Delta Kappan* (1976), it was estimated that, by 1980, as many as 90% of the school districts in America will use conferences as the primary mode of communicating with parents. Parent-professional conferences can provide a variety of important opportunities such as:

1. to share and receive information about the home and school environments and activities pertinent to the child's development.
2. to work together to enhance the child's learning.
3. to develop a rapport and partnership with one another.
4. to cooperate in preventing and solving problems.

Research has shown that conferences not only enhance parent-professional relationships, but also have an impact on student performance. Duncan and Fitzgerald (1969) examined the impact of parent-professional conferences prior to the child's entry into junior high school. Results indicated that children whose parents attended these conferences demonstrated higher attendance rates, higher grade point averages, fewer dropouts, and fewer disciplinary problems. In another study conducted by Iverson, Brownlee, & Walberg (1981), the effects of teacher-parent conferences on reading achievement of several hundred low-achieving elementary school students were investigated. Results of this study indicated that more frequent contacts between the parents and professionals resulted in significant gains in reading performance. That a positive relationship between school achievement and parent-teacher conferences exists was also validated in a similar study conducted by Anchor and Anchor (1974). While the results of these studies appear positive, more research is needed in this area before definitive conclusions can be drawn.

Because of the many potential benefits of parent-professional conferences, conferences should not be limited to the beginning and end of the school year. Regularly scheduled conferences can do much to maintain and enhance parent-professional partnerships (Heward & Orlansky, 1984). Professionals should plan to participate in planned as well as unplanned parent-professional conferences.

Planned Conferences

Conscientious planning is the key to effective parent-professional conferences. In planning a conference, the professional must consider the three major phases of a conference: (a) pre-conference, (b) conference, and (c) post-conference. Each phase consists of a number of steps that require skill and planning on the part of the professional. A description of these phases and steps follows.

Pre-conference. Pre-conference preparation is an essential ingredient of conference success. Kroth (1985) suggests that professionals perform four basic pre-conference steps to ensure a smooth and productive conference. These steps are: (a) notify, (b) prepare, (c) plan agenda, and (d) arrange environments.

There is a variety of tasks involved when the professional notifies parents that a conference is to be called, and probably the most important is to inform the parents of the purpose of the meeting. Many school systems schedule conference days for parents of all students to discuss progress. Typically, notice of these meetings is provided in the school calendar at the beginning of the year. When this is not the case, every attempt must be made to inform the parents of the purpose of the meeting in a manner that is clear, understandable, and nonthreatening. This is particularly important because, based on their own past experiences with schools and teachers, many parents may be reluctant to attend such conferences (Mattson, 1977). In Nivens' (1978) words:

> Many parents, regardless of education and socioeconomic level, are hesitant to participate in school matters. To grow up believing that in the teacher's grade book resides an awesome potential for reward or punishment is to reach maturity as a parent with little or no inclination to resume old battle lines. Just as mature people, visiting their parents' homes, can find themselves reacting to their mothers and fathers with emotional and behavioral responses reminiscent of their teenage period, so parents called into a school setting can become students of, rather than peers with, their childrens' teachers. This is especially true when the socioeconomic level and educational achievements are diverse. (p. 5)

In a workshop designed to help parents and teachers develop communication skills, Flake-Hobson and Swick (1984) asked parents to describe what they thought and felt when their child's teacher called them for a conference. Some of the parents' comments were: "I feel worried." "I feel guilty that I haven't done enough to help my child in school." "I feel nervous, I think that Roddy has done something wrong." "I think that Dorene is not doing her work" (p. 142). Of the group of 50 parents, not one parent described experiencing positive thoughts or feelings when asked to attend a school conference.

To avoid eliciting stress reactions in parents, try to be as specific as possible about the purpose of the meeting. It often helps to send a written notification of the meeting and to follow up with a telephone call. This provides the parents the opportunity to ask questions and to understand the intent and purposes of the meeting. Another helpful method to reduce stress parents feel in anticipation of school conferences is to provide a list of suggestions in preparation for the conference.

The professional will need to let the parents know the purpose of the meeting, the conference site, the date and time of the meeting, and the expected length. Whenever possible, try to schedule a time when both parents can attend. You can also be helpful by sharing with parents the names of other professionals whom you believe should attend the conference and by seeking their advice on professionals or family members to invite. Consider at that time whether or not to include the student in the meeting (see Chapter 10 for a discussion of this issue).

The next step in preparation for the parent-professional conference can be referred to as "professional preparation." It is essential that professionals spend a sufficient amount of time preparing for conferences with parents. Insufficient preparation generally is obvious to everyone and can have unfavorable results. In preparing for the meeting there are a number of logistical and psychological tasks that can be completed. Some of these tasks include: (a) review the child's cumulative record, (b) assess child progress and areas of concern, (c) gather examples of the child's work, (d) prepare materials (such as graphs and/or data sheets) for use in the conference, (e) outline items to be discussed in the meeting, and (f) meet with other professionals (when appropriate) to solicit additional information about the child and to coordinate conference proceedings. In addition, if there are delicate issues to be discussed, spend time prior to the meeting considering ways to communicate about them. Practice alternative ways to broach the topic until your approach feels smooth and natural. Ask others to give you feedback on your style and manner of speaking (Roberds-Baxter, 1984). On the day of the conference spend some time mentally rehearsing any aspects of the meeting which you feel uneasy about. Review the items to be discussed and the materials. Wear the type of comfortable clothes that you ordinarily wear when teaching. Spend time just prior to the meeting relaxing.

Planning and developing an agenda is the third major step of preconference preparation. An agenda is important for two reasons: (a) it notifies participants about what topics are to be covered at the conference, and (b) it serves as a guide for structure and sequence during the conference. The agenda should be flexible enough to accommodate last minute additions or changes and should include topics that parents have mentioned as important.

The final step in the pre-conference preparation process involves attention to the physical environment. The goal of preparing the environment is to establish an atmosphere that will enhance the communication process among parents and professional. There are a number of factors to consider when completing this task. The first is deciding where to conduct the meeting. Parent-professional conferences can be conducted at the parents' home, at the school, or in a neutral location in the community such as the library or community building.

Conferences held at the parents' home may be necessary or preferred by parents who lack transportation or who are reluctant to come to the school/program. While home visits may mean more distractions (e.g., the TV, the telephone, neighbors dropping by), they also provide professionals with the opportunity to gather a more complete picture of the child's environment and family life. Seligman (1979) cites some guidelines for home visits, as recommended by Duncan (1978):

1. Always discuss your interest in conducting a home visit with the parents *before* scheduling such a meeting. Some parents are opposed to home visits and may regard them as an intrusion into their privacy.
2. Never drop by for an unannounced visit.
3. Be prompt; don't be early and don't be late. Both early and late arrivals can create stress for the parents.
4. To the extent possible, honor the time schedule that you initially agreed upon with the family.
5. Dress appropriately and comfortably.
6. Make every attempt not to cancel since many parents expend a significant amount of physical and psychic energy preparing for the meeting.
7. Be aware that refusing food or beverage offered by the parent may insult them or hurt their feelings. If you must refuse, mention that you have eaten shortly before your visit.
8. Anticipate distractions, as there are bound to be some.

In some cases, professionals may want to consider bringing another person along to the home visit (e.g., a social worker or school nurse). This may be particularly important when the topics to be discussed may cause conflict or when there is a history of misunderstandings between the family and the professional. This person may serve as a witness to events, a support person, or a mediator in case of serious disagreements.

When parent-professional conferences are held at the school or agency, it is the professional's responsibility to prepare the setting. According to Garrett (1972), "The physical setting of the interview may determine its entire potentiality" (p. 72). Probably the two most important considerations are privacy and comfort. Unless parents can be provided an atmosphere that is confidential, comfortable, and free of interruptions, it may be difficult to establish rapport and trust. Consider the following steps in preparing the environment for a parent-professional conference:

1. Make prior arrangements for a quiet and private room; it is preferable to have one in which the doors can be closed and where windows are not facing out to frequently trafficked areas.
2. Gather all necessary materials prior to the meeting and make arrangements not to be interrupted.
3. Be sure that the temperature and lighting is comfortable. (Indirect lighting is frequently preferential to the overhead fluorescent variety.)

4. In selecting and arranging furniture, be sure to choose adult-sized chairs and tables. Sitting through an hour-long conference in chairs designed to accommodate preschoolers can be very uncomfortable.

5. As much as possible, arrange the furniture in a manner that reflects equality, for example, avoid placing the "professional's chair" behind a desk, or in a position that may convey authority (e.g., at the head of a table).

6. Have tissues, beverages, papers, and pens available for all participants. Attending to certain "extra" details can make the difference between an ordinary and a pleasurable conference.

Conference. Stephens and Wolf (1980) describe four major components of parent-professional conferences: (a) rapport building, (b) obtaining information, (c) providing information, and (d) summarizing and follow-up activities. The rapport building phase of the conference sets the tone for the remainder of the meeting and is therefore very important. After greeting the parents and introducing conference participants, devote a few minutes to relevant conversation. It is desirable to begin with something positive about the child or the family instead of resorting to superficial topics such as the weather or traffic (Hochman, 1979).

Once conference participants are seated, spend a moment previewing the meeting. Begin by reviewing the purpose of the meeting, state time limitations, and clarify the role of other individuals in attendance. It is especially important to acknowledge your appreciation for the parents' interest and attendance and to encourage them to participate by asking questions and providing input. Emphasize the importance of their thoughts, feelings, and insights. If you wish to take notes during the meeting, let the parents know at this time. When taking notes, do so openly so that the parents can see what you are writing. Some professionals take notes on carbon paper so that they can provide the parents with a copy at the end of the meeting.

A second component of the conference entails obtaining information from the parents. This phase provides the professional with the opportunity to practice many of the communication skills described in Chapter 6. Encourage parents to share information by asking open-ended questions. Demonstrate your interest in both verbal and nonverbal ways (i.e., maintain eye contact and an open posture, use minimal encouragers such as head nods and "um-hums," ask relevant questions). When unclear regarding a parent's point of view, ask for clarification or for specific examples. Do not make assumptions based on limited or unclear information. Respond empathetically if and when parents have difficulty expressing a thought or a feeling. Provide feedback to the parents regarding their ideas and, most importantly, reward their contributions. Use the technique of summarization as a means for checking out the accuracy of your perceptions and also to let the parents know that you are interested and listening attentively.

Sharing information with parents, a third component of the conference process, should be accomplished through the use of jargon-free language. Dembinski and Mauser (1978) found that parents of children who were learning disabled or gifted were especially concerned about professionals' use of jargon. When sharing information, begin on a positive note, such as by pointing out the child's strong points, before mentioning areas of deficit or concern. Provide specific examples either by telling anecdotes or by showing the parents examples of the child's work. Be aware of and responsive to the impact on the parents of what you are saying. For example, if they are frowning or appear puzzled, stop for a moment to provide an opportunity for questions or comments. As much as possible, encourage a give-and-take atmosphere in which all members of the conference can interact and share information. Avoid the following verbal roadblocks to communication:

Moralizing:	"You should . . . " "You ought" "It is your responsibility to . . . "
Lecturing:	"I told you . . . " "Do you realize . . . " "One of these days . . . "
Judging/Criticizing:	"You're wrong . . . " "One of your problems is . . . " "That was a mistake . . . "
Prying:	"Why?" "How?" "When?" "Who?"
Providing Answers Prematurely:	"Here's what you do . . . " "I suggest . . . "
Threatening:	"If you do that I'll . . . " "Unless you take my advice . . . "
Ordering:	"You must . . . " "You will . . . " "You have to . . . "
Consoling/Excusing:	"You'll be just fine . . . " "You didn't know any better . . . "
Diagnosing/Analyzing:	"You're just going through the stage of . . . " "You're behaving that way because . . . "
Using Sarcasm/Cynicism:	"You think you've got it bad . . . " "Life's just a barrel of laughs . . . "
Overusing clichés/phrases:	"You know . . . " "I mean . . . " "That's neat . . . " "Far out . . . "

Other verbal barriers to communication are interrupting excessively, dominating the conversation, and excessive use of leading questions and self-disclosure (Hepworth & Larsen, 1982). Overuse of any of these approaches may negatively influence a conference by discouraging parent participation and damaging rapport. Professionals need to be aware of any tendencies within themselves to engage in these potentially destructive behaviors. One strategy that has proven helpful in assessing one's own communication skills is through use of audio tapes and/or video tapes. If possible, get permission from families to occasionally tape conferences. Following the conferences, review the tapes, and analyze your performance. Take note of the good points as well as those that need modification. Set goals for improving your communication skills.

The last component of the conference involves summarizing and follow-up activities. In summarizing, the professional should review the high points of the meeting with special emphasis upon next-step activities. It is important at this point to restate who is responsible for carrying out next-step tasks and the date by which they are to be completed. Options for follow-up strategies should be discussed and agreed upon. If another meeting is to be scheduled, use this time to decide on the time and place. End the meeting on a positive note. Be sure to thank the parents for their interest and contributions and offer to be available should any relevant questions or issues arise.

Post-conference. The professional must attend to a number of tasks following the conference. If the student was not present at the meeting, it may be appropriate to spend some time reviewing the meeting with the student. Give special attention to the ways in which the meeting will directly impact upon the student, and be sure to provide the opportunity for questions. In addition to meeting with the student, it may also be appropriate to share the outcome of the conference with other professionals involved in the student's program. These contacts can be made in person, over the telephone, or through a written report.

A third task, recording conference proceedings, is important for parent-professional accountability, particularly in the event of a due process hearing at some later date. This should be done as soon as possible following the meeting when the information is still fresh in your mind. Included in the written proceedings should be the time of the meeting, the location, agenda topics, nature of interactions, and decisions made. It is a good practice to keep a permanent file of each of your meetings in the event you may need to access them at some later date, to mark your calendar for agreed upon follow-up dates, to list the tasks you agreed to complete as a result of the meeting, and to complete an evaluation of the conference. The University of New Mexico Institute for Parent Involvement in Albuquerque, New Mexico has developed a form that can be used to evaluate parent-professional conferences; this form is included in Table 7–2. There are many other similar forms available for other types of conferences, or you may wish to develop your own. Regardless of which procedure you select, we are confident that you will find conference

---

Table 7–2
Conference Rating Scale

Filled out by_____

Persons in Attendance _____

Approximate length of conference _____

Purpose of conference _____

_____

_____

Rate the following items from (1) most agreeable to (7) least agreeable:

1. *Environment (Space)*

Comfortable	1	2	3	4	5	6	7
Private	1	2	3	4	5	6	7
Stimulus-Free	1	2	3	4	5	6	7

2. *Time*

Hurried	1	2	3	4	5	6	7
Uninterrupted	1	2	3	4	5	6	7
Adequate	1	2	3	4	5	6	7
Controlled by Professional	1	2	3	4	5	6	7
Controlled by Family Members	1	2	3	4	5	6	7

3. *Multiplicity factor*

Purposeful	1	2	3	4	5	6	7
Numerous Topics	1	2	3	4	5	6	7
Smooth Transitions (Topics)	1	2	3	4	5	6	7

4. *Level*

Appropriate Language level	1	2	3	4	5	6	7
Appropriate Probing	1	2	3	4	5	6	7

5. *Communication*

One-Way	1	2	3	4	5	6	7
Interested	1	2	3	4	5	6	7
Listens	1	2	3	4	5	6	7

6. *Relationship*

Warm	1	2	3	4	5	6	7
Concerned	1	2	3	4	5	6	7
Trustful	1	2	3	4	5	6	7
Respectful	1	2	3	4	5	6	7
Overall Quality of the Conference	1	2	3	4	5	6	7
Success of Conference	1	2	3	4	5	6	7

Estimated Percentage of "Teacher Talk" Time_____

Note. From University of New Mexico Institute for Parent Involvement, Albuquerque, New Mexico, 1979. Adapted by permission.

evaluation a valuable process to help you identify ways that future conferences can be modified and improved.

Unplanned Conferences

Unplanned conferences with parents or other family members inevitably occur, and professionals need to be prepared for them. Preparation is particularly important because unplanned conferences can often serve as a forum for parents to manifest their most intense thoughts and feelings (Simpson, 1982). Unplanned conferences can occur at any time and in any place. Professionals have had parents unexpectedly drop in at school before, during, and after school hours; they have received telephone calls at home in the evenings and on weekends; and they have been approached with child-related concerns at such unlikely places as the beach, the theater, and the grocery store.

Although it is probably impossible to avoid being caught somewhat off-guard at such times, there are a number of things that you can do to prepare for these encounters. The first step is to decide what is acceptable to you as a professional, given the other demands on your time and energy. It is often helpful to talk with other professionals regarding their strategies for handling such issues. You may decide that telephone calls at home on weeknights are acceptable, but that conferences at the beach are out of the question. Make a list of options that you consider are, and are not, open to consideration. Once this is done, set your priorities and then seek support from the administration of the program. This support is important both for your own sense of security and in the event future problems arise concerning these issues. In addition, some administrators wish to have this information so that consistency can be established across programs.

Once priorities have been established and endorsed by the administration, it is important to inform the parents of your preferences. Ideally, this should be done at the beginning of the year before any unplanned conferences have had the chance to occur. Preferences should be communicated both verbally and in written form to avoid misunderstanding and to allow the parents to ask questions. When communicating preferences, be sure to cover the following topics: First, explain your philosophy and rationale regarding meetings in noneducational settings. A rationale for an unwillingness to engage in these conferences can be as simple a statement as the following: "I want to be able to meet your needs and answer your questions as well and completely as possible; however, I am not able to do so without sufficient preparation and access to your child's records." Second, specify the times and conditions under which you will and will not receive drop-in visits at school, as well as telephone calls at school and/or home. Third, clarify any rules, guidelines and/or protocol regarding meetings during class time and/or classroom observations.

Drop-in meetings by parents during class time can be especially disruptive to the professional as well as to other students in the program. To avoid potential disruptions, Simpson (1982) suggests that professionals consider adopting a policy that requires all visitors to the school or agency to check in at the central office. This places the responsibility in the hands of the administration regarding whether or not a conference is required and can provide the professional with advance notice of the parent's arrival. In addition, it is a good practice to provide parents with some suggestions on how to conduct themselves when visiting or observing the classroom. When communicating preferences, be specific and use many examples so parents can be certain about your meaning. The better a parent understands your preferences, the greater the chance is that your preferences will be respected. It is also important to communicate your preferences in these matters to other service delivery or school personnel, particularly the administration. This will help to ensure consistency and avoid misunderstandings between you, your colleagues, and the families whom you serve.

Having well-organized files, data sheets, permanent products of the child's work, schedules, graphs, and charts can make a difference between disastrous and successful unplanned conferences. In addition, often it is helpful to have community resource guides and names, addresses, and phone numbers of other agencies, parents, and professionals who may be of assistance to parents. Sometimes an on-the-spot referral to a school or community-based professional may be more appropriate and wise than attempting to assist a parent with a problem that may be more adequately addressed by other professionals.

Last, but not least, is the importance of good communication skills for unplanned conferences. Without good communication skills even the best prepared professionals can fail at their attempts to meet the needs of parents. We cannot emphasize strongly enough the importance of practicing the communication skills presented in Chapter 6. In addition to those skills, you may need to work on assertiveness, conflict resolution, negotiation, and ways to diffuse anger and aggression. Table 7–3 includes some valuable tips for dealing with aggression. We cannot guarantee that these tips will completely resolve conflict; but, used effectively, they often can do much to diffuse anger and aggression to a point of workability. While there is not sufficient space here to discuss the issues of assertiveness, conflict resolution, and negotiation, much has been written about these topics (e.g., Gordon, 1970; Kroth, 1985; Lombana, 1983; Lombana & Pratt, 1978; Nivens, 1978; Simpson, 1982, Warschaw, 1980). We encourage you to use this information.

Table 7–3
Tips for Dealing with Aggression

DO

_____ 1. Listen
_____ 2. Write down what they say
_____ 3. When they slow down, ask them what else is bothering them
_____ 4. Exhaust their list of complaints
_____ 5. Ask them to clarify any specific complaints that are too general
_____ 6. Show them the list and ask if it is complete
_____ 7. Ask them for suggestions for solving any of the problems that they have listed
_____ 8. Write down the suggestions
_____ 9. As much as possible, mirror their body posture during this process
_____ 10. As they speak louder, you speak softer

DON'T

_____ 1. Argue
_____ 2. Defend or become defensive
_____ 3. Promise things you can't produce
_____ 4. Own problems that belong to others
_____ 5. Raise your voice
_____ 6. Belittle or minimize the problem

Note. From University of New Mexico Institute for Parent Involvement, Albuquerque, New Mexico, 1979. Adapted by permission.

NONCONFERENCE STRATEGIES FOR COMMUNICATION

Most parents appreciate receiving information regularly about their child's activities and progress at school. Likewise, most professionals appreciate information and feedback from the home. Since weekly conferences are time-consuming and impractical, it is necessary to develop alternative strategies for keeping open the lines of communication between the families and the professional. A number of studies have shown that ongoing two-way communication between the home and school program can improve both home and school performance (Dickerson, Spellman, Larsen, & Tyler, 1973; Imber, Imber, & Rothstein, 1979). There are many different nonconference strategies for communication. These strategies can be divided into two general categories: written messages and use of the telephone.

Written Strategies for Communication

While there are many different written strategies for communication, we will present six: (a) the handbook, (b) handouts for specific situations, (c) the newsletter, (d) letters, notes and log books, (e) progress reports, and (f) occasional messages.

The Handbook. While most programs have developed handbooks for parents to outline general policy and procedures, these handbooks typically are very general and often do not include information about the specifics of the programs for children with exceptional needs. For this reason, it is often helpful to develop a handbook with information specific to your program that accompanies, and does not duplicate, the general program handbook. Kroth (1985) emphasizes that the handbook should be concise, attractive, and written in simple and understandable language. Professionals who serve children and youth who speak English as a second language should consider having the handbook printed in other languages. A variety of different kinds of information can go into a handbook. Kroth (1985) describes some of the topics that can be included in Table 7–4.

Handouts. A second written strategy for communication is the use of handouts for specific situations (Kroth, 1985). Handouts mainly provide information to parents. They can pertain to a variety of subjects, including resources in the community, safety and travel tips, tips for preparing one's child for trips to the dentist and eye doctor, a list of restaurants, shops, movie theaters and museums that are accessible to wheel chairs, places to go on field trips, and summer enrichment programs and activities for rainy days. Be creative when selecting or compiling handouts for parents. Individualize them by placing stars next to the items particularly pertinent to specific families or family members. While the collection and compilation of handouts may require some time and effort on your part, the time and effort that you invest will undoubtedly be noticed and appreciated by many of the families with whom you work. Often the small, thoughtful gestures indicate to parents that you care and have their best interests in mind.

Newsletters. Probably one of the most enjoyable ways to encourage parent-professional communication is to create and disseminate a newsletter. Newsletters can be developed by a single teacher and class, an entire grade, or the entire school. A variety of different types of information can be included in newsletters, such as drawings, quotes and essays written by the children, comic strips, announcements of upcoming special events, children's birth dates, a parent column, horoscopes, updates on ongoing school projects, and an advice column. If family members are interested, recruit them to help with the editing and development of the newsletter, as this often is a good way to give them the message that their input is valued and needed. A sample newsletter developed by Sandie Kelly's class at the Kansas State School for the Deaf is included in Figure 7–1 (p. 158).

Newsletters can also be created by family members. These newsletters can contain such information as tips for other families, stress reduction

---

Table 7–4
Topics to Include in a Special Handbook

Special Personnel. This section would include the names and phone numbers of the school personnel the parents may need to contact during the year—i.e., the principal, teacher, counselor, nurse, school psychologist, bus driver. It might also include office hours or preferred times to call and how to make an appointment.

Classroom Procedures. Any technique that is unique to that classroom should be emphasized. This might include the use of material rewards, the use of study carrels, the time out room, early dismissal time, etc. Usually the fewer surprises the parents have, the smoother the year passes. If there are special testing or field trip request forms that are different from the general school forms, then these should be included.

Classroom Materials and Supplies. Special education teachers often use and need special materials to be supplied by the parents. A list of supplies that parents are suppposed to provide at the beginning of and throughout the year should be brought to the parents' attention.

Transportation. Exceptional children are often bused to school. This can be a problem area, and usually there are special rules and regulations that need to be clearly pointed out to parents.

Conference and Reporting System. Usually a section on when regularly scheduled conferences will be held and how parents can arrange for special conferences is important. If report cards are used, parents need to be informed of the type of card and when they can expect to receive it.

Additional Information. There are many other important pieces of information that might be included, some of which depend on the age of the child and the type of program. For instance, if it is a program for secondary-age children, the parents may need to know about work study arrangements and how children will receive high school credit. A section on tips to parents on managing child behavior might be useful if the program is for younger children. There might be a section on agencies that the parent can contact for special services or books that they might want to read to receive additional information. If the children use the cafeteria, the prices of lunch programs and what provisions are made if the child brings his own lunch should be included.

Note. From *Communicating with parents of exceptional children: Improving parent-teacher relationships* (pp. 82–83) by R. L. Kroth, 1985, Denver, CO: Love Publishing Co.

techniques, descriptions of adaptive devices, advertisements for toy swaps, methods for managing child behaviors, information about workshops and seminars, and an opportunity to brag. You may consider suggesting this as an option to the families served by your program.

Letters, notes, and log books. Letters, notes, and log books are other options for communicating with families. These methods are particularly good vehicles for exchanging information and strengthening relationships.

Mrs. Kelly's Class

Issue #21   **February 1, 1985**

Monday- Today in Career Ed. Troy had the opportunity to work on the computer! (He was the only student at school at that time.) In the next few years, <u>all</u> of the kids will have computer time. We planted another potato. We put carrot tops in water. We put a bird feeder outside.

Tuesday- We helped clean up the room (it was getting dirty!). We worked on our paper puppets in Day Program in Mrs. Montgomery's class.

Wednesday-We worked on our Snowmen Cards – What a perfect day for that! It's really snowing. We planted another potato (that makes 5 now). The carrots are growing fast! We started cleaning up an old mailbox for Valentine's Day.

Thursday- We spray painted the Valentine mailbox. It looks great! We worked on our paper puppets in Foods. We worked with clay in Art. We had library. We all got to sit at the Honor Table at lunch time – we had ice cream sundaes! Kerry and Kim earned seeing the special movie "Bambi."

Friday- In Career Ed. today, Kerry had time to work on the computer! We have decorated the room for Valentine's Day! We took the SAT Screening Tests. We had our popcorn party today!

♡ **Valentines**

Don't forget to send Valentines for your child to exchange (it's a super learning skill- writing and identifying names!).

Personal Notes:

Figure 7-1
SAMPLE NEWSLETTER

Some professionals and families prefer the use of log books over notes and letters since the latter are sometimes difficult to locate and may be more easily lost or misplaced. In addition, log books offer a record of communication over time that some families like to keep at the end of the year. Sensitive, confidential or controversial information should not be shared in this manner and is best reserved for private, face-to-face conferences. Examples of information that would be appropriate to share by this method include information regarding details of routine care (e.g., eating and toileting habits), special accomplishments, and special activities. As much as possible, professionals should strive to communicate positive information about the student while attempting to keep negative com ments to a minimum. Negative comments are best relayed in person, where there is an opportunity for the parents to ask questions and seek clarification. It is a good idea to involve the parent in deciding how frequently to write, who will write, and what kinds of information will be exchanged. Encourage family members to also write notes if they are so inclined.

Progress Reports.   Progress reports are a more traditional means to provide parents feedback about how their child is doing at school. These reports can be complex or simple, and can be sent home once a day, once a week, or once every few weeks. The professional may elect to communicate information about a single subject or area of development, or about many. Samples of various formats for reporting progress are included in Figures 7–2 through 7–4 (pp. 160–162).

Occasional Messages.   Finally, professionals may wish to use occasional messages to provide information to parents specifically about positive aspects of the child's performance. These messages can take many forms including mini-diplomas, certificates of recognition, sticker cards, and mock telegrams. Hochman (1979) recommends sending "happy grams" home to parents. An example of an occasional message format is provided in Figure 7-5 (p. 163). Furthermore, many school supply companies have "happy grams" available.

The Telephone

The telephone can be a convenient and effective tool for communicating with parents. Occasional telephone calls to parents may even result in improved student performance. In a study conducted by Heron and Axelrod (1976), it was discovered that calling in a report to parents on the

How'd I do with . . .	Needs Some Help	Real Good	Great!!

Name: _____ Date: _____

Parent Signature: Teacher Signature:

_____   _____

- You might want to add student signature and include the student in the actual reporting. For example, ask him or her to help you complete the report or to read what you wrote. If the student approves, he or she signs it.
- Be sure to establish what each category means (i.e. what is "Great!"). Discuss this beforehand.
- Topics under "How'd I do with . . ." can change from day to day.
  Examples: Stayed on task   Reading completed
             Didn't talk out   Writing
             Listened carefully   or
             Completed work
- Under "Needs Some Help," a brief notation can be made about what the child can do to improve.
- IEP goals or objectives can be inserted periodically to update progress. For example, under "How'd I do with . . ." the teacher might insert an IEP objective the student has been working on and explain the student's progress.

Figure 7–2
EXAMPLE OF A DAILY OR WEEKLY REPORT

results of their child's word recognition test resulted in increased scores as well as an increase in parent tutoring. As a general rule, telephone conversations with parents should be brief and to the point. Longer, more involved, conversations should be conducted in person. It is a good idea to make prior arrangements for the specific times at which you will call so as to avoid interrupting or disrupting the parents' schedule. Be sure toinquire whether a parent wishes to receive telephone calls at work. There are certain disadvantages to conversing over the telephone, such as not

Name: _____

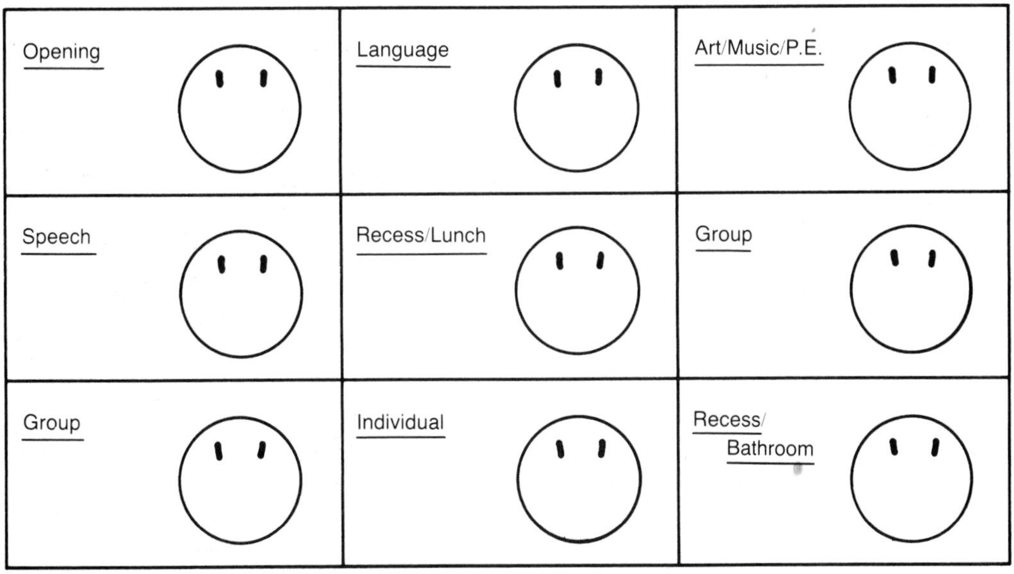

Opening 😐	Language 😐	Art/Music/P.E. 😐
Speech 😐	Recess/Lunch 😐	Group 😐
Group 😊	Individual 😊	Recess/ Bathroom 😊

Uses: - For immediate reinforcement after each period.
- For students who are non-verbal, younger, or
  those who cannot read to share with parents who
  may have the same disabilities.
- Modify to fit individual needs and subjects.
- Fill in the "smiley" face to indicate how the
  student did each period.

Figure 7–3
DAILY REPORT

being able to see the parents' nonverbal reactions and messages; for this reason, it is particularly necessary to listen carefully and to check out perceptions by asking questions. The Parent Center of the Albuquerque, N.M., Public Schools (1985) recommends the following good telephone habits and manners:

1. Treat every message (coming or going) as an important call.
2. Always identify yourself as you place a call or answer one.
3. Personalize your conversation at every opportunity by using the caller's name.
4. Don't use the telephone for criticism. Criticism is tricky enough even in an eye-to-eye encounter. When the parent must depend completely on your voice, criticism is doubly difficult.

Dear _____

This week I have been working on _____
_____
_____
_____

I need to improve some in _____.
_____
_____

I did very well this week on _____
_____
_____

Some things we might work on at home are _____
_____
_____
_____

SINCERELY,

_____
STUDENT

                                            _____
                                            TEACHER

                                            _____
                                            PARENT

Figure 7–4
PROGRESS LETTER

5. Be sure to ask the parent if you have called at a convenient time. If not, ask him to name a time when he'll be free to talk.
6. Jot down in advance what you want to find out from the parent and what you want to tell the parent.
7. When taking down information briefly double check the information.
8. If it is necessary to leave the line during a call, explain the reason and excuse yourself. When you return, thank the caller for waiting. (On long-distance calls, make every effort to avoid putting a parent on "hold.")
9. Always offer the caller or person being called your help or assistance.
10. Allow time for the parent to ask you their questions.
11. Return all calls promptly; the exception, of course, is if you are involved in the classroom with students.

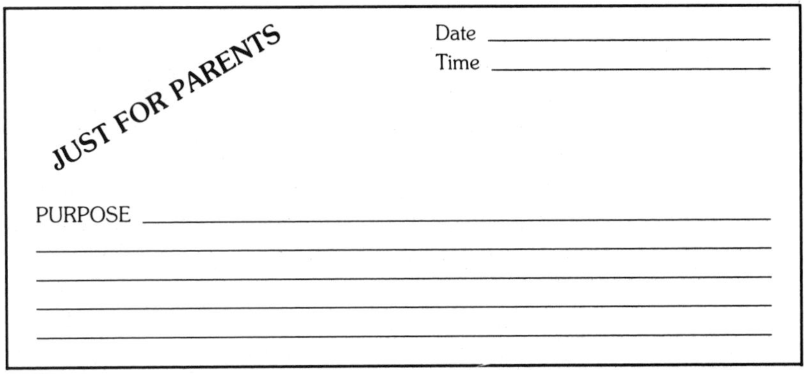

```
┌──────────────────────────────────────────────────────────┐
│  JUST FOR PARENTS          Date _____      │
│                            Time _____      │
│                                                          │
│  PURPOSE _____        │
│         _____        │
│         _____        │
│         _____        │
│         _____        │
└──────────────────────────────────────────────────────────┘
```

Occasional notes may be used to identify special events that parents need to know about, to notify parents of special meetings that will be occurring, or to thank parents for support or feedback.

Figure 7–5
SAMPLE OCCASIONAL MESSAGE

12. Give definite information and offer positive information.
13. Avoid the use of vague statements; it forces the caller to dig for information; this is irritating and wastes time.
14. As the conversation ends, thank the caller before you say good-bye. (n.p.)

Heward and Orlansky (1984) suggest that another way professionals can use the telephone is to organize a telephone tree. A telephone tree is an extremely efficient way to get information to several people with little effort. Using the telephone tree, the professional phones one to two parents with a message; those two parents, in turn, each call two more parents and so on until all parents have been contacted. This system has the additional advantage of providing parents with opportunities to get involved and to interact with one another.

A third way to use the telephone as a communication tool is to record daily messages on an automatic answering machine that parents can call in to access. Heward and Orlansky (1984) cite a study (Heward & Chapman, 1981) in which the teacher of a primary class for students with learning disabilities recorded messages such as the following on an answering machine:

Good evening. The children worked very hard today. We are discussing transportation. They enjoyed talking about the airport and all the different kinds of airplanes. The spelling words for tomorrow are: train, t-r-a-i-n;

plane, p-l-a-n-e; truck, t-r-u-c-k; automobile, a-u-t-o-m-o-b-i-l-e; and ship, s-h-i-p. Thank you for calling. (Heward & Chapman, 1981, p. 13)

During the six weeks that the program was in effect, the teacher received an average of 18.7 calls per week as compared with an average of 0.16 calls per week prior to intervention. In addition, scores on daily spelling tests improved for all students despite the fact that prior to the study spelling lists were sent home each day with a request for parents to assist their children in studying.

SUMMARY

The importance of good communication among parents and professionals cannot be emphasized strongly enough. Good intentions and fond feelings are necessary elements for good communication, but they are not enough. To establish and maintain productive and meaningful partnerships with families, the professional must acquire both skills and strategies for communicating. In Chapters 6 and 7 we have provided a variety of communication skills and strategies that have proven both valuable and effective. We encourage you to aspire toward mastery of these skills for the benefit of yourself as well as the students and families whom you serve. In the next chapter, we discuss special education law and its implications for parent-professional interactions.

Chapter 8

The Law of Special Education: The Six Principles of the Education of the Handicapped Act

We have emphasized the history of parent-professional relationships, described the family as a system, and discussed important skills and strategies for communicating with families.

It is now appropriate to introduce another system that affects family-professional relationships, a legal system established by federal laws regulating the education of children with disabilities. Those laws so dominate professional practice in all states that they deserve full attention. They do not, however, affect the education of gifted and talented children, unless, of course, those children also are disabled. Many states, however, include such children under their special education laws. As you read this chapter, remember that federal laws apply only to children with disabilities. Also, state and local laws often supplement federal laws and regulate the education of all children. Obviously, you should check your state and local laws, regulations, and policies as you carry out your professional duties.

This chapter will describe the federal law of special education by listing the reasons for the federal law, discussing the early legal responses to education discrimination, presenting a brief history of Congress' actions, discussing in detail each of the six principles of federal law, the Education of the Handicapped Act (1966), as amended by the Education of All Handicapped Children Act (1975), commonly called P.L. 94–142, and subsequent amendments (as enacted by Congress, implemented by the U.S. Department of Education, by regulations (Code of Federal Regulations) and interpreted by the courts), and describing the meaning of the law for family-professional relationships. All references in this chapter are to the Education of the Handicapped Act, as amended, and its implementing regulations.

Under the federal law, the parents of the child who is disabled are authorized to be involved in the child's education. The laws of each state specify who the parents are, and federal law adopts state definitions. Thus, we refer in this chapter to parents, but we recommend that you consider as you work not only the legal parents but also those people who act as parents. For example, if a child is living with an uncle while the father and mother are out of the country, you would involve the uncle in the child's education.

REASONS FOR THE FEDERAL LAWS

There are three major reasons why Congress decided that it is appropriate for the federal government to have a role in the education of children with disabilities.

First, for many years and in many ways schools had excluded those children from any education at all. These were practices of "pure exclusion," such as prohibiting a child who could not walk, was not toilet trained, was behaviorally aberrant, or was not able to profit from the educational program offered, from attending school. Indeed, when Congress enacted the Education for All Handicapped Children Act (P.L. 94–142) in 1975, it found that one million children with disabilities were receiving no education at all.

Second, Congress found that nearly half of the nation's children with disabilities were not receiving an appropriate education. The denial of an appropriate education is what Turnbull (1986) has called "functional exclusion"—that is, the child is included in a school program in name only but is not truly benefiting from it and therefore is excluded from the "function" of the program.

Third, schools were using psychological or intelligence tests incorrectly and with inappropriate results. For example, a child who speaks only Spanish might have been given a test in English; a child with a learning disability might have been required to take a test in the same way and in the same period of time as children who have no disabilities; poor Black children might have been asked questions that are appropriate only for White middle-class children; or a child with cerebral palsy might be asked to write answers to a test when she has so little manual dexterity that she cannot hold a pencil. In these and other similar circumstances, the test cannot measure the child's abilities or disabilities. The results therefore are not educationally reliable. As we show in this chapter, the Congress and courts have been generally unwilling to uphold such tests and the ways they were administered.

As some have pointed out (Children's Defense Fund, 1974; Milofsky, 1974; Turnbull, 1986), there were many reasons for these practices. One is that the cost of educating children with disabilities normally is higher than the cost of educating other children, and the governments that funded schools were unwilling to spend the extra money. Another is that children with disabilities had relatively little political power in legislatures or in school systems. A third is that many educators did not believe that children with disabilities could learn well or fast enough to be educated. A fourth is that children with disabilities were not regarded as important enough to educate, as being worth educating as a matter of public policy. As Blatt, Biklen, and Bogdan (1977), Sarason and Doris (1979), Gliedman and Roth (1980), and Turnbull and Wheat (1983) all argue, the very fact that a child was mentally disabled was sufficient reason to practice all sorts of discrimination. Indeed, Elizabeth Boggs (1985), Janet Bennett (1985), and Frank Warren (1985) illustrate poignantly how pervasive a form discrimination has taken. Elizabeth Boggs (1985) describes the situation in New Jersey in 1950 as she speaks about the special education that a local ARC provided:

The charter members of the Essex (County, N.J.) Unit were a remarkably foresighted lot. By the time (my husband) Fitzhugh and I came on board late in 1949, they had organized an interdisciplinary diagnostic clinic, to which a hardy band of professionals were contributing their time. The initial applicants were accepted by age groups so that the needs of a group could be identified for service planning. Soon there were enough six- to nine-year-olds identified as trainable to justify organizing some classes. This was my first volunteer organizational task. Two classes were opened in October 1950—one in a Sunday school room, the other in a neighborhood house.

These children had been denied admission to local schools. However, we had a social mission in mind, so we, too, had some eligibility criteria. The children had to be toilet-trained and able to understand simple commands. Our mission was to persuade the county superintendent of schools, and through him the local superintendents, that such children could respond to skillful teaching in a classroom setting and should be accommodated in public schools.

We were, in fact, going backward to the practices of 1911 to 1930 when "imbecile" children had been accepted and provided with an approved curriculum in the larger communities in New Jersey. A state Department of Education publication of 1918 prescribes sense training, speech training, manual training, and "exercises of practical life." It then goes on to note "while results with this group are crude, the improvement in children is marked" (Anderson, 1918). It is hard to recreate now what these classes developed by the Essex Unit meant to parents as well as children (Boggs, 1985, pp. 45–46).

EARLY RESPONSES TO EDUCATIONAL DISCRIMINATION

Despite state and federal laws, children with disabilities were faced with such widespread discrimination in education that their advocates decided early in the 1970s on a new approach. Led by parents in the Pennsylvania Association for Retarded Children (here, parents were in the role of advocates—see Chapter 1), parents, some special educators, and some civil rights groups sued school officials (Weintraub, Abeson, & LaVor, 1976). They claimed that children with disabilities have a legal right to an appropriate education. They argued that the federal constitution guarantees the right to an education for those children.

One basis of their claim was really very simple. Because the states have chosen to educate children who are not disabled and even to educate some (but not all) children who are disabled, schools violate the equal protection clause of the fourteenth amendment to the United States Constitution when they fail to educate *all* children with disabilities. The equal protection clause says that no state shall deny the equal protection of its laws to any citizen. The courts generally agreed with these advocates.

They held that there is a violation of equal protection when children who are not disabled are given an education, or when some children who are disabled are given an education, but other disabled children are not, because some children (the excluded children) are treated less equally than the included children (*Pennsylvania Association for Retarded Children v. Commonwealth,* 1972; *Mills v. D.C. Board of Education,* 1972).

A second basis for their claim was also quite simple. The fourteenth amendment prohibits states from depriving a person of due process, (Courts had come to interpret due process as an opportunity for a fair hearing before a right or privilege is taken away.) Because the denial of an education adversely affects the child, the schools violate the due process clause of the fourteenth amendment when they deny the child an education without giving a reason for that action or granting the child's advocates an opportunity to protest the denial (*Lebanks v. Spears,* 1973; *Maryland Association for Retarded Children v. Maryland,* 1974).

The courts quickly ordered important remedies. They generally required school systems to identify all school-aged children with disabilities, give them non-discriminatory tests, provide them with an appropriate education, educate them with students not having disabilities to the greatest extent beneficial for the children with disabilities, and give parents notice of proposed changes in educational classification, programming, or placement and opportunities to consent or protest (Turnbull, 1986; Weintraub, Abeson, & LaVor, 1976).

As Turnbull (1986) and Weintraub, Abeson, & LaVor (1976) have demonstrated, even before these legal victories Congress had been sensitive to the problems of special education. In 1966 it enacted P.L. 89–750, Education of the Handicapped Act. This law provided federal grants to help the states initiate, expand, and improve special education. A later law, P.L. 91–230, Elementary, Secondary, and Other Educational Amendments of 1969, had a similar purpose—namely, to stimulate the states to develop special education programs.

In 1973, Congress enacted Section 504 of the Vocational Rehabilitation Act. Section 504 is a civil rights act for people with disabilities which prohibits any recipient of federal funds, including schools, from discriminating against people who are disabled solely on the basis of their disability.

By 1974, however, Congress had become so dissatisfied with the states' efforts, and so aware of the major victories that advocates for children with disabilities had won in the courts, that it realized the need for more significant laws. In that year it substantially increased federal aid to the states and required them to adopt a goal of providing full educational opportunities to all children with disabilities, as a condition of receiving the federal funds (P.L. 93–380, Education Amendments of 1974).

In 1975, Congress acted with such finality that the education of such children and the schools of the nation were forever changed. It enacted P.L. 94–142, Education of All Handicapped Children Act. Not all of the legal requirements of federal special education law are contained in these laws, since Congress could not write laws with such specificity, but the Department of Education has implemented it with specificity by promulgating regulations that are published in the Code of Federal Regulations (1984).

P.L. 94–142 was an amendment to Education of the Handicapped Act (the original 1966 law). Many people refer to P.L. 94–142 as though it were the only federal law. It is not, and, to be accurate, we refer in this book to the federal law as the "EHA"—the Education of the Handicapped Act, as amended (20 U.S.C. Secs. 1401–1461) and as implemented by U.S. Department of Education regulations (34 CFR Part 300, Subpart A).

SIX PRINCIPLES

The EHA established new ground rules for schools, parents, and children with disabilities. Turnbull and Turnbull (1978) called these rules the *six principles* of special education law. They are

1. Zero-reject: Schools must educate all children with disabilities and may not exclude any school-aged children with a disability solely because the child has a disability.
2. Nondiscriminatory evaluation: Schools must test and classify children fairly, essentially by administering non-biased tests in ways that do not put children at a disadvantage but that allow them to display their educational abilities and disabilities.
3. Appropriate, individualized education: Schools must provide each child with an individually tailored education.
4. Least restrictive educational placement: Schools must educate children who have disabilities with their peers who do not have disabilities to the greatest extent consistent with their educational and social needs.
5. Procedural due process: Schools must provide opportunities for children's parents to consent or object to their children's educational identification, classification, program, or placement.
6. Parent participation: Parents of children with disabilities may participate in various ways in their children's education.

We will describe these six principles and their implications for professional-family relationships at greater length later in this chapter and in chapters 9, 10, and 11, where we discuss, respectively, nondiscriminatory evaluation, appropriate education, and due process. For now, note that the six principles essentially require professionals to act professionally and schools to follow a course of conduct that is both logical and helpful. They must enroll the child, evaluate fairly, provide a beneficial education, integrate to the maximum extent appropriate, follow fair procedures, and allow parent participation. Before discussing the six principles, we will point out the similarities and differences between the EHA and Section 504.

The two laws are somewhat different and somewhat similar. Like the earlier laws, the EHA provides federal funds to state and local educational agencies if they comply with certain conditions set out in the law itself and the regulations that implement it. By contrast, Section 504 is a civil rights law that prohibits state and local agencies that receive federal money from discriminating against a person with a disability solely because of the disability.

Both laws have similar results in the way they define children with handicaps. Such children are those of school age who need special education and are mentally retarded, hard of hearing, deaf, speech or language impaired, visually handicapped, seriously emotionally disturbed, orthopedically or otherwise health impaired (e.g., have a heart condition or autism), or who have a specific learning disability.

"Special education" means specially designed instruction provided free to the child's parent to meet the child's unique needs. It includes classroom instruction, instruction in physical education, home instruction, and instruction in hospitals and institutions.

If a child is entitled to special education, he or she also may be entitled to "related services," that is, services required to assist the child to benefit from special education. They include transportation, speech pathology and audiology, psychological services, physical and occupational therapy, recreation, early identification and assessment of disabilities, counseling services, medical services rendered to diagnose or evaluate, school health services, social work services in schools, and parent counseling and training.

Zero-Reject

The zero-reject principle requires schools to provide a free education to all school-aged children with disabilities. It prohibits schools from excluding any such child solely because the child has a disability. The purpose of the zero-reject principle is to remedy the practices of "pure exclusion" and "functional exclusion." It rests on the proposition, first announced in *Pennsylvania Association for Retarded Children v. Commonwealth*

(1972), that all children with disabilities can learn, and that state and local educational agencies therefore have no right to exclude any of them from school. The zero-reject principle has components that have implications for the manner in which professionals work with parents.

Free Appropriate Public Education. All school-aged children are entitled to a free appropiate education, without exception. A child is of school age when the state's compulsory education laws require school attendance. Under the EHA, state and local school systems have an option to serve children from birth through five years of age and from ages 18–21. But they have the duty to continue to serve them from age 6 until they are 18. State and local school systems ultimately must bear the entire cost of the education, even if the child is in programs operated by other state or local agencies or if the child is put in a private school at the request of the schools.

Courts have been rigorously interpreting the zero-reject principle in children's favor. For example, they refused to rule that there is such a child as one who cannot learn; they say there is no such person as an "ineducable" one (*Levine v. N.J.,* 1980; *Matthews v. Campbell,* 1981; *Christine L. v. Milan School Dist.,* 1983). They have not allowed schools to expel a child if the disability is related to or causes the behavior that the school seeks to punish, as, for example, violating rules of school conduct having to do with sexual activity, smoking, and hitting. Instead, schools may only change the child's evaluation, placement, or program (*S–1 v. Turlington,* 1981). Courts have generally not allowed schools to exclude children from athletic or extra-curricular activities (*Kampmeier v. Nyquist,* 1977; *Poole v. Plainfield Bd. of Ed.,* 1980). But courts also have allowed state and local schools to administer competency tests to children and youth as long as there are accommodations in the way the tests are administered and adequate notice that the tests will be given so the students can prepare for them; if students fail the tests, the schools may withhold graduation diplomas (*Brookhart v. Illinois St. Bd. of Education,* 1982; *Board of Education v. Ambach,* 1982).

Obviously, these provisions offer professionals many ways to work with parents. They may help parents enroll children for school, obtain services for preschool children, plan for the transition of their children from school to adult services, work with their children on school discipline matters, plan for appropriate extra-curricular or athletic activities, and work with students who are given competency tests to prepare for and accept the results of the tests. The key is this: parents now may assume their child will be educated at public expense and appropriately, and professionals now must respond to the child's legal rights to be educated appropriately.

Coverage. All children and youth are entitled to a free appropriate public education, no matter where they are educated. Thus, a child who is in a hospital because of a long illness, or confined to home because of a chronic illness, is entitled to an education. Likewise, children in state institutions for people who are mentally ill, mentally retarded, blind, or deaf are entitled to an education. Similarly, children placed in private schools by public schools are entitled to an education. In short, all school-aged students with a disability are entitled to an education, no matter where the students are. In addition, students for whom no appropriate program exists locally have the right to attend an appropriate program elsewhere, such as at a private school, a state institution, or a regional cooperative school.

The role of facilitator or coordinator is especially appropriate for professionals to consider in the cases of local school-private school or local school-institution/ hospital placement, where parents may feel they need a "case manager" or "program coordinator." We will discuss this coordination in the last section of this chapter.

Child Census. School systems, working in cooperation with health, social service, and other child-service agencies, must identify all school-aged children and youth in their jurisdictions. In addition, they must plan for the education of those students and, naturally, allow them to enroll when they are age-eligible.

Clearly, professionals in schools, health, social service, and other child-service agencies may work with parents to have their children included in this "child find."

Service Priorities. State and local school systems are required to spend their federal funds on two types of children and youth (the so-called "service priority" children). First, they must provide funding for any age-eligible student who is not receiving a free appropriate education. Second, they must provide funding for the children who have the most severe disabilities within each category of disability. For example, if there are 5 children who have multiple disabilities and 25 who are mildly mentally retarded, the 5 have a higher claim to the federal funds than the 25, but all have a right to a free appropriate public education (and the schools must provide to the 25 out of state or local funds if there are not sufficient federal funds).

Professionals may work with parents of unenrolled children to have these children included, and with parents of all children, particularly those with severe disabilities, to have them served appropriately. Professionals must bear in mind that (as a legal matter) they do not thereby impair the claims of other students, because the state and local agencies must provide for those students even if it means using non-federal funds (as it usually does). Parents of unenrolled children or children who are severely disabled now have a special claim, and this changes the ground rules dramatically. Parents now may require their children to be educated, and professionals now must recognize the validity of those claims.

Single-agency Responsibility.   The state educational agency (SEA) is ultimately responsible for the education of all children and youth with disabilities. It usually does not operate programs itself, although in some states the SEA is the "local school board" for state schools for students who are deaf or blind and in some situations the federal law authorizes the SEA to operate programs directly. Normally, the SEA delegates its authority to local educational agencies (LEAs), or state law makes that delegation. In the case where LEAs directly operate special education programs, they are responsible in the first instance for providing for each eligible student. Sometimes, however, parents have been unable to enforce their child's right at a local level, usually because of local school resistance or inability. For that reason, the SEA is responsible for educating all eligible children and youth, whether they are in an LEA, a private school, a state institution, or a hospital or home-bound program.

Parents and professionals may work together with the knowledge that, ultimately, the SEA is responsible for making the student's education appropriate. Thus, they may look to the SEA to give advice, help monitor LEAs, provide assistance and information to professionals and parents, render other technical assistance, coordinate the providers of related services, enforce compliance with federal and state law, and generally be both helper and watchdog for LEAs and professionals.

Personnel Development.   The SEA and the LEAs are required to develop and implement programs of personnel development, particularly inservice training of professionals and parents (the program referred to as the Comprehensive System for Personnel Development). In addition, the SEA is required to provide "parent surrogates" appointed by the SEA to represent, in special education matters, children who do not have parents or other legal guardians, have parents who cannot be located, or are wards of the state.

The personnel development requirements make it possible for professionals to seek and obtain training, including training on how to work with families, to make them more competent to respond to the student's rights.

Effects of Zero-reject Principle.   Clearly, parents now may make the following assumptions (contrary to the "no assumptions" rule described in Chapter 1): their child will be given free access to the schools; education will be free; they will work with professionals to provide a free appropriate public education to children; professionals will acknowledge that their children are able to learn and that professionals are able (or can be taught) to teach them effectively; some preschool education may be provided by theschools; related services will be available for their children; and the quality of their children's education will be enhanced by parent participation.

The issue no longer is whether the schools will educate their children. That problem has been laid to rest by the law. The only issues now are quality and duration: what type of education the student will have, where, and by whom education will be provided, and how soon and for how long it will be furnished. One parent sagely noted:

> I can enroll my child and get her into school. But the question is: what has she gotten into?

Thus, the zero-reject principle has changed fundamentally the assumptions that parents and professionals may make.

The zero-reject principle has had other parent-professional effects. It imposes a duty on professionals and creates a legal right for parents and children. It abolishes the privilege of an education and replaces it with a right to an education. Many a parent now says, "I've got rights," and many a professional now replies, "Yes, and I've got duties." Not long ago, parents and professionals would have talked about "privileges" and "charity," not rights and duty.

Zero-reject changes professional practices as they affect children and parents. It gives rise to the potential for the student to be integrated with others who are not disabled and to receive education for an extended period of time. It is a means to the mainstream of adult life and the first step in a lifetime of services to people with disabilities. It therefore allows and encourages growth, not only in the student but also in the parents and professionals. And, for that reason, it changes the nature of schools and thereby the nature of society. It alters dramatically the norms of school and society by saying that it is normal to include persons with disabilities. It also changes the form of society by integrating students with and without disabilities in the nation's schools. The difference is profound: children and parents today are served, not excluded. "We've been counted in, at last," said one parent. "We are now part of them. We belong in the schools, with the other kids. It's so normal, but why was it so long in happening?"

Nondiscriminatory Evaluation

The principle of nondiscriminatory evaluation exists to help professionals accurately assess the student's strengths and weaknesses. That goal has several rationale. That type of assessment—and nothing less—is necessary to assure that students are not wrongly identified as disabled (when they are not) or as having a certain type or extent of disability (when they do not). In turn, fair evaluation is necessary to assure proper placement, which, of course, helps provide an appropriate education. Clearly, the principle of nondiscriminatory evaluation is a means to an end, and the key is for professionals to translate evaluation results into instruction.

In addition, professionals may use the nondiscriminatory evaluation to defend any categorical label they assign to the student. There is much disagreement about whether labelling is acceptable professional practice, and many states have resorted to noncategorical (i.e., label-free) identification of the child as having "special needs" or "exceptionalities." But other states still adhere to categorical labelling (e.g., the categories of the EHA—learning disabilities, hearing impaired, health impaired); in those states, professionals will be able to classify students on the basis of the evaluation results.

The EHA requires professionals to adhere to multiple strategies to assure nondiscriminatory evaluation:

1. Testing and examination materials and procedures must be selected and administered so as not to be racially or culturally discriminatory.
2. Materials and tests must be given in the student's native language or mode of communication (e.g., signing) unless it is not feasible to do so.
3. No single evaluation procedure may be used as the only criterion for determining an appropriate educational program.
4. Only those materials and tests may be used that have been validated for the specific purpose for which used.
5. Tests must be administered and interpreted by trained personnel in conformance with the instructions from their producers.
6. Tests must be administered in a way that accommodates the student's manual, speaking, or sensory disabilities.
7. All evaluations must be made by a multidisciplinary team or group of persons, including at least one teacher or other specialists with knowledge in the area of the student's suspected disability.
8. The student must be assessed in all areas related to the suspected disability, including, where appropriate, health, vision, hearing, social and emotional status, general intelligence, academic performance, communicative status, and motor abilities.
9. No student may be placed in a special education program until a complete and individual evaluation, which meets the above standards, has been completed.
10. Professionals must draw upon information from a variety of sources about the student, including aptitude and achievement tests, teacher recommendations, physical conditions, social and cultural background, and adaptive behavior.
11. Professionals must ensure that information obtained from all those sources is documented and carefully considered.

12. Professionals must ensure that the placement decision is made by a group of people, including those knowledgeable about the student, the meaning of the evaluation data, and the placement options.

13. Professionals must obtain the consent of the student's parents for the initial evaluation for special education programs.

14. Professionals must re-evaluate the student, in conformity with these requirements, every three years or more often if "conditions warrant" or the student's parents or teachers request re-evaluation.

15. In the case of students with suspected or documented learning disabilities, professionals must adhere to special requirements for nondiscriminatory evaluation. You should comply with your state and local rules as well as the special federal rules for assessing learning disabilities.

16. Under some circumstances, parents have the right to have their child evaluated by an independent professional free of cost to them. Of course, parents always have a right to an independent evaluation at their own expense.

It is clear that many different professionals will be involved in evaluation. Certain professionals must be involved. Others—such as the student's present or future teachers, including those in regular education—may request to be involved. All professionals who will work with the child, therefore, may participate in the evaluation. This means professionals need to know how to work as members of a team.

Professionals also may have access to the evaluation data so they will know more about the student and, therefore, how to be more effective in their work. Professionals must bear in mind that, because evaluation is a means to an end, they should use the evaluation for the purposes for which it is conducted—for placement and program decisions, such as with respect to academic, social, extra-curricular, and behavioral interventions and programs.

Working with Parents. Professionals must obtain parents' consent for initial evaluation. In some states, state or local laws or regulations also require consent to the mandatory re-evaluations. In addition, parents may request re-evaluation when they think there are reasons to do so; for example, the student may have had a serious illness that affects one or more skill areas functions, and therefore the student requires reassessment for possible re-placement or re-programming. Finally, professionals themselves may request re-evaluation when they think there are reasons to do so; for example, there may be a change in the student's condition that the parents do not think warrants re-evaluation but the professionals do. In all instances when professionals think they need an evaluation, it is either required by state or local law or good practice to follow the "touch-base" rule by informing and obtaining consent from parents. One parent probably spoke for most when she said:

I know Nathan so very well that I can't imagine not being helpful to his teachers. But there's another point: He's my son, not theirs. I have him over the long haul, and I appreciate being kept in touch with. That's how he and I can face the long haul—together, with teachers beside us to guide us.

As we point out in greater detail in Chapter 9, professionals also may work with parents by obtaining their input to the evaluation. The same is true with respect to other members of the child's family. Those people have a great deal of information such as what their child can or cannot do in various activities. Moreover, parents and family members are especially important to consult when ethnic or sociocultural differences may exist with respect to them and professionals. This is so because the child's adaptive behavior and language may be shaped at home by ethnic or sociocultural factors that differ from those in the schools.

Jane Schulz (1985) is both a parent (her son has Down syndrome) and a special educator. Here is her observation:

> A final factor that is detrimental to the parent-teacher relationship is the reluctance on the part of the teacher to accept the abilities of the parents. Since I was a parent so many times I wanted to say, 'I have a son who is retarded. I taught him to walk, to use the bathroom, to feed himself, to say his first words, to interact with the family. I know my son; I can help you to know him and to teach him.' (Schulz, 1985, p. 5)

You can help families by carefully explaining the nature of the tests to be given, the purpose of the evaluation, how the evaluation results will be used, and how parents can help provide information about the child's abilities and disabilities. We encourage you to: (a) consider the parent as a partner and a rich resource for information, not simply as the person with legal rights to consent or as a recipient of information you provide; (b) be balanced in your discussions about the child, stressing abilities as well as suspected or confirmed disabilities; and (c) avoid jargon, as such language does not communicate and may even set up barriers between parents and yourself. In short, you can regard nondiscriminatory evaluation procedures as a way to work constructively with parents for the benefit of everyone involved.

Effects of Nondiscriminatory Evaluation Principle.   The principle has had many salutary effects (Turnbull, 1986). It has required professionals to be more careful in classifying and providing curriculum and related services for children. It has led to fewer children being classified as mentally retarded or speech-impaired who otherwise might have been so classified. It also has led to many children being classified as learning disabled (Office of Special Education, 1984), arguably to their benefit.

It has validated the use of standardized tests (*PASE v. Hannon,* 1980), even though there are legal objections in some states to using those tests without special safeguards to assure that they do not discriminate against ethnic minority children on the basis of their ethnicity (*Larry P. v. Riles,* 1984). But it also has recognized that intelligence testing has a potentially hypnotic effect (i.e., professionals will pay too much attention to a student's IQ) and it has tried to mitigate that effect by requiring that other procedures be brought to bear in classification.

It has required professionals to spend more time in evaluation and classification. But that extra effort should have the effect of giving professionals a more comprehensive picture of the student and therefore a greater ability to identify the student's strengths (and build on them) and weaknesses (and remediate them). Thus, it also has required professionals and parents to work together and in particular to evaluate more carefully a student's strengths and weaknesses. In turn, it has required professionals to make more relevant, data-based, and objective educational decisions.

Finally, it has given parents and other family members an opportunity to participate in the evaluation process and its outcomes; it has been a bridge to greater family-professional partnership.

Appropriate Education

It will achieve little for professionals to enroll and evaluate a student unless they also provide an appropriate, individualized education. The cornerstone of the principle of appropriate education is the individualized education program (IEP). We describe parent participation in the IEP and explain the process of developing IEPs in Chapter 10. Here, we will describe only the legal requirements for an IEP. We also will describe other ways that the law defines "appropriate education."

IEP. The IEP is a written document developed in a team meeting. A representative of the school who is qualified to provide (or supervise the provision of) special education and the student's teacher (or teachers) must attend. Parents must be invited and may attend. The student may attend. The school and parents may invite others to attend. When the student is evaluated for the first time, the IEP committee also must contain a member of the team that performed the nondiscriminatory evaluation. The purpose of the special requirements for the first IEP is to assure that the evaluation results are translated into the student's program.

The IEP must contain the following contents: a statement of the child's present levels of educational performance; a statement of the annual goals and short-term instructional objectives in each area requiring specially designed instruction; a statement of the specific educational services to be provided and the extent to which the child will be able to participate in regular education programs; the projected date for beginning, and the anticipated duration of, such services; and appropriate objective criteria and evaluation procedures and schedules for determining, at least on an annual basis, whether the instructional objectives are being met. The IEP may be revised annually or more often if warranted in the judgment of the professionals or parents.

If the public schools enroll the student in a private school, there are special provisions for developing the IEP. These provisions basically require the public and private agencies to work together to develop and ensure the IEP is carried out. Of course, the school pays the private tuition.

Because the law places a high premium on parent participation and because parent participation is valuable, there are special requirements for assuring that a student's parents have a chance to attend the IEP conference. These include advance notice of the meeting, mutually convenient scheduling of the meeting, and arranging for interpreters for deaf or non-English-speaking parents. If parents are unable to attend, they may still participate through individual or conference telephone calls. The chronically ill mother of a child with a disability once told us how useful the telephone IEP conference was:

> If it were not for the telephone, my daughter would have been disabled in two ways—one, educationally, and, two, by not having me involved in her IEP. And I too would have been disabled in two ways—one, by being bedridden and, two, by not being able to be involved in Susie's IEP.

The school may have an IEP meeting without the parents only when it can document that it unsuccessfully attempted to have the parents participate. The documentation should include detailed records of telephone calls, copies of letters to or from the parents, and the results of visits to the parents' home or place(s) of work. The school must give a copy of the IEP to the parents, upon request.

The IEP is the most important technique for an appropriate education. The law itself makes that clear. The EHA defines appropriate education as one that is provided at public expense, under public direction and supervision, without charge; meets the standards of the state educational agency; includes preschool, elementary, and secondary school education; and is provided in conformity with the requirements for the IEP. This statutory definition does not flesh out the meaning of appropriate; it is just a skeleton.

Determining What Is Appropriate. Another definition is the "process definition" (Turnbull, 1986). The student's education is appropriate if professionals follow the specified procedures of the EHA: (1) they make a nondiscriminatory evaluation; (2) they develop the IEP with the proper people, at the proper times, and in a proper way, using the evaluation results; (3) they place the student in the least restrictive environment; and (4) they grant parents rights to due process and to participate in the student's IEP development. This approach to an appropriate education has been sanctioned by the United States Supreme Court in the very first special education case it decided, *Board v. Rowley* (1982).

In the *Rowley* case, the Court was faced with a claim that Amy Rowley, a young teen-aged girl with significant hearing loss, required an interpreter as a "related service" in order for her to have an appropriate education. Without an interpreter, Amy heard only 59% of what transpired in her class, but she also had passed from grade to grade without ever being held back and without using an interpreter. The Court ruled that Amy did not require an interpreter. In doing so, it affirmed the "process definition," stressing that all of the professionals involved in developing her IEP were of the opinion that she could be educated appropriately without an interpreter, that the law allowed her parents to be involved in her education in multiple ways, and that in fact they had been so involved.

The Court also ruled that Congress intended only that the EHA shall open the doors of public education to children and youth with disabilities, giving them a reasonable opportunity to learn. Congress did not intend that the schools must develop students' capacities to their maximum. Accordingly, Congress' intent is satisfied when professionals provide students with a reasonable opportunity to learn. Since they had done this in Amy's case (as proved by her passing from grade to grade), they had satisfied the EHA's requirements of an appropriate education, and an interpreter was not required.

This "reasonable opportunity" rule has taken on a new meaning in those few states that have been ordered by courts to provide summer schooling to students with severe disabilities. In those states, courts have ruled that the law's requirements of individualized education mean that schools must provide summer schooling to children whose disabilities are so severe that they will experience significant regression in their learning unless their education continues during the summer (*Armstrong v. Klein,* 1980, 1981; *Georgia ARC v. McDaniel,* 1983). Here, "reasonable opportunity" and "individualized education" are the bases for summer training.

In a later case, *Tatro v. State of Texas* (1984), the Court ruled that an appropriate education depends on the availability of related services. In that case, the issue was whether clean intermittent catheterization for a child who has spina bifida and cannot toilet herself is a related service or a medical service (which is not a related service unless it is performed for diagnostic and evaluation purposes). The Court ruled that catheterization is a related service, since it is required to assist Ambur Tatro to benefit from special education.

Thus, there are four ways to define "appropriate education": (a) by the language of the law itself, which requires individualization and relies greatly on the IEP; (b) by the process definition; (c) by the "reasonable opportunity" rule; and (d) by the availability of related services (Turnbull, 1986).

Implications for Professionals.   In chapter 10 we describe in detail the implications of the IEP for parent participation, emphasizing the research on parent participation, the barriers to parent participation, and how to overcome them. Here, it is useful to make a few preliminary points. By having parents and professionals develop the IEP, the EHA turns the IEP meeting into a vehicle for communication among these people. They may decide what the student's needs are, how they can respond to those needs in the most appropriate and integrated program, and what results can be anticipated. Just as the law assumes that parents will (and will want) to participate, so it also assumes that they have equal standing with professionals to make these decisions.

Professionals who want to carry out the parent-professional opportunities of the IEP will do the following: (a) strive to have parents present, (b) inform parents that the student may be present and even suggest that the student should be present; (c) respect parents' opinions about the student's abilities and disabilities; (d) be particularly careful to respect parents' opinions about what program the student should have, because, in most cases and in the final analysis, parents (not professionals) are the people ultimately responsible for their children; (e) avoid using educational jargon and be clear in communicating with parents, especially in communicating why they believe the student should be placed in a certain program and why the objectives and evaluation methods in the proposed IEP are proposed; and (f) look on the IEP meeting as an opportunity to work with each other and with parents to obtain shared decision making, shared accountability for the student's program, and shared commitment to appropriate education. At an IEP meeting recently, a parent said to a teacher:

> "Look, we're all in the same boat." And the teacher replied, "Don't think I don't know it! Or that I don't appreciate being there with you. I do!"

Effects of Principle of Appropriate Education.   The effects of appropriate, individualized education have been far-reaching. Turnbull (1986) discusses them in detail. Among others, it has turned schools into a child-centered agency. The student is no longer required to fit the school, but the school is required to fit the student. Second, it has helped schools become providers of a wide range of services, as when they provide related services. The function of schools, therefore, has become more than traditional academic training; the schools have become multi-service agencies, providing education, health, mental health, social service, and other programs to children and parents. It has required professionals to work in multidisciplinary teams and to learn to work with many other types of professionals. Third, it has made it possible for professionals and parents to establish new relationships, ones that recognize the necessary and legitimate roles of shared decision making. It also has recognized that students themselves have legitimate roles to play in shaping their own special education and their own lives, and that changes professional, family, and student relationships. Finally, it has overcome the practice of "functional exclusion" by assuring the provision of services that are truly beneficial to students.

Least Restrictive Environment

The principle of the least restrictive environment (i.e., placement or LRE) is a technique for preventing the unwarranted segregation of students with disabilities from their peers who do not have disabilities. There are two important reasons to prevent segregation by disability. First, segregation can have an adverse effect on the ability of students with disabilities to learn. Second, segration can have an adverse effect on their ability to associate with non-disabled peers. As Turnbull and his colleagues have pointed out in reviewing these two points (Turnbull, Brotherson, Cyzewski, Esquith, Otis, Summers, Van Reusen, & DePazza-Conway, 1983; Turnbull, 1981), the LRE principle seeks to maximize the child's educational and social-associational opportunities. It therefore is a mistake to view the LRE principle only for education; it is a technique that has two objectives. A parent has told us:

> It's not so much the program that helps Ryan as it is the other students. They respond to him, and he to them, in ways that make his physical disability— his not walking—so minimal.

Moreover, the least restrictive environment rule rests on a basic principle of constitutional law. That principle says that when any state has a legitimate goal to pursue and that goal requires the state to restrict the liberty or opportunity of any of its citizens, it must pursue that goal in the way that is least restrictive of citizens' rights and opportunities. In Chambers' memorable metaphor, if it is permissible for a state to kill mosquitoes, it must use a fly swatter, not a bazooka, if the fly is on a citizen's back (Chambers, 1972).

In its attempt to carry out the educational and associational goals of the LRE principle and comply with the constitution in so doing, the EHA and its regulations require schools to assure that (a) to the maximum extent appropriate, children and youth with disabilities (including those in private schools and public institutions) are educated with those who are not disabled and (b) special classes, separate schooling, or other removal of a student with disabilities from regular education occurs only when the nature or severity of disability is such that education in regular classes cannot be achieved satisfactorily with the use of supplementary aids and services.

To carry out these two basic requirements, schools must (a) provide a continuum of alternative placements, including regular classes, resource rooms, special classes, special schools, homebound instruction, and instruction in hospitals and institutions, (b) provide supplementary services, such as speech therapy and adaptive physical education, for a student who is educated in regular classes, (c) provide education as close to a student's home as possible, and (d) allow a student to participate in extracurricular and nonacademic activities to the maximum extent appropriate. As Turnbull, Brotherson, Wheat, and Esquith (1982) have shown, courts interpret these provisions to allow the removal of the student to special placements, particularly those in institutions, only when the extent of the student's disability is very great and local programs are inadequate.

Working with Parents.   Throughout this book and particularly when we discussed family system concepts in Chapters 2–5, we emphasized the variety and complexity of families and the implications for your work. Here, it is sufficient to point out only a few obvious points that relate to families and the principle of the least restrictive education of their children.

Some parents will want their children in the "most normal" program possible (i.e., as close to regular education and the "mainstream" as possible), but others will prefer separate education, even institutional placement (Abramson, Willson, Yoshida, & Hagerty, 1983; Boggs, 1985; Turnbull & Winton, 1983; and Ziskin, 1985).Professionals should acknowledge that parents are expressing a preference for certain values— either educational or associational values related to their child.

But parents also may be saying that their child's educational placement reflects their needs and those of their other family members. As several parents have noted in *Parents Speak Out: Then and Now* (Turnbull & Turnbull, 1985), there is a delicate balancing of values and individual interests that occurs when special education placement is determined. But parent preferences also may take into account that some necessary educational or other services are not available. Leah Ziskin (1985) is a physician whose daughter, Jennie, has severe mental retardation. Having had Jennie at home for 10 years, here is what she said about balancing family interests:

> When Jennie was almost ten years old, the family had an opportunity to accompany my husband to Australia on his sabbatical leave. We obtained guest-placement status for Jennie at a state institution during the four months that we were away. From all reports Jennie's adjustment was uneventful; she did well. However, we missed her. Someone didn't always have to be watching her or feeding her; in other words, we felt suddenly unburdened. When we returned to New Jersey, we brought Jennie home. But our attitude had changed—probably mine most of all. I realized that our family had interacted better when Jennie was not always there. In retrospect, it appears that we did not realize how we were functioning as a family when we were dealing with Jennie on a full-time basis. (p. 76)

Professionals should be particulary sensitive and tactful when they discuss special educational placement with parents, remembering that values, competing interests, and service availability are three important components of parental decisions. Where the parents' preferences are based on values, professionals should acknowledge the legitimacy of those values, even when they have other values. Where parents' preferences are based on problems of service availability, professionals should try to make services available so parents' values can be realized.

In some cases, parents have concerns about placing their children in regular education. They may recognize that children who do not have disabilities and their parents may not welcome their child—the "backlash" is indeed something they fear. They may believe that their child will receive more appropriate and individualized education in special programs. They may not want to share the stigma of their child's disability when they have to associate with other students and their parents. They may have worked particularly hard to develop good special education programs and they may not be willing to leave them—they may have a psychological investment in their own volunteer work.

You may want to ask tactfully why parents prefer special or regular placement, what can be done to respond to those reasons so that the law can be carried out, and what experiences and preferences the student has so that they can be responsive to the student as well as the parents. Professionals also may want to suggest to their supervisors, principals, superintendents, school board members, or state department of education personnel how changes can be made to accommodate individual needs in LRE placements. They may want to urge parents to become involved in state or local advisory boards that specify needs and how they can be met. Paul, Turnbull, and Cruickshank (1977) describe a procedure for cooperative planning among professionals and parents.

Effects of the LRE Principle. The LRE principle has had some important effects. It has enabled parents, regular educators, and special educators to plan for and deliver programs in a collaborative way, and it has made it possible for regular and special educators to work together and for special and regular education systems to become more integrated. It has made it possible for many students who otherwise would have received special education to receive an education in regular programs (Office of Special Education, 1983, 1984). It has made it possible for some children to avoid institutional placement (Office of Special Education, 1983, 1984). Most importantly, it has helped students with disabilities to receive a more effective education and to associate with and enhance the sensitivity of peers who are not disabled (Turnbull, Brotherson, Cyzewski, Esquith, Otis, Summers, Van Reusen, & DePazza-Conway, 1983).

Procedural Safeguards and Due Process

The reasons for due process make clear why the EHA contains procedural safeguards. Those reasons are as follows:

1. Due process is a requirement of the federal constitution, a requirement that says that citizens have a right to be treated fairly whenever government takes action that may have an adverse effect. The essence of fair treatment is the right to receive notice of the proposed action and an opportunity to protest to an impartial person, have a chance to present one's case, and have an appeal.
2. Due process is a means for helping parents and students hold schools accountable. The first four principles—zero-reject, nondiscriminatory evaluation, appropriate education, and least restrictive placement—are the "inputs" from the school to the student. Due process is a means of making sure the school has done its job under those four principles.
3. Due process is a way of changing the balance of power between professionals and parents, between those who traditionally wielded it and those who felt they had no effect on their children's education.
4. Due process is a new way to focus on the rights and needs of students, parents, and professionals. It gives parents and professionals new chances to address rights and needs and to do so with an impartial decision-maker.

The EHA requires that school systems have two basic components in place. The first is the "pre-hearing" component; the second is the "fair hearing" itself.

Pre-hearing. The procedural safeguards for parents and students include the right to have access to the students' educational records. They also include the right to limit access to those records except by people who need to know what is in them so they can provide or monitor services. In addition and as noted above, parents may obtain an independent evaluation of their child.

Children who have no parents, whose parents cannot be found, or who are wards of the state have the right to "surrogate parents"—people appointed to represent them in special education matters. Professionals should ask these surrogates how they want to be involved in the child's education, remembering that the EHA requires schools to treat surrogates as though they were the child's parents but that good practice may mean using the communication skills and strategies of Chapters 6 and 7 and the implementation skills of Chapter 9 and 10 but not the family system considerations of Chapters 2–5.

Parents (including surrogates) have a right to a written notice whenever schools propose to change or refuse to change the child's identification, evaluation, educational placement, or the provision of a free appropriate education. Parents' consent must be obtained before any initial evaluation or initial placement of a child in special education. Strategies for providing notice and obtaining consent are included in Chapter 9.

Hearing.   When parents or professionals disagree about a child's iden-tification, evaluation, placement, program, or other elements of a free appropriate education, they may obtain a hearing (the so-called due process hearing) to resolve their differences. Note that schools, not just parents, may call for a hearing. Professionals should become familiar with how their employing schools or other service agencies can request a hearing.

At the hearing, both parties (i.e., parents and schools) have the right to be advised by a lawyer and other experts; to call witnesses to testify; to introduce evidence, including documents; to examine and cross-examine witnesses; to have a record of the hearing; to have written findings of fact by the hearing officer; and to appeal the decision. The decision of the first hearing officer usually is appealed to the state educational agency; from that agency, it may be appealed to a state or federal court.

The parents and service-providers must exhaust their administrative remedies before they may file a lawsuit in a state or federal court (*Sessions v. Livingston Parish,* 1980). That is, they must go through a due process hearing with a local hearing officer and then complete the appeal to the state agency before they may file their lawsuit. However, they need not exhaust their remedies if the requirement to exhaust their remedies would be futile in that it would have no power to correct the situation (*Miener v. State of Missouri,* 1982).

By the same token, parents may not unilaterally remove their child from publicly funded education, make a placement in a program that charges tuition, and expect to recover the tuition unless they first exhaust their administrative remedies (*Foster v. D.C. Board of Ed.,* 1981). This "stay-put" rule has two exceptions. First, they may make the unilateral removal and obtain tuition reimbursement if the child's physical or mental health is in serious and imminent danger in the present program (*Anderson v. Thompson,* 1981). Second, they may do likewise where the school has acted in "bad faith" (such as by unreasonably delaying the child's evaluation) (*Doe v. Anrig,* 1983; *William S. v. Gill,* 1982).

Working with Parents.   As we point out in Chapter 11, you have many opportunities to work with parents within the due process principle. You will want to be particularly careful about keeping records, because parents have access to those records that are shared among professionals. This means that you will want to record accurate, current, and relevant information, both of a positive and critical nature, about the child and the parents (if relevant to the child's education), but you should record only that which you can defend on the basis of facts and would want to defend in an open hearing.

You must comply with *every* requirement of the EHA as it relates to the child's identification, evaluation, program, and placement, since violation of any of a large number of rights can trigger a due process hearing (Turnbull, Turnbull, and Strickland, 1979). This means you should advise parents about all of their rights and should do so in a way that is comprehensive and informative—that is, paying attention to *what* you say and *how* you say it when giving notice and seeking consent (Turnbull, 1978). In addition to this legal requirement, you would do well to engage in those types of professional conduct in relationships with parents that we have described throughout this book. Finally, you should be willing to appear at due process hearings as an advisor or witness, although you must recognize that you should be able to defend your actions.

Effects of Due Process Principle.   There is no doubt about the many powerful effects of this principle. In summary (see chapter 11 for more detail), it has made professionals and parents more accountable to each other. It has made each deal more fairly with the other, and in particular it has required professionals to change the "power relationships" that they had with parents and to be more sensitive and accommodating to parent values, concerns, and information. It has helped sharpen the focus on the student's needs and the schools' duties to be student-centered and family-system-minded. It brings the essence of fairness to parent-professional relationships, and it assures, to a great degree, that fair procedures will result in acceptable results. It has exacted very high costs in terms of money, emotions, and time when there have been due process hearings. It has increased the use of mediation as a way to prevent, contain, and resolve parent-professional disputes. In some cases, it does not satisfactorily resolve all the long-standing disputes between parents and professionals but instead gives a quick answer that professionals or parents may subvert over the long haul. In many cases, however, it provides not only an answer but also a solution to differences.

Parent Participation

Because this entire book concerns parent-professional relationships and parent participation in the education of students, we will summarize only the components of the EHA. The book sets out many reasons for parent participation. As Turnbull, Turnbull, and Wheat show (1982), and as we described in Chapter 1, the EHA assumed that parent participation helps students, parents, and professionals and that it is a way to make schools accountable to parents and students.

The EHA requires each state to establish procedures for consulting with people involved in or concerned with the education of students with disabilities, including their parents and guardians. It also requires the state agency to establish procedures for making the state special education plan available to the public and parents, having public hearings, giving adequate notice of those hearings, and allowing public comment on proposed policies, programs, and procedures before they are adopted.

The EHA also requires the state agency to create an advisory panel composed of individuals involved in or concerned with special education, including at least one representative of individuals with disabilities, teachers of students with disabilities, parents of such children and youth, state and local education officials, and administrators of special education programs. The panel is to advise the state agency on unmet needs, comment on the state's special education plan, policies, and regulations, and assist in developing and reporting data and evaluations of special education.

Parents and other members of the public may have access to information about state and local school special education programs. Not all information about every student is accessible, but generally parents and other members of the public may obtain all information concerning the programs (if not the individual children) that the state or local agency runs. (This is different than right of parents to have access to their child's education records. That type of access does not belong to the public).

Parents have the right to consent or object to the release of personally identifying information about their children. This protects family privacy. In addition to the right to assure confidentiality, parents also have the right of access to their own children's educational records. This assures that parents have an opportunity to hold schools accountable and helps them redress the parent-school power relationships. Parents also are entitled to a due process hearing to challenge the content of any school records. It is advisable for educators to offer to explain the child's records, have the records present at evaluation and IEP and other meetings with parents, agree to enter parent notes into the records, and practice good communication skills in explaining records to parents.

EFFECTS OF SIX PRINCIPLES ON SCHOOLS AND OTHER HUMAN SERVICES

Throughout this chapter we have emphasized the effects of the six principles on professionals, parents, children, and their mutual relationships. We also have emphasized those effects as they relate to schools. Yet it is clear that schools are not the only agencies that provide services to students who are disabled and their parents. Many other agencies do just that. For example, a student who has spina bifida may be a patient of a physician and a local hospital (health services) as well as a student in special education (education services). Another child, who is seriously emotionally disturbed, might be a client of a psychologist and a local mental health clinic (mental health services) as well as a student in special education (education services). And still another child might be a ward of the state and placed in a foster home under social services protection (social services) as well as be a student in a program for students who have moderate mental retardation (education services). It also may be that the health, mental health, and social services are paid for in part or in full by the school in which the student is enrolled. For that reason, as well as because the child's various services should be coordinated to become more effective, school professionals also must deal with professionals in the other service agencies as well as with the student's parents as they themselves negotiate the maze of service agencies.

One effect of the six principles has been to require professionals to work within a single system (e.g., education, health, mental health, or social services) but also to work with professionals in other systems and with parents who are involved in multiple systems. Let us see how that occurs and why it is important for professionals to understand and work within the service systems framework while they simultaneously work with a family systems framework.

The zero-reject principle, for example, has interesting effects on schools and other service systems. That principle requires all-inclusive coverage of children with disabilities, wherever they are and by whichever agency they are served. It also establishes a first-priority class of children, e.g., those who are the most severely disabled within each category of disabilities.

And it imposes on the state educational agency the responsibility for assuring that all children are appropriately served.

There are equally interesting effects of the other principles. The principle of nondiscriminatory evaluation requires multidisciplinary evaluation of students and mandates that the evaluation be multi-faceted. The principle of appropriate education turns the schools into student-centered agencies that provide a wide range of services, principally because of the related-services mandates. In turn, the principle of appropriate education compels professionals to work in interdisciplinary teams. The principle of the least restrictive placement makes regular education and special education relate to each other; it also requires schools to relate to other providers, such as local health, mental health, and social service agencies, private schools, hospitals, and public residential facilities. Due process requirements tend to hold school systems accountable for providing an appropriate education, which can mean coordinating services with a variety of other agencies. Finally, the parent participation principle requires coordinated state and local planning that involves parent representatives and the control of how information (i.e., records) is shared with other agencies.

What are the effects of these components of the six principles? A useful way to answer this question is to consider the education of Deidre: She is a 16-year-old student with mild mental retardation. She is in her first year at the local high school. She lives at home with her parents and has been involved in pre-vocational training at the junior high school. Now, she attends class at the high school for half of each day, and is involved in work-training and, sometimes, work-for-pay under the sponsorship of a vocational rehabilitation during the other half of each school day. From time to time, she works at the sheltered workshop, but, most of the time, she has supported-work training or employment in a competitive employment setting. Her school services consist of functional academics, occupational therapy, and vocational education. She also receives services in regular education. In addition, Deidre also is a client, from time to time, in mental health services from the school psychologist who teaches her self-control techniques to minimize her impulsivity.

Deidre's special education teacher must relate to several faculty members at the school as well as to several other professionals, not just educators, since all of the services are school-based. In a very real sense, the school has become a provider of or home-base for several types of services, not just special education. It has become a multi-faceted service system, requiring its own employees to be able to work (within it) with professionals from a variety of professions. It also has become a microcosm of the service systems that interact outside the school system, as in the cases of Angelino, Bobby, and Chrissy:

Angelino's middle-class, Hispanic American mother and father are divorced. His mother has legal custody of him, but his father has visitation rights. Angelino himself has serious health problems (heart and lung weakness from very premature birth). He is two-and-a-half years old, is often hospitalized for treatment, and has been enrolled in an early education program ever since he was discharged from a neonatal intensive care unit. Angelino has spent nearly half of this school year in the hospital undergoing heart surgery. While recuperating, his early education is furnished in the hospital. At other times, it is furnished in a center-based school program. He has four siblings, two living with his mother and two with his father.

Bobby is a ward of the state, and his legal guardian is the State Director of Human Services. His mother and father, who are White and whose socioeconomic status is "low," had their parental rights terminated by a court when a local Department of Social Services brought charges against them of abuse and neglect. Bobby has been classified as seriously emotionally disturbed. He is now 18 years old, and thus is regarded as an adult under his state's laws, but he also is still entitled to special education. Bobby has been involuntarily committed to a state psychiatric hospital as dangerous to himself or others. At the hospital, he is enrolled in a post-secondary vocational training program. He also receives a variety of psychiatric and psychological services, is on a regimen of psychotropic medication, and is a candidate for deinstitutionalization to a community group home under the supervision of a social services case worker and a psychologist at a community mental health center.

Chrissy is a Black ten-year-old whose father and mother are upper-class professionals; she lives at home with her parents. Chrissy has been classified as learning disabled and attends the local public schools. She is in a fourth-grade regular class and attends a resource room daily for instruction in reading and math. Chrissy receives psychological counseling once a week from a psychologist who is employed by a local mental health center. Once a month her parents join her for family therapy. Her parents were adamant in their insistence that the counseling be provided out of the school setting. They want to prevent at all costs Chrissy developing a reputation as a "problem student." Her two older sisters, both school-aged, are classified as academically gifted.

In each of these illustrations, the following are the common elements:

1. Each family has varying characteristics and interaction patterns, and each is at a different life-cycle stage. There are differences in the nature of the marriage, socioeconomic status, race, composition, and family-student-school relationships.

2. Each student is of a different age and has a different exceptionality but each is receiving special education (preschool, post-secondary, and elementary).

3. Each student is in a different setting (ordinary hospital and preschool, state psychiatric hospital and post-secondary program, and community-based elementary school).

4. Each student is served by a dominant service system and by at least one secondary service system. In Angelino's case, the health care system is dominant and the preschool special education system is secondary. In Bobby's case, the mental health system is dominant and the post-secondary school and social services systems are secondary. In Chrissy's case, the regular education system is dominant and the special education and mental health systems are secondary.

5. Each student is served by more than one professional, such as health, mental health, and social services providers. But for each child, special education professionals have primary or secondary roles in these service systems. Thus, each professional must interact with people from his or her own profession as well as with professionals from other disciplines and, sometimes, other systems.

What is important about these illustrations? It is that they show how complex schools and other systems have become, and how the interaction of systems requires educators to interact with other professionals and other agencies. Perhaps there was a time when these complex illustrations were not typical, when the ordinary case was one where the professional usually was the teacher, the parent was the mother, and the relationship was much simpler, e.g., teacher relating to child and mother. But if that situation ever really existed, it exists no more. Now, the ordinary situation involves manifold relationships. Educators, physicians, mental health experts, social workers, rehabilitation counselors and their respective systems (education, health, mental health, social service, and vocational rehabilitation), all relate to each other. Equally important, they relate in a variety of settings, such as schools, hospitals, mental hospitals, mental health clinics, social service agencies, and employment settings that are based in the community or on special campuses. Even when the services are campus-based, as in the case of the state psychiatric hospital, there are important linkages with community-based families and providers.

It may help to describe the service systems at the state and local levels graphically, individual by individual. In each, there is a primary service system—i.e., one that has initial responsibility for the child. There also is a secondary service system—i.e., one that is collateral to but supportive of the primary system. Remember this: in Angelino's case, the primary

Table 8–1
SYSTEMS CONCERNED WITH THE WELFARE OF EXCEPTIONAL
INDIVIDUALS (Community-based unless noted.)

PRIMARY	SECONDARY	POTENTIAL
ANGELINO State Department of Health *Health services*	State Department of Education *Special education*	State Department of Mental Health *Mental health out-patient care*
BOBBY State Department of Mental Health *Campus-based psychiatric care*	State Department of Education *Campus-based post-secondary education*	State Department of Social Services *Social services* State Department of Education *Local high school, junior college, or vocational-technical college*
CHRISSY State Department of Education *Special education*	State Department of Mental Health *Mental health*	State Department of Vocational Rehabilitation *Vocational rehabilitation*
DEIDRE State Department of Education *Education* Special Education Functional Academics Vocational Education Related Services Occupational Therapy School Psychology Regular Education	State Department of Vocational Rehabilitation *Vocational rehabilitation, sheltered workshop employment and train-ing, and competitivework employment*	

service system is health; in Bobby's, mental health; in Chrissy's, special education; and in Deidre's, special and regular education as well as related services. Each also is involved with a secondary service-provider system and some of these students have potential providers who are likely to serve them in the future. Finally, each is receiving special education, which is the permeating system. (See Table 8–1.)

THE HUB OF SERVICE SYSTEMS

For each of these children to receive a free appropriate public education and to have other services that support them and their family, it is important for these service systems and the professionals in each system to interact positively. Each professional must realize that he or she depends on, and is depended on by, other professionals; the effective professional is interdependent. No professional acts alone; each acts as part of separate but interlocking systems. Thus, the professional can be more effective in working with families and other professionals if he or she understands human service systems, the primary, secondary, and potential service systems. And each, being a specialist as well as a generalist, must be effective in interdisciplinary or interagency work.

To accomplish this, each professional has to give up some autonomy and work at being a collaborator in order to function as a member of a team. Cooperation must replace competition. The effective professional is a collaborator, one who has a specialization (such as special education, social work, psychology, educational administration, or a related service field) and a broad understanding of, and ability to contribute to, the many systems that serve families and students who have exceptionalities.

The effective professional recognizes that special education permeates the services that students and families receive. It is the hub around which other service systems operate; it is the connector of services. It is not always the primary service system—sometimes, for example, a student and family will be served principally by a health or mental health system. But it is a constant system, always present so long as the student is enrolled in school. This is because federal and state law require the provision of a free appropriate public education to all disabled children and youth, and many states have additional special education laws for gifted and talented students.

In the best of all worlds, the manifold service systems and the various professionals would relate positively to the student and each other by regarding the special educational system as the hub of the service network. They would envision it as the system where all other service systems and professionals converge. Figure 8–1 depicts such a view of the service system (see p. 196).

Here, the point of the greatest system interaction is special education, which is legally responsible not only for specially designed individualized instruction but also for the related services, such as health (for diagnostic purposes only), and for linking the student to mental health, social services, and vocational rehabilitation.

Of course, not everyone would agree that special education *should* be the point of convergence, the point of greatest professional interaction, if the result would be that special education would serve as the dominant or controlling system. Indeed, we do not advocate that special education—and special educators—should be the dominant or controlling system and professionals. Instead, we believe that there should be no such thing as a dominant or controlling system or professionals. We believe that there

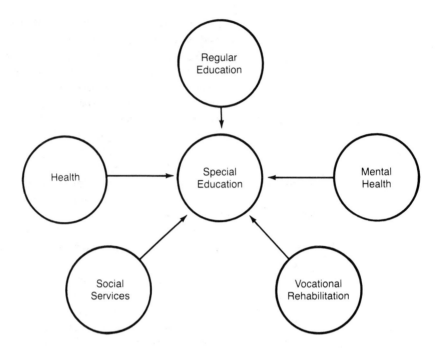

Figure 8–1
SPECIAL EDUCATION AS THE HUB

should be primary and secondary systems, where there has to be more than one system, with primary and secondary professionals. We also believe that the primary and secondary roles should be determined on the basis of a student's individual needs. Moreover, we believe that no role is necessarily permanent. For example, Angelino may have to be served by the health system as the primary system for some time but not always, or Bobby need not always be served by the mental health system in its primary role. Systems and professionals should take on primary or secondary roles as a student's needs change. But as long as the student is eligible to attend school and is enrolled, education (special and regular) always has a role. Likewise, other systems do not necessarily have that same permanence in the student's life. They may come into play and later recede as the individual's needs change.

The point is, the six principles have given education a permanent role as long as the student is eligible for education and is enrolled in it. They declare that it properly is the point of convergence. This means that professionals in health, mental health, and social services will have to relate to education. It also means that educators will have to relate to professionals in the other systems; and they also will have to relate to professionals from other disciplines who work in the education system. Finally, it means that all professionals, whatever their discipline or service system, will have to relate to families. This is so for two reasons: education is the point of convergence, and families have special rights to participate in the education of their children.

Of course, in the real world there are many instances where there is no convergence—where systems and professionals do not interact or interact in a counter-productive fashion. Consider that fact in light of the report by Mary Akerley (1985), the mother of a son with autism, as she discusses educators and physicians:

> . . . We worked with two doctors—sequentially—at that school, neither of whom ever came right out and said, "You caused the problem", even though both based everything they said on that premise. . . .
>
> The worst professional damage—not to us but to Eddie—occurred during this time. We took him back to the neurologist for a re-evaluation, as she had suggested we do as soon as we felt he could endure all the testing involved. When we advised Doctor Number One of our plans, she came close to losing her professional cool. "You didn't ask my permission! You're going to put him through all that for nothing; you're clutching at straws just to prove it's not your fault! If you go through with this, he can't stay here."
>
> Her diatribe produced a fury in me that was quelled only by her last sentence. Fear took over. There is not exactly a wealth of choices when it comes to schools for autistic children, and this one was doing a good job. We didn't want Eddie to lose this help that he needed so badly, but we didn't want him deprived of any helpful medical intervention either. It was a cruel choice, especially since it was so unnecessary and artificial. Thank God we again had the guts to take over and be proper parents. Eddie and I moved into Children's Hospital for three days for the most complete neurological evaluation possible. We had, in effect, called the school's bluff. They didn't want to give up what they had termed, in our presence, "an interesting case" (us or Eddie?)—especially one which looked more and more like a success story. Doctor Number One even visited Eddie in the hospital. (p. 26)

In this case, we see damaging competition between educators and physicians. How much better it would have been if there had been cooperation, both for Mary as well as for Eddie. The purpose of this book is not to describe how professionals can work together to prevent this and other problems; rather its focus is on parent-professional collaboration. Nonetheless, many of the communication techniques that we discuss inChapters 6 and 7 are likely to be useful in professional-to-professional relationships.

It is also true that there are many road blocks to professional-to-professional relationships and to effective relationships between school systems and other human service systems. Again, it is not the purpose of this book to describe them and suggest how they can be overcome. The purpose of this portion of this chapter is to show how the six principles vastly change the nature of relationships among parents and professionals by requiring parent-professional interaction among school and other systems. Precisely because of this complicating change, parent-professional relationships, and professional responses to family systems and within professional systems, are critical to develop. This book addresses those relationships and responses.

Unfortunately, there are times when parents themselves believe they have to be the ones who must force the professionals to cooperate. That was the experience of Jim and Rani Gallagher (1985) when they were seeking help for their son, Sean, who had serious asthma problems:

> One of the mysterious factors, from a parental standpoint, is why the professionals consistently have difficulty in working cooperatively with one another to the patient's benefit. At one time, since we had become aware of the wide range of factors involved in severe asthma, we tried to bring together the relevant disciplines to create a single treatment program. This meant bringing together a triumvirate of psychiatrist, endocrinologist, and asthma specialist to see if they could agree on a single, comprehensive treatment program. Our attempt to get such people together to talk was only a partial success; it took months before we could get a meeting. It is not encouraging for parents to see that professional roles, status, and internal conflicts so manifestly obstruct the benefits to their child. (p. 238)

It should not be necessary for the Akerleys and Gallaghers and for so many other parents and professionals to experience so much diversion from the ultimate task, which is bringing benefits to the child and the family. That is precisely why professionals must understand the family systems approach and how to apply the six principles to bring the school, as a multi-faceted and multidisciplinary system, and the other human service systems to bear on the child and family. The next chapters elaborate on the child-family centeredness, primarily of special education and secondarily of other human service systems.

Chapter 9

Referral and Evaluation

Students and their families enter special education through the process of referral and evaluation. This chapter will describe how these processes relate to implementation of the legal requirements discussed in Chapter 9 and provide meaningful opportunities to involve families in information dissemination and decision making. By handling referral and evaluation processes in competent and sensitive ways, you can help ensure that families' initial experiences with special education are positive. Initial success is an excellent predictor of ongoing success. Thus, the outcomes of referral and evaluating experiences have both short and long-term implications for family-professional partnerships. As one father stated:

> Finally, after years of vague doubts and haunting fears, there was a reason why Melissa was experiencing problems. As the psychologist explained the test results to us, our daughter was no longer "lazy" or "crazy." She had a learning disability and there was something we could all do to help. I'll never forget that first conference and I'll be eternally grateful. They gave us more than information—they gave us moral support.

COORDINATION OF THE REFERRAL AND EVALUATION PROCESS

The Education for the Handicapped Act (EHA) does not address the referral process, yet it contains many regulations pertaining to nondiscriminatory evaluations. State and local school districts have established their own policies covering both processes of referral and evaluation. This general process is outlined in Figure 9–1.

The school-based committee with overall coordination responsibility is the special services committee. The role of this committee is to coordinate the process of identification and placement. It typically is comprised of special services personnel (i.e., teachers, psychologists, social workers, counselors, therapists) and administrators. The committee is named differently in different schools, e.g., child study team, eligibility team, multi-disciplinary team, or special education committee. If you are not a member of the special services committee in the program where you work, we encourage you to talk with the chairperson of the committee to inquire about the particular procedures, schedules, and forms used throughout the process of Figure 9–1. It is important you know how this general process is applied within your particular setting. Each of the steps identified in Figure 9–1 will be discussed, in turn, in this chapter.

Figure 9–1 ▶
SEQUENCE AND FUNCTIONS OF REFERRAL AND EVALUATION

Note. From Developing and Implementing Individualized Education Programs *by A. P. Turnbull, B. Strickland, and J. C. Brantley, 1982, Columbus, OH: Charles E. Merrill Publishing Co.*

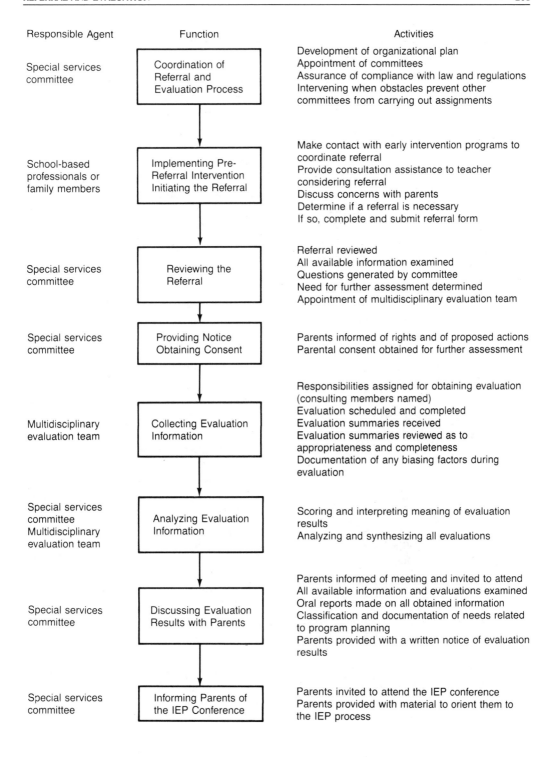

Responsible Agent	Function	Activities
Special services committee	Coordination of Referral and Evaluation Process	Development of organizational plan Appointment of committees Assurance of compliance with law and regulations Intervening when obstacles prevent other committees from carrying out assignments
School-based professionals or family members	Implementing Pre-Referral Intervention Initiating the Referral	Make contact with early intervention programs to coordinate referral Provide consultation assistance to teacher considering referral Discuss concerns with parents Determine if a referral is necessary If so, complete and submit referral form
Special services committee	Reviewing the Referral	Referral reviewed All available information examined Questions generated by committee Need for further assessment determined Appointment of multidisciplinary evaluation team
Special services committee	Providing Notice Obtaining Consent	Parents informed of rights and of proposed actions Parental consent obtained for further assessment
Multidisciplinary evaluation team	Collecting Evaluation Information	Responsibilities assigned for obtaining evaluation (consulting members named) Evaluation scheduled and completed Evaluation summaries received Evaluation summaries reviewed as to appropriateness and completeness Documentation of any biasing factors during evaluation
Special services committee Multidisciplinary evaluation team	Analyzing Evaluation Information	Scoring and interpreting meaning of evaluation results Analyzing and synthesizing all evaluations
Special services committee	Discussing Evaluation Results with Parents	Parents informed of meeting and invited to attend All available information and evaluations examined Oral reports made on all obtained information Classification and documentation of needs related to program planning Parents provided with a written notice of evaluation results
Special services committee	Informing Parents of the IEP Conference	Parents invited to attend the IEP conference Parents provided with material to orient them to the IEP process

IMPLEMENTING PRE-REFERRAL INTERVENTION AND INITIATING THE REFERRAL

A referral is a formal request for multi-disciplinary assistance in identifying the special needs of students. Referrals for special services can be initiated by parents, other family members, community professionals, or school professionals. Typically children with severe congenital disabilities are identified during infancy and increasingly are enrolled in early intervention and preschool programs. Thus, their referral to the public school program frequently occurs from early childhood professionals. By the time children who have received early intervention enter the school system, they typically have already received one or more comprehensive evaluations which have been reviewed with their families. For parents, the initial impact of diagnosis discussed in Chapter 5 has already started. Also, they are already somewhat familiar with referral, evaluation, and program planning procedures. We suggest that members of special services committees familiarize themselves with the community early intervention and preschool programs and establish strategies to help children and their families make a smooth transition from early childhood service delivery system to the school system. (Chapter 12 includes a discussion of ideas to assist families to make this transition.) Once these children become eligible for public school services and are referred by their families or by early childhood professionals, they follow the sequence outlined in Figure 9–1.

A different situation occurs with children who initially manifest characteristics creating concern about their academic or behavioral performance after they enter school. Children identified as disabled during school years typically have milder disabilities than those identified shortly after birth. Also, later-identified children may live in geographical areas that do not have a comprehensive identification program during the preschool period.

Whatever the reason, the important point is that in many cases, problems are initially identified during the school years. School-based professionals need to know the indicators of special needs related to every category of exceptionality (Schulz & Turnbull, 1984; Pasanella & Volkmor, 1981). A major indicator is school achievement that is significantly below expectation levels. It is necessary to document concerns by reviewing the student's classwork, homework, tests, and behavioral observations in order to pinpoint general levels of performance and any patterns in performance that tend to be associated with success or failure (e.g., individual versus group activities, oral versus written work). Many schools have checklists to help you identify your concerns.

Before initiating a referral for a student with a suspected mild disability, we suggest that schools adopt the policy of providing consultation assistance to the teacher. This process involves conducting an assessment of the discrepancy between the student's performance and the teacher's and parent's desired expectations and then implementing an instructional program to narrow this discrepancy (Graden, Casey, & Christenson, 1985). The rationale for more attention to the pre-referral phase is provided by the learning disabilities research team at the University of Minnesota:

> In their summary of 5 years of research on the assessment and decision-making process for learning disabled (LD) students, Ysseldyke et al. (1983) described the current situation as one in which students are referred in increasing numbers (often for reasons less to do with the student's classroom functioning than with teacher, school system, and other variables) and, once referred, tested almost automatically (often with technically inadequate tests). Once tested, a large majority of the students are placed in special education (often on the basis of LD-definitional criteria that are inconsistent and inherently problematic). (p. 378)

It is important in pre-referral intervention to discuss your concerns and possible interventions with the student's parents either at a regular parent-teacher conference or at a specially called conference.

The communication skills and strategies discussed in Chapters 6 and 7 will serve you well in sharing concerns with parents. Parents' understanding can be enhanced by using specific descriptors of performance levels:

> Stuart completed 13 of 100 additional facts on his timed test; every other student in the class was able to complete 85 or more. Stuart hid his paper and appeared to be embarrassed by his score.

You can also show parents samples of their child's work. If prior communication on report cards or in conferences about the child's performance has been accurate and explicit, parents already will have initial warnings that their child's performance is not totally satisfactory or that their child's performance is accelerated in the case of giftedness. One good reason for honest and full disclosure all along is that parents have a more gradual recognition that special help may be needed. Thus, information about special needs will not totally surprise them.

A parent conference to share concerns also enables parents to verify observations at home or information received previously from professionals outside the school with the concerns you have noted at school. Information from families can provide relevant documentation and detail to analyze the concerns in the most precise way.

What if the parents do not agree with your concerns and express strong objection to your view of their child? If the parents do disagree, it is important to consider their perspectives carefully. We must always allow for the possibility that their perspective is accurate. As one mother commented to the author:

> Roberta's teacher told me that she wanted Roberta to get special testing because of her poor reading skills. I told her that I didn't think Roberta read so badly. She reads comics, cookbooks, road signs, and written messages on TV. That's what my older kids did when they were in second grade. The teacher didn't believe me—she thought I was just sticking up for Roberta. She said Roberta couldn't do that. I told her that I see it with my own eyes at home. Why would I lie? What she does at school is not everything she does.

This mother has a good point—performance at school is not everything. Often students perform differently in different environments. When parents' observations differ from yours, ask them to describe their view of their child's performance and reasons they think can account for the discrepancy. Strive to identify procedures for observing the child at both school and home to gather more information to verify or disconfirm concerns.

The pre-referral intervention may be successful and preclude the need for formal referral and evaluation. Preliminary data indicate that some schools have substantially reduced the numbers of students who proceeded through the total process of referral evaluation and placement (Graden, Casey, & Bonstrom, 1985). If the pre-referral intervention is unsuccessful in improving the student's performance and appropriate modifications cannot be made, a referral for evaluation should be sent forward to the special services committee. Since referral forms vary from school to school, you will need to use the one approved in your school.

To the greatest extent possible, try to obtain parent cooperation before initiating a formal referral. The EHA does not require parent consent for referral; however, some states and local school districts do. Even if consent is not required in your school district, we will shortly discuss the requirement that parents give their consent for their child to receive an *initial* evaluation. Thus, the earliest parent cooperation and support possible will help to facilitate the total process. We encourage you to involve parents in the decision to initiate the referral as much as possible. It is understandable that the decision to refer their child for evaluation will create anxious and sad feelings for many parents. Your communication with the parents needs to be sensitive to their feelings.

REVIEWING THE REFERRAL

The special services committee is responsible for reviewing the information on the referral form to decide the most appropriate response for addressing concerns. They may suggest such alternative actions as gathering more information on the pre-referral intervention, waiting several months on the suspicion that the problem is temporary, providing remedial education rather than evaluating the student for special education, or deciding to pursue a multidisciplinary evaluation of the student. Parents need to be informed if an evaluation is not pursued, the reasons for the decision, and the plans developed to respond to the concerns initially triggering the referral. If parents disagree with this decision, they can request an evaluation and expect to have their request honored. This is so because, typically, the special services committee decides in favor of pursuing an evaluation. One study indicated that 92% of students referred were subsequently evaluated (Algozzine, Christenson, & Ysseldyke, 1982).

PROVIDING NOTICE AND OBTAINING CONSENT

As we noted in Chapter 8, the EHA provides parents an opportunity to participate in educational decisions. A major strategy for accomplishing this is to require schools to inform parents on their child's performance (notice) and to involve parents in decision making (consent). Typically, one member of the special services committee assumes responsibility for communicating with the family to provide notice, obtain consent, and carry out the other aspects of parent contact discussed in this chapter. Committee members use various criteria in selecting the most appropriate person for these responsibilities, e.g., the professional who has already established a positive relationship with the parents, the one who has had or is likely to have in the future the most frequent contact, the one whose ideological or communication style is most complimentary to the parents, or the one who has some time available.

We will now review how the requirements pertaining to notice and consent apply to the evaluation process.

Providing Notice

The EHA requires that schools provide a written notice to parents in their dominant language within a reasonable time period before the student's evaluation status is changed. Parents must be notified when the school:

1. Proposes to initiate or change the identification, evaluation, or educational placement of the child or the provision of a free appropriate public education to the child, or
2. Refuses to initiate or change the identification, evaluation, or educational placement of the child or the provision of a free appropriate public education to the child. (*Federal Register,* 1977, p. 42495)

The primary purpose of notifying parents (in writing) is to provide them with information on the reasons for the special service committee's decision. The EHA statute specifies the content requirements of the notice:

1. A full explanation of all of the procedural safeguards available to the parents . . . ,
2. A description of the action proposed or refused by the agency, an explanation of why the agency proposes or refuses to take the action, and a description of any options the agency considered and the reasons why those options were rejected,
3. A description of each evaluation procedure, test, record, or report the agency used as a basis for the proposal or refusal, and
4. A description of any other factors which are relevant to the agency's proposal or refusal. (*Federal Register,* 1977, p. 42495)

"Procedural safeguards" refers to some legal rights of parents. Typically, school districts have a written list of rights that they send to all parents. If the school district in which you work has such a list, we suggest that you review it to assess whether or not you believe it is comprehensible to the parents with whom you work. You might even suggest changes to eliminate jargon and to enhance clarity and relevance.

The second required component of the notice is a description of the school's proposed course of action, rationale, and alternatives. At this point in the process, the proposed action is to evaluate the student from a multidisciplinary perspective to determine whether a disability exists and the most helpful type of individual programming. Even if the reasons for this recommendation have previously been explained to parents during conferences, it is important to iterate them in writing and to identify why other possible options are less appropriate than evaluation. For example, it will essentially help to summarize the information on the referral form and the major points of discussion from the special services committee meeting in your explanation to parents.

Third, the notice must contain descriptions of assessment procedures, data, and other information used to make the decision to pursue a multidisciplinary evaluation. You can summarize information from the pre-referral intervention or from the discussion of the special service committee. It also helps to include the names and purposes of tests the evaluation team plans to administer to the student. The purposes of each test will probably be more meaningful to most parents than the actual names.

Finally, any relevant information the special services committee considered in its decision to pursue an evaluation should be shared with families. Aside from academic information, this could include information associated with health status, peer relationships, or other relevant issues.

Obtaining Consent

Requiring parental consent for the initial special education evaluation means that parents must participate in the decision of whether or not a multidisciplinary evaluation should be conducted. The EHA definition of consent is

1. The parent has been fully informed of all information relevant to the activity for which consent is sought, in his or her native language or other mode of communication;
2. The parent understands and agrees in writing to the carrying out of the activity for which his or her consent is sought, and the consent describes that activity and lists the records (if any) which will be released and to whom; and
3. The parent understands that the granting of consent is voluntary on the part of the parent and may be revoked at any time. (*Federal Register,* 1977, p. 42494)

There are two instances in which parental consent must be obtained. These include

1. Conducting a preplacement evaluation and
2. Initial placement of a handicapped child in a program providing special education and related services. (*Federal Register,* 1977, p. 42495)

A *preplacement evaluation* is the initial evaluation following the child's referral. As you learned in Chapter 8, students must be re-evaluated by a multidisciplinary team every three years. The re-evaluation requires parental notice but not parental consent. The *initial placement* refers to the first time a student is placed in special education. Parental consent is required for the initial placement but not for subsequent changes in placement.

The concept of consent implies both the right to give and withhold it. Consider a conflict that could arise:

> You have been very concerned about Eddie's sullenness and withdrawal. Some days you believe he is pulled so far into himself that you absolutely cannot reach him. He stares blankly, cries frequently, and has practically no interaction with you or his peers. Meanwhile, his school performance is plunging downward. You have met with his parents individually on several occasions, as has the school counselor. His parents refuse to acknowledge his problems and assert emphatically that no child of theirs will ever be identified as emotionally disturbed. You believe it is your professional duty to Eddie to try to locate special help for him and you realize you simply do not have the expertise to deal with his needs. You completed a referral form with thorough documentation and reviewed it with the special services

committee. They concurred with your recommendation of a psychiatric and psychoeducational evaluation. When the school counselor met with Eddie's parents to review the notice with them and request their consent, they refused to even consider the possibility of an evaluation. Frustrated, you are caught between Eddie's needs, his parents' needs, and your professional judgment.

What legal options do you have when parents refuse to give their consent? EHA provides the following options:

1. Where state law requires parental consent before a child is evaluated or initially provided special education and related services, state procedures govern the public agency in overriding a parent's refusal to consent.

2. Where there is no state law requiring consent before a child is evaluated or initially provided special education and related services, the public agency may use the hearing procedures (outlined in the law) to determine if the child may be evaluated or initially provided special education and related services without parental consent. (*Federal Register,* 1977, p. 42495)

We advocate the use of negotiation and mediation to resolve conflict whenever possible (see Chapter 11). When negotiation and mediation are unsuccessful, however, it is important to recognize that parental refusal to give consent does not end the process of providing an appropriate education to students with exceptionalities. On the contrary, school professionals may challenge the decisions made by parents. A family systems perspective can help to provide insight into the intended and unintended consequences of such action for the parent-child relationship. The ethical implications of parent-professional-child conflicts are discussed in Chapter 14.

Supplementing Written Communication

Even though the notice to parents must be provided in writing and their consent must also be obtained in writing, face-to-face contact can be very advantageous at this point in the evaluation process. All communication does not have to be restricted to a written format. You can consider several options: (a) send parents the written notice and consent form to review and schedule a follow-up meeting to discuss the need for an evaluation and answer any questions; (b) have a meeting in which you give the notice and consent form to parents and review the written information with them; and (c) have a meeting to share information with parents orally and then follow-up the meeting with a written notice and consent form. It is puzzling to second-guess the preferences of parents. Your best approach is usually simply to ask parents which option they would prefer. The face-to-face meeting can be helpful in developing a trusting relationship, providing support for parents' anxieties and concerns, and orienting them to what they can expect throughout the evaluation and IEP process.

COLLECTING EVALUATION INFORMATION

We discussed the legal requirements for nondiscriminatory evaluation in Chapter 8 and made some suggestions about the meaning of those requirements for professionals. Here, we want to discuss the meaning in greater detail.

The special services committee is responsible for appointing a multidisciplinary team to collect evaluation information. The purpose is to determine if the student has an exceptionality and to identify the nature and extent of special education and related services that the student needs. The only EHA requirement for multidisciplinary team composition is that the team must include at least one teacher or other specialist with knowledge in the area of the suspected disability. There is no explicit requirement that family members be involved in the actual collection of evaluation information. There is a requirement, however, that the team must:

> Draw upon information from a variety of sources, including aptitude and achievement tests, teacher recommendations, physical condition, special or cultural background, and adaptive behavior. (*Federal Register,* 1977, p. 42497)

Family members can provide valuable information from a unique perspective, but often family perspectives are not sought. In a two-year study examining the EHA impact on nine children and their families representing diverse exceptionalities and backgrounds, Halpern (1982) reported that parents' perspectives during the evaluation process are not actively sought. He concluded that parents have to take the initiative to share their perspectives.

Many options exist for families to participate in the evaluation process. One option is for them to participate in a family systems interview to inform professionals of family needs, interests, and preferences. This interview can follow the protocol included in Appendix A, or that protocol can be adapted to special considerations of a particular family and multidisciplinary team. Social workers and counselors have special training in family interviewing and can assume this responsibility within the context of the multidisciplinary team. This interview can provide valuable insight into the families' perceptions and expectations about the evaluation and their child's potential participation in a special education program. We advocate the inclusion of a family systems interview as an integral part of the evaluation process to ensure that the child's evaluation is viewed within the ecological context of family life. Furthermore, such an interview provides an excellent way to gain insight into family needs, priorities, and preferences.

A second option for including families in the process of collecting evaluation information is to ask them to provide information on their child's developmental skills in home and community environments. As we discussed earlier in this chapter, students perform differently in different environments. Thus, a comprehensive view of a student necessitates collecting performance data from settings in addition to the school. Vincent and her colleagues suggest that at least one report from parents or family members should be included in every multidisciplinary evaluation (Vincent, Laten, Salisbury, Brown, & Baumgart, 1981).

A variety of family inventories has been developed. Traditionally, most of these have been in the area of adaptive behavior; however, more recently, the focus of families as evaluators has expanded to a variety of other domains. An extremely helpful inventory enabling you to pinpoint a young child's behavior outside of school has been developed by Vincent et al. at the University of Wisconsin (1983). This inventory, called the Parent Inventory of Child Development in Nonschool Environments, is divided into five sections:

1. Affective Behavior—Completed by everyone,
2. Age of Dependence—Birth to 24 months,
3. Age of Exploring—24 to 36 months,
4. Age of Beginning Independence—36 to 48 months, and
5. Age of Independence—48 to 60 months.

The child is rated on a list of skills based on his or her consistency in performing the skill and whether or not the skill would represent a relevant instructional goal. Some typical questions relating to the affective behavior section are:

> Does your child: show a consistent sleeping pattern? want to be held a reasonable amount of time (that is, does not want to be held all the time)? adapt easily to changes in routine such as relatives coming to visit or taking a trip? respond appropriately to car seat, crib, or playpen, (that is, fusses a little bit sometimes but eventually settles down)?

The inventory can be completed by a variety of family members or child care providers.

Although most family inventories occur at the early childhood level, families can also participate in evaluations at the secondary level. Table

9–1 illustrates a portion of a family inventory for secondary students with moderate and severe disabilities in the area of home living. This inventory was developed as part of an intervention program aimed at assisting families in planning for the adult future of their son or daughter (Turnbull, Brotherson, et al., 1984).

This same future planning program developed another inventory—Student Preference and Choice Questionnaire—that is relevant to include in the evaluation process. Because many students with severe disabilities are unable to participate actively in their IEP conference by verbally

---

Table 9–1
FAMILY INVENTORY

Person Completing Inventory: _____

For: _____ Date: _____

DOMESTIC/HOME LIVING

Here are some specific home living activities which people perform on a daily basis. Please indicate: at what level your son or daughter participates, if this is an activity needed for the future, and if you feel any of these activities should be addressed in the IEP conference.

1—Child participates independently.
2—Child participates with assistance.
3—Child does not participate.

4—Child needs skill for future environment.
5—Parent needs to discuss activity at IEP conference.

A. *Self–care*
_____ 1. Indicates he/she wants to go to the bathroom
_____ 2. Toilets self
_____ 3. Dresses/undresses self with fasteners (buttons, zippers, etc.)
_____ 4. Dresses self without fasteners (velcro, pullovers, etc.)
_____ 5. Grooms self (e.g., hair care, brushes teeth, applies deodorant, etc.)
_____ 6. Selects own clothing (seasonally appropriate, color-coordinated)
_____ 7. Feeds self
_____ 8. Indicates he/she wants to be repositioned or placed in different location
_____ 9.
_____ 10.

B. *Clothing Care*
_____ 1. Puts laundry in hamper
_____ 2. Puts laundry in washing machine
_____ 3. Washes/dries his/her own clothing
_____ 4. Able to apply iron-on patches/hemming tape on clothing
_____ 5. Folds clothes and puts them in drawers
_____ 6. Hangs clothes on hangers/hooks
_____ 7.
_____ 8.

C. *Meal Preparation*
_____ 1. Makes own drinks (juice, coffee, iced tea, etc.)
_____ 2. Makes sandwiches
_____ 3. Puts dishes on table for mealtime
_____ 4. Clears table after meals
_____ 5. Places dishes in sink after meals
_____ 6. Selects two or three items at grocery store
_____ 7. Puts groceries away in cabinet or refrigerator
_____ 8. Selects food/drink items for meals
_____ 9.
_____ 10.

D. *House Maintenance*
_____ 1. Dusts furniture
_____ 2. Sweeps floor
_____ 3. Mops floor
_____ 4. Makes bed
_____ 5. Cleans own room
_____ 6. Empties trash
_____ 7. Waters indoor plants
_____ 8. Feeds/waters pets
_____ 9. Grooms/brushes pets
_____ 10.

List, in order of importance, three domestic/home living activities that you would most like your son/daughter to learn. Under each activity, describe what you feel your son/daughter needs to learn that would enable him/her to perform the activity more independently:

1. _____
   _____
   _____
   _____

2. _____
   _____
   _____
   _____

3. _____
   _____
   _____
   _____

Note: From How to Plan for My Child's Adult Future: A Three-Part Process to Future Planning *by A. P. Turnbull, M. J. Brotherson, G. J. Bronicki, H. A. Benson, J. Houghton, C. Roeder-Gordon, and J. A. Summers, 1984, Future Planning Project, University Affiliated Facility, Bureau of Child Research, Lawrence, Kansas.*

explaining their preferences, we developed an inventory that family members can complete to identify the student's preferences and choices as a basis for instructional planning. We have excerpted sample questions from the inventory (see Table 9–2). Special educators are increasingly recognizing the importance of tailoring instructional programs to student

---

Table 9–2
STUDENT PREFERENCE AND CHOICE QUESTIONNAIRE

---

1. How does _____ indicate his/her likes/dislikes?

		Likes	*Dislikes*
a.	Laughs	_____	_____
b.	Cries	_____	_____
c.	Facial Expressions	_____	_____
d.	Screams	_____	_____
e.	Tantrums	_____	_____
f.	Looks at people	_____	_____
g.	Looks at objects	_____	_____
h.	Moves body	_____	_____
i.	Points/Reaches	_____	_____
j.	Imitates actions	_____	_____
k.	Vocalizes	_____	_____
l.	Gestures	_____	_____
m.	Other _____	_____	_____
n.	_____	_____	_____
o.	_____	_____	_____

2. What kinds of choices does _____ usually have the opportunity to make? Please provide examples:

_____

_____

_____

_____

3. What types of choices are most comfortable for _____ to make?

_____

_____

Why do you think these are most comfortable? _____

_____

4. Do you want an objective included in _____'s individualized education program (IEP) that will help him/her learn the skill of making choices?

Yes   No

5. Has _____ ever indicated what kind of job he/she would like to have? If so, what is it?

_____

_____

Have you or the school personnel identified the critical skills _____ will need to perform this job?

Yes   No

If yes, which skills would you like included in _____ 's next IEP?

_____

_____

_____

If no, discuss with the school personnel how these skills could be identified and by whom.

6. Has _____ ever indicated where he/she would like to live after high school or later in adulthood?

Yes   No

If yes, where? _____

_____

Have you or the school personnel identified the critical skills _____ will need in the place he/she chooses to live?

Yes   No

If yes, which skills would you like included in _____ 's next IEP?

_____

_____

_____

If no, discuss with the school personnel how these skills could be identified and by whom.

7. In general, at what time of day does _____ prefer to be active and productive?

_____

_____

8. At what time of day does _____ prefer to rest and relax?

_____

9. Most of the time, _____ prefers to be:
   (circle the appropriate response)

a.	Alone	With one other person	With small group	With large group	Unable to assess

b.	Independent	Supervised	Dependent	Unable to assess

c. With age peers	With persons older	With persons younger	Unable to assess
d. Involved in: Activities of fast pace	Activities of moderate pace	Activities of slow pace	Unable to assess
e. Engage in: Highly repetitive activities	Moderately repetitive activities	Nonrepetitive activities	Unable to assess
f. In highly competitive situations	Moderately competitive situations	Noncompetitive situations	Unable to assess
g. In highly structured situations	Moderately structured situations	Loosely structured situations	Unable to assess

The information in this questionnaire can help parents and educators develop an individualized education program (IEP) based upon the choices and preferences of your child. This questionnaire can help identify the appropriate evaluations, goals, objectives, and related services that need to be included in the IEP document. It can also help identify the time of day and in what environment your son or daughter prefers to learn. It can be a valuable tool for planning an individualized education program.

Note. From *How to Plan for My Child's Adult Future: A Three-Part Process to Future Planning* by A. P. Turnbull, M. J. Brotherson, G. J. Bronicki, H. A. Benson, J. Houghton, C. Roeder-Gordon, and J. A. Summers, 1984, *Future Planning Project, University Affiliated Facility, Bureau of Child Research, Lawrence, Kansas.*

preferences and teaching choice-making skills (Guess, Benson, & Siegel-Causey, 1985; Turnbull & Turnbull, 1985).

An issue of particular concern is insuring that the needs of families from diverse ethnic backgrounds are addressed during the evaluation phase. A disturbing finding discussed in Chapter 2 is that a significantly higher percentage of minority, as compared to majority, students are referred for psychological testing; however, psychologists contact parents of minority students less often than parents of majority students (Tomlinson, Acker, Canter, & Lindborg, 1977). Helpful guidelines for addressing the special needs of minority students and their families throughout the evaluation process is provided by Sales and Fox (1982) and Marion (1979).

Families can provide many different kinds of information during the evaluation process. The multidisciplinary team can match the evaluation needs of the student with the particular appropriate opportunity for families to share information. As in all other areas, some families will welcome involvement in this process, while others will shy away from it.

ANALYZING EVALUATION INFORMATION

The multidisciplinary team assumes responsibility for analyzing evaluation information. This is done at two levels: (a) scoring and interpreting the meaning of each evaluation instrument, and (b) analyzing and synthesizing all evaluations to obtain an overall composite of the student's performance. The first task typically is done individually by multidisciplinary team members and the latter task at a team meeting. The goal of the meeting should be to determine whether the student has an exceptionality, the particular type of exceptionality, and a profile of the student's strengths and weaknesses for the purpose of individual program planning. This analysis provides the basis of the decision on the appropriateness of the student's placement into special education. It also enables the team to present a composite view to the family rather than the fragmentation of discrete scores from several different instruments.

Family members usually do not participate at this point of the process. The scoring, analysis, and synthesis of evaluation instruments requires technical expertise that most families do not have. Some families, however, are knowledgeable in this area and may value the opportunity to participate with the multidisciplinary team in this preliminary review of information. Additionally, some families value being present at any discussion related to their child's possible identification for special education. They may perceive that the best strategy for having their perspective considered is to be part of the decision-making process from its earliest point. Involvement in the task of analyzing evaluation information can vary depending upon its appropriateness for a given family.

DISCUSSING EVALUATION RESULTS WITH PARENTS

How Parents Are Informed

As we previously noted in Chapter 8 and in this chapter, parents must receive written notification any time school personnel propose or refuse to change a student's identification, evaluation, educational placement, or provision of a free appropriate education. This means that written notification (or a written summary) of evaluation results must follow the initial evaluation. The required content of the notice was described in this chapter. Re-evaluations every three years do not require a written notice. However, we recommended in Chapter 8 that professionals should follow the "touch-base" rule. In addition, a good rule of thumb is to always give families a copy of the re-evaluation summary. Full disclosure of information on a continuing basis frequently enhances parental trust and the probability of their making informed decisions.

Thus, after initial evaluations are completed, parents must be informed in a written fashion. It is also very important to have an opportunity tointerpret findings orally to them. As we pointed out earlier, evaluation information can be highly technical; written explanations may not be fully informative. Another clear benefit of discussions is that family perspectives concerning the evaluation data can be extremely helpful in validating or disconfirming them. Parents can share information on the child's special needs, confirm whether or not the performance described by professionals is typical, and make connections between the current and previous evaluations completed by persons outside of the school such as pediatricians and preschool teachers.

What options are available for interpreting evaluation findings to families in a written and oral fashion? The two major options are to hold an evaluation interpretative conference with the parents (for the sole purpose of reviewing the evaluation information) or to incorporate the review of evaluation information into the IEP conference. The advantages of a separate conference, particularly for the initial evaluation, is that it allows more time to discuss findings in depth and allows the family to assimilate evaluation information prior to making immediate programming decisions. The advantage of incorporating the interpretative conference into the IEP conference is that it can be more time-efficient to eliminate an additional meeting. We suggest that you strongly consider a separate interpretative conference in the case of initial evaluations and the multidisciplinary re-evaluations if families are interested in this option. Our experience suggests that it is practically impossible to do justice to reviewing and discussing a formal evaluation and planning the IEP in one meeting. Further, most parents (including the Turnbulls) are unable to assimilate the implications of evaluation information quickly enough to translate them immediately into IEP decisions concerning goals, objectives, placement, and related services. When formal evaluations have not been administered, however, a performance update on the child can be shared at the IEP conference.

Now, let us consider strategies for coordinating the use of oral and written notification of evaluation results. Parents may receive written notification prior to the conference, during the conference, or as a follow-up to the conference. Table 9–3 includes a summary of the advantages and disadvantages of each of these strategies (see pp. 218–219). Since it is impossible to always second-guess parent preferences, we suggest again that you ask them which strategy of sharing information they would find most helpful.

In addition to meetings and written notification, one study found that parents who were able to hear an audio and video tape replay of the evaluation conference significantly increased their understanding of their child's speech and hearing problems (Marshall & Goldstein, 1969). Thus, mechanical feedback can be used for a replay of important information. Most people's comprehension is increased from hearing emotionally laden and complex information more than one time.

Table 9—3
TIMING OF WRITTEN NOTIFICATION TO FAMILIES

Timing of Written Notification	Advantages	Disadvantages
A. Send written notification of evaluation results to families prior to the conference.	• Families can review and reflect on results that enable them to pinpoint areas of agreement and disagreement. • They can observe their child as a basis for confirming or disconfirming results. • They can review the report with the child. • They can make a list of questions to ask at the conference. • They can identify important areas not covered by the evaluation. • Essentially they can be ready to *discuss* the report at the meeting.	• When the initial evaluation is done and parents are receiving "formal" information for the first time, a written notice can seem impersonal and brusk. • Many families may have difficulty reading or comprehending the report. • Families may misinterpret information creating erroneous impressions about the child's performance.
B. Share written notification of evaluation results with families during the conference.	• Professionals can explain the evaluation results beyond the scope of that in the written notice. • A face-to-face explanation can be helpful and supportive to families who are learning for the first time that their child has an exceptionality. • Providing a copy of the written notice during the evaluation prevents families from having to take notes and provides written clarification for them to refer to immediately after the conference.	• The families' advanced planning is eliminated if they have no evaluation information to consider prior to the conference. • Hearing evaluation results for the first time at the conference may prevent families from being able to pinpoint their areas of agreement and disagreement. This could necessitate an additional meeting.

Timing of Written Notification	Advantages	Disadvantages
C. Share written notification of evaluation results with families after the conference.	• Professionals can explain the evaluation results beyond the scope of that in the written notice. • A face-to-face explanation can be helpful and supportive to families who are learning for the first time that their child has an exceptionality. • Writing the notice after the conference enables professionals to incorporate family perspectives shared at the conference into the report.	• The families' advanced planning is eliminated if they have no evaluation information to consider prior to the conference. • Hearing evaluation results for the first time at the conference may prevent families from being able to pinpoint their areas of agreement and disagreement while they are in attendance. This could necessitate an additional meeting.

Note. From Developing and Implementing Individualized Education Programs by A. P. Turnbull, B. Strickland, and J. C. Brantley, 1982, Columbus, OH: Charles E. Merrill Publishing Co.

Agenda for Discussing Results

Many professionals perceive their role to be one of interpreting evaluation results *to* parents, but such a perception implies one-way communication. It implies that the purpose of the conference is for professionals to tell parents how their child is performing. On the contrary, the purpose of the conference is for professionals and parents (and others whom they invite) to discuss the evaluation findings and reach the most complete understanding possible of the student's instructional needs. Some parents prefer to be passive recipients of information and their preferences need to be respected. Others, however, want to share in making evaluation decisions.

An agenda for you to consider in discussing evaluation results is included in Table 9–4. This agenda is appropriate whether a separate evaluation conference is held or the evaluation results are shared as a component of the IEP conference. (See p. 220.)

During initial proceedings, an important step is to ask parents their perceptions of their child's functioning (I-C). This will provide you with clues to their current level of understanding and can help you take the "shoes test" with them—put yourself in their place. Perhaps you can incorporate some key words they use (e.g., "lagging behind") in your explanations.

One of the key aspects of this agenda is Part II-A, overview of evaluation results. Providing clear descriptions of evaluation results is an important

---

Table 9–4
AGENDA FOR DISCUSSING EVALUATION RESULTS

Initial Proceedings
A. Introductions
B. Review of evaluation procedures
C. Parents' perceptions of student functioning
D. Restatement of referral concerns
Presentation of findings
A. Overview of evaluation results
B. Reaction by parents (and student, if present)
C. Detailed findings
   1. Strengths
      a. Identification of strengths
      b. Parent reactions
      c. Implications for instructional programming
   2. Weaknesses
      a. Identification of weaknesses
      b. Parent reactions
      c. Implication for instructional programming
   3. Classification of student according to an exceptionality
Recommendations (only after time has been allowed for reactions)
A. Restatement of concerns
B. Recommendations—one at a time
C. Reactions after each recommendation
D. Determination of whether the student should receive special education
E. Strategies for sharing evaluation results with the student
Summary
A. Repetition of findings, in varied wording if possible
B. Restatement by parents
C. Planning for next step

Note. *From "Discussing Diagnostic Findings with Parents," by R. J. Rockowitz and P. W. Davidson, 1979,* Journal of Learning Disabilities, 12, *p. 13. Copyright 1979 by The Professional Press, Inc. Reprinted by special permission of The Professional Press, Inc.*

skill to develop. Hirsch (1981) developed a training program to teach parent conference skills through the combination of programmed learning materials and role-play practice sessions. A major component of this training was communicating evaluation results. He developed an outline of steps for professionals to follow which we hope you will find helpful. It is included in Table 9–5, along with an example of each step. The communication skills that you learned in Chapter 6 are very useful to incorporate into the discussion of evaluation results. Many parents have had many clues that problems exist. They usually appreciate direct yet sensitive communication. Helpful tips include using jargon-free language, offering suggestions for follow-up reading material, and conveying the clear message that you have the child's and family's interests in mind.

Table 9–5
OUTLINE OF STEPS FOR PROVIDING AN OVERVIEW OF EVALUATION RESULTS

Introduce the skill: label skill or concept; give skill definition; give skill examples.	We tested Vicki's self-help skills [*skill label*].Those are things she needs to do every day to take care of herself [*skill definition*] like washing her face or going to the bathroom [*behavior examples*].
State student's current level of functioning on the skill: state student's function level; state how this compares to chronological age peers.	Vicki is at about the two year level on these skills [*function level*], about a year behind average children her own age [*amount of delay*].
Give examples: give examples of skills child can and cannot perform.	Vicki can do such things as eat with a spoon and fork, tell what is and is not food, and walk up the stairs by herself [*skills child can do*]. But she has not learned to go to the toilet, get a drink by herself, or put on her own coat, things most three-year-olds can do [*skills child has not learned to do*].
Address the importance if any discrepancy noted between age and achievement: discuss in terms of how discrepancy may affect student's development at present and in future.	If Vicki does not learn to take better care of herself, she will have a difficult time adjusting to school since she will be so dependent on the teacher to help her with things other children can do on their own [*possible future effect of discrepancy*].

Note. Training Development Disability Specialists in Parent Conference Skills *by G. P. Hirsch, 1981, Doctoral Dissertation, The University of Kansas, Lawrence, Kansas, p. 43. Copyright 1981 by G. P. Hirsch. Adapted by permission.*

When you put yourself in the parents' place, it is totally understandable that hearing evaluation results can be a painful and emotionally searing experience. As sensitive as you try to be, many parents, particularly those who strongly value academic achievement and success, will be sorely disappointed by the *confirmation* of a problem. Many parents are starved to hear good news about their child:

Ramon has been tested so many times. I guess he started a program when he was seven-and-a-half months old. I was constantly being updated on where he was in relation to where he should be. Maybe they were saying strengths, but it seemed to be they were just saying how he compared to others. His weaknesses were in all areas—motor, speech, just everything was delayed. Wasn't there anything positive to say?

Some parents may experience feelings of guilt that they created the problem or could have attended to it earlier. They may worry about their child's future and fear an escalation of problems. A defense mechanism may be to doubt the credibility or expertise of the multidisciplinary team. Some parents will need more time than others to come to grips with the reality of the evaluation results. You can help by responding to their questions, providing them with clear descriptions and concrete examples of their child's performance, and offering to arrange for additional evaluatións by persons not involved in the initial evaluation. Sometimes professionals are frustrated by parents who do not immediately accept the evaluation results. We hope you will strive to put yourself in the parents' shoes and realize how much they love their child and how strong their parental need is to "stack the deck" in favor of their child. Your support and patience will pay off in the end.

In sharing evaluation results from a multidisciplinary perspective, an important consideration is to formulate a composite view of the student's strengths and weaknesses rather than a string of isolated disciplinary reports. The family is dealing with the whole child—not a child segmented into mind, muscles, larynx, eyes, ears, and personality. A parent shared her frustration concerning isolated evaluation reports:

> Specialists see her from their own point of view. I guess the hardest thing is that I want answers. I wanted them to say she is going to make it or she isn't going to make it. I guess the hardest thing is not getting answers and everyone looking at their particular area and no one giving me the whole picture. Everyone is just looking at one area and forgetting she is a whole child.

A major outcome of the evaluation discussion should be to reframe the conception of the student's problem. This reframing was described by Fulmer, Cohen, & Monaco (1985) as follows:

> Feedback of test results inevitably affects the way in which a family conceives of their child's problem. It may serve to answer questions the family has already framed, such as "is he able to perform his schoolwork?" It may also serve to introduce whole new viewpoints from which to see a certain behavior. That is, a child whom the parents see as "bad" or "disobedient" may be reframed by the consultant as "disabled". One who is seen as "lazy" may be reframed as "depressed".
>
> The main purpose of "reframing" a child's problem is to "construct a workable reality" (Liebman, 1975) for the family. That is, to state the problem in a way that permits a solution. (p. 145–146)

The process of reframing proceeds on different schedules for different families. Again, the majority of parents will need a period of time to integrate the evaluation information fully and develop new perceptions about their child. Switzer (1985) describes a cognitive problem-solving seminar she offered for parents of children who recently received the diagnosis of learning disabilities. The purpose was to provide factual knowledge, decrease feelings of anxiety, and increase receptivity to interventions. She reported a positive evaluation by families. Interestingly, parents recommended that such a seminar be delayed for two months after diagnosis to provide needed "distance" before readiness to learn disability-related information.

Sharing evaluation results with children is also important. Colley (1973) provides a transcript of a sample discussion he had with a child whose IQ and achievement were in the slow learner range.

Two major outcomes can occur as a result of discussing evaluation results: (a) it can be determined that the student does not qualify for special education, the referral concerns can be addressed in an alternative way, and parents can be notified accordingly; or (b) the student can be identified as an appropriate recipient of special education services. If the latter case occurs, the next step in the process is to arrange for the IEP conference.

INFORMING PARENTS OF THE IEP CONFERENCE

The next chapter will discuss the IEP conference in detail. At this point we want to call your attention to the fact that the EHA requires that parents be notified (in writing or orally) of the IEP conference. This notice must be provided early enough so that the parents can make arrangements to attend, and it must indicate the purpose, time, location, and persons who will attend. Furthermore, the IEP conference must be scheduled at a mutually agreed upon time and place. In cases in which a separate evaluation conference is held, informing parents of the IEP conference can be included as one of the recommendations. Since many parents do not know what an IEP conference is, it can help to provide a thorough explanation of what will happen at the conference and even to give parents some written material to prepare for their role in the conference (a discussion of the use of printed material to provide information is included in Chapter 11.).

SUMMARY

This chapter has described the steps involved in the referral and evaluation process. These steps and the activities associated with them are summarized in Figure 9–1. The referral and evaluation process is a long one with many component parts, but it is a critically important process. When referral and evaluation are soundly and humanely accomplished, the relationship of trust and collaboration among parents and professionals will start on a firm basis. It is upon this strong foundation that the IEP conference is built. Chapter 10 will describe this next phase of implementing the legal rights and responsibilities of students and their families.

Chapter 10

Parent Participation in Developing the IEP

Extensive parent participation in the IEP process is a hallmark of the Education for the Handicapped Act (EHA). As we indicated in Chapter 8, the EHA requires schools to invite parents to attend the IEP conference. Indeed, parents are usually expected to participate actively in educational decision making. A policy interpretation of IEP requirements, prepared by the Office of Special Education in the U.S. Department of Education, clarifies these expectations:

> The parents of a handicapped child are expected to be equal participants, along with school personnel, in developing, reviewing, and revising the child's IEP. This is an active role in which the parents (a) participate in the discussion about the child's need for special education and related services, and (b) join with the other participants in deciding what services the agency will provide to the child.

It is obvious that passing a law providing the opportunity for parents to participate equally and actively in educational decision making does not necessarily ensure that they will (Turnbull & Turnbull, 1982). We made a similar point in Chapter 1 that in the not-so-distant past parents were expected to be the recipients of professionals' decisions and to comply with their suggestions. Thus, the new requirements for parent participation in the IEP process create a major role shift for parents and professionals alike.

This chapter summarizes research on the extent to which parents participate in IEP conferences, identifies barriers to more active parent participation, and presents a framework for conducting IEP conferences so that parents have the opportunity to participate according to their preferences.

REVIEW OF RESEARCH ON PARENT PARTICIPATION IN IEP CONFERENCES

We will review three studies that have investigated the extent of parent participation in the decision-making process of IEP conferences. The studies were completed since 1979 in different parts of the country and used different research methodologies. None involves special interventions to increase parent participation; rather, they portray the nature of parent participation without special attempts to influence it.

One of the earliest studies was conducted within the first two years of EHA implementation (Goldstein, Strickland, Turnbull, & Curry, 1980). It involved observation of IEP conferences of 14 elementary students with mild disabilities. The two variables coded in the study included the topics of discussion and the frequency of contributions by each conference participant. After the conference, all participants completed a questionnaire to rate their satisfaction with their role in the conference and the decisions made. The study concluded that:

1. parental contributions (mothers in 12 of 14 cases) accounted for less than 25% of the total conference contributions;
2. the mean length of conferences was 36 minutes;
3. curriculum, behavior, and performance were the most frequently discussed topics;
4. the topics of placement, related services, legal rights and responsibilities, individual responsibility for implementing goals and objectives, the child's health, future contacts among parents and professionals, and future plans for the child were each coded on the average of less than once per conference; and
5. the satisfaction data from parents, resource teachers, classroom teachers, and principals indicated an overwhelmingly positive response (the mean rating for parents on a 5-point scale for 8 satisfaction questions was 4.6).

Overall, these conferences consisted of the resource teacher describing a previously developed IEP to the mother. While parents were by no means "equal participants" or "actively involved," a high degree of satisfaction was reported by all conference participants.

A second study focused on the nature and extent of parental involvement in IEPs for elementary students with learning disabilities (McKinney & Hocutt, 1982). A portion of the study involved interviews with 32 parents to probe their involvement in the development and implementation of their child's IEP. (The original sample had included 36 parents; however, 4 parents were eliminated because they had no knowledge of their child's involvement in special education.) Findings included these:

1. 75% were able to recall the IEP document;
2. 43% indicated they did not participate fully in its development, 31% said they had helped write it, and 16% could specify the contribution they made;
3. 59% could recall at least one objective or reported that there were no objectives in the plan; and
4. 58% said they had received feedback about the IEP after it was developed, but only 9% had participated in a follow-up conference.

The final study surveyed 400 parents of students representing a broad spectrum of types and levels of disabilities, ages (i.e., 4–20), and ethnicity (Lynch & Stein, 1982). Families were interviewed in their homes using a 64-item questionnaire administered in their native language. Highlights of the results are as follows:

1. Of the 71% of parents who reported active participation in IEP development, 14.6% stated they had expressed opinions and made suggestions, 11.2% stated they helped and trusted the professionals, 7.5% stated they listened to and agreed with the teacher's recommendations, and 6.3% stated they understood everything going on;
2. 76% reported to be satisfied or very satisfied with their child's special education program;
3. parents of students with physical disabilities and parents of 13- and 14-year-old students reported significantly less participation than parents of students in other programs and age categories;
4. Caucasian parents were significantly more aware of the related services identified on the IEP than Black or Hispanic parents; and
5. Hispanic parents tended to offer fewer suggestions in the IEP conference than Black or Caucasian parents (the population was too small to allow for statistical comparison).

In summary, these studies show key trends and parallels. On the whole, parents can be characterized as passive participants in IEP conferences. Generally, they report satisfaction with both their child's special education program and their relatively low degree of involvement in IEP development. Trends of negative, disgruntled parental perceptions are noticeably absent from these data. (It is important to note that research trends do not represent *all* parents. Many parents do actively participate in IEP conferences, but the majority of parents do not.) Also, all of these studies focused on the IEP conferences of students with disabilities. Research is needed on IEP conferences involving parents of gifted students. A major contribution of the Lynch and Stein (1982) study is the identification of participation variations according to disability type, family life cycle stage, and cultural background.

The research finding that the majority of parents participate passively in conferences cannot be interpreted to mean that this is necessarily the parents' preferences. For this reason, we now need to explore barriers that prevent more active involvement.

BARRIERS TO PARENT PARTICIPATION

There are many different ways to interpret the trend of passive parent participation. One way is to recognize there are numerous barriers that preclude parents from achieving more active participation. Indeed, Lynch and Stein (1982) asked low-income parents and special education teachers to identify barriers (U.S. Department of Education, 1984) and learned that discrepancies exist between those barriers identified by parents and those identified by teachers. Parents identified logistical problems (e.g., lack of transportation, babysitting, time), communication problems (e.g., language and cultural differences), lack of understanding of the school system, feelings of inferiority, and uncertainty about their child's disability and ways they and the school can help.

Teachers identified barriers as parent apathy, parents' lack of time, energy, and understanding, and the devaluation of parent input by the school personnel.

Parents and teachers apparently have different opinions about the source of barriers. Given the vast variations among parents, professionals, and the conduct of IEP conferences, we believe that different barriers exist in different circumstances for different parents and professionals. Thus, it is important to recognize all potential barriers and to learn strategies for minimizing each one. To accomplish this goal, we will individually address each of the barriers identified.

Parent-Identified Barriers

Logistical problems. It is true that many parents do have logistical barriers, such as unavailable transportation and child care. Providing these services can increase parent participation in IEP conferences (Pfeiffer, 1980) and in IEP-related training sessions (Thompson, 1982). To overcome the transportation barrier, school personnel might consider meeting in parents' homes or in a neighborhood church, synagogue, or community center, helping parents arrange transportation through a community volunteer group, or having a school fund available to defray public transportation expenses.

Transportation is particularly problematic for families whose children attend residential schools geographically separated from their home. Because of long-distance travel, many parents may come to school three times a year—at the beginning of the year, at December break, and at the end of the year. In such situations, it is especially important to plan ahead to arrange the conference at one of these times.

Likewise, child care problems can be minimized by conducting the meeting in parents' homes or in a location with access to a playroom or playground, by helping parents brainstorm a number of alternatives for locating child care assistance, by arranging for volunteer helpers through school or community service clubs, or by having a school fund available to pay child care helpers when all other alternatives have been exhausted.

Another important logistical issue involves fathers. IEP meetings are almost always attended by one parent—the mother (Cone, Delawyer, & Wolfe, 1985; Goldstein et al., 1980; Scanlon, Arick, & Phelps, 1981). The importance of the father's role, however, is recognized in both research and model programs (LaBarbera & Lewis, 1980; Pfeiffer & Tittler, 1983). Parent contributions increase when both parents attend the conference (Pistono, 1977). A teacher commented:

> It may sound crazy, but I know I am more "on my toes" when a dad attends the conference. I think of myself as being liberated. Why is it that I listen and respond more when the dad is talking? It's a fact.

School personnel should schedule IEP conferences when interested fathers can attend. In the past, an assumption has been that mothers, because they are homemakers, could attend conferences during the school day and fathers could not attend because of employment. Given that the majority of mothers of school-age children are employed (Masnick & Bane, n.d.), both mothers and fathers frequently need flexible scheduling options early in the morning, late in the afternoon, during evening hours, or over the lunch hour.

Time is another logistical barrier for many families. In fact, this is one of the barriers identified by both parents and teachers. Strategies for dealing with this barrier include arranging meetings to the extent possible at the convenience of the parents; insuring that meetings are conducted in a time-efficient fashion; and helping families separate decision-making opportunities into those that are more and less essential (if there is not time available to participate in all decisions).

The many functions for which families are responsible, discussed in Chapter 4, make it clear that families have many other demands on their time, attention, and energy than just their child's education. As we also pointed out earlier, education is the only one of seven functions in which there are guaranteed rights to services. This may explain why many parents, facing inordinate time demands, relegate educational decision-making authority to teachers and give their attention to other family needs. From a family systems perspective, we can see that this response may have the consequence of improving the parent-child relationship or decreasing family stress. Such outcomes may be more important or more necessary for some families during periods of major stress than active involvement in IEP conferences. As one parent stated:

> Sometimes I get to the end of my rope and can't handle one more thing. The kids are crying, my husband is down and out with no job, the car is parked because we can't afford to run it, and the doctor tells me I'm pushing my luck to postpone surgery. About that time the teacher calls for me to come talk about Danny. I just can't hack it. She's a good lady and she's helped Danny. But I've got all I can handle at home. (Turnbull & Summers, 1985)

Communication Problems. We addressed the importance of language and cultural sensitivity in communicating with parents in Chapter 6. Obviously, clear language and cultural sensitivity are critically important in the IEP conference. To minimize language and cultural barriers in the IEP process, professionals might try working with churches and outreach organizations within minority communities to enlist the participation of parents in IEP conferences; making a home visit to encourage participation; having a translator present if necessary; verbally summarizing the decisions made at the meeting; and giving parents a concise written copy of the summary (Marion, 1979).

Lack of Understanding of the School System. Many parents, particularly those from minority backgrounds, lack information on legal rights pertaining to special education (Budoff, 1979; Mitchell, 1976; Strickland, 1983; Turnbull, Winton, Blacher, & Salkind, 1983). We discuss how to provide information in Chapter 12. At this point, however, we want to report two research studies that sought to increase parents' understanding of the IEP process.

The first provided training to mothers of Head Start children who had disabilities on the topics of legal rights and IEP participation skills. The training involved a one-day workshop for mothers by professionals to address competencies related to IEP conference participation. They used a combination of lecture, discussion, audio-visual, and simulated activities. The researchers then observed IEP conferences of the mothers who received training and a group of mothers who had not participated in training (Thompson, 1982). The results showed that the mothers who received training made twice as many contributions in the conference as compared to mothers who did not receive training. These same mothers also expressed slightly more satisfaction with their conference.

The second study involved the development and field-test of a set of parent education materials designed to encourage parent participation in the IEP meeting. The materials included two booklets—one for parents and one for a parent support person (friend of the family who attends the conference to provide support). The parent booklet covered the topics of procedures to be followed, terminology, and strategies for gathering, organizing, and presenting information about the child. The booklet for the parent support person included information on how a friend or advocate can assist the parent before, during, or after the conference. The field test involved interviewing a small group of parents and observing their conferences after they had had a chance to read the materials. The researchers reported that the materials influenced meeting preparations and more active conference participation for some parents. Pre-meeting planning questions were identified by parents as one of the most helpful portions of the booklets. Interestingly, none of the parents in the field test sample elected to invite a support person to attend the conference with them; however, they did report reviewing the support materials with a spouse or friend before or after the conference. A special educator involved in the field test sample made the following comment on the impact of the materials on conference participation:

> . . . compared with other parents from this school, the parents know what to do. Usually, where you get to the point when you ask for questions (after the reports), parents tend to be sitting back as if to say, "Oh, whatever you want to do." The booklets appear to have made them focus more on the purpose of the meeting—what's appropriate for the child. (Malmberg, 1984, p. 108)

We encourage you to develop, implement, and evaluate programs designed to minimize parents' lack of understanding. Legal rights are hollow unless parents have the knowledge and skill to put rights into action.

Feelings of Inferiority.   A number of factors may cause parents to feel inferior to school personnel. These include a diminished sense of status or power in decision making, feelings of intimidation associated with being outnumbered by professionals, and guilt feelings related to the cause of the child's exceptionality.

Parents' diminished sense of status and power in decision making is a documented fact. For example, approximately 1500 IEP team members were asked about the activities in which they thought parents should engage. Only 2 of a possible 24 activities were selected as appropriate for parental participation. These involved gathering and then presenting information about the child. Only 26% of these professionals said parents should influence professionals to accept a specific program or finalize education decisions (Yoshida, Fenton, Kaufman, & Maxwell, 1978).

These findings were corroborated by Gilliam and Coleman (1981). They asked IEP conference participants to rank the relative "status" or importance of the participants. Although parents were rated high in importance before the meeting, they were ranked low in terms of their actual contribution after the meeting. The researchers suggested that parents either do not possess expertise, or are not perceived as possessing expertise, commensurate with other conference members. They also suggest that the most influential roles (e.g., special education teachers, special education consultants, and psychologists) are assigned to those members who are familiar with test scores, diagnostic reports, and cumulative records. They recommended a case manager to coordinate the entire conference process and to provide increased access to parents in the assessment and data-gathering phases (Gilliam & Coleman, 1981).

These are good suggestions, but we also encourage you to convey both directly and indirectly to parents that they are valued members of the decision-making team. Pistono (1977) found a positive relationship between the attitudes of professionals (attending conferences) regarding the ability of parents to contribute and the frequency of parental contributions during the meeting. It is likely that parents' feelings of inferiority will be minimized when they are approached as partners rather than as the passive recipients of previously formulated decisions. A parent commented about the differential power as follows:

> One group has power and the other doesn't. I think the ultimate lack of power is to have a child who needs. (Ferguson, 1984, p. 44)

You can help equalize the power relationship by such conference behavior as letting parents know that they have contributions to the process that can be made *only* by them.

A second reason for the parental sense of inferiority is that parents sometimes feel outnumbered by professionals at IEP meetings. Marion (1979) warns: "The single greatest deterrent to minority parent participation is that they might feel overwhelmed when they walk into a meeting and feel all the school people are lined up against them" (p. 9). He suggests having in attendance only those people who are most familiar with the child and having other professionals "on call" to join the meeting upon request.

By contrast, a survey of 243 parents (whose ethnicity was not identified) in Colorado showed that having large numbers of professionals at conferences did not make it difficult for parents to ask questions and did not prevent good discussions. Indeed, some parents viewed the large number as a show of concern and interest (Witt, Miller, McIntyre, & Smith, 1984). Thus the number of people at conferences affects different parents in different ways. The more people present, the greater the breadth of expertise and the greater the chance of including all persons who have implementation responsibility. The benefit of smaller conferences is they can be less intimidating and more focused. The individual preferences of parents need to be respected in planning which professionals should attend.

It is important to recognize that parents are, indeed, "outnumbered" even in conferences when only three professionals attend (given that both parents attend) or when two professionals attend (in typical cases when only one parent attends). Intimidation itself probably has more to do with professionals' communication style than with the actual number of persons attending.

Communication that is sensitive to the inclusion of parents in decision making is an effective conference strategy. A study was conducted to assess the impact of two interventions on increasing parent contributions during conferences (Goldstein & Turnbull, 1982). These interventions were: sending parents questions prior to the IEP conference, making a follow-up telephone call, and having the school counselor present as a "parent advocate." The counselors were given one sheet of instructions asking them to engage in five behaviors: introduce parents, clarify jargon, ask questions, reinforce parental contributions, and summarize decisions at the end of the conference.

Forty-five parents of students with learning disabilities were chosen from five elementary schools in one local education agency to be observed at IEP conferences. The parents selected from each school were divided randomly into three groups—questions in advance, parent advocate present, and control group. All conferences were observed, and speakers and topics were coded.

Results indicated that significantly more parent contributions occurred in conferences in which a parent advocate was present as compared to the control group. No differences in participation were found between the control group and the parents who had been sent questions prior to the conferences. Thus, adherence to basic principles of good communication during the conference was effective in increasing parent contributions. One interpretation of this result is that their feelings of intimidation were reduced.

A third and final factor related to parents' feelings of inferiority is that some parents believe school personnel blame them for the child's disability. In their study of variables associated with parental satisfaction with conferences, Witt et al. (1984) found one of the major variables influencing satisfaction was that professionals attributed blame to sources other than the parents. As we stated in Chapter 1, you need to be particularly sensitive to direct comments or innuendoes that parents might perceive as blaming them for the child's problem. In addition, we encourage you to adopt the practice in every IEP conference of making several statements to parents highlighting the positive contributions they make to their child.

Uncertainty about the Child's Exceptionality.   Many parents do experience uncertainty about their child's exceptionality. This is particularly true for parents of children with mild to moderate developmental delay, unknown etiology, and no physical problems. Professionals working with families of children with no clear-cut diagnosis need to be especially supportive. A common theme in interviews with mothers of preschool children with disabilities is the need for competent teachers who have more expertise than they do in designing a relevant educational program (Winton & Turnbull, 1981). One mother described this need as follows:

> You've got to have a staff that is smarter than you . . . I'm no genius, I mean, my background is giving enemas . . . but you've got to know that the people that are teaching your child know their stuff. Now I leave him off in the morning and I feel like . . . people more competent than me are taking him and that's a great feeling. (p. 15)

Parents who experience uncertainty can be helped by professionals to recognize the important contributions that they can make. For example, parents may make a comment, such as:

> When Mark gets stubborn, I give him a two-minute warning. Then he has to do what I say. It usually works.

Then professionals might respond:

> Thank you for sharing that with us. It's very helpful to know what works at home. We haven't tried a warning period, but it sounds like a good idea. It's also important for both home and school to give Mark consistent messages.

This kind of response immediately lets parents know that their contributions are valued.

Teacher-Identified Barriers

As we mentioned, teachers in the Lynch and Stein study (1982) identified the three major barriers to parent participation as being apathy, parents' lack of time, energy, and understanding, and the devaluation of parent input by the school. The latter two were also identified by parents and discussed in the previous section. Here we will discuss parent apathy and two additional barriers that educators have reported in the literature—time constraints and expertise constraints.

Parental Apathy.   Some parents are apathetic or indifferent about their involvement in IEP conferences. Apathy can occur for a variety of reasons, including those discussed in the previous section. You will most likely encounter some parents who are apathetic and unwilling to be involved in decision making you consider very important. There will probably be instances in which you put a 100% effort into developing the IEP and find that the parents do not show any interest in even learning about it. Sometimes you will try every positive step you can think of and still not get a response. It is important for you to remember that you are not a failure.

It is not your job to *make* families do something that they choose not to do. We encourage you to use the communication skills discussed in Chapter 6 to try to stand in the parents' shoes and see the issues from their perspectives. Further, the family systems framework (Chapters 2–5) can assist you in gaining insight into their own unique pattern of family interaction. Perhaps you can come to understand and even accept parents' apathy by finding out a family's priorities and responding accordingly. We also encourage you to be on your guard to intensively with the student or maintain contact with the family even when there is no response by parents.

Professional Time Constraints. The IEP process can be extremely time-consuming. The amount of time required to develop new IEPs has been estimated around six hours according to data collected in the first several years of EHA implementation (Price & Goodman, 1980; Safer, Morrissey, Kaufman, & Lewis, 1978). One-third of the time for IEP development was reported to evolve from the teachers' personal time (Price & Goodman, 1980). Many professionals feel harried by what can seem as overwhelming time requirements to complete IEP-related paperwork. As stated by one teacher:

> I cannot ask my wife and children to put up with me, depressed and tense for months each spring because I must finish my testing, must begin testing with the new kids we've identified, must get the reports in on time, must complete reams of papers (the law says so, and tells me how much time I have to do it), and can't teach. When I am in class, I am tense and harried because the testing isn't getting done on time. I don't have any time to plan, to diagnose, to remediate, and I can't get on top . . . (Katzen, 1980, p. 582)

It is essential that professionals address directly the barrier of time. Its importance is underscored in a study by Witt et al. (1984) showing that, compared to five other variables, allowing enough time for the conference was the most important variable associated with parent satisfaction. Strategies for minimizing the time barrier include using computer technology in IEP development, dictating reports and having them transcribed by a secretary hired by the school, using volunteer assistance to schedule and arrange rooms for meetings, and providing preservice and inservice training on the efficient use of time and on small group management (Turnbull, 1983).

Professional Expertise Constraints. Interdisciplinary teams are characterized by complex group dynamics for all parties involved (Bailey, 1984; Chase, Wright, & Ragade, 1981). Providing opportunities for individualized parent participation is only one of many challenges. Professionals have been expected to function well in IEP conferences in the absence of adequate preparation. We have observed that the emphasis in preservice and inservice training programs related to parent participation in IEP conferences has been on legal rights as distinguished from educational decision making and communication. A parent shared her perspective on how professionals conduct conferences:

> Accordingly, these professionals do not tell anything to parents that they do not feel is necessary. They cover the bases legally, though; they rush through a meeting, get the parent's signature, and breathe a sigh of relief as they go on to the next "case". While they might not intentionally mislead a parent, they will withhold important information because it is safer and easier. (Ferguson, 1984, p. 43)

As an alternative to a hurried conference, we will now discuss six components of IEP conferences and strategies for involving parents in each.

SIX COMPONENTS OF THE IEP CONFERENCE

The IEP conference typically has six components: preconference preparation, initial conference proceedings, review of formal evaluation and current levels of performance, development of goals and objectives, specification of placement and related services, and conclusion. Structuring the IEP conference into separate components for the purpose of planning and conducting conferences can enhance systematic decision making (Ysseldyke, Albozzine, & Mitchell, 1982). We will provide a brief overview of each component with specific suggestions for involving parents. These suggestions are summarized in Table 10–1 (p. 238). Readers interested in more detailed information on the IEP process are referred to Turnbull, Strickland, and Brantley (1982). Again, our philosophy is that parents should have an opportunity to participate to the extent they want to. More involvement is not necessarily better involvement.

Preconference Preparation

The tasks completed during the preconference period can greatly influence conference success. We suggest you start by appointing a "case manager" (really, no one likes being a "case" nor do they like being "managed," so we will use the term "conference chair") to assume responsibility for conference planning, implementation, and follow-up (Gilliam & Coleman, 1981; Marion, 1979). Centralizing responsibility with one person can help ensure continuity and coordination. Select a confer-

Table 10–1
SUGGESTIONS FOR INVOLVING PARENTS IN THE IEP CONFERENCE

Preconference Preparation

1. Appoint a conference chair to coordinate all aspects of the conference. The conference chair should assume responsibility for coordinating preconference preparation, chairing the conference, and coordinating follow-up.
2. Solicit information from parents on their preferences related to their participation: persons who should attend, convenient time, convenient location, needed assistance (child-care, transportation), and the type of information that they would like to receive in advance. (See Table 10–2 for a sample questionnaire.)
3. Specify the persons appropriate to attend the IEP conference in light of parent and professional preferences. Be sure to consider carefully the possibility of including the student.
4. Arrange a convenient time and location for the meeting.
5. If needed, work with parents in assisting them with logistics such as childcare and transportation.
6. Inform parents (in writing or verbally) of the purpose, time of conference, location, and names of participants.
7. In light of parents' preferences, share information in advance of the conference that they believe will help them prepare for participation—e.g., evaluation reports, evaluation checklists to complete, list of subject areas which school personnel think should be covered by the IEP, summary of child's strengths and weaknesses in each subject area, ideas from school personnel on possible goals and objectives, information on legal rights, and information on placement options and related services.
8. If several placements are being considered for the student, encourage parents to visit each program prior to the conference.
9. Discuss the conference purpose and procedures with students and assist them in specifiying their own preferences for educational programming. Encourage students to discuss their preferences with their parents.
10. Encourage parents to share any information with school personnel in advance of the conference that the parents believe will be helpful during the preparation period.
11. Gather all information from school personnel that will help prepare for the IEP conference.
12. Prepare an agenda to cover each of the remaining five components of the conference.

Initial Conference Proceedings

1. Greet and welcome parents upon arrival and welcome any persons whom the parents bring with them.
2. Introduce all conference participants and share sufficient information to identify roles and areas of responsibility. If parents are being introduced to several professionals for the first time, consider the use of name tags or make a list of the names and positions of conference participants for the parents
3. State the purpose of the conference and review the agenda. Ask the parents and their guests if there are any issues they would like to add to the agenda.
4. Ask participants the amount of time they have available for the conference. State the intention to use time wisely but to avoid rushing through important decisions. Share the option of re-scheduling another meeting if necessary.
5. Ask parents and their guests if they would like to have a clarification of legal rights. If so, fully provide the information they request.

Review of Formal Evaluation and Current Levels of Performance

1. If a formal evaluation of the student has been conducted and a separate evaluation conference to review results has not been held, ask the appropriate diagnostic personnel to identify the tests administered, the specific results of each, and the options for consideration based on the evaluation results.
2. After evaluation information has been shared, summarize the major findings and encourage parents to point out areas of agreement and disagreement and their corresponding reasons.
3. Ask parents if they would like to have a written copy of evaluation results. If so, provide it to them.
4. If a formal evaluation has not been conducted (one must be conducted every three years), review the child's developmental progress and present levels of performance in each subject area.
5. Identify current implications of all test results for instructional programming and future implications for the next lifecycle stage of the child.
6. Clarify any diagnostic jargon that is used.
7. Solicit parental input on the student's current performance levels. Identify areas of agreement and disagreement.
8. Strive to resolve disagreement through discussion or examples of student performance. If your disagreement cannot be resolved within the conference, develop a plan for collecting further evaluation information by school personnel or an independent evaluator. Solicit parental suggestions on the procedures to follow in collecting further information.
9. Proceed with the development of the IEP only when you and the parents agree on the student's type of exceptionality and current levels of performance.

Development of Goals and Objectives

1. Based on the current levels of performance, identify all subject areas requiring specially designed instruction. For each subject area, collaboratively specify appropriate goals and objectives.
2. Encourage parents and their guests to share goals and objectives they believe are important for current and future functioning in the home, school, or community environment.
3. Prioritize goals and objectives in light of relevance for the student. Discuss future educational and vocational options for the student to insure that the goals and objectives provide sufficient preparation for future needs.
4. If the student receives instruction from two or more teachers, clarify the manner in which the responsibility for teaching the objectives will be shared.
5. Ask parents if they are willing to assume responsibility for teaching or reviewing some of the objectives with their son or daughter at home. If so, discuss their preferences for which goals and objectives they will work on.
6. Insure that evaluation procedures and schedules are identified for goals and objectives.
7. Explain to parents that including goals and objectives in the IEP does not represent a guarantee that the student will achieve them; rather, it represents a good faith effort that school personnel will teach these goals and objectives.

Determination of Placement and Related Services

1. Based on the student's current levels of performance and the goals and objectives deemed appropriate, review the full continuum of viable placement options by identifying benefits and drawbacks of each. Solicit parent input on benefits and drawbacks from an academic and social perspective of the different placement options for their child.

2. If parents have not already visited possible placements, encourage them to do so. Agree on a "tentative placement" until the parents can visit and confirm its appropriateness.
3. Select the placement option consistent with the goals and objectives to be taught. The placement should be as close to peers who do not have exceptionalities as possible. Specify the extent of the student's participation in the regular education program.
4. Identify the related services the student needs. Discuss the benefits and drawbacks of each service and options for scheduling (i.e., frequency, the portion of class that will be missed).
5. Specify the dates for initiating each related service and the anticipated duration of each.
6. If the parents have not had an opportunity to meet the teacher of the selected placement or the related service providers, share the names and qualifications of these professionals.

Concluding the Conference

1. Summarize to review major decisions and follow-up responsibility. Take notes to record this summary.
2. Assign follow-up responsibility for any task (e.g., arranging for physical therapy) requiring attention.
3. Review with parents the responsibility (teaching objectives, increasing socialization opportunities during after-school hours, visiting adult programs) they have expressed interest in assuming.
4. Set a tentative date for reviewing the IEP document on at least an annual basis and preferably more frequently.
5. Identify strategies for ongoing communication with parents, in light of the preferences of all involved parties.
6. Express appreciation for the shared decision making that occurred and reiterate to parents how much their participation is valued.

ence chair who has responsibility for a portion of the child's educational program or someone who is likely to be successful in communicating with parents. Frequently, the person who assumes this role is a special education teacher, counselor, social worker, or principal. An important aspect of the chair's responsibility will be to serve as a liaison between school personnel and the family.

One of the first tasks of the conference chair should be to solicit information from parents concerning their preferences. The chair should consider these ideas for obtaining information: ask parents to complete a questionnaire such as the one in Table 10–2 (p. 242); discuss preferences with parents more open-endedly, such as in a conference or over the telephone; or ask for advice from professionals who have worked successfully with a family in the past (e.g., teachers) or who have a positive current relationship (e.g., social worker, public health nurse). Whichever method seems most appropriate for each family, it is important to gather information early enough to consider parents' preferences in planning. Also, the chair should remember that professional team members are entitled to their preferences and should let families know what they are. For example, if it is impossible for you to have a conference before school in the morning, families should be alerted to your scheduling preferences.

Next, the conference chair should consider whether it is appropriate to include the student. Research on this issue indicates that the majority of secondary students with mild disabilities prefer to be involved (Gillespie & Turnbull, 1983) and that attitudes of mothers and resource teachers toward IEP conferences were more positive when elementary students were involved (Fifield, 1978). We advocate the inclusion of students whenever possible in light of student, parent, and teacher preferences, as a strategy for teaching self-advocacy skills (Turnbull & Turnbull, 1985) and as a means of addressing the student's concerns (Daniels, 1982). Parents who want or need to talk privately can always stay after the student leaves or arrange another conference. As stated by a mother of a 12-year-old student with a physical disability:

> He knows how to tell what he likes and doesn't like and what he wants to do. It does no good to decide something for someone else. If he decided, maybe he would be more eager to do it. (Gillespie & Turnbull, 1983, p. 27)

A 13-year-old student with an emotional disability expressed why involvement in the IEP conference would be beneficial for her:

> The teachers and parents get everything out and students have feelings and want to get them out, too. (Gillespie & Turnbull, 1983, p. 28)

Parent and teacher suggestions for including students are provided by Gillespie and Turnbull (1983). Furthermore, Van Reusen (1984) has developed and validated an instructional strategy to teach secondary students with learning disabilities to participate effectively in their own conferences. The instructional strategy teaches students to:

1. inventory their learning needs and interests,
2. provide their inventoried information during a conference,
3. ask appropriate questions during a conference,
4. respond appropriately to questions during a conference, and
5. verbally summarize their understanding of their IEP goals before the conclusion of the conference. (Van Reusen, 1984, p. 11)

The IEP documents of students who demonstrated these skills included more student-initiated goal statements when compared to IEPs of students who had not received training. Additionally, the other participants indicated higher levels of satisfaction with conferences in which students had been prepared for involvement.

In addition to considering students' involvement, you may encourage parents to consider their preferences for inviting other family members or friends to participate in the conference. Often other family members, such as siblings or grandparents, have valuable perspectives to share and can benefit from having access to educational information.

Third, the conference chair should take into account the items on the questionnaire that address scheduling, size and location of conference, and

Table 10–2
PARENT PREFERENCES INVENTORY FOR THE IEP CONFERENCES

The purpose of this questionnaire is to find out your preferences for the IEP conference. We believe your ideas will help us have a better conference. Please share them with us.

Persons to Attend

There are many different options for you to consider in identifying the people you want to attend the IEP conference. A major question to ask yourself is: Who are the people who can be helpful in developing an educational program tailored to my child's current and future needs? A very important consideration is to decide if your child should attend. Attending the meeting allows students the opportunity to share important information about their educational needs. Also, they can benefit from gaining an understanding of their current performance and the reasons that their educational program is designed in a particular way. We hope you will do the following:

Review the list below and consider the people you would like to bring to the conference.
Talk with the people you identify to find out if they would be willing to attend and if they think they can be helpful in designing your child's program.
Check the people you actually plan to bring.

_____ Mother	_____ Person who works with my child in other programs such as in scouting or recreation
_____ Father	
_____ Step-mother	_____ Advocate or a person who can be helpful in making sure that the educational program is in my child's best interest
_____ Step-father	
_____ My child with an exceptionality	
_____ Brothers or sisters	_____ Other (Please state) _____
_____ Grandparents	_____
_____ Other family members	

The next important consideration is for you to identify the school personnel whom you would like to attend the conference. Again, you should ask yourself: Who are the people from the school who can be helpful in developing an educational program tailored to my child's current and future needs? Some parents feel more comfortable in smaller conferences when they are not so "outnumbered" by school personnel. Other parents prefer that every professional who has a role in their child's education attend the conference. Please check below to indicate your preference:

_____ Current teachers (write the names of which teachers)	_____ Physical therapist
	_____ Adaptive physical education teacher
_____ Paraprofessional	_____ Principal
_____ Next year's teachers	_____ Director of special education
_____ Psychologist	_____ Staff from adult programs which my child will enter in the future
_____ School social worker	
_____ Counselor	_____ Other (Please state) _____
_____ Occupational therapist	_____
_____ Speech therapist	

(By law the people required to attend include one teacher and a person responsible for providing or supervising special education.)

Time of Conference

To the greatest extent possible, we will arrange the conference at a time that is convenient for you and the persons you want to bring. We must also consider the schedule and responsibilities of the school personnel who will attend. Please check the days that will be possible for you and the persons you want to bring along:

_____ Monday   _____ Thursday

_____ Tuesday   _____ Friday

_____ Wednesday

We need to set a time for the meeting that will give us at least one hour for discussion. If we do not need this much time, we can finish early. If more time is needed, we can schedule another meeting. Please check to indicate the times that will be possible for you and the person(s) you want to bring:

_____ 7:00–8:00 A.M.   _____ 12:00–1:00 P.M.

_____ 8:00–9:00 A.M.   _____ 1:00–2:00 P.M.

_____ 9:00–10:00 A.M.   _____ 3:00–4:00 P.M.

_____ 10:00–11:00 A.M.   _____ 4:00–5:00 P.M.

Location of Conference

We can consider different locations for the conference. It is important for us to find a location convenient for all participants and one in which you feel comfortable. Please check below to indicate the locations that are agreeable with you:

_____ School

_____ Your home

_____ Community building (This could be a church, library, community center or another place you might suggest.) If you would like to meet in a community building, please write the name of the one you have in mind: _____

(It is likely that more school personnel will be able to attend the conference if it is held at school.)

Needed Assistance

Will the lack of child care or transportation prevent you from attending the IEP conference? If so, we will try to assist you in locating some help. Please check below if you need some assistance:

_____ I need help arranging child care

_____ I need help arranging transportation

Pre-Conference Communication

Parents vary in their preferences for receiving information prior to the IEP conference. In deciding whether and what kind of information you would like in advance, ask yourself the following questions: *Would it help me in developing my child's educational program to have information in advance of the conference? What kind of information would be helpful to me?* Please check below to indicate the kind of information you would like to have in advance:

_____ Evaluation reports of how my child performed on formal tests

_____ An evaluation checklist for me to complete to identify the skills my child uses at home and the ones that are needed

_____ List of the subject areas which the school personnel think should be covered on the IEP

_____ Summary of my child's strengths and weaknesses in each subject area

_____ Ideas from school personnel on goals and objectives they think should be discussed at the conference

_____ Information on my legal rights related to my child's education

_____ Information on placement options

_____ Information on the kinds of related services available

_____ Other (please state) _____

_____

_____

_____ I prefer to wait until the IEP conference to receive information.

If you are interested in receiving information in advance of the conference, please indicate how you would like to be provided with the information:

_____ Written notes

_____ Phone calls

_____ Individual conference

_____ Other (please state) _____

_____

_____

You may also have information that you would like to share with school personnel in advance that you think will be helpful in planning your child's educational program. Examples of information that could be helpful include evaluations done by professionals outside the school, statement of any concerns, suggested goals and objectives, description of your child's responsibilities at home, and your preferences for future educational and vocational options. We would be happy to receive any information you believe is important for us to have. Please check to indicate your preference:

_____ I do have information on my child that I will share in advance of the IEP conference with school personnel

_____ I do not have information that I am interested in sharing in advance of the IEP Conference with school personnel

Thank you very much for providing us with this information. We look forward to your participation in the IEP conference.

_____
Signature of Respondent

_____
Relationship to student

_____
Date

advance preparation. The option of exchanging advance information such as draft ideas for goals and objectives is important to consider. (Advance information of possible ideas for considerations should not be misconstrued to mean completed IEPs.) Although providing advance information might be viewed as extra work, it can be a helpful strategy and can save time later. Parents frequently find it helps them to have an opportunity to reflect on information—such as current levels of performance, goals, objectives, placement, and related services—so they may feel confident to agree or disagree with professionals' opinions and recommendations. By exchanging information in advance, parents and professionals alike can use the IEP conference time for clarification and decision making. When information is not exchanged in advance, participants are likely to spend the majority of time reviewing information and generating ideas. Then, they tend to hurry decision making into the last few minutes. When parents prefer not to exchange written information in advance, if time allows, two meetings—one to review information and one to make decisions—may be useful. Issues of both personal preference and time efficiency need to be considered.

Initial Conference Proceedings

The atmosphere of open communication is set during the initial part of the conference. We have discussed the fact that many parents feel intimidated in the conference. The conference chair, therefore, should start the conference in a positive and constructive way to enhance the mutual efforts of all participants in working toward common goals. A clear statement of purpose early in the conference can help direct everyone's attention to the important decisions that need to be made. Surprisingly, observations of conferences indicate that a statement of purpose is usually not made, the roles of team members are not defined, and individuals present are not encouraged to participate (Ysseldyke et al.,1982). A teacher commented on how the roles of team members can create barriers in conferences:

> I was recently at a conference in which a psychologist was also present. It was not until after the conference that we discovered the father thought the psychologist was a truant officer.

Suggestions, as outlined in Table 10–1, include greeting parents and their guests, making introductions, reviewing an agenda, addressing timelines (time schedules) for participants, and providing information on legal rights.

Review of Formal Evaluation and Current Levels of Performance

The IEP must include the student's current levels of performance. This information is the direct result of the evaluation process and provides the foundation for developing an appropriate instructional program. The conference chair can consider two options (both discussed in Chapter 9). First, the IEP conference can be used to review formal evaluation results *and* to develop the IEP. Second, a separate meeting (before the IEP conference) can be held only to review evaluation results. The decision of when to report evaluation results should be based on a consensus of parent and professional preferences. Many of the suggestions for this portion of the IEP conference which are included in Table 10–1 are repeated from the discussion of the last chapter.

Development of Goals and Objectives

Goals and objectives are the heart of the IEP. They represent the content or substance of a student's educational program. All participants must address the central issue: What are the most important goals and objectives for this student to learn based on the student's current and future needs and his/her family's needs? It is important for the conference chair to direct the group's attention to this consideration throughout the conference.

Different conference participants may answer this question in different ways. Phil Roos (1985), the father of a child with a severe disability, shared his perspective on this issue:

> Parents and professionals may have different ideas regarding specific program objectives and their relative importance. For example, professionals may focus on academic and abstract achievements whereas parents may be interested in practical objectives that make the retarded child easier to live with. Professionals may emphasize development of new skills, such as number concepts or color recognition, while parents may wish to eliminate socially inappropriate behavior, such as tantrums or screaming. As a result of these different priorities, professionals may feel a child is making good progress while his parents may feel that nothing is happening. I recall, for instance, that some years ago my wife and I were told with pride that Val was beginning to recognize colors. Rather than reacting with obvious enthusiasm, we expressed dismay that she had managed to yank all her hair from her head. We suggested that eliminating this self-destructive behavior should take precedence over color recognition. (pp. 253–254)

Chapter 9 included a discussion of evaluation surveys that parents may complete to indicate their child's current levels of performance, as well as skills they would most like for their child to learn. The chair can ask parents to share their preferences at the conference. Parent and professional preferences need to be merged and translated into IEP goals and objectives (Vincent, Laten, Salisbury, Brown, & Baumgart, 1981).

The conference chair also can consider using a questionnaire, such as the one in Figure 10–1, to aid in selecting the most important goals and objectives for a particular student. Additional criteria can be added or criteria now included can be deleted based on professional and parental recommendations. In its present form, these criteria are more geared to older students. The chair may ask all conference participants to complete a questionnaire individually before, during, or after the conference and then collectively discuss the results. Goals and objectives can be selected on the basis of computed scores or through consensus following discussion. The major advantage of this questionnaire is that it makes explicit the criteria for selecting goals and objectives. (See Figure 10–1 on p. 248.)

It is important to recognize that nonacademic and enrichment opportunities need to be considered in formulating goals and objectives in addition to academic areas (Crawford, 1978). Consider Tony's case:

> Tony is a 17-year-old student with moderate mental retardation. His major needs relate to independent living and vocational skills. Considering his many deficits, it would be easy to identify more than enough goals and objectives for the year in these two areas alone. But Tony also has a special interest and talent in music. He believes that "music is magic." Music was identified as an important subject to include on Tony's IEP. One of the objectives was to teach Tony to play a guitar. As the year progressed, the music program and the guitar—as contrasted to the independent living and vocational programs—provided the spark for Tony to turn off the alarm clock and get out of bed every morning.

Determination of Placement and Related Services

The determination of placement and related services is a critical decision to be made at the IEP conference for two reasons. First, very few aspects of education are more important to the child than placement and related services. Second, placement and related services specified on the IEP make the school legally responsible for providing them.

Parents unfamiliar with placement options need a specific description of the various options available. Based on observations of 34 conferences, a team of researchers (Ysseldyke et al., 1982) concluded that the concept of least restrictive placement was neither explicitly stated nor used as a basis of making a placement decision in any of the conferences. They stated: "In general, teams presented data, and then someone on the team recom-

mended a placement. The efficacy of the placement was seldom discussed" (p. 311). It cannot be assumed that parents know the meaning or
implication of terms such as resource room, mainstreaming, itinerant
teacher, and job station. In a survey of 50 parents of kindergarten children

---

Figure 10–1
IEP ADULT LIFE SKILLS CRITERIA CHECKLIST

Instructions: These IEP goals/objectives should be rated according to their relevance to adult life skills.

Student's name _____

Completed by _____

Date _____

Key   1–Definitely No   4–Probably Yes
        2–Probably No   5–Definitely Yes
        3–Maybe/   NA–Not Applicable/
          Sometimes   Cannot Assess

IEP Goals/Objectives

1. Will acquisition of this skill allow student to function more independently in the residential environment?

2. Will acquisition of this skill allow student to function more independently in the school/educational environment?

3. Will acquisition of this skill allow student to function more independently in the community environment (e.g., social activities, shopping, transportation)?

4. Will acquisition of this skill enable student to function in vocational environments?

5. Will acquisition of this skill promote integration with non-disabled peers?

6. Will acquisition of this skill promote integration with disabled peers?

7. Will this skill improve student's quality of life?

8. Is acquisition of this skill a stated or implied preference by the student?																							
9. Will acquisition of this skill enhance student's ability to make choices?																							
10. Is this skill commonly reinforced in natural environments?																							
11. Is this a skill that will be taught in the natural environment?																							
12. Is this a skill that the student will have an opportunity to practice on a regular basis?																							
13. Is the skill age appropriate?																							
14. Are the settings, materials, cues and strategies that will be used to teach this skill age appropriate?																							
TOTALS																							

Note. Adapted from "A Systematic Procedure for Prioritizing IEP Goals," by J. C. Dardig and W. L. Heward, 1981, The Directive Teacher, Summer/Fall, p. 582. Copyright 1981 by Thomas M. Stephens, Publisher. Reprinted by permission.

with mild disabilities (all of whom were mainstreamed), 90% of the parents indicated they would like to have more information on mainstreaming (Turnbull, Winton, Blacher, & Salkind, 1983).

Furthermore, it is important to recognize that parents vary in their preferences for mainstreamed or self-contained placements (Davidson,

1980; Turnbull & Winton, 1983). A research study with parents of students with learning disabilities reported:

> Parents of learning disabled children felt that additional classes with nonhandicapped children would be beneficial for their child if he/she had a minor, school-related handicap. Similarly, parents who felt that their child's academic performance would decline if placed in more classes with nonhandicapped children thought that their child would have fewer friends and would be unhappy. Some parents noted that their child could perform at a higher academic level but in segregated classrooms. Based on these findings, parents sometimes have anxieties or beliefs that conflict with professional judgments about educational practices. (Abramson, Willson, Yoshida, & Hagerty, 1983, p. 193)

Thus, the conference chair and other professionals should ask for and consider parental views on alternative placements. Also parents should be encouraged to visit different settings which might be appropriate for more firsthand information. Sometimes professionals are resentful of parents who want to visit programs and perceive it as a threat to their expertise or an indication of lack of trust. We encourage you to view visits as a positive strategy for gaining sufficient information to make wise decisions. Chapter 7 includes suggestions for assisting parents with classroom observations.

Just as with placement, parents need information about the nature of related services and the possible benefits and drawbacks of different services. They also need information about classroom instruction that would be missed while the student would be receiving special services.

Concluding the Conference

The concluding portion of the conference should be used to synthesize recommendations and develop a plan for follow-up responsibility. Because there are many important decisions made at IEP conferences, the chair should summarize them to ensure that consensus has been achieved. The chair also should identify any tasks requiring follow-up attention, (e.g., locating instructional materials, arranging transportation) and assign individuals to assume responsibility for each. Finally, the chair should make plans for reviewing or revising the IEP and identify strategies for ongoing communication among school personnel and the family about the student's progress. The suggestions in Table 10–2 are designed to help ensure that closure is reached and future steps are identified.

POSITIVE OUTCOMES OF THE IEP CONFERENCE

There has been surprisingly little research on the results of IEP conferences. More research is needed on the outcomes of parental participation. Several outcomes, such as professional accountability, parental well-being, and student gain have been suggested in the literature, but they have not been researched thoroughly.

Regarding professional accountability, one study investigated the effect of parental participation in team meetings in a residential institution for persons with mental retardation (Singer, Bossard, & Watkins, 1977). Results indicated that more staff members attended conferences and more recommendations were made when parents were in attendance. A teacher described a similar reaction:

> Whether we acknowledge it or not, our staff puts a lot more effort into evaluations and IEPs when we know that the parents are going to participate actively. It's motivation for us—it helps us do our best. (Winton, Turnbull, & Blacher, 1984, p. 137)

Parent well-being is suggested in the following view of a father who described his reaction to the IEP conference:

> Attending the IEP meeting gave me a psychological boost. I looked around the table and felt very fortunate that every person there really cared that Cindy gets a quality education. It made me realize that my wife and I are not alone in our concerns and in our hopes. (Winton, Turnbull, & Blacher, 1984, p. 136)

Furthermore, the high level of satisfaction reported in the studies in the first section of this chapter indicates that parents have a positive perception of their role in the IEP conference. It is important to note, however, that one study found a less positive attitude toward the IEP process by parents of students classified as gifted as contrasted to parents of students classified as disabled (Lewis, Busch, Proger, & Juska, 1981). A teacher of secondary students in the gifted program shared her interpretation of this finding:

> IEPs designed for students with disabilities are used for gifted education indiscriminately. They are often not appropriate. The stress on IEP goals for gifted education can be too restrictive and place too much emphasis on too little material. (Morse, 1985)

Finally, the ultimate outcome is the determination of whether parent participation increases the appropriateness of the student's educational program. Research studies on this important topic have not been reported. It represents a priority area of inquiry for the next decade.

SUMMARY

Research on parent participation in IEP conferences indicates a general trend for passive involvement in decision making. We have discussed barriers to more active parent-professional partnerships from the perspectives of parents and teachers and suggested strategies for your consideration that have been verified by research studies. Furthermore, we have shared a model that we have found helpful in planning IEP conferences—a model that divides the conference into six components. Suggestions for involving parents in each of the six components are summarized in Table 10–2. We believe that adherence to these suggestions will increase the relevance and success of conferences.

Despite your best efforts, however, there will be instances in which satisfactory agreement cannot be reached in IEP conferences. When such an impasse occurs, other forums of decision making are necessary to pursue. Chapter 11 provides you with information on the due process hearing, which is the legally sanctioned mechanism for resolving disputes that can arise in IEP conferences or otherwise.

Chapter 11

Due Process: Using the Law to Resolve and Prevent Conflict

As we pointed out in Chapter 8, one of the six principles of the federal special education law is due process. There, we gave a shorthand definition of due process as the legal requirement that schools must provide opportunities for families to consent or object to their children's educational identification, classification, program, or placement. The underlying concept of due process is fairness, as manifest in the opportunity to consent or object. Due process is the legal technique that seeks to assure fairness among professionals, service systems, families, and students. Taking this theme of fairness as the fundamental characteristic of due process, it is helpful to remember the reasons for due process as we outlined them in Chapter 8:

1. Due process is a requirement of the federal constitution. It says that each citizen has the right to be treated fairly whenever government takes action that might have a personally adverse effect. The essence of fair treatment, we said, is the right to receive notice of the proposed action and the opportunity to protest to an impartial person, to present one's case, and to appeal.

2. Due process is a way to help families and students make schools accountable. The first four principles of law—zero reject, nondiscriminatory evaluation, appropriate education, and least restrictive placement—are the "inputs" from the school to the student. Due process is a way to ensure the school has done its job under those principles. It also is a way that schools can make parents accountable, since schools may bring a due process hearing against parents who object to the schools' proposed course of action.

3. Due process is a way of changing the balance of power between professionals, who have traditionally wielded power, and families, who have felt they could not affect their children's education.

4. Due process is a new way to focus on the rights and needs of students, families, and professionals, particularly students. It gives parents and professionals new opportunities to address their rights and needs.

Later in this chapter we will show how these purposes have been accomplished. But we also will point out some of the new problems that due process has created in family-professional relationships. Throughout this chapter we will suggest ways for professionals to avoid the family-professional conflict that the due process provisions seek to resolve.

In Chapter 8, we organized the elements of due process, as it is guaranteed by the Education of the Handicapped Act (EHA), into two categories. One deals with pre-hearing rights and the other deals with hearing rights. In doing so, we used the impartial hearing or due process hearing (the actual "trial" of the dispute between professionals and service systems, on the one hand, and families, on the other) as the centerpiece of our presentation. Here, we will continue that same organizational scheme but will discuss each of the due process rights of the EHA in greater detail.

Under the EHA and its regulations, any public or private agency that uses federal funds to educate a child with a disability is required to follow due process requirements. For purposes of brevity, we will refer to "schools" but we mean, of course, all public and private agencies (including schools, hospitals, and institutions) that provide special education.

PRE-HEARING

The pre-hearing components of due process relate to the schools' records, evaluation of the student, consent to services, surrogate parents, notice, public consultations and hearings, and advisory panels. We will discuss each in detail.

Access to Records

Families have rights to obtain access to, and to control others' access to, their child's educational records. A child's parents or guardians have the right to examine all relevant records relating to the child's identification, evaluation, placement, and education. This means that generic and specific information must be available to families. For example, certain generic information about school programs for all students with disabilities (e.g., the number, ages, and races of all such students) and about the children themselves is public information, available to all people, not just the families of the students. Teachers should refer parents to school administrators when parents request these records. This is because administrators, not teachers, are the recordkeepers.

But there are specific requirements that relate to individual families and children. Schools must notify families (in the parents' native language) that personally identifiable information is on file. This information includes the name of the child, parents, and other family members; address; any personal identifier, like a social security number or student number; and any list of personal characteristics or other information that would make it possible to identify the child. Schools also must explain the type of information they plan to collect and how they plan to use the information. One mother remarked, "I like knowing what Dr. Grason and his teachers have on file about John, and why. It takes Big Brother out of the scene, and makes me more comfortable." A school therefore may collect information on the number of children with a particular disabling condition, or it may seek data for a description of the educational achievement of a group of such children. Typically, school administrators, not teachers (or other direct-service staff), are responsible for these duties and records.

In addition, schools must give parents a summary of policies and procedures to be used by "participating agencies" (*any* agency or institution that collects, maintains, and uses or provides information) for storing information, releasing it to third parties, or destroying it, as well as their plans for protecting personally identifiable information. These plans should strive for exact compliance with the law. Schools must publicly announce, through the newspapers or other appropriate media, any activities they plan to identify and evaluate children who may be disabled. Thus, they have responsibility for developing policies for access to system records and protection of student records to be followed by all other agencies involved in children's education. Again, school administrators have primary responsibility for these duties.

Parents and their representatives have the right to inspect personally identifiable information in their child's records within 45 days maximum after requesting to inspect the records. For example, a parent may want to see the child's records of intelligence testing. If the record includes information on more than one child, parents are entitled to see or be informed only about the portion relating to their child. As one father said, "I don't want to know about the other children, and I don't want their parents knowing about Jesse. That's good law!"

Obviously, professionals will want to be careful to record information that is accurate, current, and relevant and impressions or conclusions that can be supported by facts. A good rule of thumb is this: put into the record only what you would be willing to defend in court. Another good rule is to consider whether you would want the information that you are about to enter to be filed about you. That is, take the "shoes" test— regard your action as you would if it were taken with respect to you. Both of these criteria—the "defense-in-court" and "shoes" tests—should help you understand the fairness doctrine that underlies the due process principle.

If a parent requests access to these records, the teacher or other direct-service staff should state that access is available and that the school may have policies that must be followed (and they, of course, should follow those policies), and should refer the request to the appropriate administrator. Under no circumstance should any professional refuse access. It is proper, however, to follow school policies and inform appropriate administrators of the request.

A school may presume that the parent has access rights unless it is advised otherwise in cases of guardianship, separation, and divorce. If a professional doubts the authority of a parent, any parent representative, or any other person to inspect a child's records, the professional should refer all requests to the school or other agency chief executive. A teacher has noted this bind, and how she worked out of it:

> The mother told me that, as a result of a divorce agreement, she has legal custody of her child. But the child's father told me the same thing a few weeks earlier. I referred both to the administrators of my school and also asked for copies of the court order that determines custody. That'll settle my doubts about Henry's custody!

Parents may request an explanation or interpretation of the information and must be given copies. All school staff should be willing to make explanations, when qualified to do so. A fee for copies may be charged, unless the fee would prevent a parent from having access to the record. Typically, school administrators should handle the billing.

Upon request, parents must also be provided with a list of the types and locations of information collected and used by the agency. The school must keep a record of who has had access. A good practice for professionals is to offer to explain the content of records and, in doing so, to follow the suggestions we made in Chapter 6 about communicating with parents. Again, school administrators usually have those lists and the duty to comply with this duty.

After reading the records and having them appropriately interpreted, parents may ask the school to amend the information in them. For example, a child may be classified as having one disability but the parent may believe the child's disability is different than is stated in the record. Or, the record may say that the parents neglect the child or somehow cause problems for the child (even, that they are the cause of the child's disability), although the parent has reason to believe that such is not the case. The school—acting through its administrators and direct-service staff—must consider the request and give an affirmative or negative response within a reasonable time. If the school disagrees with the request, it must inform the parents of their right to a hearing to protest this decision. Thus, parents have rights to challenge the contents of the student records. This again underscores the necessity for professionals to recognize the importance of their responsibilities for maintaining accurate student records and documenting educational progress.

In commenting on the "fairness" element of due process, with specific reference to the provisions for access to records, Turnbull (1985) has concluded that "access is not only invaluable to parents and professionals, it is imperative as a course of decent conduct between people and as a weapon against charlatanry" (p. 111). When parents and professionals alike have access to records, they can be more equitable in their dealings with each other. This fact alone can evoke more positive, more respectful, and more decent parent-professional relationships. This is the "fairness doctrine" at work. In addition, access can be a powerful tool for accountability—a way for parents and professionals to assure themselves, by knowing the facts and impressions recorded in the child's record, that they are not being taken advantage of.

The records often reveal whether schools have complied with the EHA. Records transmit information from one professional to another; therefore, their accuracy, completeness, and relevance determine the effectiveness of professional intervention. For that reason, parental access helps to keep the records useful, and that in turn helps professionals. Records may contain information about the family, not just the student. For the sake of the family, then, access is important. Finally, records reveal much about people. As one parent remarked to us recently:

> Those records are our lives, our child's and our family's. All that any professional may know about us is in those records. We are our records! So, we'd better be able to control them and thus what people know about us! That's only fair . . . it's what everyone wants.

Confidentiality of Records—Privacy

The EHA also provides for the confidentiality of student records. The "Buckley-Pell Amendment" (the Family and Educational Rights and Privacy Act, which has been incorporated into the EHA) assures the confidentiality of any personally identifiable data, information, and records collected or maintained by the state education agency, all schools, and all other education agencies. This law also requires agencies to give parents, guardians, and, in some cases, pupils access to their own public school records, an opportunity for a hearing to challenge the content of the records, and the right to prevent the release of certain parts of the records without consent.

There must be one person at each school appointed to assume overall responsibility for ensuring that personally identifiable information remains confidential. This person might be the director of special education, the director of special services, or some other administrator who has concomitant responsibility. All persons who participate in the collection or use of confidential information must receive training related to state and local policies and procedures on the confidentiality of personally identifiable information. Each school also must maintain an updated roster of persons (and their positions) employed by the agency who have access to personally identifiable information. For example, the list may authorize the teachers or related service providers who work directly with a child, but not every teacher in the school and certainly not parents of other children. This list must be available for public inspection. Professionals should know who that person is and whether they themselves have access to personally identifiable information. Teachers, related service providers, and other professionals who work directly with a child should exercise the right to see the child's records, particularly evaluation data, IEPs, and year-end summaries. "I like that right," one teacher told us. "It sure helps us know the students better and coordinate my work with their other teachers!"

Schools must obtain parental consent before releasing personally identifiable information to anyone other than the officials authorized to collect and use the information, unless otherwise authorized to do so under the "Buckley-Pell Amendment." For example, schools should get parental consent to release information to Special Olympics or parent-advocacy groups such as ARCs or ACLDs. Generally, the administrators should prepare the consent forms and, together with the direct-service professionals, give them to parents with the request for parental consent.

Agencies must notify parents when personally identifiable information is no longer needed for educational services; on the request of the parents, the information must be destroyed. Permanent information that may be kept indefinitely includes a student's name, address, phone number, grades, attendance record, classes attended, grade level completed, and year completed. School officials should advise parents that their child's records may be needed for such purposes as securing social security benefits or qualifying for certain income tax deductions. In addition, they should fully explain the safeguards for maintaining confidentiality of records before asking parents to make a decision about whether or not to destroy the records. Typically, school administrators fulfill those duties.

The EHA specifies that parents' rights pertaining to educational records automatically are transferred to the student (or his or her legally appointed guardian, if the student has been adjudicated incompetent) at age 18. As one teacher said:

> Just imagine Virginia wanted her school records, because she was 18, and her parents didn't want her to have them . . . all because she and they disagreed about her placement in an LD class. Thank heavens the law settled that fight.

This requirement has major implications for schools serving students in the 18 to 21 age range. With respect to such students, professionals should know whether the child has been adjudicated incompetent (i.e., a court has ruled that the child, although having attained the age of majority, is not mentally competent and therefore should be placed under the legal authority of a guardian). Professionals also should know who the judicially appointed guardian is. They also should consider whether the student and his or her parents want the parents to continue to have access to records and otherwise exercise the rights of parent participation. It is a good idea for administrators and direct-service staff to confer on these matters and settle upon a uniform course of action.

Evaluation

Parents are entitled to an independent educational evaluation of their child. Evaluation under the EHA refers to procedures used to determine whether a child is disabled and the nature and extent of the special education and related services that the child needs. Such procedures are those used selectively with an individual child and do not include basic tests administered to or procedures used with all children in a school, grade, or class. A person who may make an independent evaluation is any qualified examiner that has responsiblity for educating the child and is not employed by the school. A qualified person is one who has met state certification, licensing, registration, or similar requirements. It is likely, therefore, that professionals in one school district will be asked to serve as independent evaluators for other schools.

Upon request, schools must give parents information about where they may have independent educational evaluations made. Under some circumstances, the independent evaluation must be made at public expense; the public agency either pays for the full cost of the evaluation or ensures that the evaluation is otherwise provided free to the parents. Parents have the right to an independent evaluation at public expense if the due process hearing officer requests one for use in a hearing or if the parents disagree with the school's evaluation. If in a due process hearing that it initiates, however, the school can prove that its evaluation was appropriate, the parents may be required to pay for the new evaluation. When parents obtain an independent evaluation at their own expense, the agency must consider this evaluation as a basis for providing the child with an appropriate education, as evidence in a due process hearing, or both. For example, if a child's family employs a psychologist to evaluate the child, the school must consider that person's report in evaluating the child for special education, classifying that child into a disability group, preparing and implementing an IEP, and contesting the parent if there is a due process hearing. Also, the psychologist's report must be admitted into evidence at the hearing. A mother describes how she obtained an independent evaluation:

> Our daughter, Debbie, has always had significant language delays. At the age of 5 her distortions of sounds and vocabulary were similar to that of her younger brother who is 3. For several years, Debbie had almost constant ear infections that resulted in a temporary mild hearing loss. During those times, she could not adequately hear the sounds of words. She was evaluated by

the public school and classified as learning disabled. My husband and I were shocked, to say the least. We had never considered the fact that her language problems would have this result. We believed that such a classification was totally ridiculous. After learning about our right to an independent evaluation, we wrote a letter to the superintendent of schools and told him that we intended to pursue this evaluation and that we expected to send the bill to him. We told him that we were willing to request a due process hearing unless our request was honored. I don't think he particularly liked it, but he did agree to pay for the independent evaluation. As I look back, that was one of the best decisions we have ever made. Debbie was evaluated at a private clinic by a speech clinician, an audiologist, and a psychologist. Their results indicated that Debbie qualifies for special education because of her language delay; however, they were emphatic in stating that she does not have a learning disability. The school system accepted this independent report. Thank goodness we took the time to do this. Debbie has enough problems with language without having the further complication of another label (Winton, Turnbull, & Blacher, 1984, pp. 102–103).

The provisions for obtaining and using independent evaluations reflect some of the major purposes of the due process doctrine. Clearly, they let parents challenge the schools and their experts by their ability to obtain and use the work product of experts whom they employ. That is accountability at work. They also allow parents to deal on a more equal basis with professionals. When fortified with their own experts, parents have an ability to change the balance of power between themselves and professionals. Third, they tend to keep the professionals and parents focused on the child, who is, after all, the person evaluated.

Notice.   Schools must give prior written notice to parents, a guardian, or the surrogate parent whenever they propose to initiate or change, or refuse to initiate or change, the child's identification, evaluation, placement, or the provision of a free appropriate public education. The elements of notice are set out in Chapter 9.

The requirements for notice obviously serve several purposes. First, they make it possible for parents and professionals to speak *with* each other, to have at least the same basic information. When notice must contain certain information (the ''what'' or the content and substance of the notice) and when their information must be provided in understandable ways (the ''how'' or the method of communication), there begins a certain sharing; there is an opportunity for dialogue, a chance for speaking with each other. Second, the ''power relationship'' between the professional and the parent can be equalized. With roughly equal knowledge, parents and professionals can deal in roughly equal ways with each other. Third, knowledge can relieve some of the anxiety that parents naturally feel about the authority of the school and their child's attendance. Janet Bennett (1985) describes that constant anxiety:

> Whether parents like or dislike their children's special classes, they're held back from voicing criticism by oblique reminders of the early days when there were no classes at all. (Those were the days, remember, when closets and attics across the land presumably harbored a supply of sluggish and slovenly retarded children.) After a long Christmas holiday when the youngster goes back to his class, parents say with relief, "Well, it's better than nothing." Just the term *special class* somehow suggests concession and a veiled threat that if parents get picky, the class will be eliminated. It would obviously be illegal, obviously won't happen; but the nagging primordial fear stays alive among parents just the same. (p. 168)

Just because these purposes for notice exist does not mean they will be achieved. In fact, notice sometimes does not enable professionals and parents to speak with others because it does not adequately inform, does not change the power relationship, and does not relieve parent anxiety. That is often so because the notice is written for the purpose of satisfying the legal requirements and therefore tends to be stated in terms that lawyers or school administrators use with each other. In those instances where the written notice does not inform, professionals may prefer face-to-face explanations, simplified written notice, or both. They also may have an ethical duty to give more adequate notice (see Chapter 14).

Of course, some parents will not respond to notices. There may be many reasons for their nonresponse, and professionals should seek to determine by other means why parents do not respond. They may telephone, make a home visit, ask the student, or consult other professionals involved with the parents. If they do not learn in these ways why parents do not respond, they are legally entitled to seek a due process hearing if parental consent (following notice) is required. Likewise, they may proceed with their plans if parental consent (following notice) is not required. Of course, the legal solutions do not provide solutions that create responsive parents. Professionals therefore should continue to give notice when legally required to do so, follow the "touch-base" rule, and try to learn why parents do not respond. These efforts can be frustrating, but they also, if undertaken politely and persistently, may evoke parental responses.

Consent.   As we discussed in Chapter 9, the school must obtain the parents' consent for preplacement evaluation and for the child's initial placement in a special education program. Consent, in this and in all contexts, means that: the parents have been fully informed in their native language, or in another suitable manner of communication, of all information relevant to the activity (e.g., evaluation) for which consent was sought; the parents understand and agree in writing that the activity may be carried out; the consent describes the activity and lists the records (if any) that will be released and to whom; and the parents understand that they give consent voluntarily and may revoke it at any time. Professionals should use the consent forms that their agencies have prepared, and they should offer to explain those forms and make careful notes of their conversations with parents when seeking consent. Typically, administrators have those forms and usually prepare them (often with the advice of legal counsel). But the duty to explain does not rest solely with them—all professionals should be available and able to seek consent and explain their request for consent.

Turnbull (1985) makes a telling point about consent in his description of his son's early intervention program. He had been asked to observe a psychologist work with his 6-month-old child, Jay, who is mentally retarded, after Jay had undergone surgery:

> Jay's surgery went well, his hernia was repaired successfully, and he came back home with the recommendation that he be put into a behavior program at the Kennedy Institute, an adjunct of Hopkins Hospital. Trusting and hopeful, we duly enrolled Jay and were obliged, as part of his program, to watch a professor of psychology try to get him to say "Aaah" in exchange for a spoonful of banana pudding. "We want to teach him to react to his environment, to control it," we were told. And that's all we were told, even after questioning. We saw failure after failure. And to what purpose—helping Jay? collecting data?
>
> Leaving aside (if one can) the irreparable injury Jay's repeated failures did to my ex-wife and me, and not daring to calculate the almost numberless times parents have had their children's deficiencies so pointedly and callously highlighted by helping professionals, I wonder whether the concern that we attorneys have with consent is sufficiently impressed on all of us. I shudder to think how many programs children have been enrolled in without their parents ever truly knowing the who, what, where, how, why, and how long. When did my trust turn to skepticism? When I first asked, "What's in it for Jay?" That simple question is not asked often enough. Informed consent troubles us all, and rightly it should—we don't have enough of it. (p. 111)

If parents refuse to consent when consent is required, the parties must first attempt to resolve the conflict by complying with any applicable state law. (Better yet, it is a matter of good professional practice for professionals to communicate clearly, even repeatedly, to explain the reasons that consent is sought.) If there is no consent, the school may initiate a due process hearing. Should the hearing officer rule in the school's favor, the parents' refusal will be overruled and the school may evaluate or place the child and notify the parents of its actions so that they may appeal. Again, school administrators are responsible for deciding whether to seek a hearing. It is proper, however, for direct-service staff to consult with them, and be consulted by them, in reaching these decisions.

The requirements for consent clearly address some of due process' purposes. They help assure accountability by requiring schools to explain what they want to do and why. In that way, they also change the balance of power between parents and professionals by giving parents an opportunity to veto, subject to a due process hearing, what the school wants to do. Finally, the consent provisions mean that schools must focus on the student, adapting their services to him or her; they do this by requiring schools to justify themselves.

Surrogate Parent.   Each state education agency must ensure that the rights of a child are protected if his or her parents are unknown or unavailable or if he is a ward of the state. (The provision for surrogates does not apply when the parents are simply uncooperative or unresponsive.) The state education agency may comply with this requirement by assigning a "surrogate parent." (Some states use different terms than the EHA, e.g., "educational advocates.") It must devise methods for determining whether a child needs a surrogate and then for assigning one to him. There are two criteria for selecting a surrogate: there should be no conflict of interest, and the individual should have the skill to represent the child. A superintendent or other employee of an institution in which a child resides may not serve as a surrogate for him. If there is a disagreement about who the surrogate will be, the conflict may be resolved by a due process hearing. The surrogate may represent the child in matters affecting identification, evaluation, placement, and right to a free appropriate public education. Professionals should know whether a child has a surrogate parent and generally should deal with that person just as they would with the child's own family members (see Chapter 8).

Of course, fundamental fairness calls for protection of the vulnerable child, the person without parents. The surrogate also has the same opportunities as natural parents or other guardians to hold the schools accountable, redress any imbalance of power, and require schools to focus on the child.

Notice, Consultation, and Hearings

The state education agency must establish procedures for consultation with persons involved in or concerned with the education of students with disabilities, including those individuals and their parents or guardians. Each state agency also must make available to the public and to parents its annual plan for complying with the law; for conducting hearings at which the public may comment on the education of such students and the state's annual plan; for giving adequate notice of those hearings; and for allowing the general public to comment on proposed policies, programs, and procedures before they are adopted.

The state education agency also must give public notice of hearings at which it seeks public comment on its special education policies, provide an opportunity for public participation and public comment, review the public comments before adopting the annual plan, and publish and make the plan generally available. In addition, the agency must give assurances that, in giving full educational opportunities to children with disabilities, they will provide for the participation and consultation of the parents or guardians of the children. State-agency professionals generally have input into the state plan, and sometimes so do local-agency professionals. All may attend the public hearings and may want to encourage parents and other interested people to attend those meetings.

Advisory Panels

The Secretary of Education must establish a 15-member national committee on children with disabilities. That committee must advise the Secretary concerning the administration of federal law and recommend improvements in its administration and operation.

Similarly, each state education agency must create an advisory panel whose members are to be appointed by the governor or other official authorized to make such appointments. The panel should be composed of individuals involved in or concerned with the education of children with disabilities, and the panel should include at least one representative of individuals who are disabled, teachers of children who are disabled, parents of such children, state and local educational officials, and administrators of programs for such children. The panel is to advise on the unmet needs of students, make public comment on the annual plan and on pertinent state rules or regulations, and assist the state in developing and reporting relevant data and evaluations. Professionals may attend the meetings of the state advisory panel and may want to encourage parents and other interested people to attend them.

Up to this point, the pre-hearing provisions of the due process principle have tried to emphasize the "fairness" component and, in doing so, prevent any conflict between professionals and parents. But conflict is inevitable in some cases. That is why another component, the "hearing" provisions, provide a means for resolving conflict. We now turn to the "hearing" provisions.

DUE PROCESS HEARING

The EHA's provisions for a hearing address each of the major purposes of the due process principle. First, they advance the fairness doctrine by allowing parents or schools to protest what each other does. Second, they enforce accountability by making it possible for each party to require the other to justify and defend a course of conduct. Third, they redress the power relationship by allowing parents to seek a resolution of a dispute from an impartial person, thus preventing unilateral decision making. "I like being able to pull the trigger on the schools, and it's okay if they can do the same to me . . . it gives us an equal shot at each other," said one parent. Finally, they make parents and professionals alike focus on the student's identification, evaluation, classification, placement, and program; they give the rights to the child, and require parents or professionals to discharge duties to the child. It is now appropriate to describe the hearing rights in detail.

Each school must give the parents, guardian, or surrogate an opportunity to present complaints relating to any matter concerning the child's identification, evaluation, placement, or right to a free appropriate public education. If the parents, guardian, or surrogate file a complaint with the school, they are entitled to an impartial hearing. The school must inform the parents about any available low-cost or free legal aid in the geographical area (e.g., about legal aid clinics).

The right to a due process hearing is not limited to parents, guardians, or surrogates. A school also may initiate a due process hearing on its own proposal or refusal to initiate or change a child's identification, evaluation, placement, or free appropriate public education. Normally, the school's decision to seek a due process hearing is made by its administrative officers. Professionals may be asked to help school administrators decide whether to file a due process hearing. In addition, they may request the appropriate administrators to initiate one. For example, schools may want to initiate due process when parents refuse consent for the initial evaluation of a child who has an obvious disability. However, it is not usual for schools to initiate hearings.

Unless the parties agree to an extension, the hearing must be held and a final decision reached within 45 days after the hearing is requested, and a copy of the decision must be mailed to the parties. (The hearing officer may extend this deadline.) The time and place of the hearing and each review of that decision (i.e., when parents or schools file an appeal) involving oral argument must be reasonably convenient to the parents and student (e.g., in the local school district, not at a distant state capitol).

Professionals may be involved in due process hearings in a variety of ways. They may be asked to be witnesses for one side or the other. They may even volunteer to be a witness, although there are some ethical issues involved when they do so (see Chapter 14). Professionals' records may be put into evidence at the hearings. In some cases, professionals may be asked to give their expert opinions on what should be done for the student. In cases where professionals serve as expert witnesses, and indeed in all cases where they testify or their records are admitted as evidence, professionals should be careful to testify from facts and data before reaching a conclusion. Of course, they may feel conflict about their loyalties (see Chapter 14), but their professional conduct should be above reproach. If it is, they will have discharged their duties to the student, parents, and schools. It is only natural for professionals to feel bias toward one party or to experience conflicting loyalties, but their feelings and conduct should be separate entities.

Typically, teachers, other direct-service staff, and school administrators will be involved in a due process hearing. They will be asked, in most cases, to bring school records to the hearing, testify, and, when appropriate, give opinions. Before the hearing, they will be working with the school's lawyer in preparing the school's case.

Each school must keep a list of the hearing officers and their qualifications. The hearing may not be conducted by an employee of the school involved in the education of the child. A due process hearing also may not be conducted by any person having a personal or professional interest that might conflict with his or her objectivity in the hearing. A person who otherwise qualifies to conduct a hearing is *not* considered an employee solely because he is paid by the school to serve as a hearing officer. Sometimes hearing officers are employees of other schools or are retired educators, university professors of education, lawyers, or interested citizens with no particularly relevant experience or training.

At the initial hearing and on appeal, each party has the right to be accompanied and advised by an attorney and by other persons with special knowledge or training with respect to children and youth with disabilities; to present evidence and confront, examine, cross-examine, and compel the attendance of witnesses; to make written and oral argument; to receive a written or electronic verbatim record of the hearing; and to receive a written account of findings of fact. No evidence may be introduced by any party unless it was disclosed at least five days before the hearing. The parents have the right to have their child present and to have the hearing open to the public. Some parents will want to close the hearings because of privacy. Others may want to have open hearings in order to let the public know about a problem. Typically, hearings are not attended by anyone except the participants.

Unless a party appeals from the initial hearing or begins a court action after the appeal, the decision of the initial hearing is final. If the hearing is conducted by a local education agency, an aggrieved party may appeal to the state education agency, which is required to conduct an impartial review of the hearing, reach a decision, and send a copy of the decision to the parties within 30 days. The hearing officer on appeal must make an independent decision after reviewing the matter.

The parties thereafter may file a civil action in either a state court or a federal district court. The court, whether state or federal, is to receive the records of the administrative proceedings, hears additional evidence if offered, and, on the basis of the preponderance of the evidence, grants appropriate relief. The decision whether to initiate or appeal typically is made by school administrators upon advice by school lawyers. The decision whether to go to court involves a careful assessment of the chances of winning, but there also are factors of cost, time, and effects of prolonged school-parent conflict on the child.

During the initial hearing or appeal, the student remains in his or her current educational placement unless the school and the parents, guardian, or parent surrogate agree otherwise. When applying for initial admission to school, the student will be placed in the public school program, with the parents' consent, until all the hearings (including appeals) have been completed. The school may use its normal procedures for dealing with children and youth who are endangering themselves or others (e.g., suspension or expulsion; see Chapter 8 on the law regarding suspension and expulsion).

EFFECTS OF DUE PROCESS PRINCIPLE

There is no doubt about the many powerful effects of the due process principle. At the beginning of this chapter, we stated that due process seeks to achieve the four results of fair treatment, accountability, a new balance of power, and a focus on rights and needs. Has it succeeded? Generally, it has.

The requirements for notice have been the core of the fair treatment that due process seeks. Without notice, families would have no way of knowing what schools are doing or proposing to do with their children. With notice, families can acquire that knowledge and, with it, sometimes assure themselves that the schools either are or are not providing their children with a free appropriate public education.

Due process has sought accountability and achieved it. The fact that families may take legal action against schools, and schools may do likewise against families, has made it possible for parents to hold schools accountable, and schools to hold parents accountable, for their actions. Indeed, the United States Department of Education reported (1982) that 1,412 due process hearings were conducted in 49 states during 1981. The Department also has reported (1984) that there has been a 7.2% decrease across the states in the number of due process hearings between 1979–80 and 1981–82. Of course, given the number of children with disabilities served in school (over 4 million), the percentage of due process hearings is very small. Still, Turnbull (1982, 1983, 1986) has concluded that even this small number of hearings has made schools more accountable to students and families involved in those hearings as well as to other students and families. This is because the decision in one case often sets a precedent for decisions in other cases. In addition, Strickland (1982) observed that due process helps assure accountability by bringing important educational issues to the public, to policy-makers, and to those charged with carrying out public policy. She also stated that due process has the potential for clarifying difficult policy issues, and Turnbull (1986) has shown how such clarification takes place through the courts and becomes precedent for subsequent policy decisions.

Due process sought to redress the balance of power between schools and families—to redress the power relationship. There is substantial but not conclusive evidence that it has succeeded. Budoff and Orenstein (1982) maintained that due process, particularly the system of hearings and appeals, has legitimized the rights of parents and students, lent credence to parents' right to question educators and other professionals concerning the services offered to their children, served to bring pressure on political and administrative organizations to become more responsive to the needs of students, and caused some school systems to reconsider their modes of operation and to make appropriate changes in their relationships with families and students. Of course, these conclusions do not apply universally; there still are intransigent school systems, policy-makers, and professionals, as evidenced by the continuing use of due process hearings to resolve family-school conflict. Yet the frequency of due process is down and the federal special education agency has observed on several occasions that compliance with the EHA is widespread (U.S. Department of Education, 1982, 1983, 1984).

Finally, due process sought to create a new forum for focusing on the rights and needs of children and youth. It certainly seems to have succeeded, for the very issue in a due process case is whether the school and parents have responded satisfactorily to the legal rights of students. In case after case, as Turnbull (1986) shows, the courts have required schools to reshape their policies and practices to discharge their duties to students.

PROBLEMS WITH DUE PROCESS

In many respects, then, due process has accomplished its goals. But, in so doing, it has caused new problems. In brief, these results have been costly. It will be helpful to highlight those problems and suggest how professionals can act with respect to families to accomplish due process' goals without also creating new problems.

As we pointed out in Chapter 8, the due process principle has resulted in some important adverse consequences. There, we stated that it has exacted very high costs in terms of money, emotions, and time; it has increased the use of mediation as a way to prevent, contain, and resolve parent-school disputes; it has not satisfactorily resolved all the disputes beteen parents and schools; and it even may have added to some of the parent-school problems. It is now appropriate to examine these points in detail.

Costs

There are two elements of "costs." One deals with the financial costs that families and schools must bear when they use the due process hearing and appeals as a method of resolving disputes. The other refers to the emotional or psychic costs that the affected individuals experience.

Families and schools alike must pay for attorneys, expert witnesses, independent evaluations, consultations, and communications (telephone, duplicating records) when they enter into an adversarial hearing. These costs can be as low as $200 or as high as $4000 per case (Budoff & Orenstein, 1982; NASDSE, 1978; Strickland, 1982; Yoshida, 1979). In addition, some parents must devote so much time to a case that they cannot attend to their job responsibilities and even lose their jobs (Budoff & Orenstein, 1982). In light of the high costs, it is not surprising that the parents who exercise their due process hearing rights generally are from middle to upper-middle socioeconomic classes (Budoff & Orenstein, 1982; Lay, 1977; NASDSE, 1978).

Schools also must absorb high financial costs (Budoff, 1979; Budoff & Orenstein, 1982; NASDSE, 1978; Yoshida, 1979), including costs of up to $8000 per hearing, with an average between $800 and $1000 (NASDSE, 1978). There also are costs associated with staff time, typically 73 hours per hearing (Kammerlohr, Henderson, & Rock, 1983). Staff time spent on due process arguably is staff time not spent on other aspects of students' education.

Emotional or psychic costs also are high. Budoff and Orenstein (1982) report parents and educators experienced emotional trauma and anxiety. Staff morale and confidence can diminish, particularly when parents attack professionals who see themselves as advocates for children or when they cast doubt on their professional judgment and competence (Budoff & Orenstein, 1982). But Strickland (1982) has documented that there are also emotionally satisfying aspects to the hearing, for parents and educators alike. Both Budoff and Orenstein (1982) and Strickland (1982), thus, note both negative and positive psychic outcomes.

How may a professional act to reduce these costs? Obviously, any conduct that avoids the need for a due process hearing is a way of containing costs. Professionals therefore should act legally and professionally, in the ways we suggest in this book. That will do much to prevent the causes of conflict. More, they should try to de-personalize any conflict that does arise. Of course, it is very difficult not to take personally or not to act defensively at any suggestion of error, misjudgement, wrong-doing, or other behavior that might trigger conflict. But a professional who acknowledges that some conflict is inevitable and regards the due process hearing as a means for working out conflict is less apt to be emotionally injured or to attack and try to emotionally wound a parent or other professional. Professionals may want to try, with renewed vigor, to follow the communication skills and techniques that we discussed in Chapters 6 and 7, particularly after a hearing or mediation.

Mediation

From the very start, many people thought due process could harmonize the separate but similar interests of parents, professionals, and children—the interests of each in the free appropriate public education of the student (Turnbull, 1986). Yet research has demonstrated that adversarial confrontation typically does not bring these common interests together and even may cause the deterioration of relationships (Budoff, 1979; Budoff & Orenstein, 1982; Mitchell, 1976; Strickland, 1982; Yoshida, 1979). In part because of the financial and emotional costs and in part because due process can exacerbate the feelings of conflict between parents and professionals (Strickland, 1982), some people (Budoff & Orenstein, 1982; Turnbull & Barber, 1984) have concluded that mediation, or some other way of preventing or informally resolving conflict without a win-lose result, is a desirable policy.

Mediation is a process that seeks compromise, not victory. It consists of meetings between the parties who are in disagreement, with an impartial person, selected by the parties and therefore trusted by them, presiding over the meetings. The person, the mediator, tries to find ways of helping to resolve differences by compromise, and the parties are asked by him or her to identify points of agreement, points for compromise, and points that cannot be compromised. In mediation, some agreement can be obtained, and some differences may remain. When differences still exist, the parties may choose to go to a due process hearing.

For example, the parties may have differences at the outset concerning a child's evaluation (is he learning disabled or emotionally disturbed?), program (should he be in a resource-room program or in a separate, self-contained program?), and related services (should the family and child have psychological counselling?). After mediation, they may have differences only about the child's program, in which case they may go to due process.

Of course, mediation will never fully take the place of the due process hearing, because the hearing is required by the EHA and ultimately by the federal constitution. It can, however, be a useful prelude to the hearing, because it may make the hearing unnecessary by resolving the parties' differences. (Of course, it also can prolong conflict.)

The desire for an alternative to the due process hearing has several sources. Some professionals have criticized the over-legalization of special education, claiming that the "moral and ethical issues of contemporary life, including issues in education" are best decided "outside" a courtroom or a due process hearing (Kauffman, 1984). Others have argued that the due process approach is too rigid and forces an either-or choice, so that one party necessarily wins and another invariably loses (Agard, 1980; Folberg & Taylor, 1984). Some say that schools practice "defensive education" and concentrate on technical compliance with the law at the expense of "quality" education (Hassell, 1982). Some have observed that the parties generally do not seek compromise or problem-solving solutions (Losen & Diament, 1978), and some think this is so because they become too intent on "winning" the case (Budoff & Orenstein, 1982). Those who have criticized the due process approach as too "adversarial" have suggested that mediation is a preferable approach, and Turnbull and Strickland (1981) have even described how to conduct mediation as a type of parent-professional negotiation.

Mediation is a method of settling disputes by negotiation rather than by decision of a third party who is not involved in the dispute. It necessarily requires compromise by the parties, and it uses the mediator—a disinterested third party—as the means for promoting agreement by consensus. Mediation has the advantage of drawing attention to the points of agreement and using them as the springboards for reconciling the points of conflict (Turnbull & Strickland, 1981). Many states now require the parties to a dispute to resort to mediation before they are entitled to engage in a due process hearing.

Professionals who find themselves in disputes with parents would do well to suggest mediation, to avoid the threat of a due process hearing, to try to identify the common ground and seek (and be prepared to make) compromises on disputed issues, and to the greatest extent possible actively use the knowledge and techniques for enhancing interpersonal relationships that we have described in this book.

DISPUTE RESOLUTION

We stated in Chapter 8 that, in some cases, the due process principle and its various techniques do not satisfactorily resolve all the long-standing disputes between parents and schools but instead give a quick answer that schools or parents may subvert over the long haul. In other cases, the principle and techniques provide not only an answer but also a solution to differences. It is appropriate to examine both the negative and positive aspects of dispute resolution through the due process principle and techniques.

There is evidence that the due process hearing reduces not only the confidence of parents and professionals in the approach itself but also the confidence of parents in the schools themselves and their support for public education (Budoff & Orenstein, 1982). Indeed, the due process hearing in some instances has escalated the conflict between parents and professionals (Essex, 1979; Winer, 1982), left professionals feeling cynical and suspicious about parents (Daynard, 1980), widened the gulf between parents and professionals (Budoff & Orenstein, 1982), foreclosed constructive future communication (Budoff & Orenstein, 1982), and created a "win-at-all-costs" situation, not a problem-solving one (Budoff & Orenstein, 1982). These results are not universal. For example, Strickland (1982) did not find that the due process hearing caused a significant change in parent-professional relationships—there was neither improvement nor deterioration in the relationships. Indeed, she reported that parents noted a significant improvement in the way they were treated by professionals after the hearing—they were respected as knowledgeable, courageous, and committed to their children, and they were dealt with in a more conciliatory way by professionals because they were regarded as "willing to go to bat" for their children.

What about the child? Both Budoff and Orenstein (1982) and Strickland (1982) reported that some children can experience little to no effects, or can experience negative consequences from due process hearings. Their attitudes toward school sometimes become more negative during the due process hearings (Budoff & Orenstein, 1982) and they may experience informal sanctions from professionals (Strickland, 1982), such as negative teacher attitudes that are manifest by unwarranted "correction" procedures or unfairly depressed grades.

These data seem to suggest that the due process hearing will produce mainly negative consequences for parents, children, and professionals. They also suggest that, over the long haul, the quick remedy of the hearing can be easily countered by the negative consequences. To conclude that the due process hearing is more problem-producing than problem-solving, however, is to focus only on one aspect of parent-professional relationships, which is the personal or affective nature of the relationship.

If the focus is on the results with respect to students' identification, classification, program, and placement, it is clear that there have been and will continue to be highly positive results for children and youth, families, and even school systems, particularly from the due process hearing. Turnbull (1982; 1983; 1986) has gone to great lengths to document the changes that the due process hearing, as an enforcement and dispute-resolving technique, has caused. Those changes affect not just individual children and their families, but also whole systems—from state to local education agencies. According to Turnbull's analysis of the judicial decisions arising from due process disputes, all of the four major "input" principles of special education law—zero reject, nondiscriminatory evaluation, appropriate education, and least restrictive placement—have been interpreted by the courts in ways that prevent exclusion, discrimination, inadequate programming, and unwarranted segregation of students who are disabled. By keeping the focus on the systemic changes in public education, Turnbull has demonstrated that the due process principle, including the hearing technique, provides not only an answer but also a solution to differences where the differences are over the question whether the schools must educate students effectively, not whether disgruntled parties can reconcile their attitudinal problems by legal means.

SUMMARY

The first challenge for professionals is to prevent conflict by carrying out the skills that this book seeks to teach, complying regularly and rigorously with federal, state, and local laws and policies, and seeking and accepting parental and professional collaboration. The second challenge is more specific. It is to follow the suggestions that we have made about how to comply with the law and work with families within the law's structure. The third is to make the promise of due process—its purpose—into the reality for each student and family. This means having a strong desire and the skill to deal fairly, to hold oneself and one's employer accountable, to recognize that professionals do not (and should not) have a monopoly of power over the student and family, and to keep one's focus clearly on the child and his or her family. In keeping that focus sharp, the professional will want to know how to provide information to the child's family, a topic we address in the next chapter.

Chapter 12

Providing Information to Families

Professionals can satisfy an important component of educational programs for children and youth having exceptionalities by providing information to family members in many different ways ranging from informal (e.g., suggestions on how to explain visual impairment to neighborhood children) to highly formal (e.g., workshop on enhancing social interaction). This new emphasis (providing information to families) contrasts with the older concept of "training" parents to implement educational programs at home. The latter concept, mainly one of the 1970s, was based on the premise that parents can be effective in changing their children's behavior and increasing their skills (Johnson & Katz, 1973).

The rationale for "parent training" emanated more from professional ideology than parent-stated preferences (Shearer & Shearer, 1977; Turner & Macy, 1980). The role of parent as teacher has been particularly strong in early childhood education programs. Its wide acceptance is exemplified in the following passage describing the type of parent involvement expected during the 1970s in the Handicapped Children's Early Education Program Network (early childhood projects), funded by the U.S. Department of Education:

> It thus becomes mandatory that projects develop training programs for parents with the objective of teaching parents to be effective in working with and teaching their own child (Shearer & Shearer, 1977, p. 213).

Given the strong priority of the 1970s for training parents, it is not surprising that the Education for the Handicapped Act (EHA) gave rights to parents to receive training and imposed responsibilities on schools to provide it. There are three legal requirements:

1. inclusion of parent training in the definition of related services,
2. inclusion of parents as one of the groups to receive inservice training through the mandatory Comprehensive System for Personnel Development, and
3. preparation of surrogate parents to represent the child in educational decision making.

There are many reasons why parent training has been considered an important component of special education programs over the last two decades. One is the recognition that parents can be effective teachers of their children. Other reasons include the continuity that parents provide in their children's lives, an increased probability that parents would learn to handle future problems, and the innate strength of parents' reinforcement of their children (Altman & Mira, 1983).

A classic review article on parent training states another reason: "The advantage of parents as change agents is that they constitute a cheap, continuous treatment resource which is able to augment existing therapeutic manpower capabilities and work conveniently within the home" (Johnson & Katz, 1972, p. 181). It is instructive to analyze this statement from a family systems perspective. Several interpretations are possible: parent time is not necessarily cheap (e.g., some mothers may forego employment outside the home because of the need to work with their child), "continuous treatment" may be detrimental to positive family interaction, some parents' ideological style may not value "augmenting existing manpower capabilities," and the competing functional responsibilities of parents may reduce the possibility of working "conveniently within the home."

The family systems perspective has influenced how training is now conceptualized. First, there has been a shift in terminology from "parent training" to "parent support," "family support," or simply "providing information to families." This semantic change represents a philosophical shift away from the view of parents as the students of professionals.

Jane Schulz (1985), the mother of a son with Down syndrome and a leading teacher educator in special education, shared her view on this issue:

> The current concept of parent training is extremely insulting. Some colleagues told me of an encounter with a young mother and her two boys, aged 7 and 12, both mentally retarded and blind. My associate suggested that parent training was indicated. I wondered at the time who we knew that could tell this mother anything. In fact, I immediately wanted to meet and learn from a woman who had raised children with such complicated problems. Since that time I have had the distinct pleasure of working with her and her children. We pooled our resources; we learned from each other. Parent training? This mother and father were good parents long before I came along. (p. 6)

Second, models for parent involvement have broadened from clinic-based and formal workshops to include more diverse options for providing information. This diversity is consistent with parents' preferences on ways to receive information in consideration of their schedules, available time, and competing responsibilities. For example, many parents want to receive information through informal conversations rather than participate in didactic sessions.

Third, there has been a shift from singular focus on "training" parents (usually mothers) to providing information to different family members (e.g., fathers, mothers, sisters, and extended family). This new emphasis enables family members to address their own priorities, not just the child's progress, because the family systems approach acknowledges the right of the family to identify their own priorities rather than priorities imposed by professionals.

Family members vary in their interest in receiving information, the priority of their topics of interest, the desired format of the information to be shared, and the choice of a person with whom to work. We will provide an overview of options to consider in individualizing your approach to providing families with information.

OVERVIEW OF TOPICS

Many different topics are relevant to the concerns and needs of families. Based on our review of the literature and our own experiences in working with families, we have chosen four topics to highlight in this section—managing behavior, teaching pre-academic and academic skills, educational advocacy, and future planning. The families with whom you work may be interested in obtaining information on these topics, or they may prefer pursuing others.

Managing Behavior

The most prevalent and well-documented model for providing information is in the area of managing behavior—particularly in the case of children and youth who have difficulty in complying with parental rules and requests. Different training approaches, based on different learning theories, have been developed—transactional analysis (Sirridge, 1980), Parent Effectiveness Training (Gordon, 1980), and behavioral approaches (Altman & Mira, 1983; Dangel & Polster, 1984). This section will focus on behavioral approaches, because they have been used far more frequently than any other approach with children and youth having behavioral and learning problems. We were unable to locate any research studies or model programs using behavioral approaches with students who are gifted.

Behavior management interventions seek to change parent-child relationships by modifying parent and child behaviors alike. Parents learn principles that enable them to increase the positive behaviors of their child and decrease or eliminate the negative behaviors. These principles typically include defining the behavior, measuring its rate and occurrence, intervening by arranging consistent consequences, and evaluating the effectiveness of the intervention.

Many different types of behaviors have been the focus of training sessions, including acting-out behavior (Brehony, Benson, Solomon, & Luscomb, 1980; Fleischman, 1982), self-help skills (Adubato, Adams, & Budd, 1981), communication skills (Arnold, Sturgis, & Forehand, 1977; Casey, 1978), and academic skills (Blechman, Kotanchik, & Taylor, 1981;

Wedel & Fowler, 1984). Behavior management instruction has been provided to parents who have children with mental retardation (Brightman, Ambrose, & Baker, 1980), autism (Koegel, Schreibman, Johnson, O'Neill, & Dunlap, 1984), physical disabilities (Feldman, Manella, & Varni, 1983), emotional disturbance (Thomas, 1977), language impairment (Schumaker & Sherman, 1978), and hearing impairment (Lowell, 1979).

A comprehensive program focusing on behavior management topics is the Project for Developmental Disabilities at UCLA (Baker, 1983). This project has used many approaches and has generated research to document the intervention outcomes. The approaches include:

1. Self-instructional manuals—The *Steps to Independence Series* includes eight instructional manuals to teach parents concepts and skills related to play, speech and language, behavioral problems, self-help skills, and independent living skills (Baker, Brightman, Heifetz, & Murphy, 1976–1977; Baker, Brightman, Carroll, Heifetz, & Hinshaw, 1978; Baker, Brightman, & Hinshaw, 1980; Baker, Brightman, & Blacher, 1983).
2. Individual sessions—The family comes to a clinic for a series of individual sessions with a professional.
3. Home visits—Professionals and families meet in the home to discuss content.
4. School-based model—Parents are provided with information in conjunction with an ongoing school program.
5. Group sessions—Ten two-hour sessions are conducted, with pre- and post-assessments and several follow-up visits. Group leaders guide parents through the *Steps to Independence* series and use active learning strategies such as demonstrations and role-plays.

The program has obtained consistent increases in parent knowledge, parent teaching skills, and child development (Baker, 1984). An important study investigated whether or not parents continue to use newly learned behavior management skills after the completion of training (Baker, Heifetz, & Murphy, 1980). Ninety-five parents were followed up 14 months after training to find out if they were using the skills they had learned. Sixteen percent of the families were setting aside time for planned sessions several times a week, 22% had carried out a behavior management program related to their child's problem, and 76% reported incidentally incorporating behavioral principles into daily routines.

Baker (1984) identified low SES-status as a critical variable in the parents' comprehension of behavioral principles and their follow through in teaching their child with mental retardation. In order to individualize training to the needs of these families, the UCLA Project has made several adaptations such as using a central and familiar location, recruiting families through counselors who have personal relationships with them, providing child care, providing or reimbursing for transportation, earning lottery tickets for attendance and homework, giving diplomas for program completion, and increasing the use of modeling and supervised child teaching during group sessions (Baker, 1983). Spanish-speaking parents who averaged a fifth grade education were successful in a training program (Prieto-Bayard & Baker, in press).

Brothers and sisters also have been given opportunities for training on behavior management (Powell & Ogle, 1985; Schreibman, O'Neill, & Koegel, 1983). Schreibman and her colleagues (1983) taught behavior management principles to brothers and sisters of children with autism. The evaluation indicated that the siblings were able to use the behavior management skills effectively and their brother or sister with autism made consistent progress. An excellent review of research on providing information to brothers and sisters and guidelines for setting up programs can be found in Powell and Ogle (1985).

More commercial materials are available on behavior management issues than any other training topic. A 1978 survey (Bernal & North, 1978) identified and described 26 commercially available information manuals including ones developed for parents to use and others for professionals to use in working with parents. In addition to self-instructional books for parents, films/videocassettes and workshop kits focusing on behavior management skills are commercially available.

Assisting parents in becoming better managers of their child's behavior has many potential advantages—decreasing parent-child conflict, increasing positive communication, increasing children's progress in social and self-help skills, and increasing parents' competence as a disciplinarian. There are also some cautions with this approach. Bernal (1984) describes characteristics of families who do not seem to benefit as much from training:

> There are some personal and demographic characteristics of parents that have the potential for reducing the effectiveness of parent training, even if the parent does not drop out before the end of treatment. Among these characteristics are marital problems (Cole & Morrow, 1976; Johnson & Lobitz, 1974; Margolin & Christensen, 1981; Oltmanns, Broderick, & O'Leary, 1977; Wahler, 1980b), depression (McMahon, Forehand, Griest, & Wells, 1981), social isolation (Wahler, 1980b); low socioeconomic status (Blechman, et al., 1981); child-rearing philosophies that conflict with parent training philosophy (Bernal & Klinnert, 1981; Sloop, 1974), a severely negative, critical view of the child (Bernal & Klinnert, 1981; Cole & Morrow, 1976), and an inability or unwillingness to devote sufficient time to carrying out parent training programs . . . (Bernal & Klinnert, 1981)

My personal view of behavioral parent training is that it is best suited for white middle- and upper-class families, since it was developed for service to these families. Issues arise relevant to the match or mismatch between parent training (as well as parent trainers) and diverse populations, such as low-income and culturally or ethnically different families. The parent trainer who attempts to work with low-income families soon learns that the required appointments, homework, and monitoring of parent and child behavior are not family priorities when economic pressures and uncertainties disrupt schedules, plans, and availability of resources on a daily basis. These families may have needs for which a parent training approach may be inappropriate . . . In general, the less acculturated and the more linguistically different the family is in relation to the white culture, the greater the need is for a cultural and linguistic match between the family and the parent trainer, in order to facilitate the adaptation of parent training procedures to the culture in the appropriate language. (pp. 487, 488)

Despite these limitations, the state-of-the-art in assisting families to learn to manage their child's behavior more proficiently is more advanced than any other informational topic. Readers interested in a comprehensive review of research in this area are referred to Snell and Beckman-Brindley (1984), Dangel and Polster (1984), and Baker (1984).

Teaching Pre-Academic and Academic Skills

Many parents are interested in learning how to help their son or daughter at home with the skills they are being taught at school. In an observational study of IEP conferences, it was reported that the majority of parents asked how they could help their child at home, but none of them received a definitive response from the professionals at the meeting (Goldstein, Strickland, Turnbull, & Curry, 1980). Parents of gifted students are thought to have special responsibilities for ensuring that the home environment is challenging (Karnes & Karnes, 1982), yet many of these parents experience concern and anxiety about how to best support their child's achievement (Dettmann & Colangelo, 1980).

A comprehensive approach to providing parents with information on teaching pre-academic and academic skills was developed by the staff of an early intervention program for young children with developmental delays (Sandler & Coren, 1981). Parents were first provided an eight-week instructional program to learn skills they could use to teach the same education program at home that was being used at school. After the completion of this program, a team meeting (i.e., parent, teacher, program co-ordinator, and therapist) was held every six weeks to review each child's progress on IEP objectives and to make necessary revisions in objectives or instructional approaches. The parents then received a written copy of the evaluation report and IEP revisions. An individual session was held with parents during the week after the team meeting to observe their child being instructed, to receive teaching suggestions, engage in a practice teaching session while being videotaped, view the video tape, and receive feedback on their performance.

Parents and teacher sent a data sheet back and forth to record the child's progress on specific skills and to review progress being made in the other setting. They met once every week to coordinate programming efforts, share educational materials, and provide and receive support and encouragement.

The parents expressed a high level of satisfaction with the program (100% valued observing their child being instructed; 92% believed the team meetings should be held at least every six weeks). It is also noteworthy that 87% of the parents reported occasionally inventing data and 15% indicated the pressure was too great on occasions to record data at home. The parents were described as well-educated and middle to upper-middle class in socioeconomic status. Of the 26 mothers who participated, 3 were single parents and 24 were full-time homemakers.

Another parent training program that links home and school activities is the Parent Education Model in the Follow-Through Program (Gordon, Olmsted, Rubin, & True, 1978). This Follow-Through Program was not developed for children who are disabled but rather for ones from a lower socioeconomic background and at-risk for academic problems. The Parent Education Model recognizes the important role parents play as the teachers of their own children. The major strategy used is a weekly home visit program by a paraprofessional who also works with children and teachers in the classroom. The paraprofessional helps to coordinate instruction between home and school by participating in both settings. During the home visit, the paraprofessional describes the child's classroom expectations and performance to the parents (mostly all from minority background) and reviews with parents home learning activities that they are requested to teach during the following week. The paraprofessional stresses desirable teaching behaviors with the parents, behaviors such as giving clear directions, removing environmental distractions, and praising the child for attending and performing correctly. In 1977, over 153,000 home visits were made to over 6,000 families (Gordon, 1978). A group of parents who had been involved with the Parent Education Model for at least one year were compared with a matched group of parents who had not been associated with the program. Parents in both groups were videotaped while they presented a learning activity to their child. Parents who had participated in the Parent Education Model used an average of 24 desirable teaching behaviors; the control group of parents used an average of 14.5.

Programs to provide information to families on pre-academic and academic skills do not have to be as extensive as the previously described one. Many school districts do not have the personnel resources to implement programs of such comprehensiveness; furthermore, many families are not interested in such extensive involvement. A first grade teacher who had a group of students gifted in reading successfully implemented a program to send enrichment homework activities for parents to work on co-operatively with their child in the evening. A thorough description of this program and sample assignments are described in an article written by the teacher (O'Neill, 1978).

A training alternative on a smaller scope involved a school district providing five workshops for parents of elementary-aged children on "survival reading" (Cassidy & Vukelich, 1978). The workshop leaders were reading specialists and teachers whose goals were to assist parents in learning to develop games to reinforce survival reading skills at home. Pretests were sent to parents prior to the workshop so they could informally assess their child's skill levels. The identification of skills was helpful in ensuring that the games constructed during the workshops were at the appropriate level of difficulty. Parents were given instruction sheets, as illustrated in Figure 12–1 (p. 286), as a guide to constructing and playing the games. Parents reported that they shared instruction sheets with neighbors and that their children enjoyed playing the games.

Providing information to families on teaching academic skills has the potential advantages of enhancing the child or youth's academic or developmental progress and strengthening the partnership between families and teachers. A drawback for some families could be increased stress created through the tension of teaching. You might reflect on your own experience. Was tension ever created in your family when your parents attempted to help you with a school assignment? Depending upon family dynamics, involving parents in teaching academic skills can be an asset or liability.

Maddux and Cummings (1983) provide excellent suggestions, consistent with a family systems perspective, of when home tutoring should not be done:

- if there is parental disagreement over whether or not the child should be tutored;
- if no quiet, non-distracting place is available in the home;
- if tutoring might result in neglect of the needs of other family members (in cases where there are many children or where someone suffers from a chronic illness);
- if either parent resents the time spent tutoring or feels guilty if tutoring sessions are skipped or cut short;
- if time spent in tutoring deprives the child of opportunities to make friends with other children or develop necessary social skills. (p. 31)

Materials
egg carton for 12 eggs
marble
driver's manual
glue
cardboard
pen

Directions for construction
1. Look in the driver's manual and find 12 traffic signs; make or cut out 2 of each and 3 extras.
2. Glue one set of signs in the bottom of an egg carton, a different sign in each depression.
3. Make bingo cards:

a. For Level I, glue the second set of signs and the extras randomly on 3 bingo cards, 5 per card.

b. For Level II, print the descriptions of the 12 signs randomly on the 3 bingo cards, 5 per card.

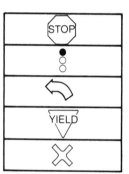

stop
yield
one way
go
railroad crossing

How to play
1. Each player takes a bingo card.
2. Players take turns shaking the egg carton with the marble inside. The marble lands in one of the depressions. The player matches the sign the marble landed on with the same sign on the card (Level I), or matches the symbol that the marble landed on with the appropriate written description of a sign (Level II).
3. The first player to cover his/her bingo card wins.

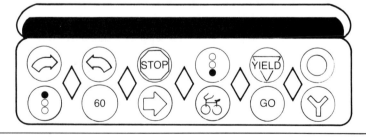

FIGURE 12–1
TRAFFIC BINGO

Note. From "Survival Reading for Parents and Kids: A Parent Education Program" by J. Cassidy and C. Vukelich, 1983, The Reading Teacher, 31, *pp. 638–641.* Reprinted with permission of the authors and the International Reading Association.

Another warning is to avoid the "perpetual patient" syndrome for the students (Gliedman & Roth, 1980), described by Sondra Diamond, a psychologist with a physical disability:

> Something happens in a parent when relating to his disabled child; he forgets that they're a kid first. I used to think about that a lot when I was a kid. I would be off in a euphoric state, drawing or coloring or cutting out paper dolls, and as often as not the activity would be turned into an occupational therapy session. "You're not holding the scissors right." "Sit up straight so your curvature doesn't get worse." That era was ended when I finally let loose a long and exhaustive tirade. "I'm just a kid! You can't therapize me all the time! I get enough therapy in school every day! I don't think about my handicap all the time like you do!" (Diamond, 1981, p. 30)

Sometimes students do get enough instruction or therapy in school and teaching pre-academic or academic skills might be overkill. All students— those who are disabled and/or gifted—have the potential for "burning-out" on learning. As we discussed in chapters 3–5, balance is the key.

Educational Advocacy

Since the passage of the EHA, educational advocacy has been a major training emphasis. Specific topics include legal rights, involvement in the IEP process, and assertive communication. Ferguson (1984), the mother of a child with a severe disability involved in a parent-run advocacy program, pointed out one reason advocacy training is important:

> Although parents do have a lot of information, it is not the "right" kind. When we go to speak to administrators at school we hear about IEP's, MA's, criteria, auditory processing, regulations, and, sometimes, due process. At first, there seems to be no correspondence between what we know and what the people in schools are talking about. Difficult initial experiences can cause some parents to stay silent. Others begin to search out information and eventually learn to speak the language of the schools. . . . One of our members suggested, "If you say 'perseveration' instead of 'he does it again and again and again and again,' it makes it sound as though you know what you are talking about." (p. 41)

Families with advocacy skills are able to represent their child's interests in securing appropriate educational services. Furthermore, the need for advocacy does not end with high school graduation but continues in settings such as group homes, as Jane Schulz (1985) points out:

> We as parents of handicapped children have fought for the rights of our school-aged children. We have not fought as hard for the rights of handicapped adults . . .
>
> During our weekend visits I watched Billy revolt against the forced companionship of an unchosen roommate, the rage of an ill-tempered house parent, and the confusion of group living . . . I watched Billy regress

for two years before I re-examined the situation and my own behavior. I could no longer relinquish my parental rights, my professional judgment, and my ultimate responsibility for my son's welfare. In an impassioned effort to remedy the situation, I wrote a letter to Billy's landlord. I referred to the exorbitant rent, the substandard housing, the lack of adequate utilities. I stated that I had tried to stay out of the situation because there were agencies working with Billy, but that I could no longer live with it. I asked for satisfaction and an immediate reply.

I sent copies of the letter to the agencies involved. One agency member called to express his indignation at my writing such a letter and to ask if I would meet to discuss the situation. I responded that I would welcome a meeting. No meeting was called. No action was taken. We brought Billy home and helped him move into a trailer. (pp. 12–13)

An excellent advocacy resource for special education professionals is the federally funded parent center. These centers, usually staffed by parents of persons with exceptionalities, have advocacy training as a primary mission. An example of a parent center is the PACER program in Minneapolis, Minnesota. PACER was funded in 1976 with the philosophy of "parents helping parents." Its main function is to inform parents of their legal rights and responsibilities related to special education. Over 9000 persons received information from PACER in 1983–84. The primary means of sharing information include workshops, newsletters, phone calls, and letters. The recipients of this information have evaluated the services in an extremely favorable way (PACER Center, Inc., 1984). A teacher commented on the value of attending a PACER workshop:

I have received more information about the rights of the handicapped in the first hour of this workshop than I have received from the schools during 20 years of teaching. I teach 12th grade and I have had blind, hearing impaired, mentally retarded and emotionally disturbed children in my classroom during these years. (PACER Center, Inc., 1984, p. 13)

Parents' comments included:

I think we got what we needed because PACER was involved. When we knew where we stood regarding laws and rights the district started listening to us. (PACER Center, Inc., 1984, pp. 17, 27)

PACER and other parent centers contribute extremely useful advocacy information and assistance. The names and addresses of these centers are included in Appendix B. We urge you to write centers in your geographical area to inquire about the services they provide and the ways that the families with whom you work, along with yourself and your professional colleagues, can benefit from their services.

Another method of advocacy training has been the development and mailing of printed information by state educational agencies. Family members may write state agencies for this information. A research study was conducted to analyze the format and content of this material (McLoughlin, Edge, Petrosko, & Strenecky, 1981). The typical response by state educational agencies was described by the authors:

> In general, most states strive to send one to three items, of durable and attractive 8-1/2 × 11 inch material weighing under a pound, in 3rd class mail for about a dollar, organized for easy use in narrative format, written at the 15th grade or college reading level, taking over an hour for the average reader to read. PL 94–142 and the specific rights of the handicapped, as well as their characteristics and various services for them, should be covered. (McLoughlin et al., 1981, p. 56)

The extraordinarily high reading level of this material represents a comprehension barrier for many families. Further, this article did not report the language translations in which the material is available. The New York State Department of Education has translations in English, French, Spanish and Chinese. The extent to which other states account for language diversity is unknown.

Two approaches to preparing parents for participation in IEP conferences were discussed in Chapter 10. These approaches included a workshop on legal rights and participation skills (Thompson, 1982) and the mailing of printed materials to parents in advance of the IEP conference to help them prepare for their role (Malmberg, 1984). Both of these studies reported that the additional information positively influenced the behavior of the parents in the IEP conference. We have conducted many workshops for parents and surrogate parents related to legal rights and IEP participation. We organize workshops around the six components of the IEP conference that we discussed in Chapter 10. A sample agenda of one of these workshops is included in Table 12–1.

We also send a manual in advance to participants with printed material on legal rights, suggestions for the six components, and suggestions for assertive communication. When parents read this information in advance, they can spend workshop time on discussion and specific questions. Evaluations have indicated that parents find discussion with other parents about their experiences, practical suggestions, and the manual to be the most helpful aspects of the workshops.

Again, educational advocacy is not for all families. Given the responsibilities they have in fulfilling other family functions some families find that advocacy is not a priority. A mother commented on her need to balance priorities:

> I used to run from this meeting to that one. I wanted the people in my community to crown me "World's Greatest Mom of a blind kid". I wanted to know deep down in my heart that I was creating a better world for Angela.

Table 12–1
PLANNING FOR YOUR PARTICIPATION IN THE IEP CONFERENCE

Workshop Goals

1. Participants will be able to state the purpose of an individualized education program (IEP), both the document and the conference.
2. Participants will be able to describe their rights and responsibilities in educational planning.
3. Participants will be able to describe the six components of the IEP conference.
4. Participants will discuss and/or role play how they want to be involved with each component of the IEP conference.

Workshop follow-up

5. Participants will have the option of scheduling a home visit with project staff to identify skills and priorities for their child's next IEP conference.

Agenda

9:00–9:10 A.M.	Introduction of families, other participants, and presenters.
9:10–9:20	What is the purpose of an IEP?
9:20–9:50	Group discussion: 1) What have I liked most and least about past IEP conferences? 2) What are my expectations of an IEP conference?
9:50–10:15	What are my rights and responsibilities in educational planning?
10:15–10:30	Break and refreshments (Review of materials on display table)
10:30–11:15	The Six Components of the IEP Conference How do I want to participate in the IEP conference? Group discussion on the first three components: 1) Preconference preparation 2) Initial conference proceedings 3) Review of formal evaluation and current levels of performance
11:15–11:30	Break and refreshments
11:30–12:30	How do I want to participate in the IEP conference? (continued) Group discussion and role play on the last three components: 4) Development of the goals and objectives 5) Determination of placement and related services 6) Concluding the conference
12:30–12:45	Do you have any additional questions? Discussion of any questions you want to ask other parents, other participants, or the presenters.
12:45–1:00	Evaluation of the workshop Questionnaire on scheduling summer training sessions

> Then after Angela starting acting out really badly, it dawned on me that she needed a mother—not a community organizer. I spend more time at home making sure she gets what she needs. We are both happier.

Engaging in advocacy is extremely demanding of time and energy. One way to assist families who are not able to advocate is to suggest community resource persons who may help them in this area. Another important consideration is to teach students self-advocacy skills which can have the benefit of their assuming more lifelong responsibility in this area.

Future Planning

The importance of helping families plan for the future is well documented in the life cycle literature. As discussed in Chapter 5, a pervasive concern of many parents is the future. From life cycle literature we know that transitions or life changes are periods of greatest stress for families. These transitions frequently involve entry into or exit from school programs—preschool, elementary school, secondary school, and post-secondary education or the adult services. Educators recently have begun to realize the importance of preparing families for successful school transitions.

Training has been provided to families in a number of ways. Most of the training models developed to date focus exclusively on helping families deal with an educational transition at one particular point in time. For example, one of us (Ann Turnbull) participated with Pam Winton and Jan Blacher in writing a book for parents entitled *Selecting a Preschool: A Guide for Parents of Handicapped Children* (Pro-Ed, 5341 Industrial Oaks Blvd., Austin, TX 78735). This book, aimed primarily at parents but also relevant for professionals, is the culmination of four years of research at the Carolina Institute for Research in Early Education of the Handicapped at The University of North Carolina at Chapel Hill. The book focuses on answers to these questions:

- What do you want from a preschool?
- What kinds of preschools might be available?
- How do you gather information and select the most appropriate preschool program for your child?
- How can you best prepare your child and yourself for the new preschool?
- How can you ensure that the preschool is meeting your child's needs and your own needs?

Also included is an extensive resource list with names, addresses, and annotations of helpful resource materials for parents.

The book provides a framework within which the experiences of parents of children with disabilities are shared with other parents. Parents contributed their ideas to the book, and they provided a careful field test and critique during draft stages.

A school-based model to prepare families for making transitions from preschools to kindergarten programs is currently being developed by Susan Fowler and her colleagues at The University of Kansas. Two products are being developed and will be available by 1987:

1. A manual containing the instruments developed for identifying and assessing childrens' readiness for transition (e.g., teacher expectations regarding child skills necessary for successful kindergarten adjustment at school entry, midyear, and end of year points; parent interview which assists parents or family members to identify and prioritize family needs).
2. A curriculum manual for preschool and kindergarten teachers containing detailed procedures and ideas for assessing and teaching transition skills.

At the other end of the educational continuum is the transition from secondary school to post-secondary education or adult services. This transition can be particularly stressful for families of students with severe disabilities when limited vocational and residential options are available. A model currently being developed to address the transitional planning needs of families with adolescents having moderate and severe disabilities (Turnbull et al., 1984) contains three phases. The first phase involves working with families to select options for residential living and vocational preparation for their son or daughter. Strategies include assisting families in identifying the criteria that are important for their adolescent and for themselves in achieving a satisfactory quality of life. Families are also guided through the process of visiting and observing community programs to select the ones most consistent with their preferences. The second phase targets the IEP conference as a forum for future planning. Specifically, parents are helped to identify and prioritize the skills necessary for admission to and ongoing success in preferred programs. These skills become the basis of IEP planning during the secondary years. Information is provided to families to prepare them to participate in the IEP conference according to their preferences for involvement. An outline of the planning steps involved in phases one and two for employment are included in Figure 12–2. The third phase involves conducting a series of life-planning seminars with families on legal and ethical issues, such as estate planning, financial resources, sexuality, right to treatment, and case management. These materials will be disseminated through the Association for Retarded Citizens/US.

FIGURE 12–2 ▶
FUTURE PLANNING PROCESS FOR EMPLOYMENT OPPORTUNITIES

Note. From How to plan for my child's adult future: A three-part process to future planning *by A. P. Turnbull, M. J. Brotherson, G. J. Bronicki, H. A. Benson, J. Houghton, C. Roeder-Gordon, and J. A. Summers, 1985, Future Planning Project, University Affiliated Facility, Bureau of Child Research, Lawrence, KS.*

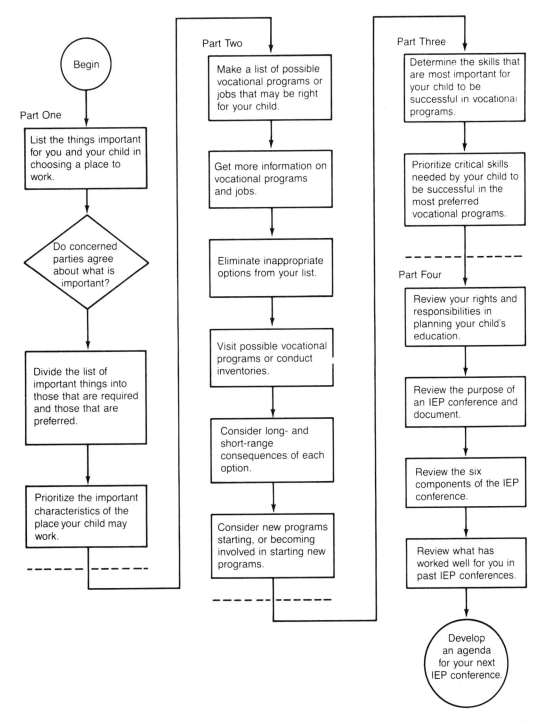

Begin

Part One

List the things important for you and your child in choosing a place to work.

Do concerned parties agree about what is important?

Divide the list of important things into those that are required and those that are preferred.

Prioritize the important characteristics of the place your child may work.

Part Two

Make a list of possible vocational programs or jobs that may be right for your child.

Get more information on vocational programs and jobs.

Eliminate inappropriate options from your list.

Visit possible vocational programs or conduct inventories.

Consider long- and short-range consequences of each option.

Consider new programs starting, or becoming involved in starting new programs.

Part Three

Determine the skills that are most important for your child to be successful in vocational programs.

Prioritize critical skills needed by your child to be successful in the most preferred vocational programs.

Part Four

Review your rights and responsibilities in planning your child's education.

Review the purpose of an IEP conference and document.

Review the six components of the IEP conference.

Review what has worked well for you in past IEP conferences.

Develop an agenda for your next IEP conference.

Future planning is an area of particular importance for parents of gifted students. Parents can create early opportunities for these students to explore and identify interests. Indeed, research indicates that individuals highly successful in artistic, psychomotor, and cognitive fields have had families who provided strong support and encouragement at an early age (Bloom & Sosniak, 1981). These researchers described the important role of families:

> In the majority of our cases one or more of the parents (sometimes a sibling or relative) had a personal interest in the talent area and gave the talented individual great support and encouragement for his or her development in the specific talent field . . . In some instances the interest and commitment of a parent was so strong that all members of the family were expected to participate in the area to some extent from an early age. It is hard to see how a young member of such families could resist becoming somewhat involved.
>
> Especially in the early years of three to seven, many of these children were encouraged to explore the field, to participate in home activities in the field, and to join other members of the family in the activity in or out of the home. Small signs of interest and capability in the talent field by any of the children in these homes were encouraged and much rewarded by the parents. (pp. 87–88)

Parents of students who are gifted can benefit from information on how to encourage career development through strategies, such as having biographies available on persons with distinguished careers, helping students become personally acquainted with adults having leadership positions in a variety of fields, arranging an adult mentor relationship with a person whose profession is particularly interesting to the students, and helping with college planning (Karnes & Karnes, 1982).

Assisting families with future planning can alleviate some of the parents' concern and worry. Once future options are explored, the future is likely to be less threatening to families. Another benefit is that identifying future goals can guide students, parents, and professionals in designing relevant educational programs to best prepare the student to meet the future goals.

But there can also be some drawbacks to future planning for some families. One drawback, discussed in Chapter 5, is that many families are more present- than future-oriented. Their ideological style is one that "takes a day at a time," believing that all things eventually work out. This style was expressed by Elsie Helsel, the mother of an adult son with cerebral palsy and mental retardation:

> We have lived long enough and through enough that we are not fretting about what will happen to Robin when we die. There is a limit to what can be accomplished by planning ahead. Who knows precisely what will happen ten years from now, or five years from now, or even tomorrow? We believe that all of us are in God's care and under His protection. Robin's deep,

abiding faith in God has helped him cope with a very frustrating existence on this earth. He truly believes that God is his refuge and strength, and that belief will sustain him as long as he lives. (DeWert & Helsel, 1985, pp. 104–105)

Thus, even though some professionals may believe it is important for a family to engage in detailed future planning, the family may not be so inclined. For such families, future planning may be stress-producing rather than stress-reducing.

In summary, this section has provided an overview of four topics—managing behavior, teaching pre-academic and academic skills, educational advocacy, and future planning—on which families may be interested in receiving information. We reiterate that families may not want to pursue these topics, but they may be very curious about other topics, such as learning more about their child's particular exceptionality. Preferences for information will vary widely; preferences for how information is shared will also vary. The next two sections will discuss alternatives to consider in individualizing *how* to provide information to families.

GROUP OR INDIVIDUAL SESSIONS

Important considerations in planning how to share information are the benefits and drawbacks of group and individual sessions. Studies of behavior management sessions have examined the relative effectiveness of these two approaches (group or individual sessions). One study randomly assigned parents of children with mental retardation to an individual training group, a 10-session group training, or a control group (Brightman, Baker, Clark, & Ambrose, 1982). The parents receiving individual and group training had almost identical results, and both performed higher on outcome measures than the control group. Group training was conducted at half the cost per family and was far more time-efficient for the professionals providing the training.

Group Sessions

Group training can provide a supportive environment in which families can learn from other families. Group training also can reassure families who learn that others face similar concerns and problems. As one mother stated in the evaluation of a group training session:

It helps to know that there are other parents who have the same concerns and problems as I do. It makes me feel normal.

Another advantage of group training is decreased cost and time as compared to individual sessions. For some families however, group training poses problems related to schedule inconvenience, transportation, child care, perceived breach of privacy, and lack of responsiveness to idiosyncratic family concerns.

There may be a stereotype of group sessions as being offered in the evening for one to two hours with mostly mothers and some fathers in attendance. Many variations exist, however, on ways to structure group sessions. One variable is scheduling. An example of an innovative group training model is the Families Together program in Lawrence, Kansas. The goals of Families Together are to strengthen families, provide an opportunity to learn and recreate together, bring professionals and parents together as equals, share information and learn from each other, and reinforce the concept that each family member is an important and vital part of the family unit. Families Together provides weekend workshops (Saturday morning through Sunday noon) for the entire family at a motel. Approximately 18 families come together for family recreation, parent discussion groups, sibling discussion groups, and child activities. Parents identified the major highlights of the weekends to be visiting and talking with other parents, information given by resource persons, and a chance to go out and not worry about the children on Saturday night because child respite care is provided. The key to this program is the balanced emphasis on enjoyment and learning.

A second variable is the persons for whom the group sessions are designed. In addition to information opportunities for mothers only or for mothers and fathers, workshops have been designed for siblings (Powell & Ogle, 1985), grandparents (Vadasy, Fewell, & Meyer, in press), and fathers (Meyer & Fewell, 1985).

Individual Sessions

By contrast to group approaches, individual sessions can enable a family and professional to develop a closer working relationship (Bernal, 1984) and to focus more specifically on the unique aspects of the family's situation. When working with just one family, professionals more likely can tailor information to the preferences of that one family.

Individual sessions frequently are conducted in the family's home. Home sessions have the advantages of enabling professionals to "get to know the family on their own turf," to assess family and child needs related to educational goals and objectives, to observe family interaction and child-related problems and expectations in the home setting, and to minimize family problems related to child care and transportation.

In addition to sessions with parents, individual sessions also can be conducted with a variety of persons who have important relationships to the child or youth with an exceptionality, e.g., siblings, extended family, neighbors, child care providers, scout leaders, and religious education teachers. An example of a well-established home teaching program is the Portage Project, which serves children from birth to six in 23 Wisconsin school districts (Shearer & Loftin, 1984). Each child is assessed and goals and objectives are identified by professionals and parents. The home teaching process includes these components:

1. the home teacher measures the previous week's activities;
2. the home teacher introduces new activities and models teaching techniques for the parents;
3. the parents model teaching techniques for the home teacher;
4. the home teacher reviews the instructional activities and recording procedures with the parents.

Evaluation results indicate positive child outcomes across developmental areas.

We need to remember, however, that all families are not comfortable with home visits. Some families consider their homes to be their own private domain, which they do not want professionals to enter. Professionals have criticized parents for not eagerly anticipating their home visits and interpret parental aloofness as "not caring about their child." This kind of generalization is unwarranted. Rather, professionals need to respect the preferences of parents for participating in home visits or not and remember that they sometimes retreat into the privacy of their homes, too.

Decisions pertaining to group or individual sessions are important areas to consider in respect to family preferences. The particular arrangement used will influence the format of materials used—print, media, or computer technology. These alternative formats are discussed in the next section.

ALTERNATIVE FORMATS FOR PROVIDING INFORMATION

Print

A variety of printed resources are available. Many of the training projects described in the previous section have developed manuals to serve as a supplement to group training (e.g., UCLA Developmental Disabilities Project, PACER) . The advantage of manuals is the organization of material into a succinct format with a substantive core of information. If parents read this material before a group session, there may be more time for discussion and such active learning strategies as role playing, modelling, and group problem-solving. The manual can also be a resource to review and update after a workshop is completed.

A second option is for manuals to be used alone, unaccompanied by group or individual sessions. A study of 106 families of children with mental retardation randomly assigned families to one of five training conditions: control; training by manuals only; manuals and phone consultation; manuals and eight group meetings; and manuals, eight group meetings, and six home visits (Baker & Heifetz, 1976; Baker, Heifetz, & Murphy, 1980; Heifetz, 1977). Families in all training conditions scored higher than the controls on their knowledge of behavioral principles and child self-help skills. Little difference was found in the effectiveness of approaches. The families who only received the manuals reported less confidence about their teaching and reported doing less teaching one year later than the parents in the other three groups; however, the manuals-only group was by far the most cost-effective group.

Professionals from a variety of backgrounds and parents have written books and manuals that are available for purchase or through most community libraries. A distinct advantage of parent-written books is that parents reading them may be able to identify with the author as a "person who has been there" and, therefore, having an authenticity deriving from firsthand experience (Mullins, 1983). Parents vary in their perspectives, however, and many parent readers may disagree with the views of parent authors. One useful approach is to offer families the option of reading materials written by professionals and/or parents.

Media

Media is increasingly being used as a format for providing information to families. The Navajo community of Rough Rock, Arizona shared information with families on the availability of special education services through videotaped vignettes (Dunlap, Ondelacy, & Sells, 1979). Families viewed these video tapes on battery-operated equipment in hogans, summer shelters, tents, and outdoors in a field of grazing sheep. The authors described the value of the video tapes as follows:

> The video tape format permitted stopping of the action, re-winding for subsequent viewings, and the selection of vignettes most likely to be of interest to the people being addressed. Moreover, it added a valuable dimension to the message of what special education was at the school. For "special education" is a difficult concept to convey in the Navajo language. Even in English, the term is vague and demands a certain conceptual foundation before it can begin to be well understood.

As many of those viewing the tapes had not attended school, and those who had, had likely attended school quite different from contemporary schools, a visual representation of the school program was seen as vital to the communication process of the identification project. The staff visiting a home or addressing a group used the tapes as a shared experience, which was always followed by a flurry of questions. A home visit alone, without the video component, would probably have been more of a one-way communication than the shared experience sought in the project. (Dunlap, et al., 1979, pp. 3–4)

In addition to use with individual families, video tapes can also be used for mass dissemination. A project of national significance is currently under way at The Young Adult Institute, a social service agency in New York City that provides residential and rehabilitative services to persons with developmental disabilities. The Young Adult Institute has conducted a comprehensive national search of videotapes, films, and slide-tape presentations that provide instruction and support to families and has compiled this information into a resource directory. You can order a copy of the directory from Young Adult Institute, 460 W. 34th St., New York, NY 10001. The Young Adult Institute is producing and evaluating a series of parent support television programs in the northeast geographical area with videotapes it has collected, as well as new ones it is producing. The use of television has tremendous potential for reaching families in their own homes. Furthermore, the fact that many families own video-cassette recorders suggests that it would be helpful for public libraries, tape rental stores, and school programs to make instructional tapes available for rent or loan.

Computer Technology

Computer technology offers opportunities for families to receive information as well as for family members to work with children and youth on home-based learning activities. One demonstration project involved home-based teaching of children from birth to six in rural areas (Tawney, Aeschleman, Deaton, & Donaldson, 1979). Computer equipment was installed in the homes of 19 families, most of whom were of a lower socioeconomic status. These families lived as far as 275 miles from the project headquarters. Instruction of children focused on motor or visual discrimination skills. The program was designed for parents and children to work on lessons for 15 to 30 minutes each day for five days per week. Parents also could discuss concerns through post-session voice communication with program specialists. The authors documented increases in child performance and noted that a positive project outcome was that families accepted the technology into their homes and worked co-operatively with project staff.

A microcomputer/video disc-based instructional system has been used with students having learning disabilities in classrooms to teach time-telling skills (Friedman & Hofmeister, 1984). Unlike the computer program above, the video disc can provide spoken instruction. We expect this type of instructional system will be used to provide information for families and home-learning opportunities for students in the relatively near future.

Families need assistance in becoming familiar with computer technology. This would be an excellent topic for informational sessions. If families are able to meet the financial expense involved in a home computer, they can learn to make judicious software selections (Huntington, 1984a) and provide opportunities for their children to increase their academic achievement at home (Huntington, 1984b).

Most available educational software programs focus on the development of skills for children and youth. But software programs for families focusing on the informational topics we previously discussed (e.g., managing behavior, educational advocacy) may become available in the future.

RESOURCE PERSONS

A variety of resource persons can be used in providing information to families, such as:

1. professionals—teachers, psychologists, social workers, counselors, physicians, and therapists;
2. family members—mothers, fathers, siblings, relatives;
3. individuals with exceptionalities; and
4. paraprofessionals.

Of course, the resource person should fit the topic. For instance, assisting parents in following up on school activities might best be done by a professional; helping parents learn to be assertive with professionals might best be taught by other parents. Certainly, one should not overgeneralize this point—many parents can effectively teach school follow-up skills, just as many professionals can teach assertiveness. Families may not feel comfortable with all professionals or parent leaders. It is important to survey parent preferences to identify the people from whom they would most like to receive assistance.

PLANNING FOR TRAINING

Knowing your options for providing information to families is not enough; you also need a planning process to design and implement training. We suggest a process that includes the following five steps:

1. identify family needs and preferences (see questionnaire in Appendix C as one alternative for identifying family preferences—this will need to be adapted to fit your particular situation),
2. analyze needs and determine individual and group priorities,
3. plan informational opportunities consistent with priorities,
4. provide informational opportunities, and
5. evaluate participant outcomes.

One way to coordinate planning efforts in a school district is to establish an advisory committee comprised of school and community professionals, paraprofessionals, adults with exceptionalities, and parents of children and youth with different exceptionalities. This committee can assume responsibility for systematically proceeding through the five steps of the planning process. You can find more information on the planning process in an article by Heward and Dardig (1978).

SUMMARY

This chapter has highlighted the important role professionals have in providing information to families. Because families' preferences vary widely, we have emphasized the need to provide a range of informational topics and formats for addressing those topics. We also suggest a planning process to assist you in organizing your efforts, to provide meaningful learning opportunities. A key aspect of planning is to develop a network of professionals and families to work together.

Many families will be interested in receiving information, but it is also important to realize that increased knowledge is not the only helpful coping strategy. The next chapter will discuss the range of alternative coping strategies available to families.

Chapter 13

Family Support: Helping Families Cope

In the previous chapter we reviewed a number of programs and strategies designed to help families make meaningful contributions to the education of their children. It should be clear by now, however, that although education is the central mission of a school, it is not a family's only goal, perhaps not even its main goal. Families must meet a variety of demands, ranging from economic survival to the nurturance of self-esteem. Also, other people in families besides persons with exceptionalities have needs which are equally important. The key, as we have emphasized, is balance. Family lives that are totally centered around exceptionalities are unfair not only to all the other family members but also to the persons with exceptionalities. In the long run, how far up the developmental ladder can students with exceptionalities climb, if the people holding up the ladder—their families—fall apart?

The school has a role in helping families cope with stresses that lie beyond the realm of education. In some cases the school may take leadership in providing these services. In others, its role may be more peripheral: appropriate referrals and interagency coordination. In still others, its role may be no more (or less) than well-placed empathic comments and moral support. Nevertheless, major or peripheral, these are roles the school can play in family support.

In Chapter 4 we outlined the variety of functions that families fulfill, the needs families must meet, and the ways in which exceptionality may shape those needs and the family's response to them. Unmet needs, tangible or intangible, are sources of stress. Most family theorists define coping as any activity that reduces stress (Pearlin & Schooler, 1978); we extend that definition as "any activity that results in meeting one's needs."

Families' reactions to situations—how much stress or unmet need they feel, or even any feeling of stress at all—vary widely with respect to their different perceptions of the event as well as the different resources they may have available to meet the challenge (Hill, 1949). Further, one of families' key resources for dealing with stress is their arsenals of coping strategies. Using categories of coping styles identified by Olson and his associates we defined these strategies in Chapter 2, (Olson et al., 1983). Briefly, coping may involve (a) one or more internal strategies designed to make an event less stressful by changing one's perceptions about it or to make it solvable, or (b) one or more external strategies designed to marshal one's resources to address needs directly and thus reduce stress (Olson et al., 1983). In this chapter we will look at internal and external coping strategies in depth and consider family support programs designed to strengthen each one.

INTERNAL COPING STRATEGIES

Internal coping involves thinking about a stressful situation either to change one's perceptions (making it feel less stressful) or to make it solvable. Perceptions involve interpretations of the personal meaning of events in our environment. The same event could be interpreted positively, neutrally, or negatively by three different people. If we interpret an event negatively, we think of it as threatening our well-being or creating needs—in other words, it is stressful to us. If we interpret an event positively, we think of it as enhancing our well-being or satisfying our needs—in other words, we cope. For example, depending on her values and beliefs, a mother with a particular religious background might view her daughter's marriage to someone of another religion as a positive event ("He's such a nice young man!") or as a negative one ("She's marrying outside the faith!"). When we use an internal coping strategy, we revise our interpretations about an event that was originally perceived negatively, so that all or part of it can be perceived positively or at least neutrally. The three major types of internal coping strategies are passive appraisal, reframing, and spiritual support.

Passive Appraisal

Uses of Passive Appraisal. Passive appraisal involves ignoring a problem or setting it aside, either temporarily or permanently. Looked at pessimistically, passive appraisal might be viewed as a kind of "helpless resignation" (Pearlin & Schooler, 1978), or more positively as a decision to "ride out" a crisis (Olson et al., 1983) in the hope that it will go away (e.g., "maybe he'll grow out of it"). Passive appraisal also could include "checking out," or relaxing, when a situation seems overwhelming by putting one's problems aside for an hour, a day, or a weekend.

We often see passive appraisal at work within the first few days or months after parents learn of their child's exceptionality. Early interventionists or professionals in learning disabilities or giftedness may see the family denying an exceptionality as they struggle against the idea that their child may be different from anyone else. For example, one father, when told by the school psychologist that his son was eligible for the gifted program, responded:

> Oh, no. You're not going to put any wild ideas in his head that he can go to college or something, because I can't afford to send him. We're just regular people, and we *work* for a living. We don't go around setting ourselves up over other people. Besides, that boy has a smart enough mouth on him already.

As discussed in Chapter 5, denial may be one of the stages in the cycle of adjustment to a distressing event, such as the death of a loved one or the birth of a child with a disability. We can see an example of denial in the reaction of one mother at the birth of her child:

> Finally my pediatrician brought the baby to me and unwrapped him for me to see. I was stunned . . . This was not my perfect baby! I was still tired from my delivery, and I felt like a spectator in a dream. I just knew I would wake up and everything would be all right. I could not take this baby when I was uncertain that it was mine. (Bristor, 1984, p. 29)

Another form of passive appraisal is refusal to think about the future. This may be a behavior caused by the fact that immediate concerns of physical care, finding services, helping the child to be successful in school, and so forth, are more than enough to handle at one time. The future seems to be an expendable item to cut from the list of stresses (Featherstone, 1980). Another reason families may refuse to consider the future is that it is too great a fear (Brotherson, 1985). For a child with an exceptionality, future adulthood is a great unknown and therefore fraught with uncertainties. Faced with their own mortality, parents may have few clues as to who will continue to provide support and guidance for their child. Adult services are a fragmented maze, and they are not mandated as they are for school-aged students. Bob Helsel refers to this fear:

> You mentioned worrying about the future. I suppose this is the biggest worry that a parent of a severely handicapped child has—what happens when I die? And there is no answer to that. As far as I know, there is no way to provide properly for him in that eventuality—at least, I don't know of any way. (Helsel, 1985, p. 90)

In *Parents Speak Out: Then and Now,* Rud Turnbull also expresses his feelings about the future:

> There is the sadness that I would experience if (my son) could not leave home or if there were no community alternatives for him. And there is the sadness I know I will feel upon his inevitable departure. My experience of surrendering Jay when he was only a child cannot help informing my emotions when it comes time for Jay to go away again. Or when my death approaches. The sense of loss, past and future, is pervasive and powerful. (Turnbull, 1985a, p. 123)

Thus, it is little wonder that families often avoid considering the future. "Take things one day at a time" is advice "passed like an amulet" from parent to parent in support group meetings (Featherstone, 1980, p. 29). One mother explained why she hadn't joined a support group:

> I don't go to any parent associations. I couldn't face people saying this is what I went through with my child and then I'd know I'd got it to go through. I'll worry in six years time, but just now I'll take each day as it comes. (Lonsdale, 1978, p. 115)

The third type of passive appraisal, relaxation, is one in which families with children having exceptionalities may indulge less often. Relaxation means taking time out for oneself, stopping to catch one's breath when little irritations or large problems become too weighty. Any activity that removes the mind and body from problems at hand could be considered coping through relaxation. Everyone seems to have a favorite style of "getting away," ranging from watching TV to hobbies like carpentry or gardening. Exercise, sports, eating out, reading, drinking, or smoking are are all examples of relaxation. One mother explained her way of coping:

> It makes me more patient and I try to grin and bear it. When things really get bad I go and soak in the bath for an hour. My husband was told I was on the verge of a nervous breakdown but I've never had it yet! (Lonsdale, 1978, p. 108)

It is difficult, however, for many families to find the time to get away. Kathryn Morton (1985) speaks of the tremendous demands placed on parents of children and youth with exceptionalities:

> Disabled children use up enormous amounts of their parents' physical and psychic energy. These children require more of everything, and those who take parenting seriously give it to them. Yet all the rest of life goes on and also demands its due from us. And the collective demands must be met within the same twenty-four hour day allotted to everyone. . . . For parents of handicapped children the fact of life which is least understood by others is this: It is difficult and exhausting to live normally, and yet we must. To take the other route, to admit that having a disabled child makes us disabled persons . . . means drifting slowly out of the mainstream of adult life. In a very real sense, we are damned if we do make the extraordinary effort required to live normally, and damned if we don't. (Morton, 1985, p. 144)

Working through Denial. Professionals are often frustrated when families seem to deny their child's exceptionality or refuse to plan for the future. From the professionals' point of view, the families are wasting precious time that could be spent more usefully to help the child make developmental or academic progress. It is important to keep in mind, however, that denial may be serving an adaptive function for the people who are engaging in it. Denial provides time for absorbing facts in small, digestible bits and avoiding a more devastating reality (Fortier & Wanlass,

1984). It may also serve as a cushion giving the family a span of time to regroup and gather the energy to go on (Bristor, 1984). Except in rare circumstances, parents will eventually turn to more active coping strategies in their own time. It is important in the meantime to maintain an open line of communication, establish trust, and consistently point out educational strategies that offer realistic opportunities for improvement without promising miracles.

For those few parents who do seem "stuck" in a denial stage, we do not recommend that professionals should confront them directly with the "reality" of their children's exceptionalities and/or bleak prospects for the future. Confrontation is a specialized therapeutic technique employed by highly skilled counselors. Its successful use requires hours of trust-building before the confrontation and many more hours of empathic support afterward to follow through with the desired changes (Northern, 1982). Even social workers, counselors, and psychologists on the school's interdisciplinary team should be reluctant to attempt confrontation if there is not adequate time to work with a particular family. If handled without empathy and trust, confrontation may result in alienation, anger, and withdrawal. The best strategies are building trust; remaining open, supportive, and available when parents do make tentative inquiries; and encouraging involvement in support groups. It also may help to provide frequent examples of the child's school work, to invite parents to observe the class, and to provide parents with information on normative expectation for a particular grade. All of this, of course, should be done with careful attention to the principles of empathic and nonthreatening communication discussed in Chapter 6.

Encouraging Relaxation. With all the demands on their time—including those made by professionals—parents may feel guilty about taking time to get away occasionally. They may need to know that they have "permission" to relax, and that professionals think it important for parents to take some time just for themselves. You might try asking parents what they do to get away from stressful days, and tell about some of the ways you do yourself. Try to help families understand the value of pacing their efforts and that recreation in whatever form they may choose is an important part of their sense of well-being. For those who protest they do not have the time, you may suggest some of the ideas discussed in Chapter 4, such as time management strategies, ideas for re-negotiating chores, or the use of social support.

Some families might be interested in an organized relaxation training workshop. There are a number of these available, either through consultants who specialize in relaxation training or through packaged instructor's manuals with accompanying audio tapes (Osterkamp & Press, 1980). For those who are not interested in such a group activity, there are relaxation tapes on the market, either with guided imagery exercises in relaxation or with instructions accompanied by soft music to encourage relaxation. You may wish to consider adding a few of these tapes to your school's resource library. By so doing, you and other school staff could also have access to the tapes.

A final way to encourage relaxation is to refer families to respite care services in your community. Respite care services provide temporary care of a person with a disability for an hour, a day, or for longer periods of time, so that the family can get away. Respite care may be provided in the family home, in the provider's home, in an activity program (in which the person with a disability attends a recreation program for a day or an evening, usually on a regular basis), or in a group home (which may keep a "guest bed" available for respite) (Zamarripa & Goldstein, 1980). Although most families prefer in-home services (Upshur, 1982), all of these types of respite care have value. Respite care providers are usually trained in such skills as first aid, adaptive equipment, handling, positioning, communication, behavior management, and so forth (Lueger, 1981).

Families report that respite care services have a positive impact on their lives, and there is some evidence that the availability of respite care may reduce the need for institutionalization (Joyce, Singer, & Isralowitz, 1983). Unfortunately, respite care services are not available in all areas. Further, some parents may be unable to use services because of prohibitive costs. Others may be reluctant to use them because of family values that avoid seeking help or because they do not know or trust the providers. Over time, however, these obstacles seem to dissipate as the respite program becomes established in the community and as families learn the value of the service (Kansas Children's Service League, 1984).

It would be helpful to have information available in your school about any respite services available in your community, including costs, contact persons, and any eligibility rules. A mentorship program for students who are gifted (or one involving adults with disabilities as mentors) not only may be valuable to the students but also could serve as a source of respite care for their families. If there are no services available, someone in your school might participate in community planning to start a program. Alternatively, the school's parent group might consider organizing a respite cooperative and drawing upon the experiences of other communities (Ferguson, 1978). Although planning and development is time consuming, in the long run, it is worthwhile. Encouraging families to relax can help develop an extremely valuable coping skill.

Reframing

Olson et al. (1983) define reframing as "the family's ability to redefine a demanding situation in a more rational and acceptable way in order to make the situation more manageable" (p. 143). Essentially, reframing involves two steps. The first step requires distinguishing situations (or parts of situations) that can be changed from those that are beyond control. The second step requires taking action on alterable situations and/or redefining what cannot be changed to make it more acceptable (McCubbin et al., 1983). Families can be assisted in both action taking and redefinition.

Taking Action: Building Problem-solving Skills. Systematic problem-solving is a technique used in a variety of settings, including individual or group therapy, educational classrooms, and corporate planning (Goldfarb, Brotherson, Summers, & Turnbull, in press). Many families use problem-solving, either formally or informally, in their daily lives. It is also a skill that can be taught, as, for example, when Intagliata and Doyle (1984) successfully taught problem-solving to a group of parents whose children have developmental disabilities.

Problem-solving essentially employs four steps. First, defining the problem involves describing the issue completely and—as suggested by Olson et al. (1983)—breaking it into resolvable and unresolvable parts. Second, brainstorming alternatives involves a free-spirited and nonjudgmental listing of all possible options for solutions. Third, evaluating alternatives includes using criteria on which all family members agree to consider the relative merits of each alternative. Finally, selecting an alternative and taking action involves assigning responsibility for tasks and following through on them (Goldfarb et al., in press). These steps are illustrated in Figure 13–1.

This bare-bones description of the problem-solving process obviously masks a number of nuances and potential complications. Families must use appropriate communication skills to work through the process together. They must be able to negotiate, compromise, and assume responsibility without attributing blame. These skills can be cultivated with practice. Your school may be interested in conducting problem-solving workshops for families (for school personnel, too!). Problem-solving can be an effective tool for resolving such educational issues as selecting and prioritizing IEP goals and objectives, deciding on placement for a student, agreeing on appropriate related services, and reaching consensus on whether to initiate a due process hearing. Problem-solving training manuals are available (e.g., Wasik, 1983). When conducting a training program is not possible, or if some families are not interested in attending workshops, there are self-help books available (Goldfarb et al., in press).

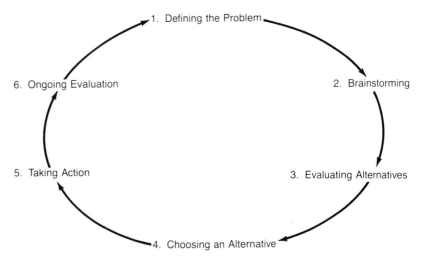

FIGURE 13–1
PROBLEM-SOLVING STEPS

Note. Meeting the Challenge of Disability and Chronic Illness—A Family Guide by L. Goldfarb, M. J. Brotherson, J. A. Summers, and A. P. Turnbull, in press, Baltimore: Brookes Publishing Co. Adapted by permission.

Encouraging Redefinition. Although many of the day-to-day problems associated with an exceptionality are within families' control to solve, the fact of exceptionality itself is not. It therefore is a vital part of families' reframing skills to be able to redefine the situation to make it less stressful. Positive redefinition was the coping strategy most often used by families surveyed in one study (Brotherson, 1985). There are two ways families can redefine their perceptions of the exceptionality and its impact on them, and a number of ways that professionals can help.

Positive comparisons, one type of redefinition, involve considering the problems and stresses that other people have, and concluding that our own are not so bad after all (Pearlin & Schooler, 1978). The effect fits the old parable: If we could put our troubles in a bag and bring them to a meeting to exchange with someone else, we would all go home again with our own. One mother philosophically summarized this effect:

> Everybody has got a cross to bear. Some people's are a bit heavier than others. You can always look around and see people worse off. (Lonsdale, 1978, p. 106)

No matter how difficult the exceptionality may seem to an outside observer, many families are amazingly adept at using positive comparisons:

> We're lucky because Carol isn't aware she's different. I know lots of others who are very hurt because they know they're retarded. But Carol is too handicapped to be hurt by her limitations. (Turnbull, Summers, & Brotherson, 1984, p. 31)

It would certainly be inappropriate to violate confidentiality and point out to parents the specific ways in which their child is less disabled, less disruptive, or less troublesome than another student. Professionals can indirectly assist families in making positive comparisons, however. For example, you can avoid implying that a particular student is the "worst one" in regard to a behavioral or academic problem, and you of course should take care to highlight the child's strengths. If possible, help families understand that their particular child's problems are not uncommon and that they are shared by many students. After all, except in very rare cases, this is true. Such assurances place the problem in a more realistic and less alarming perspective; it helps to know one is not alone. Comparisons with other students may be equally important for parents of children who are gifted. Those parents who see their children as "little adults" may find graphic examples helpful in seeing that their children have similiar needs to other children for security, assurance, guidance, peer interactions, and time for just plain fun.

A second type of redefinition is selective attention and selective ignoring (Pearlin & Schooler, 1978). This involves more attention to the positive aspects of a situation and less to the negative aspects. Contrary to the usual expectations of some professionals, there *are* positive factors associated with exceptionality, and many families recognize this fact. For example, 75 percent of a sample of 25 parents surveyed by Wikler, Wasow, and Hatfield (1983) reported that their experiences with disability had strengthened their families. Leah Ziskin (1985) lists some of the positive contributions her daughter brings to their family:

> In return for our efforts, Jennie gives us love and a sense of patience. She makes us see that all people do not learn or progress at the same rapid rate. She makes us appreciate the gift of speech, the gift of communication. She makes us marvel that she communicates with us in her own way. (Ziskin, 1985, p. 71)

Similarly, Elsie Helsel (1985) identified a number of positive contributions her son made to her development:

> To be honest and blunt, I was a smug, self-centered intellectual snob. Robin's birth . . . abruptly changed the pattern of my life. Suddenly I was thrust into a totally different world with people from all levels of society. We had common problems, and our children had common service needs. Through working together, we learned to know and appreciate each other for what we were and not for professional, financial, or social status . . . Robin has indeed brought direction, purpose, and meaning to my life. I have

achieved a degree of personal fulfillment that I think I would never have attained in my former career as a bench scientist. (Helsel, 1985, pp. 84–85)

It is important to encourage families to think of the positive contributions of exceptionality. You will note from the examples that most of these contributions are intangible, contributions to understanding, to capacity to love, to meaningfulness, and to career direction. Generally these types of attributes are not mentioned at IEP meetings as part of the student's characteristics. It might be rewarding to do so.

Parents also need to be recognized for their own contributions and successes. It may be more difficult for parents to see their own positive attributes than those of their children. Parenthood is so deeply rooted in one's self-concept that the advent of a child with an exceptionality can have a profound effect on one's self-esteem. Even parents of gifted children may feel inadequate about their perceived responsibility to nurture their children's talents. The threat to parents' self-esteem that accompanies an exceptionality makes it vital for professionals to point out the successes that parents have achieved and to praise their efforts, no matter how small. It is also important not to expect too much from parents in the way of participation in their child's education because, for parents, falling short of professional expectations could be one more blow to an already feeble self-image. Begin with small, easily achievable tasks, with predictable and, preferably, highly visible probabilities of success. For example, if you are working on a toilet training program for a child at school, you might ask the parents to keep a log of the number of diaper changes they make at home. When they provide you with the log, let them know you understand how busy they are and that you appreciate their extra efforts. Then ask for more detailed logs, such as the frequency with which the child drinks liquids. When the child is toileting appropriately at school, demonstrate your procedure for the parent in the classroom and have him or her use the procedure once or twice at school. Next, you might suggest the parents could use the procedure at home during the part of the day when they are least rushed for time. Only when both parents and child are ready should anyone expect the child to be fully toilet trained. At each step, the parents should realize clearly that toilet training a child with a severe exceptionality is no small feat and that the parents are demonstrating a high level of skill.

All this, of course, is sound behavioral practice, i.e., increasing family participation in education by making the experience rewarding. However, the point is that such a strategy does more than benefit the student by more closely coordinating home and school efforts. It also provides parents with a sense of accomplishment, a pride in success, and a feeling of mastery of the situation. They need to believe they *can*, after all, make a difference.

Spiritual Support

McCubbin et al. (1983) classify spiritual support as an external coping strategy. However, we choose to consider it an internal strategy. The type of support one might receive from organized religious participation—from clergy or from fellow religious group members—is really a type of social support and therefore another strategy altogether. In fact, many families have reported they do not receive much support from organized religious groups and that they may receive rejection or intolerance instead (Bristol & Schopler, 1983; Brotherson, 1985). The type of spiritual support most often employed by families of children with exceptionalities is personal, spiritual, or philosophical interpretation gleaned from reading religious books or drawn from their upbringing (Turnbull, Summers, & Brotherson, 1984). In this context, then, the essence of spiritual support as a coping strategy means an interpretation of the meaning of the exceptionality.

People have a strong need to understand the meaning of events in their lives. The advent of an exceptionality is a random event that must be explained somehow. Gardner (1971) suggested that, to some people, feelings of guilt may be preferable to the feeling that the world is out of control. One parent expressed a commonly heard question when he learned of his daughter's leukemia: "Oh, my God, why Ellen? Why us? What have I done to deserve this wrath?" (Zimmerman, 1982, p. 28). Some families lose their religious beliefs after the advent of an exceptionality. One parent commented:

> It shouldn't have happened to me. Why did it happen to me? Crikey, if there was a God there wouldn't be any disabled children. All children are supposed to be perfect. (Lonsdale, 1978, p. 107)

Other families, however, use their beliefs to gain a sense of meaning. For example, one parent said he believed "God has a plan for that boy," and another parent commented, "God must think I'm a pretty strong person, to trust me with all these problems" (Turnbull, Summers, & Brotherson, 1984).

Still other families may reframe their beliefs to fit the exceptionality into a new framework. Perhaps one of the most extensive examples of this is Rabbi Kushner's (1981) efforts to explain his son's severe degenerative disease in his book, *When Bad Things Happen to Good People,* which made the best-seller list. Kushner notes that when something goes wrong, one need not decide either that God is evil or that the victim is evil and is being punished. Rather, he postulates that even God must follow his own laws of nature and that his omnipotence lies in compassion and support of those who fall victim to random natural events.

More so than other professionals, school professionals have an especially delicate role to play in encouraging the use of spiritual support. Aside from the fact that it is difficult to know when one is stepping over the boundaries between church and state, spiritual beliefs are personal and are not often discussed in public situations. In addition, such beliefs are highly individual. It is difficult to know the right thing to say, because what might be comforting to one person might seem foolish to another. Thus, a better strategy is simply to listen nonjudgmentally to families' religious interpretations of the exceptionality and to refer them to religious resources in the community that can provide support and assistance.

Nearly every national religious organization has some curricula available for children and youth with exceptionalities. Special educators and other school personnel might wish to lend their expertise in integrating children and youth in ongoing classes in their own religious organizations, making the church or synagogue more accessible, or fostering greater general awareness and acceptance of exceptionalities. This is a type of informal interagency cooperation that should not be overlooked.

EXTERNAL COPING STRATEGIES

The amount of stress a family may feel is related to the nature of the event, the family's resources, and perceptions or interpretations of the event (Hill, 1949). In the previous section, we discussed coping strategies relating to perceptions, i.e., the internal strategies of passive appraisal, reframing, and spiritual support. On the other hand, external coping strategies, i.e., coping through the use of social support or formal support, relate to the family's resources. Professionals can help families effectively use both strategies.

Social Support

Uses of Social Support. Social support refers to the assistance one can get from extended family, friends, co-workers, and others in the community. Friends who feed our pets while we are on vacation and neighbors who bring food when there is a death in the family are providing social support. But more importantly, along with these material gestures of support comes the message that these people like and appreciate us, that we are *worth* supporting. Some psychologists (e.g., Cobb, 1976) believe that the main value of social support lies in giving a person the feeling that he or she is loved, valued, and belongs to a social network. Social support apparently leads to self-esteem, which in turn leads to an increased ability to deal with a stressful situation (Pearlin, Menaghan, Lieberman, & Mullan, 1981).

In families where there is an exceptionality, social support can be especially important. Of course, family members provide each other the greatest amount of support. For example, Friedrich (1979) found that a good marital relationship was the single best predictor of good adjustment in mothers who had children with disabilities. Similarly, Kazak and Marvin (1984) found it was less important to mothers that fathers help with child care than that they provide their wives with emotional support. In addition, help from outside the immediate family circle is also important. Isolation is related to all sorts of family problems, from alcoholism to abuse (Brehm, 1983). Friends can be useful in helping families deal with numerous issues. They can lend support after the family hears the diagnosis; they can provide transportation; they can be a comforting presence at IEP meetings; they can serve as mentors for gifted children and help find out about college scholarships for them. There is no end to the emotional and tangible assistance of social support.

More social support, however, is not necessarily *better*. There is increasing evidence that the quality of the support we receive is more important than the sheer amount. Not all relationships are beneficial (Brehm, 1983). For example, some studies (e.g., Embry, 1980) have found that abusing families tend not only to be isolated, but also to limit their few interactions to extended family members. We could assume that contact with relatives in these cases was not producing the kind of support that reduced stress. Other researchers have theorized that social support networks with a high density (everybody knows everybody else in the group) and high boundaries (members in the family share the same network and have few friends of their own) are less effective in reducing stress than a diverse group of friends, some shared by all family members and some not (Kazak & Marvin, 1984).

Families with children having exceptionalities may be at risk for isolation. Apparently this is not true at all stages of the life cycle but rather is a growing problem as the child becomes older. Waisbren (1980) found no differences between families with 19-month-olds with and without disabilities in regard to the social support available to them. On the other hand, families with adolescents who have disabilities tend to be more isolated (Suelzle & Keenan, 1981). This may be due to the fact that it becomes more and more difficult to maintain the image of leading a normal life as the gap grows wider between the age of the person with a disability and his or her dependency (Birenbaum, 1971). In other words, assisting a three-year-old with a handicap with feeding in a restaurant does not cause the same kind of public stir as the same assistance to that person when he or she is 18.

Stigma is a large impediment to families who are seeking social support or even going out in public. Here is an incident Ann Turnbull describes in *Parents Speak Out: Then and Now:*

. . . a stranger yelled across a restaurant at my husband and me, 'What's wrong with that strange little boy?' When we tried to ignore him, he kept pressing, 'I asked you why that little boy looks and acts so strange.' Other persons in the restaurant looked back and forth between him and us, waiting for a response. My husband told him nothing was wrong and he should mind his own business . . . The stranger left . . . My husband and I were in a state of shock. As we continued to feel the other customers looking at us and at Jay, we got up and left the restaurant. How is the best way for parents to handle such situations? (Turnbull, 1985b, p. 132)

An accumulation of rude remarks and stares from strangers can drive families into isolation. Aside from strangers, extended family and friends may withdraw simply because the exceptionality is an awkward situation and they do not know what to do, exactly *how* to provide support. Kathryn Morton (1985) makes this point:

As one looks down the list of life's other sad happenings, most bring with them a ritual or a tradition which helps people deal with them. When a person is ill, there are cards to send, visits to make, flowers to deliver, gifts that comfort. When someone dies, there are routine ways of informing people of the sad news, funerals where people can grieve together . . . Friends and acquaintances know their roles. . . . The birth and life of a retarded child has no such advantages. It is a quasi tragedy, a joyful event that got spoiled. . . . Family and friends are faced with . . . ambivalence. Just what is their role? What words should they say? Can they reassure that everything will be all right? Should they extend their sympathy? Bring supper to the family? Send flowers? None of the usual comforting gestures are appropriate, so most people, under such circumstances, do and say nothing. The absence of response to an event of such enormous significance and impact on the lives of the parents simply compounds their loneliness. (Morton, 1985, pp. 145–146)

In summary, social support can be a very effective avenue to building self-esteem and the resources to cope with stressful situations. But it can't be just *any* relationship that serves as useful social support. It has to be *quality* support to be truly helpful. Unfortunately, the kind of quality social relationships families need for support may be hard for some families with an exceptionality to find. Thus, assisting families to develop supportive relationships can be beneficial.

Building Social Support. One of the most popular forms of building social support for families with children who have exceptionalities is the self-help support group. These are groups organized with the main objective of providing emotional support for their members as distinct from educational programs. Groups that are organized and conducted by a professional social worker or psychologist may have a therapeutic goal (e.g., Intagliata & Doyle, 1984). Other groups may be organized through the leadership of family members (with perhaps a little logistical assistance from a professional) with the major purpose of sharing concerns and advice, planning recreational activities, and assuring one another that "we are not alone." As we point out in Chapter 1, many parent-founded groups perform the self-help function by design.

The majority of these support groups are attended by mothers—even when originally organized as a couples' group. A growing number of schools and other service agencies are organizing siblings' groups, which seem to meet an important need for information and support for brothers and sisters of children with exceptionalities (Powell & Ogle, 1985). A few fathers' groups have been organized, and—even more rarely—groups for grandparents. Support groups are fairly common in early intervention and preschool programs, less common in school-aged programs, and extremely rare for families with adults. These neglected family members and life cycle stages deserve some attention if your school is considering developing a support program or cooperating with another agency that is organizing one.

Another strategy for building social support is a mentorship program, such as the Parent to Parent groups springing up around the country (Reynolds & Shanahan, 1981). These are programs matching a "veteran" parent to a parent with a child whose exceptionality has been newly identified. The parent-mentor provides emotional support, information about services and—by his or her mere presence—testimony that one *can* survive the parenthood demands. These programs have proven extremely successful in communities where they have been established.

In addition to helping with family support groups, professionals can help families build their own networks of social support. Encourage parents to attend IEP meetings together and to bring a friend or extended family member as well. Consider that interdisciplinary team members often compare notes before or after an IEP meeting and imagine how valuable it would be for parents also to have that opportunity. In addition, the school's resource library can provide information about exceptionalities that families can share with friends to alleviate ambiguity and fear. It may be surprising what simple information can do to increase the social support available to families. Consider the comments of this step-grandparent, whose son had recently married a woman with a nine-year-old daughter with cerebral palsy:

> She's such a lovely child . . . She really wants to spend time with me too, but I'm afraid to. How do I help her take off her coat? How do I help her sit in a chair? I just know I'd break her arm or something (Goldfarb et al., in press, p. 58).

In a case like this, a brief lesson from an occupational or physical therapist on some basic positioning techniques could produce many hours of respite for the parents, not to mention a rewarding relationship for the child and grandmother.

Finally, it is important to remember that as a professional you provide social as well as professional support. Your encouragement and empathy play a vital role, as discussed in Chapter 6.

Professional Support

Using Professional Support.

When families turn to agencies or private practitioners for help in solving problems, they are using professional support as a coping strategy. Doctors, lawyers, mental health clinics, welfare offices, vocational rehabilitation programs, and schools are all examples of professional support. Families may receive tangible assistance with their problems—for example, a training program for their child or Medicaid reimbursement for adaptive equipment. They may also receive emotional support, either formally through counseling designed for that purpose or informally through encouragement from a caring professional. The main distinction between social and professional support is that professionals are paid to help. It is their job to provide support, which is essentially the main focus of a one-way relationship between the professional and the person or family to be helped. Social support comes from family and friends with whom we interact for a variety of reasons, and for whom we also provide support when it is their turn to face problems. This mutuality and exchange in a relationship is the coin with which we pay for social support. On the other hand, we pay for professional support with appreciation for their help and with money—either tax dollars or our own.

Families of children with exceptionalities are often more familiar than others with the professional support system. From the time of diagnosis through adulthood, a constantly changing plethora of professionals enter and exit their lives. As they grow older, the most constant—and most trusted—fixtures in this professional scene are educators (Suelzle & Keenan, 1981), a point we made in Chapter 8 when discussing special educators' relationship to other human service systems. Unfortunately, contact with professionals may produce stress as much or more than it provides support. Professionals may discount concerns about their children (Roos, 1985). Family members may learn about their child's problem indirectly, through a furtive scan of forbidden medical records (Helsel, 1985; H.R. Turnbull, 1985b), or they may be given the diagnosis bluntly, with spouse or other supportive persons absent (Lonsdale, 1978). They spend endless days in waiting rooms and school conference rooms and repeat the same medical and family histories over and over (Harris, 1983). They may be blamed for their child's problem (Akerley, 1985; Warren, 1985). The accusations against professionals go on and on.

It is difficult to know how much of this indictment is true. Some of it may be a "kill the messenger" syndrome, in which parents have difficulty separating the pain of bad news from the bearer of it. Harris (1985) described the difficulty:

> Like any parent of a handicapped child, I've encountered incompetence and insensitivity as well as genius and saint-like understanding in helping professionals . . . But I have realized only recently what burning rage I have felt because my daughter is handicapped and how bitterly I have viewed the efforts of any professional who is less than perfect. It's not easy to accept that the world is unjust, that some children are blessed and others burdened . . . Helping professionals were among the first to get in the way and catch the brunt of my unrestrained anger (Harris, 1985, pp. 262–263).

A good strategy to learn what works and what does not is to ask each family as you begin to work with them about their most positive and most negative experiences with professionals. Their answers may give you insights on individualized approaches to them.

Building Better Professional Support. Simply because parental anger at professionals may be intensified by the perceived injustice of their child's exceptionality, however, is no reason to discount entirely families' criticisms. There is always room to be more helpful, more sensitive, more encouraging. The overall goal of this book is to build professional support in the schools that is truly supportive of the well-being of all family members.

There is, however, one specific facet of professional support that should be discussed here, and that is the need to coordinate services. Development of effective coordination has been hampered by, among other details, the lingering assumption that families are responsible for finding and coordinating the variety of health, educational, and social services their child may need (Schalock, 1985). Some parents accept this responsibility. For example, Mary Akerley (1985) commented:

> One day I kept Eddie out [of school] for an appointment with the neurologist; the next day I caught hell because I had not asked permission. Would they have felt the same way if it had been a dental appointment? Oh yes, indeed. Perhaps then it was time to get something straight: Did they, by chance, consider themselves the primary case managers? Of course. Well, we did not—that responsibility was ours alone. They were providing a

service which we had determined we wished to purchase for our child; we were the customers, and we would call the shots. I did not ask permission from my other children's schools to make professional appointments, and I had no intention of mothering Eddie any differently. (Akerley, 1985, pp. 29–30)

However, there is a difference between acknowledging parents as the primary managers and decision-makers for their children and leaving them to their own devices in the search for, and coordination of, services. Some children may need a wide variety of services, both within and outside the school. Also, some communities may have a large number of professional services that overlap in function. The task of finding services, deciding which is best for a particular person, and then co-ordinating the various agencies involved can be time-consuming and exhausting. Families usually have no way to undertake a systematic search for available resources or to make informed decisions about the best programs for their children.

One promising solution to this problem is a program called "direction services," an agency that perhaps has no direct service responsibility itself but which families can contact for descriptions of programs and for help in gaining access to the services their children need (Zeller, 1980). Direction services screen individuals to assess needs, help families identify goals, and refer them to appropriate services (Zeller, 1980). Such services require extensive community planning and interagency agreements to be effective. Agencies must agree on such issues as who will pay for what service for which clients (the schools? social services? Medicaid? the family?); such agreements are hard to reach and usually complex. Other issues include participation on the interdisciplinary team, coordination of generic with specialized services, how to guide families in the selection of providers when services overlap, and so on (Schalock, 1985). The bottom line in co-ordination, of course, is the human factor—overcoming professional conflicts in philosophical approaches to services and developing mutual trust and respect across disciplines and agencies (Hall, 1980).

Schools, of course, are critical participants in interagency co-ordination. Some schools participate in co-ordination and direction services that are set up as a separate agency; others, like the Portland (Oregon) Public School District, are the primary organizers and administrators of direction services (Zeller, 1980). These programs maintain extensive files of community resources that may be helpful to families with an exceptionality, including descriptions of services, costs, contact persons, admissions or eligibility criteria, and so forth. Some direction services may do all the leg work for families, including contacting agencies, providing case files, and linking two or more programs. Other families may want to use the direction service primarily to find out what is available. Regardless of the way direction services may be designed or utilized by families, they are a critical link between families and the professional support they and their children need.

SUMMARY

This chapter has described a variety of support services within the framework of natural coping strategies families may use to reduce stress. The range of coping strategies, from passive appraisal to professional support, provides families with a wide array of help in managing the presence of exceptionality in the family. Many families use some or all of these strategies instinctively. Professionals can help build these natural strengths in a number of ways. Some help is in the form of structured programs, like direction services, respite care, or problem-solving workshops. Other help is more incidental to the professional's day-to-day interaction with families, e.g., encouraging families to think of positive contributions of the child with an exceptionality, pointing out successes, and giving parents encouragement to relax once in awhile.

It is important to note, however, that not every family can use every coping strategy, and, even if they do, they might not want it in the format professionals present. For example, some families want nothing to do with organized support groups and prefer to stay away from the "handicapped establishment" (Bennett, 1985). Others might have no place in their belief structure for spiritual support. Still others might have no need for respite care and feel perfectly comfortable getting their rest and relaxation by their own firesides (Lonsdale, 1978). Preferred coping strategies may change over the life cycle (McCubbin et al., 1983). Finally, some coping strategies may be more useful for some family functions than for others (see Chapter 4). As we have emphasized again and again, professionals should work with, not against, individual family preferences. The questionnaire included in Appendix C includes sections on coping strategies. You can modify it to suit your program offerings and use it to identify family preferences.

Furthermore, we should note that some coping strategies are more appropriate for some situations than for others. Thus, as much as possible, families should be encouraged to have a variety of coping strategies at their disposal. In a way, reframing is the first step to any action—internal or external—one might take to reduce feelings of stress. The first question is: Is this something we can change or is it something we must learn to live with? Once that question is answered, the next step is to choose the coping strategy that will best fit the situation as well as the individual family's style. As a professional, your role is to suggest, not dictate; to provide options, not to select. It is through seeing yourself and your school as a *resource* for coping, rather than a manager, that you can best provide support.

Throughout this book and particularly in this chapter, we have discussed the strengths and weaknesses of families, the family systems approach, and family-professional relationships. This chapter on coping is the last chapter on those subjects in which direct solutions to family-professional problems are available. In the next chapter, we continue to focus on those relationships, but we do so from a radically different perspective, one that does not admit of direct or simple solutions—the moral perspective.

Chapter 14

Professional Ethics and Morals

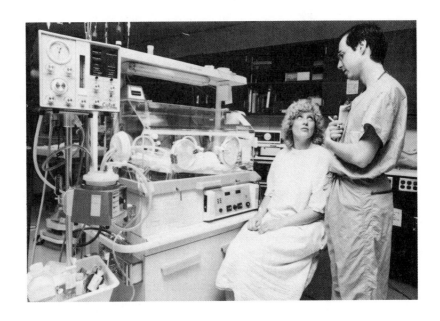

In studying this book, you have familiarized yourself with the family systems perspective, which states that professionals should take into account the interests of all members of a family when addressing the needs of one of them. You also have considered stategies for communicating with and providing information to families, so that you can carry out the family systems perspective. And you have learned about the legal rights of students, family members, and professionals in special education, so that you may act lawfully.

Perhaps you said to yourself, "I know what the family systems concepts and communication skills are, and I know the law, but I still have questions about what is right to do in this particular situation."

If questions like this have crossed your mind, you are apparently interested in looking into the morals of special education and other intervention. If, however, such questions have not presented themselves, perhaps you have not considered deeply enough some of the right-wrong problems that can and usually do arise. There are, after all, situations that do not have a clear-cut, right-wrong answer and that require you to exercise professional, legal, and moral judgments. In this chapter, we will discuss some of those problems and show how you can begin the difficult process of making reasoned, articulated *moral* judgments about them. We begin by stating a problem involving self-injurious behavior and a proposed intervention, by presenting the moral issues of that problem from a family systems perspective, by showing why it is important to consider the problem from a moral perspective, and by defining "moral perspective" through "ethics" and "morals." We then point out the source of ethics and morals, offer more case problems and help you in reaching judgments, and, finally, return to the first problem.

A MORAL PROBLEM FOR FAMILIES AND PROFESSIONALS

For example, consider this case. A teen-aged girl who is moderately mentally retarded has begun to bite her nails so often and severely that she has torn her skin and requires bandages that impair her work at school and at her job. A school psychologist suggests to her teacher and parents that the most effective way to stop the nail-biting is to shout "no" loudly, shake a finger at the girl, point to her hand, and slap her hand. The teacher agrees that this would be effective. The parents have doubts, the mother being inclined not to use the slap and the father being inclined to use it, perhaps too heavily. The school social worker is well-known for reporting cases of abuse to the child protection agency and is opposed to the intervention. By contrast, the school principal still practices corporal punishment (which is legal in many states).

What is the right thing to do? Consider it from these perspectives: the student's, the teacher's, the mother's, the father's, the social worker's, and the principal's. Will they agree with each other? How do you determine, and who decides, what is right in this situation? Why does it matter what is right?

"What is the right thing to do?" asks about the ultimate resolution of the problem. "Will they agree with each other?" deals with the issue of a universal right answer as distinguished from a relative right answer. "How do you determine?" deals with the process for resolving the issue. "Who decides?" deals both with the process for decision making and the power to make decisions. "Why does it matter?" deals with the relevance and, indeed, necessity for making moral judgments when formulating a course of action.

Let us consider those issues. It is not likely that these people will all agree on whether the intervention is right. After all, each has a different view about whether to use the shout-point-slap method. It may be that they can tell us why they think they are right. For example, the psychologist and teacher may say it is right to use that intervention because it will be effective (thus, right equals effective), but the social worker may say it is wrong because it is not the least restrictive/drastic (Turnbull, 1981) intervention (thus, right equals least intrusive, a concept discussed in chapter 8). It is not clear how they will resolve their differences or who will make the decision.

There are several reasons why it matters what is right. One, the student has a behavior that interferes with her learning, may be socially isolating, and may be physically harmful and non-hygienic. Two, no law or codes of professional ethics adequately govern the situation (as long as the slap does not constitute child abuse). Three, a family systems perspective teaches us that there is a variety of considerations. These include the wishes of the student, the wishes of the parents, the effect of the procedure on the siblings when the procedure is followed at home, and the effect of the procedure on other functions of the family, such as the affection and socialization functions. Thus, we have no choice except to think about right and wrong actions.

From this example, we learn why we should be concerned with the moral right and wrong of professional interventions. Tymchuk (1976) suggested the reason is to have consistent treatment by professionals. Allen and Allen (1979) contended that the extreme vulnerability of students with mental retardation requires professionals to consider the ethics of intervention. Mesibov and LaGreca (1981) made the case that professionals must consider ethical issues in order to be more effective in their work. Turnbull (1982) argued that the law requires professionals to consider their ethical duties because they set the standards of professional conduct over and above those standards required by the U.S. Constitution as a matter of the child's lawful rights. Heshusius (1982) and Rosenberg, Tesolowski, and Stein (1983) said ethics are important to consider because professionals have a moral duty to be advocates for their clients. Bateman (1982) and Guess et al. (1984) stated that ethics are important because the law often does not provide guidance for professionals. There are many other good reasons to consider ethics:

1. Studying ethics can help us answer difficult questions, such as the shout-point-slap enigma.
2. Other sources of answers to difficult questions may not be available (in this case, the law was not helpful and professional codes of ethics were not sufficiently helpful).
3. Thinking about issues of right and wrong usually will provide thoughtful and reasoned answers which generally are better—because they can be defended and justified—than a knee-jerk or gut-feeling response.
4. It usually is better to think through problems for oneself and reach a conclusion that is personally satisfactory than to be guided solely by what another person thinks (e.g., in this case, the teacher could have acquiesced to the psychologist and principal, even though neither of them was required to do the shout-point-slap). We thereby become more independent and autonomous when we think for ourselves, especially concerning the hard questions of right and wrong in education. As the Greek philosopher Socrates pointed out, the unexamined life is not worth living.
5. We ought to do right and not wrong, and we must therefore think about right and wrong carefully because we act as trustees and stewards for children and as caretakers of their bodies and minds.
6. The professional who carefully considers moral issues is truly acting in a professional manner by applying broad concepts to a problem in an attempt to answer it.

DEFINING ETHICS AND MORALS

What do ethics and morals mean? The word *ethics* refers to the science of thinking about and studying morals, and the word morals refers to right and wrong behavior. Thus, ethics is systematic reasoning about right and wrong behavior (Frankena, 1973; Mann & Kreyche, 1966). In this chapter, we refer to decisions about the right or wrong action as moral decisions, and we try to help you reach decisions by using ethics.

Let us apply that definition to the teen-ager in our example. The individuals involved in her life were not likely to reach consensus on the rightness or wrongness of the shout-point-slap. Even the reasons they gave (e.g., effective is right; least intrusive is right) would not resolve the disagreement. Yet it is clear that right and wrong matter in this case and that it is important to consider the moral issues of the case.

When reasonable people disagree about the right or wrong thing to do in a particular situation, like the one we have described, it will help to think carefully about what you would do and why. To do that, it will help you to know about the sources of ethics and morals in special education.

SOURCES OF ETHICS AND MORALS: PROFESSIONAL CODES

There are some obvious and useful sources of ethics and morals for special education professionals. For example, the Council for Exceptional Children (CEC), the nation's special education professional organization, has published a Code of Ethics and accompanying Standards for Professional Practice (1983). The CEC begins by stating a Code of Ethics. The Code is based on the obligation of special educators to the student, the employer, and the special education profession. These obligations are described in eight principles that are to form the basis for all professional conduct. The CEC then lists minimum standards of conduct, the Standards for Professional Practice. Together, the Code and the Standards "provide guidelines for professional etiquette, for effective interpersonal behavior, for resolution of ethical issues, and for making professional judgments concerning what constitutes competent practice" (p. 205). The CEC Code and Standards are reproduced in Appendix D of this book. After we describe various situations that raise problems of moral behavior, we will refer to the applicable Code and Standards.

The CEC is not the only organization that has developed a professional code of ethics. Such codes include those of the American Psychological Association (1981), National Association of Social Workers, American Psychiatric Association, and American Speech-Language-Hearing Association.

Rather than adopt Codes or Standards, some organizations have adopted statements of policy. For example, the American Association on Mental Deficiency (AAMD) has formulated policies concerning the basic rights of persons with mental retardation including the right to habilitation and the use of physical, psychological, and psychopharmacological procedures to affect behavior. The Association for Persons with Severe Handicaps has adopted position papers and resolutions concerning treatment, education, and habilitation.

If you have questions about the morality of a behavior, you may consult any number of professional organizations' views. You are not bound to follow the organizations' codes, standards, or policy positions, which are guidelines and recommendations, not obligations that can be enforced by law. They can, however, be useful to you in defense of what you did if you acted consistently with them. And, in some cases, noncompliance can result in expulsion from the professional organization.

The codes, standards, and policy positions are valuable in other respects. First, they represent the careful thought of a large number of professionals; obviously, they also represent the accumulated experience and wisdom that go into the professionals' consideration of the moral problems. The codes, standards, and policy positions usually have been adopted only after debate and consideration by various delegate bodies to professional meetings (such as the AAMD Council, which is its governing body) or by delegates to professional meetings (such as the delegates to the CEC annual meeting in 1983). This assures that the codes are widely accepted.

Second, the codes deal in general terms with a large number of problems; they give general guidance and cover many issues. Although someone might wish that they were specific and answered all the questions that any individual may have, that clearly is neither practical nor desirable. It is not practical because they cannot possibly address all of the problems that may arise. It is not desirable because individual professionals are responsible for their own behavior and should be encouraged to consider and apply moral solutions to particular problems.

Finally, the codes, standards, and policies have the effect of supplementing the laws of special or regular education by providing moral guidance. Those laws—whether in the form of the Education of the Handicapped Act (EHA) and its regulations, state or local laws and regulations, or court interpretations of those statutes and regulations—do not always apply to a problematic situation. Thus, you may need extra guides to moral conduct; indeed, there are likely to be situations in which the laws do not apply or seem to be inadequate in determining what is right or wrong. After all, in cases in which the law does apply but seems inadequate, the laws merely state what is lawful, not necessarily what is right or wrong from a moral perspective. In those cases, a professional may choose between the law or morals. This is a choice of civil obedience or civil disobedience, a topic well beyond this chapter's boundaries.

SOURCES OF GENERAL MORAL PRINCIPLES

Let us assume that you have a moral problem concerning the education of a child and the relationship between the child and the family. After consulting the CEC Code and Standards, you determine that they do not address your problem in a way that seems entirely sufficient or satisfactory to you. What can you do?

One way to proceed is to begin to think systematically about moral behavior. How do you do this? After all, you are not necessarily trained to think about moral behavior. You may have some conceptions about the right thing to do; indeed, you probably do. But you have not been trained to apply your conceptions of morality to the situation at hand, and you may realize that your conceptions are different from those of other professionals.

It may help, therefore, to have some philosophical landmarks from which you may make moral decisions. You may want to know, for example, how the classical Greek philosophers would have answered the moral questions. You may want to know whether their answers are consistent with the Judeo-Christian ethical tradition. You may want to apply a utilitarian philosophy. In any case, you want to know the major philosophical principles so you can apply them to the situation at hand. In short, you will be trying to base your response on some chosen moral ground. In that case, it will be helpful for you to be given a brief description of each of the major philosophical principles and some guidance about how to apply them to particular cases.

Naturally, it is not the role of this chapter to reach final answers; that is something you must do for yourself. Nor is it the role of this chapter to describe fully all the major philosophical doctrines; that is best left to texts on philosophy (Frankena, 1973; Taylor, 1967; Mann & Kreyche, 1966) and to the words of the philosophers themselves. This chapter seeks only to describe briefly some of the major philosophies and show how they might be applied to some of the problems. Thus, it has these inherent attributes: The description of the philosophies will only briefly show how they might apply, and it will not answer for you what is "moral" because that is within the scope of your own professional responsibility. For that reason, we will pose unanswered questions in the hope you will try to answer them for yourselves. Moreover, we do not say what we would do in a particular situation because a more important objective of this text is for you to make your own judgments.

Some readers may criticize us for not disclosing our judgments, the reasons we reached them, and the reasons we rejected other judgments. That indeed may be a shortcoming. (Of course, in some cases our judgments can be inferred.) Nonetheless, we adhere to our plan of setting forth the principles, applying them, and showing how you may reach certain judgments.

We do so because we believe that the family systems approach makes it undesirable for us to give our answers. An advantage of the family systems approach is that it clarifies professional-family relationships by analyzing families more carefully than most approaches to the relationships. But a disadvantage of the approach is that it complicates the effort to find solutions to hard problems, especially moral problems. We believe we will undermine the essential didactic message of this book—that professionals must take family systems into account in their work with people with exceptionalities—if we say what moral judgments should be reached in each problem we give, when taking a family systems approach. What is right for one family is not necessarily right for another.

A second reason for our declining to give our judgments is that a judgment stated in one case can become a precedent in another case. That is how it should be, but facts of cases can change enough to justify different judgments. Given our brief statement of principles, cases, and application, we are wary of the precedential problems that judgment-giving can create.

Third, in each of the problems matters of fact are entwined with questions involving moral judgments. In real life, these are intermingled, as in this chapter. Thus, for example, whether a shout-point-slap intervention works is a matter of fact; whether such a procedure should be used is both a matter of fact (will it work?) and moral judgment (if it won't, how can it be justified, and if it will, should it nonetheless be used as a moral action?). Because mixed questions of fact and morals are present, we think it best for you to sort out the questions of fact from the moral issues and, having done so, complete the task of making moral judgments.

Finally, matters of moral judgment are different from matters of taste. We emphatically deny that any one moral judgment is as worthwhile as any other. It may be a matter of political doctrine to establish an all-Aryan race, but that did not make the Holocaust moral. It may be a matter of social preference to want to improve the condition of mankind, but that does not make compulsory sterilization of all people who are mentally ill or mentally retarded moral. It may be a matter of taste to apply shock therapy for inappropriate behaviors, or even a matter of programmatic desirability, but that does not make the use of shock morally right in every case (Turnbull, Guess, Backus, Barber, Fiedler, Helmstetter, & Summers, 1985). Thus, not all matters of taste or desirability can be justified on moral grounds, and, too, matters of taste or desirability must be distinguished from matters of moral judgment. The recent effort at values clarification has tended to accord all values, and hence all moral judgments, equal status, as if they were merely matters of taste. That may be insufficient for some readers, as it is for us, but it has the advantage of forcing readers to clarify for themselves what are matters of taste, what are matters of moral judgment, and when, why, and under what circumstances one or more moral judgments prevail over other plausible ones. We adopt that advantage here but not elsewhere, (e.g., Guess et al., 1984).

The Greeks and St. Thomas Aquinas

Ancient Greece is a fertile source for philosophy still applied in our western world. Socrates, Plato, and Aristotle were the leading thinkers of ancient Greece and thus most deserving of attention today. Centuries later, St. Thomas Aquinas reiterated their views. All of them argued, first, that the essence of a human is the ability to reason, the characteristic that sets a human apart from other species. The human faculty of greatest value therefore is intellect—the power that enables reasoning, conceptualization, and rational judgment. For this reason the power of the intellect provides human satisfaction, fulfillment, or happiness; it is also the faculty that has the primary claim for development. This is why Socrates said that the unexamined life is not worth living. To fulfill this unique trait, we must use our reason and intelligence. In addition, the Greeks maintained that, to have a "happy" life, we must act reasonably, with intelligence and thoughtfulness, and we must avoid excesses of action. Thus, we must live according to a "Golden Mean"—a course of conduct that avoids extremes.

Judeo-Christian Doctrine

The Judeo-Christian ideal is for people to be more like God. This ideal is most often perceived in terms of love between persons. Precepts such as "Do unto others as you would have them do unto you" and "Love thy neighbor as thyself" are the cornerstones of the Judeo-Christian doctrine of reciprocity. This is a doctrine that expresses love and concern for others. The Old Testament stresses the concept of the brotherhood of man and responsibility to each other. The New Testament stresses the commandment to treat others as you would want to be treated.

Empathetic Reciprocity

The Judeo-Christian doctrine of love is very much like a secular doctrine of empathetic reciprocity. That doctrine says that we should recognize in other people the same needs to be loved, fulfilled, and respected as we see in ourselves (Allen & Allen, 1979). The doctrine of empathetic reciprocity is secular because it does not explicitly rest on religious authority. But it is like the Judeo-Christian doctrine of reciprocity in that it urges us to put ourselves in the position of others as fully as we can. We should do this by adopting their needs and wants and by laying our own aside. Because this doctrine emphasizes the humanness of each individual as reflected in each person's need for love, fulfillment, and respect, according to this doctrine, each action that we take concerning another is right or wrong to the extent that it contributes to the capacities of others to acquire love, fulfillment, and respect.

Kant's Categorical Imperative

The German philosopher Immanuel Kant stated a rule by which to judge maxims of conduct. He argued that an act is moral only if it can be applied to all rational beings without contradiction or exception. Thus, non-dichotomous (i.e., equal or unexceptional) treatment of all people in similar circumstances is the right action. An action is right if a rational person would decide upon and approve that action for *all* persons in the same circumstance. Any action that one takes toward a student with exceptionalities must therefore be appropriate for all other students with exceptionalities and indeed, in most cases, for all students of any type.

Utilitarianism

In contrast to the exceptionless nature of the Categorical Imperative are the doctrines of the utilitarians. Jeremy Bentham and John Stuart Mill, English philosophers, were leading utilitarians who argued that the "right" action is the one that promotes the greatest good for the greatest number of people. Thus, we must judge the effect of our actions from the viewpoint of not only their effect on ourselves (the actors) but also their effect on people directly and indirectly affected. We must also determine what constitutes a good effect or a less good, or bad, effect.

Causalism

A different way to define moral action is to ask about an act, "What harm does the act do?" This approach, called causalism, requires us to determine if an action will have a negative effect on society, on the general welfare. If it does, the action is wrong. In this view, the individual is the means to a general welfare. For example, causalism disallows the nontreatment of a mildly injured newborn who is reasonably likely to become a gifted child, but it may allow nontreatment of children who will always be wholly dependent on others because of their severe disabilities. Similarly, causalism may compel postgraduate education of gifted children even when they do not want it, but causalism may not require adult training for people with disabilities. The only proper perspective in causalism is societal harm: What harm will an action cause to society?

CASES WHERE ETHICS AND MORALS MAY BE INVOLVED

In this section, we will present some of the most common situations where right and wrong may be involved. We will describe a factual situation, ask questions from the family systems perspective about the right or wrong thing to do, and briefly show how one or more of the major philosophical doctrines can be applied to resolve each situation. As you read the problems and the questions, remember that we are approaching situations from the family system perspective. That perspective asks you to consider the interests of all affected people; our questions help you to do that. Also remember that reasonable people can disagree about the right action. As you think about the right action, remember that you are increasing both your ability to think as well as your tolerance of the different points of view of others. Those abilities may help you in interdisciplinary team decision making.

When we apply one or more of the principles, we try to accomplish two tasks with you. First, we show you more adequately the *meaning* of the principles, as our initial definitions were brief. Second, we show you *how* a principle might be applied to a particular case. Remember, however, that it is your decision, not ours, *whether* the case *should* be approached that way.

You will probably experience several responses as you read these situations and our discussion of them. First, you may be somewhat overwhelmed by the number of questions we raise concerning the moral thing to do in each situation. Please recall, however, that the family systems approach requires you to take into account the interests of all family members. You also will notice that, in some cases, we ask you to consider the interests of people outside the family of the child, including the interests of various professionals and the interests of other children. Of course, considering their interests means the family system perspective is not the only legitimate perspective. There are other competing interests.

Second, you may observe that the moral action in each situation depends on which principle you apply and that different results are approved or disapproved by different doctrines. This conflict is unavoidable. However, you should not give up seeking an answer simply because there are conflicting results. You may prefer to apply one philosophical principle—such as the reciprocity principle or the utilitarian principle—and apply it to all of the situations. If you do this, you will have chosen to act on the basis of a consistent philosophy. Or, you may prefer to reach a result that consistently is child centered; you may always rule in the child's favor. If you do this, you usually will not apply consistently any given philosophy but, instead, you will be acting as an advocate of the child.

Third, you may find that the CEC Code and Standards are sufficient to provide you with guidance. That is, of course, an entirely understandable result because the Code and Standards reflect a national consensus that resolves these matters for you from the perspective of a national special education organization. But even then, you are exercising your own independent judgment to adhere to them. Let us now turn to the problems.

Screening, Evaluation, and Referral

An early childhood screening program has been established in your state (where early education begins at age 5 for children with disabilities). The screening consists of cursory examination of each child to determine if there may be visual, hearing, motor, intellectual, or emotional problems. Two-year-old Sally is screened, with her mother's consent, and found to have a moderate hearing loss. Unfortunately, Sally lives in a rural community. There are no appropriate diagnostic or treatment clinics within 100 miles of her home or school. Sally's mother does not have transportation and is a single parent.

Should the professionals tell Sally's mother about the hearing problem? Unquestionably, they should tell Sally's mother the truth about her daughter. For one reason, telling the truth is a matter of moral duty under reciprocity and Categorical Imperative doctrines. For another, not telling the truth, or withholding a substantial portion of it, is normally indefensible professional conduct as a matter of tradition. There are times, some people think, when falsification or withholding is defensible (Bok, 1978; Katz, 1984.) By contrast, there are questions about the consequences of telling the truth. Should the professionals make a referral to an agency that is, for all practical purposes, unavailable because it is so far away, or try to intervene in some other way (such as by learning what intervention to use and using it themselves, even though they may not be fully trained and may be doing some harm as well as some good)? What would be the effects for Sally and her mother of doing nothing? Of making an impractical referral? Of putting together a makeshift intervention?

What is the right action? It may be that a "Golden Mean" approach would require a makeshift intervention. This is so because doing nothing or referring Sally to the distant clinic are extremes that do not yield acceptable results. Doing nothing is unacceptable from the standpoint of developing Sally's capacities to hear and thereby to use reason and intelligence. Referring Sally to the distant clinic is unacceptable because it is unlikely in this case that any intervention will occur at all—the distances are too great. But a different result can be defended. Thus, it may be that the "Golden Rule" or reciprocity doctrines would put us in Sally's or her mother's shoes and have us at least make the referral to the distant clinic. Less desirable but more practicable, we might choose the makeshift intervention. Sally's mother may be able to arrange transportation to the distant clinic and she and the clinicians together might devise a way to carry out its intervention in her rural community. Or, we might conclude as a matter of fact (i.e., after evaluating the efficacy potentials) that a makeshift intervention would do some good until Sally enters the early childhood education programs three years from now. Note, however, that this is a judgment of fact, not a moral judgment.

Establishing Educational Opportunities

A family recently has arrived in America from Vietnam after surviving the Vietnam war and subsequent internal strife. There is only one child in this family, Kim, a 15-year-old boy whose older brothers and sisters were killed in Vietnam. After two years in public school programs for non-English speaking students, Kim has mastered English and demonstrated a brilliant grasp of mathematics, physics, and chemistry. Kim's teachers urge his father and mother to send Kim to a school for students who are gifted, nearly 2500 miles from Kim's family's home. There, Kim would receive a full-tuition scholarship, free room and board, and intensive training that almost certainly would qualify him for a full scholarship at any of the nation's best universities.

Kim is ambivalent. His mother and father are strongly opposed to the idea and say that they would lose their only son. It is clear that they have strong values of family togetherness. But the professionals at the school, which has no program for gifted secondary students, are eager to see one of their "own" excel and have these chances.

In Kim's case, there are conflicting values and beliefs about what is important. Kim's parents think that their family's unity is more important than Kim's education; the professionals believe otherwise. Kim is caught in the middle, perhaps feeling (as the only son of immigrants who have lost their other children in war) an obligation to his parents, to himself, and to his deceased brothers and sisters to "make it" in America.

What is the right thing to do (and whose perspective prevails?) when professional, family, and student values conflict? The Greek approach may favor the out-of-home education because that intervention will maximize Kim's intelligence and ability to reason, which the Greeks valued so much. The reciprocity doctrines, however, also can be applied. If Kim's parents adopt a reciprocity approach, they perhaps would favor Kim's intellectual development and allow him to go away to school. But Kim himself may prefer to stay home, also because of reciprocity (putting himself in his parents' place). And Kim's parents might argue that he should stay home because that is what they would do if they were in his position. Thus, the reciprocity doctrine will yield different results, depending on one's perspective. Or, all may be persuaded by the utilitarian argument that everyone will benefit in some way by Kim's leaving home and acquiring benefits for himself, his parents, and his present school.

Establishing Intervention Goals

A very young boy has been diagnosed as brain-damaged. There is an early intervention project in his family's town where he would receive fairly typical special education training. His parents, however, have read about the Doman-Delacado method of intervention. Called "patterning," this method involves intensive physical intervention for nearly half a day every day. In this case, the intervention requires the assistance of a staff of volunteers. The early childhood program recommends that the parents enroll the boy in its program. The professionals in this program say that they have been effective with such children and that the Doman-Delacado method has not been proven effective. The mother wants the patterning because she believes it could cure her son as well as provide her with a support system of volunteers. The father wants to enroll the boy in the local program, avoid a "parade of do-gooders" coming to his home, and spend the cost of the Doman-Delacado tuition and equipment on the older son's college tuition.

What is the right thing to do when family members and professionals have a conflict over values, and when there are conflicting professional opinions, some of which are supported by research results? Here the utilitarian perspective may favor the father and the local educators, who also argue for spreading the benefits among all family members. This is so because, from the father's perspective, the center-based early education program will help his boy with the disability as well as leave funds for the development of his other son's talents. From the educators' perspective, the local program will help the boy (its efficacy is well-documented), his mother (who will not have to be so terribly involved in his therapy that she may overlook some of the other members of the family as well as her own needs), and the brother (because family financial resources can be preserved). The reciprocity doctrines may tip the balance toward the local program, as they focus on the boy and his mother, both of whom may benefit by the intervention and by the presence of other people in their lives. From the boy's perspective, it may be good to be the center of so much attention, and it may be beneficial to have the therapy. From the mother's perspective, she also benefits as the key person in her son's therapy and as the recipient of a support system. Obviously, this is a case where the right action will depend on three factors—the perspective taken (the father's, mother's, boy's, brother's, or educators'), the philosophical approach adopted (the utilitarian and reciprocity approaches give different results), and the efficacy of the therapy. Again, remember that the question of fact (efficacy) must be answered separately from the question of right behavior.

Granting or Denying Access to Information; Dealing with Child Neglect and Custody Disputes

Sean is a ten-year-old with a learning disability. His parents were divorced last year and he lives with his mother, who has legal custody, and her parents. Sean's father, whose interest in Sean's welfare is well-known, lives in the same town; he fought hard but unsuccessfully to obtain joint custody and alleged that Sean's mother sometimes neglected to feed Sean during the time Sean was living with her before the divorce hearing. Sean's father comes to your classroom and asks to see Sean's school records; you decline the request and refer the matter to the school principal, who also declines. Sean's father argues that, although the mother has legal custody, he is, after all, Sean's father, and Sean may be neglected still. In fact, you recently have observed Sean's lethargy and noted in the school records that Sean is extraordinarily hungry at lunch times and perks up after eating. Sean's father also says to the principal, "I know you have talked about Sean and me to a whole bunch of people in this little town because the word's come back to me. If you can blab about us to a bunch of people who have no business knowing about us, why can't I see his school records?"

It helps to think about the records, child neglect and Sean's welfare, and your role in adversary proceedings. Remember, too, that the family systems perspective is not the only one; here also is a school-system perspective to consider.

Should Sean's father be shown the records? Here the EHA denies access to the father, but the father's moral claim may seem more compelling than the mother's legal rights under the EHA. Should the principal discuss Sean and his parents with people who are not involved in Sean's education? It seems clear he should not; the EHA prohibits disclosure, and no moral principle justifies it. Does it make any difference, as the teacher points out, that Sean's maternal grandparents have seen the records without explicit permission by his mother? What is the right thing to do?

Consider the issues of child neglect and child welfare. Should the school professionals file a report of suspected child neglect, as the law requires them to do? Assuming that they comply with the law and file a report, would their action help Sean, who is having adjustment problems because of his learning disability as well as because of his parents' divorce? Suppose you have reason to believe, from Sean's school and family history, that Sean's health has deteriorated during the time he has stayed with his mother. Since the bottom line is a custody battle, would Sean be better off with his mother or his father?

Would you be willing to go to court to testify that you suspect Sean's mother may be neglecting him? Or would you testify only reluctantly, if required to appear in court? Should you volunteer to tell the father about the problem of neglect as you noted it in the records? What if the principal has said to you, "Listen, this case is closed. Let's keep out of the courts and get along with educating Sean." Do you agree that Sean's educational welfare is the school's only business? Would you volunteer to reveal the facts that you have noted in Sean's record if you were called to testify in a new child-custody proceeding? In short, are you willing to defend your actions when there are issues of privacy and confidentiality of records, potential or actual neglect or abuse, and custody disputes?

Let us consider Sean's case from the reciprocity perspective. First, Sean is the most vulnerable person in this situation, so we may want to take his point of view as the most important one. What would he want? What would you want if you were Sean? Clearly, he wants and needs both good health and an education. Without the former, the latter is more difficult to obtain. Thus, disclosing the records to the father (probably illegally) and reporting the suspected child neglect (which is legally required) are right, from a reciprocity perspective. But consider the parents. We know what the father wants, and we can assume the mother objects to disclosure and reporting. If, however, she could understand that those actions would help Sean and perhaps herself, would she object so much?

From the perspective of the Greeks and Aquinas, it is right to report the suspected neglect because Sean could be helped physically, and his physical improvement most likely will help him intellectually. Now consider the case from a utilitarian perspective. Releasing the records might promote a great deal of good, even though it may be illegal. The good might involve Sean's health and education, his father's peace of mind, his mother's getting help, and perhaps even a change in the custody arrangement.

In Sean's case, we said we should consider the morality of action from his point of view because he is the most vulnerable of the people involved. That perspective—namely, that professionals have a moral duty to give priority to the most vulnerable of the people in a situation (usually, the child who is exceptional or any child, for that matter)—has been advanced by special educators (Weintraub & McCaffrey, 1976). It is an appealing idea, and one that you might well adopt. It considers the power relationships among people and attempts to rebalance them. It gives professionals a single point of focus, which simplifies matters of moral judgment. And it is consistent with the reasons many professionals entered the business of helping people who are exceptional. On the other hand, it does not necessarily take into account the family systems perspective, which requires careful consideration of the interests of all family members. It makes moral judgments on the basis of the needs of one person, not on the basis of principles as applied to problems. And it therefore arguably will be too pragmatic and eclectic for many people (although pragmatism and eclecticism themselves are philosophical principles that one may adopt). Despite the shortcomings of the "vulnerability perspective," it has much to recommend it, not the least of which is that CEC seems to have used it as the central point of view for its Code and Standards (Weintraub & McCaffrey, 1976).

Giving Sufficient Information to Get Consent

Under the EHA, professionals must obtain consent from a student's parents to administer an initial special education evaluation and to make an initial placement into special education. Knowing this, you (the assistant director of special education in the school district) meet with Hillary's parents to seek consent from them for an initial special education placement out of the "mainstream," where she attends regular classes with children who, unlike her, are not orthopedically disabled, to a new "trainable" school, where all the children are physically disabled or mentally disabled. This will be her first special education placement or identification. Thus, parental consent is required.

Hillary's parents (Mr. and Mrs. Beaudelaire) speak only a little English. Before you meet with them, Hillary's teacher recommends continuing her present placement, which is intellectually and socially beneficial to her. The special education director has issued a policy that all school personnel shall strongly push for the transfer of students like Hillary to the new school. He is under orders to do so from the school board that proposed the new facility and staked its reputation on the bond vote for funds to build it. He also may lose a special education program (in the new facility) that is badly needed by some children if there is not a large enough number of them to justify its cost.

In your meeting with Hillary's parents, they ask you about the benefits and drawbacks of the transfer and about their rights if they do not like the transfer. They want to know how Hillary's program will be implemented there; they ask about the school district's capability to provide social integration of students who have physical disabilities with students who are not disabled. They ask why you are pressing so hard for consent to the transfer and what alternative placements there are. Finally, they ask the meaning of certain jargon such as "mainstream," "separate self-contained program," "paras," "quads," and "TMR."

Knowing that the "information" element of consent is satisfied by telling a sufficient amount of information in a way that can be understood (Turnbull, 1978), you face at least these questions. How much do you say, if anything? How do you say it so it will be understood? How do you avoid a confrontation between the parents, the principal, and school board? How clearly do you define the terms you and others so frequently use (e.g., "para" or "TMR") for the parents?

According to the Greeks and Aquinas, any action that maximizes Hillary's or her parents' intellect is right. Thus, full information is demanded. Obviously, the reciprocity doctrine also favors Hillary and Mr. and Mrs. Beaudelaire. Their futures are very much at stake, and few people would want to have so much resting on inadequate information. From a utilitarian perspective, it may also be good for full and frank disclosure to occur, as that may help in the education of other children. Conversely, it could cause considerable administrative problems for the school and teachers, and that in turn may hurt other children. From the causalist perspective, it can be argued disclosure would cause no harm for Hillary and her parents and only limited harm for the school, but long-term benefit for its students. This, of course, is a matter of fact, not moral judgment (as is the efficacy of aversive therapy in our first illustration). But facts shape moral judgments and therefore must be known before judgments are reached. From a causalist perspective, there also is an argument that Hillary would be at a disadvantage if she were placed in an environment that is intellectually impoverished and not challenging; thus, disclosure is right. Again, matters of fact affect moral judgments.

Dealing with the Cause of a Disability

Two students in your special education program (you are the school special education director) pose interesting problems in working with their parents. Jennie has been classified as autistic. Larry is moderately mentally retarded.

In Jennie's case, the cause of her autism is not clear. There are suggestions from one psychiatrist, who examined her at the school's request, that her mother is so disturbed herself that she may be a cause of Jennie's disability. Another psychiatrist, however, strongly rejects this theory, which he says is not consistent with current research.

In Larry's case, there is no doubt whatsoever that his retardation was caused by his mother's excessive drinking of alcohol during pregnancy; Larry has fetal alcohol syndrome. In both cases, Jennie's and Larry's parents are very committed to their children, and in Larry's case his mother is wholly remorseful and feels exceptionally guilty about the etiology of his retardation. It also is clear that both students and their parents would profit from counseling because both families have multiple psychological problems to resolve. The mothers, however, resist entering school-based counseling (or any other therapy, for that matter), because they do not see how it would help their children, and they accuse the school of meddlesome interference. You recognize the great desirability of having counselors work with the mothers. One of the professional staff suggests that you should "try a little guilt . . . it works wonders" (the so-called "guilt-trip technique"). She argues that, since the mothers were the cause of the disabilities, they should be willing to be the cause of a "cure." You have doubts about the causation but you think a great deal of good could result from counseling.

Do you blame the parents, using the guilt-trip technique? Do you blame each of them equally, even though the causation in Jennie's case is not clear? Do you use it only in the case of Larry, where the etiology is clear? Do you ask, "So what if the parents do not go to counseling—what difference would it make to the students?" After asking that question, do you conclude that it might make a positive difference? Again, we see mixed questions of fact and moral judgment. The lesson is the same: Be sure of your facts before making any judgments. What do you do then?

Here, the classical, utilitarian, and causalist approaches may favor the guilt-trip technique as a means to obtain a result (therapy) that may be helpful. From a classical perspective, counseling may help the parents understand their children and their development. From a utilitarian perspective, the greatest good is the mental health of the mothers and the development of their children; the greatest number of people helped is four [two sets of mother-child(ren)]. From a causalist perspective, there will be little, if any, harm to the children or their parents, who as a group already are in need of mental health intervention. But these approaches arguably are disrespectful of the parents and may make their relations with the school and their children even worse; thus, the Categorical Imperative argues against using that technique, since it treats the children as means and not ends, as ways to get to their parents. The Categorical Imperative also disapproves of the guilt-trip technique because the technique is an exception to the rule that equal treatment of people in similar circumstances fosters respect and fosters familial relations. Also, the same results may be obtained by other means; it certainly would be worthwhile to try. Finally, the reciprocity doctrine seems ambiguous, as one can argue that each parent would want counseling but would not want to be brought to that result by these methods.

Treating the Real Client

Charles is a 10-year-old child who is both gifted and severely hearing-impaired. For a variety of reasons, transferring him from the local school, where you are the school psychologist, to the state school for students who are deaf is not possible. You have seen Charles on several occasions, and principally to determine the causes of his increased withdrawal from social contact with other students (as a younger boy, he was quite gregarious with them). You have decided there is little you or anyone else can do for him except to wait out his adolescence. You are pessimistic about his future, as you know that research indicates that, as they grow older, children with severe hearing impairments become more and more isolated from people who hear normally. You have interviewed Charles' parents, Eleanor (who is hearing-impaired) and Robert (who is not), and you realize that you can do a great deal for them if they will enter into therapy with you (you have an after-school practice).

Who is the real client? Charles, or Eleanor and Robert? Or is it you, with your private practice? Suppose you also have been working with Charles' younger brother, Eric, who also is hearing-impaired but much more determined and optimistic than Charles about being accepted at school. Do you make comparisons between Charles and Eric in working with their parents? Do you even make comparisons about Eleanor's approach (she is very mothering to Charles, very sympathetic) and Robert's (he is much more demanding)? Do you side with one parent or the other?

The family systems perspective suggests that there is no conflict here, no need to decide who the real client is because it considers the family as a whole and says that professionals should try to help the family meet everyone's needs. But Charles is the student and you are employed by the school system to work with students. That seems to mean he is the real client from your perspective as a school employee. From your perspective as a psychologist with a private practice, however, it may appear that Charles' parents are the true clients. And from your perspective, again as a school employee, the true client might be Eric, for whom prevention of social isolation seems desirable and possible.

The problems here are similar to those in the immediately preceding case. But there is the extra dimension of the younger brother, Eric. Does your decision depend in any way on its effect on Eric? If so, how? If Eric can be helped by helping Charles, Eleanor, and Robert, then it seems that any decision about them is made even more right if it also can help him, too. This is a utilitarian approach, because it maximizes good among a larger number of people.

The Advocacy Issue

Miguel is the son of Rosita and Hernandez, both of whom recently immigrated to the United States illegally but have been given amnesty to stay. Miguel was born in America, so he is an American citizen. He is educationally puzzling. School evaluations show him to be either mildly mentally retarded or a slow learner-borderline student. The school district in a southwestern state is under pressure from the state education department to reduce the special education enrollment. Indeed, it has been threatened with a lawsuit if it places too many Hispanic Americans in its programs for students with mild mental retardation or learning disabilities.

You are the director of special education in the district and a firm believer in special education for Miguel and students like him. The research data and your own experience of 15 years in the district convince you that special education placement is preferable to regular education placement because of the individualized instruction and the success of eventual phase-out from special education. You believe special education also is preferable because a local attorney, herself an Hispanic American, keeps watch on the school district's special education students and often takes their cases, usually without charge, when there are school-family disputes. You know you soon will be asked to make a recommendation concerning Miguel's placement.

Is there an ethical duty to be an advocate for Miguel, as Rosenberg, Tesolowski, and Stein (1983), Heshusius (1982), and Hyman and Schreiber (1975) argue? Or is the duty to the child based on research data, local experience, and the availability of a free lawyer? Is there a duty as an administrator to be an advocate for the school district, which is under extreme pressure from the state education department and may face a lawsuit? Does it make any difference that all local, state, and federal special education funds already have been budgeted, and there may have to be a withdrawal of funds from regular to special education for Miguel?

This case poses a hard question about loyalty. The Greeks' Golden Mean may tell you that *some* (but not excessive) advocacy is required for Miguel. The reciprocity approach will move you to be an advocate for Miguel only if you put yourself in *his* shoes alone. But if you consider the risk of lawsuit to the district and the district's limited resources, you may reach a different result under the reciprocity perspective, one that favors the mainstream for Miguel and takes account of the needs of other special education students. You also may adopt a utilitarian perspective and say that the interests of the group of all special education children outweigh the interests of Miguel, who is, after all, only one child.

The Dual-Loyalty Issue

You are a classroom teacher in a school district that serves the residents of a black ghetto in one of America's largest cities. Trained in social welfare and in special education, you have become increasingly convinced that the district is taking advantage of the parents. For example, its consent forms are full of educational jargon and legalese. Although they may be legal, they are not helpful. There is another problem, which is that the way in which parents' consent for evaluation, programming, and placement is obtained seems, in your judgment, coercive. In addition to these concerns about the legality of consent, you have strong reason to believe that the school district routinely violates special education students' rights.

Thus, your concerns are two-fold: first, you are concerned about the parents, who have no real control over their children's programs; and second, you are concerned about the inadequacy of the school's programs for the children. In this frame of mind, you attend a meeting of a local teacher-parent group and listen with increasing discomfort to the school principal gloss over problems or misstate facts.

To whom does your loyalty run? To the school, which employs you and provides, after all, some programs? To the parents, who may be able to recapture some stake in their children's lives and by collective action improve the school for them and other children? To the children, who may well leave the school before any improvements occur and who also may be subject to informal discipline or casual sanctions if their parents become too involved in their education? Would you be willing to attend the next meeting of the parent group and set the record straight? Does it matter that the last teacher who set the record straight, several years ago, still has not been given lucrative summer-school teaching opportunities and has been assigned regularly to the least desirable administrative tasks in school? Does it matter, too, that there is a rumor that the school board will try to fire the next teacher who "gets out of line?"

The dual-loyalty issue is a hard one. Here, we clearly see that the right or wrong action depends on the perspective you take, whether the students' and their parents' or the school's. The doctrines do not give you clear-cut answers.

In addition to the dual-loyalty issue, there is the problem of "whistle-blowing" (Bok, 1980; Nader, Petkas, & Blackwell, 1972). The issue is this: should the employee "squeal" or "blow the whistle" on the employer and should that be done publicly, or are there less noticeable ways to be an advocate (Crary, 1980)?

From the utilitarian perspective, your duty is to the greatest number of people. You therefore need to decide if your action in setting the record straight will benefit anyone, and, if so, how many and for how long. From the perspective of the Golden Mean, you need not make a public protest because it suggests that there may be other ways to be effective and that they should be used before you resort to public protest. The reciprocity doctrines are ambiguous in application. On the one hand, they say that you should be loyal to the students and parents, as you would want them to be loyal to you. On the other hand, you may ask whether the parents and students would put their jobs at risk for you. That is *not* a proper question under the reciprocity doctrines, because those doctrines do not involve making deals. Yet many people would ask that very question (make a deal), and that fact alone makes the reciprocity doctrines ambiguous in application though they should not be.

Under the Categorical Imperative, it would be wrong for your co-employees to take formal or informal sanctions against you or the students, since that would use people as a means of retribution and not as ends in themsleves or as valued people. But you cannot be sure that the school board will behave as Kant would under the Imperative. Indeed, you think it will not and that the school board and some school officials will violate that principle in the way they deal with the students and parents. Finally, causalism may tell you that the harmful effects of your protest would be felt by you yourself as well as by the children and parents, too. So causalism may say that you should find other means for correcting the problem.

Consent and Choice by Teachers, Parents, and Students

Renee is a teen-ager who, for several years, has expressed to her parents, Murray and Kirsten, her dissatisfaction with her learning disabilities (LD) program at the high school. In talking with some university faculty who are conducting research in learning disabilities at the school, Renee learns that she has the right under the EHA to attend her own IEP conference if it is "appropriate" for her to do so. She also learns that "appropriateness" has not been defined by law but there are data that student participation in IEPs is academically and emotionally helpful to the student.

She asks you, the LD program director, for permission to attend her next IEP conference. You recognize the critical role that consent and choice play (Guess, Benson, & Siegel-Causey, 1985; Guess & Siegel-Causey, 1985; Turnbull & Turnbull, 1984; Shevin & Klein, 1984; Turnbull, 1981) in the academic, social, and emotional maturation of children. You know that in a year or two Renee will enter a transition phase from school to adult services and that her curriculum next year will be geared to independence training. You also see in Renee a squelched spirit because of constant frustration in her education.

With this in mind, you discuss Renee's wishes and her rights with her parents and the special education director. Murray, her father, thinks Renee's participation is "silly—she's still just a girl." But Kirsten, her mother, is "keen on it—she needs to be on her own one day, and we'd all better get ready for it." The special education director is adamantly opposed and cites his experience ("special education kids just can't have a meaningful role") and the precedent problem ("we'll have every kid in school telling us what to teach and how, and we're the professionals, not the kids").

Putting aside for this case the potential problems about advocacy and dual loyalty (which we discussed before), what is the "right" thing to do? When and how much consent and choice should the professional give a child? Remember that when the professional does not develop independence in the student by providing training in consent, choice, and decision making, the professional may make the child more dependent on family and professionals, and this in turn may make the family also more dependent on the child.

The classical approach will be to include Renee in her IEP, if that will increase her capacities. The reciprocity doctrine is ambiguous, and the result will depend on whose perspective you adopt. The Categorical Imperative tends to favor Renee's participation, as she will be treated as a more valued person when she participates. The utilitarian approach also may favor her participation because, in the long run, she will be more independent of school and parents. The causalist approach may suggest that little if any harm will come because her participation can be controlled or limited by adults and her participation will not be a precedent for all children.

CONSIDERING ALTERNATIVES

You may have noticed that we have described problems in which you must deal with a given intervention or action by a professional. Perhaps you even remarked to yourself that there may be alternatives to that intervention or action. If so, you are correct.

We stated problems that have specific interventions or actions to make you think about the moral thing to do. But one course of action for you in any situation may be to develop alternative interventions and actions. For example, in the case of "screening, evaluation, and referral" involving the preschool girl who had a hearing disability and who lived in a rural community, it may have been possible for the mother and local professionals to obtain training about interventions, to make trips to the distant clinic less often but for longer periods of time, or to obtain the services of an itinerant professional. Likewise, in the case of the "cause of disability," it may have been possible to persuade the mothers to enter counseling by some means other than the "guilt-trip technique." Similarly, in the case of the "dual loyalty", the professional may secretly approach an "outside" advocate (such as a spokesperson for the parent group), protest to the principal, persuade the principal to correct the impressions he created, remain quiet until such time as there is power to correct the situation without being fired, or leave the job. So, in each problem as well as in your professional life, you may seek alternatives. After identifying them, you still may have questions whether they are right or wrong. If so, you may use the same procedure for those questions as we have described.

In that case, the questions involve important ones of efficacy, i.e., whether the proposed action will be effective and have the intended results and whether there are equally effective or nearly effective alternatives. This is the situation where matters of fact must be rigorously separated from matters of moral judgment. You must determine the facts (is the intervention efficacious?) before making a moral judgment (is it right to use the intervention?). A central question in this case or a similar case of an arguable intervention, therefore, is this: Is there a duty to use only the curriculum, procedures, methods, settings, and technology that actually benefit a child, or at least does not harm the child, all according to research data and professional experience? The self-evident answer is "yes." Turn the question around: May the professional use an intervention that has no benefit and actually may harm a child without offsetting benefit? The self-evident answer is "no." Yet nonefficacious treatments have been used without moral objection, for many reasons (Turnbull, Guess, Backus, Barber, Fiedler, Helmstetter, and Summers, 1985).

In addition, consider the possibility that a curriculum, procedure, method, setting, or technology may also have a negative effect on the teacher or other professional. This may be the case when an intervention such as the shout-point-slap procedure so depersonalizes the student-professional relationship that the student becomes an "object" in the professional's mind. (A different perspective is that depersonalization is a professional coping strategy that allows more consistent application of an intervention and reduces the personal anxiety about the intervention's use.)

Consider, too, the possibility that the intervention may have harmful effects on other students. This would be the case where, for example, the intervention, when carried out in the presence of other students, has the effect of making them so afraid of the professional that any intervention by the professional will be resisted, feared, or avoided and thus less effective.

Finally, consider the family systems perspective. What effect will the intervention have on the child and other family members individually? What effect will it have on the family as a whole?

In the case of the shout-point-slap intervention for nail biting, the efficacy questions are these. First, does the intervention work—does it stop the behavior? Second, what other effects does it have on that student and are those effects negative (e.g., the child avoids contact with the professional, thus rendering any interventions ineffective)? Third, what effects does it have on other students, and are those effects positive (e.g., does it keep them from similar behavior) or negative (does it make them want to avoid the professional, thus rendering any other interventions ineffective)? Fourth, what effects does it have on the professional? Fifth, what effects does it have on family members and the family as a whole? Once these questions have been answered, it is possible to determine if the procedure is right or wrong by following the process set out in this chapter. Indeed, as we have tried to show, it is possible to apply that procedure, once the facts are known about a situation, to all situations.

It is now appropriate to review the process that we have described. Take the shout-point-slap procedure as an example:

1. State the problem: A student is injuring herself, both physically and socially, by severe nail-biting.
2. State the facts and distinguish them from moral judgments.
3. State the ethical issue: Knowing what we do about an intervention, is it moral to use a point-shout-slap method to correct the problem?
4. Consider the alternatives to that intervention: Can other interventions prevent the behavior and yet not have effects on the student, family, other students, and the professional that are more negative than the proposed intervention?
5. Repeat the issue: When is a proposed or an alternative intervention moral? Answer the question by applying professional and philosophical principles.

From some perspectives, right behavior is that which professional organizations recommend—the proposed and alternative interventions are moral only if they are recommended or at least not prohibited by the codes of ethics and professional standards of relevant professional organizations. (This does not mean that professional associations' approval of a professional behavior necessarily makes it right. Moral debate rages around interventions that have received approval by some professional associations, e.g., abortion, electric shock therapy, nontreatment of some newborns, and denial of treatment in community settings.) Thus, at least the CEC Codes and Standards come into play in a major way in the following cases (See Appendix D):

1. Screening, evaluation, and referral: Code I, and Standards 1.1, 1.3, and 2.4.
2. Establishing educational opportunities: Standard 1.4.
3. Establishing intervention goals: Codes I and III, and Standard 1.1.
4. Granting or denying access to information and dealing with child neglect and custody disputes. Codes I, VII, and VIII, and Standards 1.4 and 1.5.
5. Giving sufficient information to get consent: Codes VI, VII, and VIII, and Standards 1.4 and 1.5.
6. Dealing with the cause of a disability: Codes I, II, III, and VI, and Standards 1.4 and 3.1.3.
7. Treating the real client: Codes II, III, VI, and Standard 1.4 and 3.1.3.
8. The advocacy issue: Codes I, II, VII, and VIII, and Standards 1.1, 1.5, and 3.1.
9. The dual-loyalty issue: Codes I, II, VII, and VIII, and Standard 1.1, 1.5, and 3.1.
10. Consent and choice: Code I, and Standard 1.1.
11. Efficacy of intervention: Codes I and III, and Standards 1.1 and 1.4.

But there are other standards for determining what is a moral action. These include the following:

1. *Classical Greek and Philosophical View of Thomas Aquinas.* Right behavior is that which increases the power of the intellect. The proposed and alternative interventions are moral only if they increase (or, at least, do not decrease) the students' abilities to develop their powers of intellect and powers to engage in reasoning, form ideas and concepts, and make rational judgments.
2. *Judeo-Christian Golden Rule and Secular Empathetic Reciprocity.* Right behavior is that which we would want done to us. The proposed and alternative interventions are moral only if they are what we would want others to do to us in similar circumstances. It bears repeating that the reciprocity doctrines do not involve "making deals" (asking whether others would do the same for us).
3. *Kant's Categorical Imperative.* Right behavior is that which we approve universally. The proposed and alternative interventions are moral only if they can be approved for all persons in the same circumstances as the particular student.
4. *Utilitarianism.* Right behavior is that which obtains the greatest good for the greatest number. The proposed and alternative interventions are moral only if they increase the "good" for the greatest number of people.
5. *Causalism.* Right behavior is that which has no harmful effects to society. The proposed and alternative interventions are moral only if

they do not cause harm (i.e., negative results) for the members of society generally.

For each problem, you may want to construct a visual guide such as this one:

	Proposed Action	Alternative A	Alternative B
Principles:	*Does the Principle Apply?*		
1. Classicists	Yes	Maybe	Yes
2. Golden Rule	No	No	Yes
3. Categorical Imperative	Yes	No	Yes
4. Utilitarianism	Maybe	No	Yes
5. Causalism	Maybe	No	Yes

With this technique, you are determining the right or wrong behavior by treating each of the principles equally. That is, none has greater reason to be applied than another. The right or wrong action will then depend on the totality of the applied principles. You decide which action is right by determining which is more often right than not under each of the principles. This is, of course, a very mechanical approach, even somewhat simplistic and, for that reason, it may not be appealing. But it has the utility of giving general guidance. Of course, you may reject this approach and treat any of the principles as having an exclusive (or a greater) claim to your morals than any other.

SUMMARY

As you make your decision about the right or wrong of an action, remember to keep the family systems perspective in the front of your mind. Do this by asking questions about the interests of the members of the student's family. Remember, too, that there are other legitimate perspectives, namely those of the school system and its professionals and those of other students.

We hope we have been successful in accomplishing the purposes of this chapter, which are to:

1. Make you more aware of moral problems in your profession,
2. Help you understand why it is important to consider the ethics of a situation,

3. Help you apply the relevant CEC Codes and Standards and the major ethical perspectives that you might take into account in determining the right thing to do,
4. Show you how those perspectives can be applied, and
5. Help you think in moral terms, so that you yourself will be more able to act thoughtfully when you confront tough issues.

Since we have reached the end of this chapter, it is now time for an epilogue, a final word about this book and its messages.

Epilogue

In parts of this book, we discussed the ways in which professionals and families have changed in their relationships to each other and to children with exceptionalities. In most cases change has come slowly, even when it seems to have been precipitous (as in the enactment of the Education of the Handicapped Act). But we also have argued that there is no longer an evolution in those relationships, much less in the professions and families. The years of gradual and not-so-gradual change seem to be part of history, not part of the present.

Instead of evolution there is revolution, in the healthy sense of the word. We ourselves are witnessing and participating in revolution, in dramatic reversals of how professionals, families, and children work together and are seen by each other. More than that, we—and, we hope, you—advocate for that revolution, for the turning around of behavior and perceptions.

The revolution that we seek and hope you will join refocuses the roles of professionals and families. For so many years, professionals and the systems in which they work regarded their systems as central to the mission of delivering human services. In a system-centered world, professionals had wide discretion whether, how, and where to serve. The child with the disability or special talent was the usual focus of the service system, and the child's family often was regarded as tangential or adjunctive, as a sort of after-thought.

Today the central focus of the service delivery system is becoming, as it should be, the family and the child, each equally important. Professionals and their systems are expected to accommodate the family and the child; the child and family are no longer expected to accommodate the professional and the services system. We are firmly convinced, from our own work and that of others, that this approach is analytically accurate, doctrinally sound, and programatically efficacious.

A major cause of this revolution is the application of a family systems perspective to families whose children are disabled or gifted and talented. The family systems approach has the great advantage of showing, through multiple analyses of families, just how families behave. It reveals families to be extraordinarily different from each other, to be immensely fluid, dynamic, and interdependent. It illumines the enormous complexity of a family and demonstrates the ''ripple effect'' of intra-family behavior and professional intervention. Any action that is intended to affect one person necessarily affects others, often in unanticipated ways.

A result of the family systems work is not only clarity but, in some cases, confusion. A professional who begins to understand the family by grasping the family systems approach may experience a sense of frustration: ''Now that I know all of this, what should I do?'' This book tries to answer that very question by describing the family systems approach, its significance for professionals, and actions that professionals may take.

We ardently hope that our analysis and our advice on how to work with families will fulfill the revolution, establishing a new unity of purpose and focus for families, professionals, and children, one that helps each of them. The purpose must be to be effective with the family, not just with some people in it. That goal requires professionals to focus sharply on the family, the child, and the system, in that order.

More than that, we hope you have profited from our work and, in applying it in your work, will find it to be valuable to families, children, and professionals. Just as a journey begins with the first step, so a revolution begins with the first volunteer. You could be one of the first, and we encourage you to be just that.

Appendices

A. **Family Assessment Interview Guide (Chapters 2, 3, 4, and 5)**
B. **Parent Information Centers (Chapter 12)**
C. **Family Information Preference Inventory (Chapters 12 and 13)**
D. **CEC Code of Ethics and Standards (Chapter 14)**

APPENDIX A
Family Assessment Interview Guide

Many family system characteristics described in this book (Chapters 2–5) can be uncovered through standard psychosocial assessment instruments available to psychologists and social workers. However, the goal of most of these instruments is to measure a family's needs from a therapeutic standpoint; they are therefore far too detailed for use in a school setting. From the point of view of the school, the goal of assessment should not be to pinpoint some pathology in the family, but rather to provide information to: (a) determine the best means of interacting with the family, (b) guide the interdisciplinary team in selecting instructional objectives for the student that also serve the needs of the family, and (c) indicate areas of need that the school or a referral agency can serve. For these purposes, we have found that the best assessment strategy is a series of open-ended questions similar to those presented on the following pages. Before progressing to those questions, however, we should make some points about their use.

First, as in any open-ended interview, the questions require the establishment of rapport between the professional and the parent. These questions are by their nature personal, and it will be easy for parents to perceive them as intrusive. Therefore, it is essential for interviews to be conducted in private, preferably in a comfortable surrounding. Perhaps, if the parent prefers, it could be conducted in the home. The strict confidentiality in which the information will be held should be emphasized. It is also important to explain openly the use to which the information will be put, its relevance to the child's program, and its value in helping the school serve the family. Parents should clearly understand that participation in the interview is voluntary and that they are free to refuse to answer any or all of the questions. In no case should parents be pressed to respond to questions when they appear uncomfortable.

Second, many of these questions have a "social desirability factor." That is, people may tend to answer them in a way that they believe will make themselves and their families more acceptable to the interviewer. To reduce this tendency (although it may not be possible to eliminate it entirely), it is important to take a neutral and nonjudgmental attitude toward all responses. You should stress that there are no "right" or "wrong" answers to any of the questions, and that the purpose of the questions is to adapt the school's program and resources to the family's particular needs. Once again, the parent's levels of comfort with and trust in you are vital to the accuracy of the information you receive.

Third, the questions presented here are clearly too numerous to be used in one session. You may wish to conduct the interview in several sessions, and these sessions may even be scattered throughout the school year. Alternatively, you may select only a few questions that seem most important in establishing a good initial relationship with the family. Also, some questions are clearly not relevant for every family (e.g., questions about relationships in a blended family or questions about siblings for a family with only one child). These should, of course, be deleted when they are not relevant. A good strategy may be to select a few of the most relevant questions from each of the four sections of the questionnaire (Family Resources, Interaction, Functions, and Life Cycle).

Fourth, you should be flexible in any open-ended interview and be willing to follow tangents in whatever direction the parent's interest may seem to dictate. For example, a parent may answer other questions in the process of answering one; in such a case, you should avoid repetition by "formally" asking them later. If parents refer to some issue or seem especially interested in a particular question, you should follow up by encouraging them to clarify or provide more information for you on that topic. You can get a better idea of many family system components from some anecdote or example the parent may tell you (e.g., the family's communication style) than from directly asking the question itself.

Finally, you should follow school policy on the type of information and formats when you report information for inclusion in the student's permanent record. We encourage you to avoid interpretive comments in the report and present only facts or actual statements made by the parents. Guidelines for maintaining records are included in Chapter 11.

INTERVIEW GUIDE

Family Resources

1. Who are the members of your immediate family (please include names, ages, sex)?
2. Are there other persons (not necessarily relatives) whom you consider to be part of your family? What is your relationship with them?
3. How often do you have contact with extended family members? How do they help you with your child with an exceptionality?

4. Is there anything further you would like to learn about the nature of your child's exceptionality?

5. (If joint custody) Which parent has custody of your child during the school week? Is there a schedule the school should be aware of?

6. How are stepparents involved in the care and education of your child with an exceptionality?

7. How has your child reacted to your divorce? Are there any issues for the child that the school should be aware of?

8. Do any other members of your family have exceptional needs? If so, please describe.

9. Which members of your household are employed? What are their occupations?

10. How does work outside the home influence child-rearing?

11. How does work outside the home influence involvement with your children's educational program?

12. Is your family a member of a religious organization? If so, which one? How have your religious beliefs influenced your experience in dealing with your child with an exceptionality?

13. Are there any special ethnic traditions or customs you would like us to include in your child's program?

14. In general, how does your family approach problems? What helps you most when you are facing difficulty?

15. What family members or friends do you turn to when you are facing difficulty? How are they helpful?

16. Please describe (without using names) an interaction with a professional that was most helpful to you. Describe one that was least helpful.

17. How openly do the members of your family talk about your child's exceptionality with each other? With others?

18. What are your beliefs about the most important things parents should teach their children?

19. What do you think are the most important things schools should teach children?

20. What things do your family value most in life?

Family Interactions

1. What are your feelings and thoughts about your child with an exceptionality? Do you have any unanswered questions or unresolved needs in relation to this child?

2. What is your impression of your spouse's feelings and thoughts about your child with an exceptionality? Are there any unresolved issues?

3. What is your impression of your other children's feelings about your child with an exceptionality? Are there any unresolved issues?

4. How often do all of you spend time together as a family? What interests or activities do all of you share?

5. Do people in your family generally support an individual family member in pursuing some goal or interest? How do they show their support?

6. Do you have interests, hobbies, or friends of your own that other family members do not share? Do other family members have outside interests?

7. How are decisions made in your family? Who generally has the final say?

8. Who makes decisions about your child with an exceptionality? How are those decisions made?

9. How would you characterize your family's daily or weekly schedule or routine—is it fairly predictable or not? How do family members react when the schedule is disrupted?

Family Functions

1. How are chores divided in your family? (Who does the housework, child care, etc.) Which chores are children expected to perform? Are you satisfied with the way chores are divided?

2. Are there members of your family who require special attention or care? Please describe and indicate who provides this care.

3. Please describe the nature of your family's past involvement in the children's educational program? Which member(s) are most involved? Are you satisfied with your involvement?

4. If children have homework or special programs that need to be carried out at home, who assists them? Please describe any "special programs" that are currently carried out in your home.

5. Are children rewarded for completing chores? If so, please describe.

6. What does your family do for fun?

7. Please describe any community activities in which your family, or a member of your family, are involved? (e.g., scouts, board members, aerobics classes . . .)

8. What are some of the strengths of your family?

9. How have you and your family benefited by your experience with exceptionality?

10. As you think about your family, what are the characteristics of each person that give you the most pride? What about yourself?

Family Life Cycle

1. Tell me how you found out about your child's exceptionality. What was your reaction? Who was helpful? Who wasn't?
2. Looking back over your life so far, what has been the most difficult time for you? The best time?
3. What events or persons have had the biggest influence on your life? How did they influence it?
4. What are the short term goals that you have for yourself? For other members of your family?
5. What are the long term goals that you have for yourself? For other members of your family?
6. What do you think your child's life (with exceptionality) will be like 5 years from now? Ten years from now?
7. What do you think your life and other members of your family's lives will be like 5 years from now? Ten years from now?
8. What worries you most about the future?
9. What do you look forward to in the future with the most enthusiasm?

APPENDIX B
Parent Information Centers

Alabama

None

Alaska

Marsha Buck*
SE Regional Resource Center
218 Front Street
Juneau, AK 99801
(907) 586-6806

Arizona

None

Arkansas

Patsy Fordyce*
Arkansas Coalition for the Handicapped
701 West 7th Street
Little Rock, AR 72201
(501) 376-0378

Barbara L. Semrau*
Focus, Inc.
2917 King Street, Suite C
Jonesboro, AR 72401
(501) 935-2750

California

Mary Lou Breslin*
Disability Rights Education Defense Fund, Inc.
2032 San Pablo Avenue
Berkeley, CA 94702
(415) 644-2555

Albert C. Zonca*
Protection & Advocacy, Inc.
2131 Capitol Avenue, Suite 100
Sacramento, CA 95816
(916) 447-3324

Raylene Hayes**
TASK (Team of Advocates for Special Kids)
1800 East LaVeta Avenue
Orange, CA 92666
(714) 771-6542

Colorado

Cathy Carlson*
Denver ARC
899 Logan, Suite 311
Denver, CO 80203
(303) 831-7733

Connecticut

Nancy Prescott*
CT Parent Advocacy Center
c/o Mohegan Community College
Mahan Drive
Norwich, CT 06360
(203) 886-5250

Delaware

Patricia Herbert*
PIC of Delaware, Inc.
193 West Park Place
West Park Community Center
Newark, DE 19711
(302) 366-0152

District of Columbia

Annette Bobbitt*
Lt. Joseph Kennedy Institute
The Kennedy School Program
801 Buchanan Street, N.E.
Washington, D.C. 20017
(202) 529-7600

Ellen Abramson**
District of Columbia General Hospital
Department of Pediatrics
Handicapped Infant Intervention Program
1900 Mass. Avenue, SE, 4th Floor
Washington, D.C. 20003
(202) 727-3866

---

*Newly Funded PTI
*Continuation PTI
***Newly Funded and Continuation PTIs

Florida

None

Georgia

Mildred J. Hill**
Georgia ARC
1851 Ram Runway, Suite 104
College Park, GA 30337
(404) 761-3150

Hawaii

None

Idaho

None

Illinois

Charlotte Des Jardins***
Coordinating Council for Handicapped
   Children
220 South State St., Room 412
Chicago, IL 60604
(312) 939-3513

Donald Moore**
Design for Change
220 South State St., Room 1616
Chicago, IL 60604
(312) 922-0317

Dr. Norma Ewing**
Southern Illinois University
Department of Special Education
Pulliam Hall, 124
Carbondale, IL 62901

David W. Peterson**
La Grange Area Department of Special
   Education
1301 West Cossitt
La Grange, IL 60525
(312) 354-5730

Indiana

Becky Irvin**
Task Force on Education for the Handicapped,
   Inc.
812 East Jefferson Boulevard
South Bend, IN 46617

Iowa

None

Kansas

None

Kentucky

Gene Young*
Kentucky Coalition for Career and Leisure
   Development
366 Waller Avenue, Suite 119
Lexington, KY 40504
(606) 278-4712

Louisiana

None

Maine

Pam Rasmussen*
Maine Parent Federation, Inc.
P.O. Box 2067
Augusta, ME 04330
(207) 767-3101

Maryland

Joan Driessen*
Maryland Society for Autistic Adults &
   Children—Project Peer
1000 Grosvenor Century Plaza, #327
10630 Little Patuxent Parkway
Columbia, MD 21044
(301) 596-0793

Massachusetts

Martha H. Ziegler***
Federation for Children with Special Needs
312 Stuart Street, 2nd Floor
Boston, MA 02116
(617) 482-2915

Michigan

Eileen Cassidy*
Citizens Alliance to Uphold Special Education
313 South Washington Square
Lansing, MI 48933
(517) 485-4084

Minnesota

Paula F. Goldberg**
Marge Goldberg
PACER
4826 Chicago Avenue South
Minneapolis, MN 55417
(612) 827-2966

Mississippi

Anne Presley*
Association of Developmental Organizations
   of Mississippi
6055 Highway 18 South, Suite A
Jackson, MS 39209
(601) 922-3210

Sharon Booth*
Training and Information for Parents Project
4750 McWillie Drive, Suite 101
Jackson, MS 32906
(601) 981-8207

Missouri

None

Montana

None

Nebraska

None

Nevada

Cindy Pennington*
Nevada Association for the Handicapped
P.O. Box 28458
Las Vegas, NV 89126
(702) 870-7050

New Hampshire

Judith Raskin***
NH Parent Information Center
155 Manchester Street
Concord, NH 03301
(603) 244-7005

New Jersey

Mary L. Callahan*
Involve New Jersey, Inc.
199 Pancoast Avenue
Moorestown, NJ 08057
(609) 778-0599

Mary Vernacchia**
Montclair Board of Education
Montclair Public Schools
22 Valley Road
Montclair, NJ 07042
(201) 783-4000

New Mexico

Beatriz Mitchell*
Protection and Advocacy System
2201 San Pedro N.E., Bldg. 4, #140
Albuquerque, NM 87102
(505) 888-0111

New York

Jane Stern**
Advocates for Children of New York, Inc.
24-16 Bridge Plaza South
Long Island City, NY 11101
(212) 729-8866

Dr. Susan Polerstok**
Parent Training Project
Herbert H. Lehman College
Bedford Park Blvd. West
Bronx, NY 10468
(212) 960-8570

Joan Watkins*
Western NY Association for the Learning
    Disabled
190 Franklin Street
Buffalo, NY 14221
(716) 855-1135

North Carolina

Jennifer Seykora*
Advocacy Center for Children's Education and
    Parent Training
219 Bryan Building
Raleigh, NC 27605
(919) 821-2048

Connie Hawkins*
Exceptional Children's Advocacy Council
P.O. Box 16
Davidson, NC 28036
(704) 892-4407

Patti Gilbert**
Project PAVE
Family Infant & Preschool Program
Western Carolina Center
Morganton, NC 28655
(704) 433-2864

North Dakota

None

Ohio

Thomas Murray**
SOC Information Center
3333 Vine Street, Suite 604
Cincinnati, OH 45220
(513) 861-2475

Margaret Burley*
Ohio Coalition for the Education of Handicapped
    Children
933 High Street, Suite 200-H
Worthington, OH 43085
(614) 431-1307

Oklahoma

None

Oregon

William Moore**
Western Oregon State College
Teaching Research
Special Education
Monmouth, OR 97361
(503) 838-1220

Diana D. Bricker**
Center on Human Development
University of Oregon
901 East 18th Avenue, First Floor
Eugene, OR 97403
(503) 686-3568

Deanna Goodson**
Western Oregon State College
Special Education
Monmouth, OR 97361
(503) 838-1220 Ext. 322

Cheron Mayhall*
Oregon COPE Project
999 Locust Street, NE #42
Salem, OR 97303
(503) 373-7477

Pennsylvania

Beth Sinteff*
ARC/Allegheny
1001 Brighton Road
Pittsburgh, PA 15233
(412) 322-6008

Christine Davis*
Parents Union for Public Schools
401 North Broad St., Room 916
Philadelphia, PA 19108
(215) 574-0337

Mary Rita Hanley*
PA Association for Children with Learning
   Disabilities
Box 208
Euchland, PA 19480
(215) 458-8193

Louise Theime*
Parent Education Network
240 Haymeadow Drive
York, PA 17402
(717) 845-9722

Puerto Rico

Carmen Selles**
Associacion DePadres
P.O. Box Q
Rio Piedras, PR 00928
(809) 765-0345

John G. Henning**
11A of World University
Hato Ray, PR 00920
(809) 782-2990

Rhode Island

None

South Carolina

None

Tennessee

Harriett Derryberry*
EACH, Inc.
P.O. Box 121257
Nashville, TN 37212
(615) 327-0697

Texas

Bob Glenn**
Positive Parent Involvement
833 Houston Street
Austin, TX 78756
(512) 454-6694

Kay Lambert*
Advocacy, Inc.
7700 Chevy Chase, Suite 300
Austin, TX 78752
(512) 475-5543

Janice Foreman*
ARC/TX Early Parent Intervention
910 Seventh Street
Orange, TX 77630
(409) 883-3324

Utah

Susan McFarland*
PIE—Parents Involved in Education
c/o Developmental Disabilities, Inc.
1018 Atherton Drive, Suite 101
Salt Lake City, UT 84123
(801) 266-3939

Jean Nash*
Utah PIC
4984 South 300 West
Murray, UT 84107
(801) 265-9883

Vermont

Peggy Spaulding**
University of Vermont
Center for Developmental Disabilities
499 C Waterman Building
Burlington, VT 05405
(802) 656-4032

Connie Curtin*
VT/ARC
37 Champlain Mill
Winooski, VT 05404
(802) 655-4016

Virgin Islands

None

Virginia

Winifred Anderson**
Parent Education Advocacy Training Center
228 Pitt Street, Room 300
Alexandria, VA 22314

Washington

Pam McDonald*
King County Advocates for Retarded Citizens
2230 Eighth Avenue
Seattle, WA 98121
(206) 622-9292

Mary Christie*
Project PEP
1025 South 3rd Street
Renton, WA 98055
(206) 228-8868

Martha Gentili*
Washington PAVE
1010 South I Street
Tacoma, WA 98405
(206) 272-7804

West Virginia

William L. Capehart**
WVA Department of Education
Room 309 Capitol Complex
Building 6
Charleston, WVA 25305
(304) 348-8830

Wisconsin

Liz Irwin*
Parent Education Project
United Cerebral Palsy of SE WI
152 West Wisconsin Avenue #308
Milwaukee, WI 53203
(414) 272-4500

Wyoming

None

APPENDIX C
Family Information Preference Inventory

On the following pages are a number of different things parents often mention when they are asked about information or programs they would like to have. We would like to know which of these interests you, and we would also like to know how best to go about designing and presenting the materials you want.

Step 1: In the box immediately to the right of the items in the inventory, please rate how much you would like to have the information:

> put "0" if the information has no interest for you at all;
> put "1" if the information has a *low* priority for you;
> put "2" if the information has a *medium* priority for you; and
> put "3" if the information has a *high* priority for you.

Step 2: Next, we need to know how best to provide you with any information you might want. For example, some people prefer group meetings while others would rather have the information in written form. We also recognize that, for different types of information, you might have different preferences about the way you would like to receive it. Telling us your preferences for format will help us decide how to develop the appropriate materials and present them to you. For each of the items you prioritize, *even if it has no interest to you at all*, please check the format you prefer, as follows:

> if you would like to participate in a group meeting with other parents to receive information about the topic, put a "✔" in the box under "group meeting";
> if you would like to meet with someone individually in a private meeting, either face-to-face or over the phone, put a "✔" in the box under "individual meeting"; and
> if you would prefer to receive written information about the topic to read at your leisure, put a "✔" in the box under "written materials."

For example, Mrs. Smith filled out the first item this way:

	Priority	Group Meeting	Individual Meeting	Written Materials
How to manage my child's behavior at home and in public places	3	☐	☐	✔

Mrs. Smith's answer tells us that learning more about managing her child's behavior is very important to her, and that she would like us to send her some written information about how to do that. Now, please turn the page and tell us about the kinds of information you would like to have and your preferences for format.

INFORMATION ABOUT TEACHING MY CHILD AT HOME

In this section, we are asking about information you might want to help you teach your child at home. Some of the teaching you might want to do might involve skills the teacher or therapist is working on at school and you would like to supplement at home. Or there might be some lessons you would like to tackle on your own. Please give us your priority and the format you prefer for *each* of the following types of information:

	Priority	Group Meeting	Individual Meeting	Written Materials
How to manage my child's behavior at home and in public places	☐	☐	☐	☐
How to teach self-help skills (for example, eating, toileting, dressing, etc.)	☐	☐	☐	☐
How to teach social skills (for example, saying please and thank you, playing nicely with other children, etc.)	☐	☐	☐	☐
How to help with homework	☐	☐	☐	☐
How to work on special needs (for example, language, speech, physical therapy exercises, etc.)	☐	☐	☐	☐
How to provide a wide range of stimulating experiences for my child	☐	☐	☐	☐
How to help my child develop meaningful relationships with friends	☐	☐	☐	☐
How to help my child develop realistic concepts and expectations about him/herself and the world	☐	☐	☐	☐
How to talk with my child about sexuality and dating	☐	☐	☐	☐
(Please use this space to tell us about any other kinds of information about teaching your child at home you would like)	☐	☐	☐	☐
_____	☐	☐	☐	☐
_____	☐	☐	☐	☐
_____				

INFORMATION ABOUT ADVOCACY AND WORKING WITH PROFESSIONALS

In this section, we are asking about information you might want to help you better understand your legal rights and work more successfully with professionals. Types of information in this section include information on rights and procedures and information to improve communication between you and professionals. Please give us your priority and the format you prefer for each of the following types of information:

	Priority	Group Meeting	Individual Meeting	Written Materials
How to participate in my child's IEP	☐	☐	☐	☐
How to participate in decisions about evaluation, placement, and related services	☐	☐	☐	☐
What my legal rights are and how to use them	☐	☐	☐	☐
How to negotiate better to get what I want	☐	☐	☐	☐
How to understand jargon and other medical or educational terms	☐	☐	☐	☐
What parent or consumer advocacy groups are available in this area	☐	☐	☐	☐
(Please use this space to tell us about any other kinds of information about advocacy and working with professionals you might like)				
_____	☐	☐	☐	☐
_____	☐	☐	☐	☐
_____	☐	☐	☐	☐

INFORMATION ABOUT PLANNING FOR THE FUTURE

In this section, we are asking about information you might want to help you and your child plan for the future. Parents of all children are interested in what the future might hold for them, but parents of children with exceptionalities may need specific kinds of information to help them plan a successful and happy future for their children. Please give us your priority rating and the format you prefer for *each* of the following types of information:

	Priority	Group Meeting	Individual Meeting	Written Materials
How to locate and evaluate educational options for next year and beyond	☐	☐	☐	☐

How to locate and evaluate residential and/or vocational programs for my child when he or she leaves school

☐ ☐ ☐ ☐

How to evaluate and select colleges, universities, or vocational schools

☐ ☐ ☐ ☐

How to locate and apply for scholarships or other financial aid for training after high school

☐ ☐ ☐ ☐

How to decide what skills my child needs to learn now to prepare for the future

☐ ☐ ☐ ☐

How to plan for my childs financial future

☐ ☐ ☐ ☐

How to plan our estate to best meet the needs of everyone in the family

☐ ☐ ☐ ☐

How to consider and evaluate options for guardianship when my child is an adult

☐ ☐ ☐ ☐

(Please use this space to tell us about any other kinds of information about planning for the future you might like to have)

_____ ☐ ☐ ☐ ☐

_____ ☐ ☐ ☐ ☐

_____ ☐ ☐ ☐ ☐

INFORMATION TO HELP THE WHOLE FAMILY RELAX AND ENJOY LIFE MORE

In this section, we are asking about information you might want to help your whole family cope better with the stresses of everyday living. Stress seems to be a fact of life in our modern world, and sometimes families of children with exceptionalities seem to have more than their share. Fortunately, there are many different ways to cope successfully with stress and the problems that cause it. Please give us your priority rating and the format you prefer for *each* of the following types of information:

	Priority	Group Meeting	Individual Meeting	Written Materials
How to cope with stress	☐	☐	☐	☐

How to handle tension with relaxation methods
☐ ☐ ☐ ☐

How to manage my time
☐ ☐ ☐ ☐

How to clarify values and decide
what our family wants in life
☐ ☐ ☐ ☐

How to solve problems as a family
☐ ☐ ☐ ☐

(Please use this space to tell us
about any other kinds of information about learning to cope that
you might like to have)

_____   ☐ ☐ ☐ ☐

_____   ☐ ☐ ☐ ☐

_____   ☐ ☐ ☐ ☐

INFORMATION TO HELP FIND AND USE MORE SUPPORT

In this section, we are asking about information you might want to help you and your whole family
better use the resources you have available to you in the community. Some people turn to friends,
neighbors, or relatives for help when they need it, while others might turn to a religious organization.
Still others turn to professionals and agencies in the community established to provide different kinds
of support. Please give us your priority rating and the format you prefer for *each* of the following
types of information:

	Priority	Group Meeting	Individual Meeting	Written Materials
How to help my family and friends better understand my child's exceptionality	☐	☐	☐	☐
How to teach my family and friends to care for my child's special needs while they are babysitting or providing respite care for me	☐	☐	☐	☐
How to locate and hire professional respite care services	☐	☐	☐	☐
What support groups (where families meet and share experiences) are available in this area	☐	☐	☐	☐
How to help my religious organization better serve me and my child	☐	☐	☐	☐

How to find the services that are available in this area

☐ ☐ ☐ ☐

How to apply for and use the services we need

☐ ☐ ☐ ☐

How to co-ordinate the different services my child is receiving

☐ ☐ ☐ ☐

How to find and apply for financial support

☐ ☐ ☐ ☐

(Please use this space to tell us about any other kinds of information about community services you might like to have)

_____   ☐ ☐ ☐ ☐

_____   ☐ ☐ ☐ ☐

_____   ☐ ☐ ☐ ☐

PLEASE USE THE SPACE BELOW TO TELL US ABOUT ANY ADDITIONAL NEEDS FOR INFORMATION YOU MIGHT HAVE OR ANY THOUGHTS THAT OCCURRED TO YOU AS YOU FILLED OUT THIS INVENTORY:

APPENDIX D
CEC CODE OF ETHICS AND STANDARDS

CEC CODE OF ETHICS

We declare the following principles to be the Code of Ethics for educators of exceptional persons. Members of the special education profession are responsible for upholding and advancing these principles. Members of The Council for Exceptional Children agree to judge by them in accordance with the spirit and provisions of this Code.

 I. Special education professionals are committed to developing the highest educational and quality of life potential of exceptional individuals.

 II. Special education professionals promote and maintain a high level of competence and integrity in practicing their profession.

 III. Special education professionals engage in professional activities which benefit exceptional individuals, their families, other colleagues, students, or research subjects.

 IV. Special education professionals exercise objective professional judgment in the practice of their profession.

 V. Special education professionals strive to advance their knowledge and skills regarding the education of exceptional individuals.

 VI. Special education professionals work within the standards and policies of their profession.

 VII. Special education professionals seek to uphold and improve where necessary the laws, regulations, and policies governing the delivery of special education and related services and the practice of their profession.

 VIII. Special education professionals do not condone or participate in unethical or illegal acts, nor violate professional standards adopted by the Delegate Assembly of CEC.

CEC STANDARDS FOR PROFESSIONAL PRACTICE

1. Professionals in Relation to Exceptional Persons and Their Families

1.1 Instructional Responsibilities

1.1.1 Special education personnel are committed to the application of professional expertise to ensure the provision of quality education for all exceptional individuals. Professionals strive to:

1.1.1.1 Identify and use instructional methods and curricula that are appropriate to their area of professional practice and effective in meeting the needs of exceptional persons.

1.1.1.2 Participate in the selection of and use appropriate instructional materials, equipment, supplies, and other resources needed in the effective practice of their profession.

1.1.1.3 Create safe and effective learning environments which contribute to fulfillment of needs, stimulation of learning and of self-concept.

1.1.1.4 Maintain class size and caseloads which are conducive to meeting the individual instructional needs of exceptional persons.

1.1.1.5 Use assessment instruments and procedures that do not discriminate against exceptional persons on the basis of race, color, creed, sex, national origin, age, political practices, family or social background, sexual orientation, or exceptionality.

1.1.1.6 Base grading, promotion, graduation, and/or movement out of the program on the individual goals and objectives for the exceptional individual.

1.1.1.7 Provide accurate program data to administrators, colleagues, and parents, based on efficient and objective record keeping practices, for the purpose of decision making.

1.1.1.8 Maintain confidentiality of information except where information is released under specific conditions of written consent and statutory confidentiality requirements.

1.2 Management of Behavior

1.2.1 Special education professionals participate with other professionals and with parents in an interdisciplinary effort in the management of behavior. Professionals:

1.2.1.1 Apply only those disciplinary methods and behavioral procedures which they have been instructed to use and which do not undermine the dignity of the individual or the basic human rights of exceptional persons (such as corporal punishment).

1.2.1.2 Clearly specify the goals and objectives for behavior management practices in the exceptional person's Individualized Education Program.

1.2.1.3 Conform to policies, statutes, and rules established by state/provincial and local agencies relating to judicious application of disciplinary methods and behavioral procedures.

1.2.1.4 Take adequate measures to discourage, prevent, and intervene when a colleague's behavior is perceived as being detrimental to exceptional persons.

1.2.1.5 Refrain from adversive techniques unless repeated trials of other methods have failed and then only after consultation with parents and appropriate agency officials.

1.3 Support Procedures

1.3.1 Adequate instruction and supervision shall be provided to professionals before they are required to perform support services for which they have not been previously prepared.

1.3.2 Professionals may administer medication, where state/provincial policies do not preclude such action, if qualified to do so or if written instructions are on file which state the purpose of the medication, the conditions under which it may be administered, possible side effects, the physician's name and phone number, and the professional liability if a mistake is made. The professional will not be required to administer medication.

1.3.3 Professionals note and report to those concerned whenever changes in behavior occur in conjunction with the administration of medication or at any other time.

1.4 Parent Relationships

1.4.1 Professionals seek to develop relationships with parents based on mutual respect for their roles in achieving benefits for the exceptional person. Special education professionals:

1.4.1.1 Develop effective communication with parents, avoiding technical terminology, using the primary language of the home, and other modes of communication when appropriate.

1.4.1.2 Seek and use parents' knowledge and expertise in planning, conducting, and evaluating special education and related services for exceptional persons.

1.4.1.3 Maintain communications between parents and professionals with appropriate respect for privacy and confidentiality.

1.4.1.4 Extend opportunities for parent education, utilizing accurate information and professional methods.

1.4.1.5 Inform parents of the educational rights of their children and of any proposed or actual practices which violate those rights.

1.4.1.6 Recognize and respect cultural diversities which exist in some families with exceptional persons.

1.4.1.7 Recognize that the relationship of home and community environmental conditions affects the behavior and outlook of the exceptional person.

1.5 Advocacy

1.5.1 Special education professionals serve as advocates for exceptional persons by speaking, writing, and acting in a variety of situations on their behalf. Professionals:

1.5.1.1 Continually seek to improve government provisions for the education of exceptional persons while ensuring that public statements by professionals as individuals are not construed to represent official policy statements of the agency by which they are employed.

1.5.1.2 Work cooperatively with and encourage other professionals to improve the provision of special education and related services to exceptional persons.

1.5.1.3 Document and objectively report to their supervisors or administrators inadequacies in resources and promote appropriate corrective action.

1.5.1.4 Monitor for inappropriate placements in special education and intervene at the appropriate level to correct the condition when such inappropriate placements exist.

1.5.1.5 Follow local, state/provincial, and federal laws and regulations which mandate a free appropriate public education to exceptional students and the protection of the rights of exceptional persons to equal opportunities in our society.

2. Professional Employment

2.1 Certification and Qualification

2.1.1 Professionals ensure that only persons deemed qualified by having met state/provincial minimal standards are employed as teachers, administrators, and related-service providers for persons with exceptionalities.

2.2 Employment

2.2.1 Professionals do not discriminate in hiring on the basis of race, color, creed, sex, national origin, age, political practices, family or social background, sexual orientation, or exceptionality.

2.2.2 Professionals represent themselves in an ethical and legal manner in regard to their training and experience when seeking new employment.

2.2.3 Professionals give notice consistent with local education agency policies when intending to leave employment.

2.2.4 Professionals adhere to the conditions of a contract or terms of an appointment in the setting where they practice.

2.2.5 Professionals released from employment are entitled to a written explanation of the reasons for termination and to fair and impartial due process procedures.

2.2.6 Special education professionals share equitably the opportunities and benefits (salary, working conditions, facilities, and other resources) of other professionals in the school system.

2.2.7 Professionals seek assistance, including the services of other professionals, in instances where personal problems threaten to interfere with their job performance.

2.2.8 Professionals respond objectively when requested to evaluate applicants seeking employment.

2.2.9 Professionals have the right and responsibility to resolve professional problems by utilizing established procedures, including grievance procedures when appropriate.

2.3 Assignment and Role

2.3.1 Professionals should receive clear written communication of all duties and responsibilities, including those which are prescribed as conditions of their employmfesent.

2.3.2 Professionals promote educational quality and intra- and interprofessional co-operation through active participation in the planning, policy development, management, and evaluation of the special education program and the education program at large so that programs remain responsive to the changing needs of exceptional persons.

2.3.3 Professionals practice only in areas of exceptionality, at age levels, and in program models for which they are prepared by reason of training and/or experience.

2.3.4 Adequate supervision of and support for special education professionals is provided by other professionals qualified by reason of training and experience in the area of concern.

2.3.5 The administration and supervision of special education professionals provides for clear lines of accountability.

2.3.6 The unavailability of substitute teacher or support personnel, including aides, must not result in the denial of special education services to a greater degree than to that of other educational programs.

2.4 Professional Development

2.4.1 Special education professionals systematically advance their knowledge and skills in order to maintain a high level of competence and response to the changing needs of exceptional persons by pursuing a program of continuing education including but not limited to participation in such activities as inservice training, professional conferences/workshops, professional meetings, continuing education courses, and the reading of professional literature.

2.4.2 Professionals participate in the objective and systematic evaluation of themselves, colleagues, services, and programs for the purpose of continuous improvement of professional performance.

2.4.3 Professionals in administrative positions support and facilitate professional development.

3. Professionals in Relation to the Profession and to Other Professionals

3.1 To the Profession

3.1.1 Special education professionals assume responsibility for participating in professional organizations and adherence to the standards and codes of ethics of those organizations.

3.1.2 Special education professionals have a responsibility to provide varied and exemplary supervised field experiences for persons in undergraduate and graduate preparation programs.

3.1.3 Special education professionals refrain from using professional relationships with students and parents for personal advantage.

3.1.4 Special education professionals take an active position in the regulation of the profession through use of appropriate procedures for bringing about changes.

3.1.5 Special education professionals initiate support and/or participate in research related to the education of exceptional persons with the aim of improving the quality of educational services, increasing the accountability of programs, and generally benefiting exceptional persons. Professionals:

3.1.5.1 Adopt procedures that protect the rights and welfare of subjects participating in research.

3.1.5.2 Interpret and publish research results with accuracy and a high quality of scholarship.

3.1.5.3 Support a cessation of the use of any research procedure which may result in undesirable consequences for the participant.

3.1.5.4 Exercise all possible precautions to prevent misapplication or misuse of a research effort, by oneself or others.

3.2 To Other Professionals

3.2.1 Special education professionals function as members of interdisciplinary teams and the reputation of the profession resides with them. Professionals:

3.2.1.1 Recognize and acknowledge the competencies and expertise of members representing other disciplines as well as those of members in their own disciplines.

3.2.1.2 Strive to develop positive attitudes among other professionals toward exceptional persons, representing them with an objective regard for their possibilities and their limitations as persons in a democratic society.

3.2.1.3 Cooperate with other agencies involved in serving exceptional persons through such activities as the planning and coordination of information exchanges, service delivery, and evaluation and training, so that no duplication or loss in quality of service may occur.

3.2.1.4 Provide consultation and assistance, where appropriate, to both regular and special education as well as other school personnel serving exceptional persons.

3.2.1.5 Provide consultation and assistance, where appropriate, to professionals in nonschool settings serving exceptional persons.

3.2.1.6 Maintain effective interpersonal relations with colleagues and other professionals, helping them to develop and maintain positive and accurate perceptions about the special education profession.

CEC STANDARDS FOR THE PREPARATION OF SPECIAL EDUCATION PERSONNEL

Note: Standards recommended by the Professional Standards Committee are italicized. Other standards are those of NCATE, adopted in their existing form.

1. Governance of Basic Programs

1.1 Membership of the Governing Unit

Standard: The faculty and staff of the governing unit for basic programs possess scholarly preparation and professional experience appropriate to their assignments. They maintain an involvement in and are well informed about educational issues and are committed to the preparation of teachers to provide instruction in a multicultural society.

1.2 Functions of the Governing Unit

Standard: The governing unit is responsible for setting and achieving teacher education goals, establishing policies, fixing responsibility for progam decision making, identifying and utilizing resources, and facilitating continuous development and improvement of basic teacher education programs.

1.3 Relationship to Other Administrative Units

Standard: Policies are published that clearly delineate responsibility of the governing unit and the interdependent responsibilities of other policy-making groups and administrative offices within the institution for the overall administration and coordination of basic programs.

1.4 Official Representative

Standard: One person is officially designated to represent the teacher education unit. The authority and responsibility of this individual for the overall administration and co-ordination of basic teacher education programs are indicated in published policies.

1.5 Commitment to Exceptional Children

Standard: *Members of the governing unit responsible for basic programs understand and are committed to the preparation of teachers capable of providing an appropriate educational program for exceptional students.*

1.6 Representation by Special Education Administration Units

Standard: *Special education programs where established as administrative units shall be represented on the teacher education governing unit.*

2. Curricula for Basic Programs

2.1 Design of Curricula

Standard: Teacher education curricula are based on explicit objectives that reflect the institutions's conception of the teacher's role. There is a direct and obvious relationship between these objectives and the components of the curriculum.

2.1.1 Multicultural Education

Standard: The institution provides for multicultural education in its teacher education curricula, including both the general and professional studies components.

2.1.2 Special Education

Standard: The institution provides its graduates with the knowledge and skills necessary to provide an appropriate education for exceptional learners.

2.2 The General Studies Component

Standard: There is a planned general studies component requiring that at least one-third of each curriculum for prospective teachers consist of studies in the symbolics on information, natural and behavioral sciences, and humanities.

2.3 The Professional Studies Component

Standard: *The professional studies component shall be sufficient to provide a preparation program requisite to the development of a competent professional and shall not constitute less than one-half of a student's total undergraduate program of study.*

2.3.1 Content for the Teaching Specialty

Standard: The professional studies component of each curriculum for prospective teachers includes the study of the content to be taught to pupils, and the supplementary knowledge, from the subject matter of the teaching specialty and from allied fields, that is needed by the teacher for perspective and flexibility in teaching.

2.3.2 Humanistic and Behavioral Studies

Standard: The professional studies component of each curriculum for prospective teachers includes instruction in the humanistic studies and the behavioral studies.

2.3.2.1 Distribution of Humanistic and Behavioral Studies

Standard: *Requirements in humanistic and behavioral studies shall be determined by the specialty area and may be achieved as part of, or separate from, the general studies component.*

2.3.3 Teaching and Learning Theory with Laboratory and Clinical Experience

Standard: The professional studies component of each curriculum includes the systematic study of teaching and learning theory with appropriate laboratory and clinical experience.

2.3.4 Practicum

Standard: *The professional studies component for each specialty area curriculum offered shall provide prospective teachers with direct, qualitative, and intensive supervised teaching experience. Prospective teachers seeking multiple specialization shall be required to complete a practicum in each specialization area (as defined by individual teacher preparation programs and state education agencies).*

2.3.5 Supervision of Practicum

Standard: *Each specialty area provides supervision to practicum students by persons qualified and experienced in teaching in the specialty area (as defined by individual teacher preparation programs and state education agencies).*

2.3.6 Practicum Selection

Standard: *Each specialty area program applies a list of specific criteria in the selection of appropriate practicum sites for prospective teachers. All practicum sites are evaluated on a continuous basis to assess their continued appropriateness and quality.*

2.3.7 Practicum Placement

Standard: *Each specialty area program has responsibility for assigning students to approved placements. This responsibility includes the approval of cooperating teachers and supervisors. Criteria for the selection and retention of such persons are in writing and subjected to ongoing evaluation.*

2.4 Use of Guidelines Developed by National Learned Societies and Professional Associations

Standard: In planning and developing curricula for teacher education, the institution studies the recommendations of national professional associations and learned societies and adopts a rationale for the selection and implementation of pertinent sets of recommendations for each teacher education program.

2.5 Student Participation in Program Evaluation and Development

Standard: The institution makes provisions for representative student participation in the decision-making phases related to the design, approval, evaluation, and modification of its teacher education programs.

3. Faculty for Basic Programs

3.1 Competence and Utilization of Faculty

Standard: An institution engaged in preparing teachers has full-time faculty members in teacher education whose preparation reflects rich and varied backgrounds appropriate to the programs offered. Each has post-master's degree preparation and/or demonstrated scholarly competence and appropriate specializations. Such specializations make possible competent instruction in the humanistic and behavioral studies, in teaching and learning theory, and in the methods of teaching in each of the specialties for which the institution prepares teachers. There are appropriate specializations to ensure competent supervision of laboratory, clinical, and practicum experiences. Institutional policy will reflect a commitment to multicultural education in the recruitment of full-time faculty members.

3.2 Faculty Involvement with Schools and Other Educational Agencies

Standard: *The teacher education faculty members maintain a continuing interaction with educational programs and personnel working in both public and private schools, institutions, and state and local agencies in their specialty areas.*

3.3 Conditions for Faculty Service

Standard: The institution enforces a policy which limits faculty teaching load and related responsibilities to make possible effective performance.

3.4 Conditions for Faculty Development

Standard: The institution provides conditions and services essential to continuous development and effective performance of the faculty.

3.5 Part-Time Faculty

Standard: *Part-time faculty who meet all appointment requirements applicable to full-time faculty are employed when necessary to augment and/or enrich existing course or program offerings. No more than one-fourth or 25% of any specialty area should be delivered via the utilization of part-time faculty.*

4. Students in Basic Programs

4.1 Admission to Basic Programs

Standard: The institution applies specific, published criteria for admission to teacher education programs.

4.2 Retention of Students in Basic Programs

Standard: The institution applies clearly stated evaluative criteria and establishes time frames for the retention of candidates in basic programs. These criteria are reviewed and revised periodically, in the light of data on the teaching performance of graduates, to increase the probability that candidates will become successful teachers.

4.3 Counseling and Advising for Students in Basic Programs

Standard: *Counseling and advising provided to teacher education programs should be provided by persons qualified in and knowledgeable about the specialty area being pursued by the student. Advisement should provide for a total career understanding encompassing both preparation and practice.*

5. Resources and Facilities for Basic Programs

5.1 Library

Standard: The library quantitatively and qualitatively supports the instruction, research, and services pertinent to the needs of each teacher education program.

5.2 Materials and Instructional Media Center

Standard: *An accessible instructional materials and media center shall be maintained to support all teacher education programs offered. The responsibility for the content, materials acquisition, and operation of the center shall be that of the teacher education program or shared with the library, depending upon its location.*

5.3 Physical Facilities and Other Resources

Standard: *The institution provides accessible physical facilities and instructional resources as well as other appropriate adaptations of them to assure maximal utilization by all students enrolled in teacher education programs.*

6. Evaluation, Program Review, and Planning

6.1 Evaluation of Graduates

Standard: The institution keeps abreast of emerging evaluation techniques and engages in systematic efforts to evaluate the quality of its graduates upon completion of their programs of study and after they enter the teaching profession. This evaluation includes evidence of their performance in relation to program objectives.

6.2 Evaluation of Results to Improve Basic Programs

Standard: *The basic teacher education programs preparing persons to perform as teachers in public and private schools, institutions, and agencies offering educational programs shall be regularly and systematically evaluated in an effort to improve these programs and maximize their quality.*

6.3 Long-Range Planning

Standard: The institution has plans for the long-range development of teacher education: these plans are part of a design for total institutional development.

G–1. Governance of Advanced Programs

G–1.1 Membership of the Governing Unit

Standard: The faculty and staff of the governing unit for advanced programs possess scholarly preparation and professional experience appropriate to their assignments. They maintain involvement in and are well informed about educational issues and are committed to the preparation of school personnel to serve a multicultural society.

G–1.2 Functions of the Governing Unit

Standard: Primary responsibility for initiation, development, and implementation of advanced programs lies with the education faculty. The governing unit is responsible for setting and achieving advanced program goals, establishing policies, fixing responsibility for program decision making, identifying and utilizing resources, and facilitating continuous development and improvement of advanced programs.

G–1.3 Relationship to Other Administrative Units

Standard: *Where special education is identifiable as an organizational unit or program entity it shall be entitled to representation on the decision-making unit responsible for advanced programs.*

G–2. Curricula for Advanced Programs

G–2.1 Design of Curricula

Standard: Curricula for advanced programs are based on specified objectives that reflect the institution's conception of the professional roles for which the preparation programs are designed. There is a direct and obvious relationship between these objectives and the components of the respective curricula.

Standard: The institution provides for multicultural education in its advanced curricula—in the content for the specialty, the humanistic and behavioral studies, the theory relevant to the specialty, with direct and simulated experiences in professional practices, as defined in Standard G–2.2.

G–2.2 Content of Curricula

Standard: The curriculum of each advanced program includes (a) content for the specialty, (b) humanistic and behavioral studies, (c) theory relevant to the specialty with direct and simulated experiences in professional practice, all appropriate to the professional roles for which candidates are being prepared and all differentiated by degree or certificate level.

G–2.3 Research in Advanced Curricula

Standard: Each advanced curriculum includes the study of research methods and findings; each doctoral curriculum includes study in the designing and conducting of research.

G–2.4 Use of Guidelines Developed by National Learned Societies and Professional Associations

Standard: In planning and developing curricula for its advanced programs, the institution studies the recommendations of professional associations and national learned societies and adopts a rationale for the selection and implementation of pertinent sets of recommendations for each advanced program in teacher education.

G–2.5 Student Participation in Program Evaluation and Development

Standard: The institution makes provisions for representative student participation in the decision-making phases related to the design, approval, evaluation, and modification of its advanced programs.

G–2.6 Individualization of Programs of Study

Standard: Each advanced curriculum provides for the individualization of students' programs of study.

G–2.7 Quality Controls

G-2.7.1 Graduate Credit
Standard: Institutional policies preclude the granting of graduate credit for study which is remedial or which is designed to remove deficiencies in meeting the requirements for admission to advanced programs.

G–2.7.2 Graduate Level Courses

Standard: *Not more than one-third of the curricula requirements for the master's degree and sixth-year certificate or degree may be met by the utilization of courses, experiences, and seminars open both to graduate and advanced undergraduate students. All courses granting credit toward the doctorate degree must be graduate level offerings.*

G–2.7.3 Residence Study

Standard: *A full-time continuous residency on campus which consists of any two contiguous semesters or three contiguous quarters (or alternative pattern defined by the institution) shall be required for the doctoral degree.*

G–3. Faculty for Advanced Programs

G–3.1 Preparation of Faculty

Standard: Faculty members teaching at the master's level in advanced programs hold the doctorate with advanced study in each field of specialization in which they are teaching, or have demonstrated competence in such fields; those teaching at the sixth-year and doctoral levels hold the doctorate with study in each field of specialization in which they are teaching and conducting research. Faculty members who conduct the advanced programs at all degree levels are engaged in scholarly activity that supports their field of specialization and have experience which relates directly to their respective fields.

G–3.2 Composition of Faculty for Doctoral Degree Programs

Standard: *No less than one full-time qualified doctoral faculty member shall be provided for each specialty area (as defined by the institution) offered in special education. In addition, sufficient faculty shall be provided in those areas that directly relate to, or serve to augment the specialty area programs.*

G–3.3 Conditions for Faculty Service

Standard: The institution enforces a policy which limits faculty teaching load and related assignments to make possible effective performance and time for scholarly development and community service.

G–3.4 Conditions for Faculty Development

Standard: The institution provides conditions and services essential to the effective performance by the faculty in the advanced programs.

G–3.5 Part-Time Faculty

Standard: *The number of part-time faculty utilized in the support of any one given doctoral specialty area shall not exceed one-fourth or 25% of the total curricula delivered.*

G–3.6 Faculty Involvement with Educational Programs in Public and Private Schools, Institutions, and Local and State Agencies

Standard: *Faculty who are assigned courses and/or who are required to supervise practicum shall have demonstrated past, present, and planned involvement with public and private schools, agencies, and other institutions providing educational programs and/or services in their specialization area.*

G–4. Students in Advanced Programs

G–4.1 Admission to Advanced Programs

Standard: The institution applies published specific criteria for admission to each advanced program at each level.

G–4.2 Retention of Students in Advanced Programs

Standard: The institution applies clearly stated evaluative criteria and establishes time frames for the retention of candidates in advanced programs. These criteria are reviewed and revised periodically in the light of data on the performance of graduates, to increase the probability that candidates will be successful in the professional roles for which they are being prepared.

G–4.3 Planning and Supervision of Students' Programs of Study

Standard: The program of study for each student in the advanced programs is jointly planned by the student and a member of the faculty; the program of study for each doctoral candidate is approved by a faculty committee; the sponsorship of each thesis, dissertation, or field study is the responsibility of a member of the faculty with specialization in the area of the thesis, dissertation, or field study.

G–4.4 Admission Policies

Standard: *Students considered for admission to advanced programs shall not be discriminated against because of ethnicity, race, sex, creed, socioeconomic status, age, disability, sexual orientation, or exceptionality.*

G–5. Resources and Facilities for Advanced Programs

G–5.1 Library

Standard: The library provides resources that quantitatively and qualitatively support instruction, independent study, and research required for each advanced program.

G–5.2 Materials and Instructional Media

Standard: *Accessible materials and instructional media resources are provided advanced programs by the teacher education program directly or on a shared basis by the library in both quantity and quality sufficient to support each specialty area.*

G–5.3 Physical Facilities and Other Resources

Standard: *The physical facilities, instructional and research activities related to advanced programs shall be fully accessible to all students. Appropriate adaptations necessary to maximize instructional opportunity for all students shall also be provided.*

G–6. Evaluation, Program Review, and Planning

G–6.1 Evaluation of Graduates

Standard: The institution keeps abreast of emerging evaluation techniques and engages in systematic efforts to evaluate the quality of its graduates upon completion of their programs of study and after they enter their professional roles. This evaluation includes evidence of their performance in relation to program objectives.

G–6.2 Evaluation Results to Improve Advanced Programs

Standard: *The advanced preparation programs for practitioners in public and private schools, agencies, institutions, and higher education institutions shall be regularly and systematically evaluated in an effort to improve and/or modify these programs to assure maximum quality.*

G–6.3 Long-Range Planning

Standard: The institution has plans for the long-range development of its advanced programs; these plans are part of a design for total institutional development.

References

A

Abramson, M., Willson, V., Yoshida, R.K., & Hagerty, G. (1983). Parents' perceptions of their learning disabled child's educational performance. *Learning Disabilities Quarterly, 6*(2), 184–194.

Ackerman, J. (1985). Preparing for separation. In H.R. Turnbull & A.P. Turnbull (Eds.), *Parents speak out: Then and now* (pp. 149–158). Columbus, OH: Charles E. Merrill Publishing Co.

Adubato, S.A., Adams, M.K., & Budd, K.S. (1981). Teaching a parent to train a spouse in child management techniques. *Journal of Applied Behavior Analysis, 14,* 193–205.

Agard, J.A. (1980). Dispute settlement. In S.I. Mopsik & J.A. Agard (Eds.), *An education handbook for parents of handicapped children* (pp. 233–252). Cambridge, MA: ABT Books.

Akerley, M.S. (1985). False gods and angry prophets. In H.R. Turnbull & A.P. Turnbull (Eds.), *Parents speak out: Then and now* (pp. 23–33). Columbus, OH: Charles E. Merrill Publishing Co.

Allen, D. W. (Ed.). (1967). *Microteaching: A description.* Palo Alto, CA: Stanford Teacher Education Program.

Allen, D.F., & Allen, V.S. (1979). *Ethical issues in mental retardation: Tragic choices/living hope.* Nashville: Abingdon Press.

Altman, K., & Mira, M. (1983). Training parents of developmentally disabled children. In J.G. Matson & R. Andrasik (Eds.), *Treatment issues and innovations in mental retardation* (pp. 303–371). New York: Plenum Press.

Algozzine, B., Christenson, S., & Ysseldyke, J. E. (1982). Probabilities associated with the referral to placement process. *Teacher Education and Special Education, 5*(3), 19–23.

Ammer, J.J., & Littleton, B.R. (1983, April). *Parent advocacy: Now more than ever active involvement in education decisions.* Paper presented at the Council for Exceptional Children's 61st Annual International Convention, Detroit, MI.

American Psychological Association (1981). Ethical principles of psychologists. *American Psychologist, 36*(6), 633–638.

Anchor, K.N., & Anchor, F.N. (1974). School failure and parental school involvement in an ethnically mixed school: A survey. *Journal of Community Psychology, 2,* 265–267.

Anderson, D. (1983). He's not "cute" anymore. In T. Dougan, L.

Isbell, & P. Vyas (Eds.), *We have been there* (pp. 90–91). Nashville: Abingdon Press.

Argyle, M. (1975). The syntaxes of bodily communication. In J. Benthall & T. Polhemus (Eds.), *The body as a medium of expression* (pp. 143–161). New York: E. P. Dutton.

Arnold, S., Sturgis, E., & Forehand, R. (1977). Training a parent to teach communication skills. *Behavior Modification, 1,* 259–276.

Avis, D.W. (1985). Deinstitutionalization jetlag. In H.R. Turnbull & A.P. Turnbull (Eds.), *Parents speak out: Then and now* (pp. 181–191). Columbus, OH: Charles E. Merrill Publishing Co.

B

Bailey, D.B. (1984). A triaxial model of the interdisciplinary team and group process. *Exceptional Children, 51*(1), 17–25.

Baker, B.L. (1983). Parents as teachers: Issues in training. In J.A. Mulick & S.M. Pueschel (Eds.), *Parent-professional partnerships in developmental disability services.* Cambridge, MA: The Ware Press.

Baker, B.L. (1984). Intervention with families with young, severely handicapped children. In J. Blacher (Ed.), *Severely handicapped young children and their families: Research in review* (pp. 319–375). New York: Academic Press.

Baker, B.L., Brightman, A.J., & Blacher, J.B. (1983). *Steps to independence series: Play skills.* Champaign, IL: Research Press.

Baker, B.L., Brightman, A.J., Carroll, N.B., Heifetz, B.B., & Hinshaw, S.P. (1978). *Steps to independence series (for parents of retarded children).* (Speech and language: Level 1 and Speech and language: Level 2). Champaign, IL:

Research Press.

Baker, B.L., Brightman, A.J., Heifetz, L.J., & Murphy, D. (1976–1977). *Steps to independence series: Behavior problems, early self-help skills, intermediate self-help skills, advanced self-help skills, toilet training.* Champaign, IL: Research Press.

Baker, B.L., Brightman, A.J., & Hinshaw, S.P. (1980). *Steps to independence series: Toward independent living.* Champaign, IL: Research Press.

Baker, B.L., & Heifetz, L.J. (1976). The Read Project: Teaching manuals for parents of retarded children. In T.D. Tjossem (Ed.), *Intervention strategies for high risk infants and young children* (pp. 351–369). Baltimore: University Park Press.

Baker, B.L., Heifetz, L.J., & Murphy, D. (1980). Behavioral training for parents of retarded children: One year follow-up. *American Journal of Mental Deficiency, 85,* 31–38.

Ball, E.L., Chasey, W.C., Hawkins, D.E., & Verhoven, P.J. (1976). The need for leisure education for handicapped children and youth. *Journal of Physical Education and Recreation, 47*(3), 53–55.

Barr, M.W. (1913). *Mental defectives: Their history, treatment, and training.* Philadelphia: P. Blakiston's Son & Co.

Barsch, R. H. (1969). *The teacher-parent relationship.* Reston, VA: The Council for Exceptional Children.

Bateman, B. (1982). Legal and ethical dilemmas of special educators. *Exceptional Education Quarterly, 2*(4), 57–67.

Baumeister, A.A. (1981). Mental retardation policy and research: The unfulfilled promise. *American Journal of Mental Deficiency,*

85(5), 449–456.

Beckman, P.J. (1983). Influence of selected child characteristics on stress in families of handicapped infants. *American Journal of Mental Deficiency, 88,* 150–156.

Benjamin, A. (1969). *The helping interview.* Boston, MA: Houghton-Mifflin Company.

Bennett, J.M. (1985). Company, halt! In H.R. Turnbull & A.P. Turnbull (Eds.), *Parents speak out: Then and now* (pp. 159–173). Columbus, OH: Charles E. Merrill Publishing Co.

Bennett, J.M. (1985). A ten o'clock scholar. In H.R. Turnbull & A.P. Turnbull (Eds.), *Parents speak out: Then and now* (pp. 175–183). Columbus, OH: Charles E. Merrill Publishing Co.

Bensky, J. M., Shaw, S. F., Gouse, A. S., Bates, H., Dixon, B., & Beane, W. E. (1980). Public law 94–142 and stress: A problem for educators. *Exceptional Children, 47*(1), 24–29.

Benson, H.A., & Turnbull, A.P. (in press). Approaching families from an individualized perspective. In R.H. Horner, L.H. Meyer and H.D. Fredericks (Eds.), *Education of learners with severe handicaps: Exemplary service strategies.* Baltimore: Paul H. Brookes Publishing Co.

Bernal, M.E. (1984). Consumer issues in parent training. In R.F. Dangel & R.A. Polster (Eds.), *Parent training: Foundation of research and practice* (pp. 477–503). New York: The Guilford Press.

Bernal, M.E., & Klinnert, M.D. (1981). *Further insights on the results of a parent training outcome study.* Paper presented at the XIII Banff International Conference on Behavioral Sciences, Banff, Canada.

Bernal, M.E., & North, J.A. (1978). A survey of parent training manuals. *Journal of Applied Behavior Analysis, 11,* 533–544.

Bettleheim, B. (1950). *Love is not enough.* Glencoe, NY: Free Press.

Bettleheim, B. (1967). *The empty fortress: Infantile autism and the birth of the self.* London: Collier-MacMillan.

Birenbaum, A. (1971). The mentally retarded child in the home and the family cycle. *Journal of Health and Social Behavior, 12,* 55–65.

Blacher, J. (1984). Sequential stages of adjustment to the birth of a child with handicaps: Fact or artifact? *Mental Retardation, 22,* 55–68.

Blacher, J. (Ed.). (1984). *Severely handicapped young children and their families: Research in review.* New York: Academic Press.

Blacher, J., & Meyers, C.E. (1983). A review of attachment formation and disorder of handicapped children. *American Journal of Mental Deficiency, 87,* 359–371.

Blatt, B. (1975). Toward an understanding of people with special needs. In J.M. Kauffman & J.S. Payne (Eds.), *Mental retardation: Introduction and personal perspectives.* Columbus, OH: Charles E. Merrill Publishing Co.

Blatt, B., Biklen, D., & Bogdan, R. (1977). *An alternative textbook in special education.* Denver, CO: Love Publishing Company.

Blechman, E.A., Budd, K.S., Christophersen, E.R., Szykula, S., Wahler, R., & Embry, L.H. (1981). Engagement in behavioral family therapy: A multi-site investigation. *Behavior Therapy, 12,* 461–472.

Blechman, E.A., Kotanchik, N.L., & Taylor, C.J. (1981). Families and schools together: Early behavioral intervention with high-risk students.

Behavior Therapy, 12, 308–319.

Bloom, B.S., & Sosniak, L.A. (1981). Talent development. *Educational leadership, 39*(2), 86–94.

Blue-Banning, M. (1985). [An interview with a family with a child having a disability]. Unpublished raw data.

Boggs, E. M. (1969). Pointers for parents. In W. Wolfensberger & R. K. Kurtz (Eds.), *Management of the family of the retarded.* Chicago: Follett Publishing Co.

Boggs, E.M. (1985). Who is putting whose head in the sand? (Or in the clouds, as the case may be.) In H.R. Turnbull & A.P. Turnbull (Eds.), *Parents speak out: Then and now* (pp. 39–55). Columbus, OH: Charles E. Merrill Publishing Co.

Boggs, E.M. (1985). Whose head is in the clouds? In H.R. Turnbull & A.P. Turnbull (Eds.), *Parents speak out: Then and now* (pp. 55–64). Columbus, OH: Charles E. Merrill Publishing Co.

Bok, S. (1978). *Living: Moral choice in public and private life.* New York: Pantheon Books.

Bok, S. (1980). Whistleblowing and professional responsibilities. In D. Callahan & S. Bok (Eds.), *Teaching ethics in higher education* (pp. 277–295). New York: Plenum Press.

Brehm, S.S. (1983). *Social support processes: Problems and perspectives.* Unpublished manuscript, University of Kansas, Department of Psychology, Lawrence.

Brehony, K.A., Benson, B.A., Solomon, L.J., & Luscomb, R.L. (1980). Parents as behavior modifiers: Intervention for three problem behaviors in a severely retarded child. *Journal of Clinical Child Psychology, 9,* 213–216.

Bricker, W.A., & Bricker, D.D. (1976). The infants, toddler, and

preschool research and intervention project. In T.D. Tjossem (Ed.), *Intervention strategies for high risk infants and young children* (pp. 545–572). Baltimore: University Park Press.

Brightman, R.P., Ambrose, S.A., & Baker, B.L. (1980). Parent training: A school-based model for enhancing teaching performance. *Child Behavior Therapy, 2,* 35–47.

Brightman, R.P., Baker, B.L., Clark, D.B., & Ambrose, S.A. (1982). Effectiveness of alternative parent training formats. *Journal of Behavior Therapy and Experimental Psychiatry, 13,* 113–117.

Bristol, M.M. (1984). The birth of a handicapped child—a wholistic model for grieving. *Family Relations, 33,* 25–32.

Bristol, M.M., & Gallagher, J.J. (in press). Psychological research on fathers of young handicapped children: Evolution review, and some future directions. In J.J. Gallagher & P. Vietze (Eds.), *Families of handicapped persons: Current research, treatment, and policy issues.* Baltimore: Paul H. Brookes Publishing Co.

Bristol, M.M., & Schopler, E. (1983). Stress and coping in families with autistic adolescents. In E. Schopler & G.B. Mesibov (Eds.), *Autism in adolescents and adults* (pp. 251–278). New York: Plenum Press.

Brooks, P.H., & Baumeister, A.A. (1983). A plea for consideration of ecological validity in the experimental psychology of mental retardation. *Peabody Journal of Education, 60*(3), 45–59.

Brotherson, M.J. (1985). *Parents self report of future planning and its relationship to family functioning and family stress with sons and daughters who are disabled.* Unpublished doctoral dissertation,

University of Kansas, Lawrence.

Brotherson, M.J., Backus, L., Summers, J.A., & Turnbull, A.P. (In press). Transition to adulthood. In J.A. Summers (Ed.), *The right to grow up: Introduction to developmentally disabled adults*. Baltimore: Paul H. Brookes Publishing Co.

Bruch, C.B. (1984). Schooling for the gifted: Where do we go from here? *Gifted Child Quarterly, 28*(1), 12–16.

Budd, K.S., & Greenspan, S. (1984). Mentally retarded mothers. In E.A. Blechman (Ed.), *Behavior modification with women* (pp. 477–506). New York: The Guilford Press.

Budoff, M. (1979). Implementing due process safeguards: From the user's point of view. In Department of Health, Education, and Welfare, Office of Education, *Due process: Developing criteria for the evaluation of due process procedural safeguard provisions*. Philadelphia: Research for Better Schools, Inc.

Budoff, M., & Orenstein, A. (1982). *Due process in special education: On going to a hearing*. Cambridge, MA: The Ware Press.

C

Callahan, C.M., & Kauffman, J.M. (1982). Involving gifted children's parents: Federal law is silent, but its assumptions apply. *Exceptional Education Quarterly, 3*, 50–54.

Caplan, G. (1976). The family as a support system. In G. Caplan & M. Killilea (Eds.), *Support systems and mutual help: Multidisciplinary explorations* (pp. 19–36). New York: Grune & Stratton.

Carkhuff, R. R., & Berenson, B. G. (1967). *Beyond counseling and therapy*. New York: Holt, Rinehart & Winston.

Carnes, P. (1981). *Family development I: Understanding us*. Minneapolis: Interpersonal Communications Programs, Inc.

Carrillo, A.C. (1982). Ann Cupolo Carrillo. In A.P. Carrillo, K. Corbett, & V. Lewis (Eds.), *No more stares* (pp. 61–63). Berkeley, CA: The Disability Rights Education and Defense Fund, Inc.

Carrillo, A.C., Corbett, K., & Lewis, V. (1982). *No more stares*. Berkeley, CA: The Disability Rights Education and Defense Fund, Inc.

Carter, E.A., & McGoldrick, M. (Eds.). (1980). *The family life cycle: A framework for family therapy*. New York: Gardner Press.

Casey, L. (1978). Development of communicative behavior in autistic children: A parent program using signed speech. *Devereux Forum, 12*, 1–15.

Cassidy, J., & Vukelich, C. (1978). Survival reading for parents and kids: A parent education program. *The Reading Teacher, 31*(6), 638–641.

Castaneda, A. (1976). Cultural democracy and the needs of Mexican American children. In R.L. Jones (Ed.), *Mainstreaming and the minority child* (pp. 181–194). Reston, VA: The Council for Exceptional Children.

Chambers, D. (1972). Alternatives to civil commitment of the mentally ill: Practical guides and constitutional imperatives. *Michigan Law Review, 70*, 1108–1200.

Chase, S., Wright, J.H., & Ragade, R. (1981). Decision making in an interdisciplinary team. *Behavioral Science, 26*, 206–215.

Children's Defense Fund, Inc. (1974). *Children Out of School in America: A report of the Children's Defense Fund, Washington Research Project, Inc.*. Washington,

D.C.: Author.

Chilman, C.S. (1973). Programs for disadvantaged parents: Some major trends and related research. In H.H. Ricciuti & M. Caldwell (Eds.), *Review of Child Development Research* (Vol. 3), (pp. 403–465). Chicago: University of Chicago Press.

Chinn, P. C., Winn, J., & Walters, R. H. (1978). *Two-way talking with parents of special children: A process of positive communication*. St. Louis, MO: The C.V. Mosby Co.

Cleveland, D.W., & Miller, N. (1977). Attitudes and life commitments of older siblings of mentally retarded adults: An exploratory study. *Mental Retardation, 15*(3), 38–41.

Cobb, S. (1976). Social support as a mediator of life stress. *Psychosomatic Medicine, 38*, 300–314.

Code of Federal Regulations, Title 34, Part 300, Subparts A through G.

Cole, C., & Morrow, W.R. (1976). Refractory parent behaviors in behavior modification training groups. *Psychotherapy: Theory, Research and Practice, 13*, 162–169.

Cole, J.T., Smith, G.L., & Ranken, M.M. (1981). Providing services to exceptional students in rural areas: Some solutions. *Rural Educator, 2*(3), 7–13.

Colley, T. E. (February, 1973). Interpretation of psychological test data to children. *Mental Retardation, 11*(1), 28–30.

Cone, J.D., Delawyer, D.D., & Wolfe, V.V. (1985). Assessing parent participation: The parent/family involvement index. *Exceptional Children, 51*(5), 417–424.

Conroy, J.W. (1985). Reactions to deinstitutionalization among parents of mentally retarded persons. In R.H. Bruininks & K.C. Lakin

(Eds.), *Living and learning in the least restrictive environment* (pp. 141–152). Baltimore: Paul H. Brookes Publishing Co.

Cormier, W., & Cormier, L. (1979). *Interviewing strategies for helpers: A guide to assessment, treatment, and evaluation.* Monterey, CA: Brooks/Cole Publishing Co.

Council for Exceptional Children. (1983). Code of ethics and standards for professional practice. *Exceptional Children, 50*(3), 205–218.

Crary, D. (1980). Advocacy for children and families. *Educational Horizons, 59*(1), 47–53.

Crawford, D. (1978). Parent involvement in instructional planning. *Focus on Exceptional Children, 10*(7), 1–8.

Crnic, K.A., Friedrich, W.N., & Greenberg, M.T. (1983). Adaptation of families with mentally retarded children: A model of stress, coping, and family ecology. *American Journal of Mental Deficiency, 88*(2), 125–138.

Cummings, S.T., Bayley, H.C., & Rie, H.E. (1966). Effects of the child's deficiency on the mother of MR, chronically ill, and neurotic children. *American Journal of Orthopsychiatry, 36,* 595–608.

D

Dangel, R.F., & Polster, R.A. (Eds.). (1984). *Parent training.* New York: The Guilford Press.

Daniels, S.M. (1982). From parent advocacy to self advocacy: A problem of transition. *Exceptional Education Quarterly, 3*(2), 25–32.

Davidson, C. (1980). Parents' and teachers' responses to mainstreaming. *Education Unlimited, 2*(2), 33–35.

Daynard, C. (1980). *Due process:*

The appeals hearing under chapter 766. Unpublished doctoral dissertation, Boston University, Boston.

Deford, F. (1983). *Alex: The life of a child.* East Rutherford, NJ: Viking Press.

Deiner, P.L. (1983). *Resources for teaching young children with special needs.* New York: Harcourt Brace Jovanovich.

Dembinski, R.J., & Mauser, A.J. (1978). Parents of the gifted: Perceptions of psychologists and teachers. *Journal for the Education of the Gifted, 1*(2), 5–14.

Dettmann, D.F., & Colangelo, N. (1980). A functional model for counseling parents of gifted students. *Gifted Child Quarterly, 24*(4), 158–161.

DeWert, M., & Helsel, E. (1985). Update: The Helsel family today. In H.R. Turnbull & A.P. Turnbull (Eds.), *Parents speak out: Then and now* (pp. 101–106). Columbus, OH: Charles E. Merrill Publishing Co.

Diamond, S. (1981). Growing up with parents of a handicapped child: A handicapped person's perspective. In J.L. Paul (Ed.), *Understanding and working with parents of children with special needs* (pp. 23–50). New York: Holt, Rinehart, & Winston.

Dickerson, D., Spellman, C.R., Larsen, S.C., & Tyler, L. (1973). Let the cards do the talking: A teacher-parent communication program. *Teaching Exceptional Children, 5,* 170–17,8.

Dinkmeyer, D. C. (1965). *Child development: The emerging self.* Englewood Cliffs, NJ: Prentice Hall, Inc.

Doernberg, N., Bernard, M., & Lenz, C. (1976). Psychoeducational treatment for parents of autistic children. In E. Webster (Ed.), *Pro-*

fessional approaches with parents of handicapped children. Springfield, IL: Charles C. Thomas.

Donnellan, A.M., & Mirenda, P.L. (1984). Issues related to professional involvement with families of individuals with autism and other severe handicaps. *TASH Journal, 9,* 16–24.

Drake, E.A., & Shellenberger, S. (1981). Children of separation and divorce: A review of school programs and implications for the psychologist. *School Psychology Bulletin, 10,* 54–61.

Duncan, D. (1978). *The conduct of home conferences.* Unpublished manuscript, University of Pittsburgh, Department of Special Education, Pittsburgh, PA.

Duncan, L.W., & Fitzgerald, P.W. (1969). Increasing the parent-child communication through counselor-parent conferences. *Personnel and Guidance Journal, 47,* 514–517.

Dunlap, D.A., Ondelacy, J., & Sells, E. (1979). Videotape involves parents. *Journal of American Indian Education, 19*(1), 1–7.

Dunlap, W.R., & Hollingsworth, J.S. (1977). How does a handicapped child affect the family? Implications for practitioners. *The Family Coordinator, 26*(3), 286–293.

Duvall, E. (1957). *Family development.* Philadelphia: Lippincott. Education of the Handicapped Act, 20 U.S.C. Section 1401–1461 (P.L. 91–230), as amended by Education of All Handicapped Children Act (P.L. 94–142).

E

Ellifritt, J. (1984). Life with my sister. *Exceptional Parent, 8*(14), 16–21.

Embry, L.H. (1980). Family support for handicapped preschool children at risk for abuse. In J.J. Gallagher (Ed.), *New directions for exceptional children* (pp. 29–57). San Francisco: Jossey-Bass.

Essex, L.N. (1979). The development and evaluation of an inservice workshop training program in conflict management for school administrators. *Dissertation Abstracts International, 40,* 4822. (University Microfilms No. 8006605).

Evans, D. R., Hearn, M. T., Uhlemann, M. R., & Ivey, A. E. (1984). *Essential interviewing: A programmed approach to effective communication.* Monterey, CA: Brooks/Cole Publishing Company.

Eversoll, D. (1979). A two generational view of fathering. *The family Coordinator, 28,* 503–508.

F

Faerstein, L.M. (1981). Stress and coping in families of learning disabled children: A literature review. *Journal of Learning Disabilities, 14,* 420–423.

Falicov, C.J. (1982). Mexican families. In M. McGoldrick, J.K. Pearce, & J. Giordano (Eds.), *Ethnicity in family therapy* (pp. 134–163). New York: The Guilford Press.

Farber, B. (1960). Family organization and crisis: Maintenance of integration in families with a severely retarded child. *Monographs of the Society for Research In Child Development, 25*(1).

Farber, B., Jenne, W., & Toigo, R. (1960). Family crisis and the decision to institutionalize the retarded child. *NEA Reasearch Monograph Series.* Washington, DC: Council for Exceptional Children.

Farber, B., & Ryckman, D.B. (1965). Effects of severely mentally retarded children on family relationships. *Mental Retardation Abstracts, 2,* 1–17.

Featherstone, H. (1980). *A difference in the family: Living with a disabled child.* New York: Basic Books.

Federal Register. (1977, August). Washington, D.C.: U.S. Government Printing Office.

Federal Register. (1981, January). Washington, D.C.: U.S. Government Printing Office.

Feldman, W.S., Manella, K.J., & Varni, J.W. (1983). A behavioral parent training program for single mothers of physically handicapped children. *Child: Care, Health, and Development, 9,* 157–168.

Ferguson, D.L. (1984). Parent advocacy network. *The Exceptional Parent, 14,* 41–45.

Ferguson, J.T. (1978). *Starting a respite care co-op program.* Kalamazoo, MI: Family and Children's Services of the Kalamazoo Area.

Fifield, V.J. (1978). *Parent and school staff attitudes toward meetings to develop individualized education programs which include/exclude the child.* Unpublished manuscript, Utah State University, Department of Special Education, Logan.

Figley, C.R., & McCubbin, H.I. (Eds.). (1983). *Stress and the family. Vol. I: Coping with normative transitions.* New York: Brunner-/Mazel.

Flake-Hobson, C., & Swick, K.J. (1984). Communication strategies for parents and teachers, or how to say what you mean. In M.L. Henniger & E.M. Nesselroad (Eds.), *Working with parents of handicapped children: A book of readings for school personnel* (pp. 141–149). Lanham, MD: University Press of America, Inc.

Fleischman, M.J. (1982). Social learning interventions for aggressive children: From the laboratory to the real world. *The Behavior Therapist, 5,* 55–58.

Folberg, J., & Taylor, A. (1984). *Mediation: A comprehensive guide to resolving conflicts without litigation.* San Francisco: Jossey-Bass.

Fortier, L.M., & Wanlass, R.L. (1984). Family crisis following the diagnosis of a handicapped child. *Family Relations, 33,* 13–24.

Foster, M., Berger, M., & McLean, M. (1981). Rethinking a good idea: A reassessment of parent involvement. *Topics in Early Childhood Special Education, 1*(3), 55–65.

Fotheringham, J.B., & Creal, D. (1974). Handicapped children and handicapped families. *International Review of Education, 20*(3), 353–371.

Fotheringham, J.B., Shelton, M., & Hoddinott, B.A. (1972). The effects on the family of the presence of a mentally retarded child. *Canadian Psychiatric Association Journal, 17,* 283–290.

Frankena, W.K. (1973). *Ethics* (2nd ed.). Englewood Cliffs, NJ: Prentice-Hall, Inc.

Frankl, V.E. (1963). *Man's search for meaning.* Boston: Beacon Press.

Fraser, B.A., & Hensinger, R.N. (1983). *Managing physical handicaps.* Baltimore: Paul H. Brookes Publishing Co.

Fredericks, H. D., Baldwin, V., & Grove, D. A. (1976). Home-center-based parent training model. In D. L. Lillie & P. L. Trohanis (Eds.), *Teaching parents to teach* (pp. 107–129). New York: Walker & Co.

Friedman, E.H. (1980). Systems and ceremonies: A family view of rites of passage. In E.A. Carter & M. McGoldrick (Eds.), *The family life cycle* (pp. 429–460). New York: Gardner Press.

Friedman, S.G., & Hofmeister,

A.M. (1984). Matching technology to content and learners: A case study. *Exceptional Children, 51*(2), 130–134.

Friedrich, W.N. (1979). Predictors of coping behavior of mothers of handicapped children. *Journal of Consulting and Clinical Psychology, 47*, 1140–1141.

Frieze, I.H., Parsons, J.E., Johnson, P.B., Ruble, D.N., & Zellman, G.L. (1978). *Women and sex role: A social psychological perspective.* New York: Norton.

Frodi, A.M. (1981). Contribution of infant characteristics to child abuse. *American Journal on Mental Deficiency, 85*, 341–349.

Fulmer, R. H., Cohen, S., & Monaco, G. (1985). Using psychological assessment in structural family therapy. *Journal of Learning Disabilities, 18*(3), 145–150.

G

Gallagher, J.J., Cross, A., & Scharfman, W. (1981). The father's role. *Journal of the Division for Early Childhood, 3*, 3–14.

Gallagher, J.J., & Gallagher, R. (1985). Family adaptation to a handicapped child and assorted professionals. In A.P. Turnbull & H.R. Turnbull (Eds.), *Parents speak out: Then and now.* Columbus, OH: Charles E. Merrill Publishing Co.

Gardner, N.E.S. (in press). Sexuality. In J.A. Summers (Ed.), *The right to grow up: An introduction to adults with developmental disabilities.* Baltimore: Paul H. Brookes Publishing Co.

Gardner, R.A. (1971). The guilt reactions of parents of children with severe physical disease. In R.L. Noland (Ed.), *Counseling parents of the ill and the handicapped* (pp. 27–43). Springfield, IL: Charles C.

Thomas.

Garrett, A. (1972). *Interviewing: Its principles and methods.* New York: Family Service Association of America.

Gath, A. (1974). Sibling reactions to mental handicaps: A comparison of the brothers and sisters of mongol children. *Journal of Child Psychology and Psychiatry and Allied Disciplines, 15*(3), 838–843.

Gath, A. (1977). The impact of an abnormal child upon the parents. *British Journal of Psychiatry, 130*, 405–410.

Germain, C. B., & Gitterman, A. (1980). *The life model of social work practice.* New York: Columbia University Press.

Gillespie, E., & Turnbull, A.P. (1983). Involving special education students in planning the IEP. *Teaching Exceptional Children, 16*(1), 27–29.

Gilliam, J.E., & Coleman, M.C. (1981). Who influences IEP committee decisions? *Exceptional Children, 47*(8), 642–644.

Gilmore, S. K., & Fraleigh, P. W. (1980). *Communication at work.* Eugene, OR: Friendly Press.

Gliedman, J., & Roth, W. (1980). *The unexpected minority: Handicapped children in America.* New York: Harcourt Brace Jovanovich.

Goddard, H.H. (1912). *The Kallikak family: A study in the heredity of feeblemindedness.* New York: MacMillan.

Goldenberg, I., & Goldenberg, H. (1980). *Family therapy: An overview.* Monterey, CA: Brooks/Cole Publishing Co.

Goldenson, L.H. (1965, March). *Remarks on the occasion of United Cerebral Palsy Associations' 15th anniversary.* Paper presented at the 15th annual meeting of the United Cerebral Palsy Associations, Los

Angeles, CA.

Goldfarb, L., Brotherson, M.J., Summers, J.A., & Turnbull, A.P. (in press). *Meeting the challenge of disability and chronic illness—A family guide.* Baltimore: Paul H. Brookes Publishing Co.

Goldstein, S., Strickland, B., Turnbull, A.P., & Curry, L. (1980). An observational analysis of the IEP conference. *Exceptional Children, 46*(4), 278–286.

Goldstein, S., & Turnbull, A.P. (1982). The use of two strategies to increase parent participation in IEP conferences. *Exceptional Children, 48*(4), 360–361.

Gordon, I.J. (1978, June). *Parents as teachers—What can they do?* Paper presented at the International Conference on Parents and Children, St. Louis, MO.

Gordon, I.J., Olmsted, P.P., Rubin, R.I., & True, J.H. (1978). *Continuity between home and school: Aspects of parental involvement in follow through.* Paper presented at the fifth biennial meeting of the Southeastern Conference on Human Development: A regional convention of the Society for Research in Child Development, Atlanta, GA.

Gordon, T. (1970). *Parent effectiveness training.* New York: Wyden.

Gordon, T. (1980). Parent effectiveness training: A preventive program and its effects on families. In M.J. Fine (Ed.), *Handbook on parent education* (pp. 101–121). New York: Academic Press.

Graden, J. L., Casey, A., & Bonstrom, O. (1985). Implementing a prereferral intervention system: Part II. The data. *Exceptional Children, 51*, 487–496.

Graden, J. L., Casey, A., & Christenson, S. L. (1985). Implementing a prereferral intervention system:

Part I. The model. *Exceptional Children, 51,* 377–384.

Grossi, J.A. (1981). *Parent/advocate groups for the gifted and talented.* Reston, VA: ERIC Clearinghouse on Handicapped and Gifted Children. (ERIC Document Reproduction Service No. ED 021169)

Grossman, F.K. (1972). *Brothers and sisters of retarded children: An exploratory study.* Syracuse, NY: Syracuse University Press.

Guess, P.D., Benson, H., & Siegel-Causey, E. (1985). Concepts and issues related to choice-making and autonomy among persons with severe handicaps. *Journal of the Association for Persons With Severe Handicaps, 10*(2), 79–86.

Guess, D., Bronicki, M.A., Firmender, K., Mann, J., Merrill, M., Olin-Zimmerman, S., Wanat, P., Zamarripa, E., & Turnbull, H. (1984). Legal and moral considerations in the education of a child with herpes. *Mental Retardation, 22*(5), 257–263.

Guess, D., & Siegel-Causey, E. (1985). Behavioral control and education of severely handicapped students: Who's doing what to whom? And why? In D. Bricker & J. Filler (Eds.), *Severe mental retardation: From theory to practice* (pp. 230–244). Reston, VA: The Council for Exceptional Children.

Gumz, E.J., & Gubrium, J.F. (1972). Comparative parental perceptions of a mentally retarded child. *American Journal of Mental Deficiency, 77,* 175–180.

H

Haavik, S. (in press). Marriage and parenthood. In J.A. Summers (Ed.), *The right to grow up: An introduction to adults with developmental disabilities.* Baltimore: Paul H. Brookes Publishing Co.

Haavik, S.F., & Menninger, K.A. (1981). *Sexuality, law, and the developmentally disabled person.* Baltimore: Paul H. Brookes Publishing Co.

Hall, H.B. (1980). The intangible human factor: The most critical coordination variable. In J.O. Elder & P.R. Magrab (Eds.), *Coordinating services to handicapped children* (pp. 45–62). Baltimore: Paul H. Brookes Publishing Co.

Halpern, R. (1982). Impact of P. L. 94–142 on the handicapped child and family: Institutional responses. *Exceptional Children, 49,* 270–272.

Hammond, D., Hepworth, D., & Smith, V. (1977). *Improving Therapeutic Communication.* San Francisco: Jossey-Bass.

Hareven, T.K. (1982). American families in transition: Perspectives on change. In F. Walsh (Ed.), *Normal family processes* (pp. 446–466). New York: The Guilford Press.

Harris, G.A. (1983). *Broken ears, wounded hearts.* Washington, DC: Gallaudet College Press.

Harris, G.A. (1985). Fairy tales, beatlemania, and a handicapped child. In H.R. Turnbull & A.P. Turnbull (Eds.), *Parents speak out: Then and now* (pp. 261–270). Columbus, OH: Charles E. Merrill Publishing Co.

Harrison, R., & Edwards, J. (1983). *Child abuse.* Portland, OR: Ednick Publications.

Hassell, C.M. (1982). A study of the consequences of excessive legal intervention on the local implementation of P.L. 94–142. *Dissertation Abstracts, 42,* 7.

Hayden, A.H. (1983). Early intervention and home-based care. In J.A. Mulick & S.M. Pueschel (Eds.), *Parent-professional partnerships in developmental disabilities* (pp. 89–106). Cambridge, MA: The Ware Press.

Heifetz, L.J. (1977). Behavioral training for parents of retarded children: Alternative formats based on instructional manuals. *American Journal of Mental Deficiency, 82,* 194–203.

Helsel Family (1985). The Helsel's story of Robin. In H.R. Turnbull & A.P. Turnbull (Eds.), *Parents speak out: Then and now* (pp. 81–100). Columbus, OH: Charles E. Merrill Publishing Co.

Hepworth, D. H., & Larsen, J. A. (1982). *Direct social work practice: Theory and skills.* Homewood, IL: The Dorsey Press.

Heron, T.E., & Axelrod, S. (1976). Effectiveness of feedback to mothers concerning their children's word-recognition performance. *Reading Improvement, 13,* 74–81.

Heshusius, L. (1982). At the heart of the advocacy dilemma. *Exceptional Children, 49*(1), 6–13.

Heward, W.L., & Chapman, J.E. (1981). Improving parent-teacher communication through recorded telephone messages: Systematic replication in a special education classroom. *Journal of Special Education Technology, 4,* 11–19.

Heward, W.L., & Orlansky, M.D. (1984). *Exceptional Children* (2nd ed.). Columbus, OH: Charles E. Merrill Publishing Co.

Heward, W.L., & Dardig, J.C. (1978). Inservice for parents of special needs children. *Viewpoints in Teaching and Learning, 54,* 127–137.

Heward, W. L., Dardig, J. C., & Rossett, A. (1979). *Working with parents of handicapped children.* Columbus, OH: Charles E. Merrill Publishing Co.

Hill, R. (1949). *Families under*

stress. New York: Harper and Row.

Hirsch, G. P. (1981). *Training developmental disability specialists in parent conference skills.* Unpublished doctoral dissertation, University of Kansas, Lawrence.

Hobbs, N., Dokecki, P.R., Hoover-Dempsey, K.V., Moroney, R.M., Shayze, M.W., & Weeks, K.H. (1984). *Strengthening families.* San Francisco: Jossey-Bass.

Hochman, R. (1979). Communicating with parents about the classroom. *Exceptional Teacher, 1*(3), 6–7.

Hocutt, A., & Wiegerink, R. (1983). Perspectives on parent involvement in preschool programs for handicapped children. In R. Haskins & D. Adams (Eds.), *Parent education and public policy* (pp. 211–229). Norwood, NJ: Able.

Holroyd, J., & McArthur, D. (1976). Mental retardation and stress on the parents: A contrast between Down's syndrome and childhood autism. *American Journal on Mental Deficiency, 80,* 431–436.

Hunt, J. (Ed.). (1972). *Human intelligence.* New Brunswick: Transaction Books.

Huntington, F. (1984). Home Remedies. *inCider* (pp. 21–25).

Huntington, F. (1984). Ten tips for choosing educational software. *inCider* (pp. 31–34).

Hyman, I., & Schreiber, K. (1975). Selected concepts and practices of child advocacy in school psychology. *Psychology in the Schools, 12*(7), 50–58.

I

Imber, S.C., Imber, R.B., & Rothstein, C. (1979). Modifying independent work habits: An effective parent-teacher communication pro-

gram. *Exceptional Children, 46,* 218–221.

Intagliata, S., & Doyle, N. (1984). Enhancing social support for parents of developmentally disabled children: Training in interpersonal problem solving skills. *Mental Retardation, 22,* 4–11.

Isbell, H.M. (1983). He looked the way a baby should look. In T. Dougan, L. Isbell, & P. Vyas (Eds.), *We have been there* (pp. 19–23). Nashville: Abingdon Press.

Isbell, L. (1983). The conditional use permit. In T. Dougan, L. Isbell, & P. Vyas (Eds.), *We have been there* (pp. 179–181). Nashville: Abingdon Press.

Isbell, L. (1983). The meanest mommy on the block. In T. Dougan, L. Isbell, & P. Vyas (Eds.), *We have been there* (pp. 45–49). Nashville: Abingdon Press.

Iverson, B.K., Brownlee, G.D., & Walberg, H.J. (1981). Parent-teacher contacts and student learning. *Journal of Educational Research, 74,* 394–396.

Ivey, A. (1971). *Microcounseling: Innovations in interview training.* Springfield, IL: Charles C. Thomas.

Ivey, A. E., & Authier, J. (1978). *Microcounseling: Innovations in interviewing, counseling, psychotherapy and psychoeducation.* Springfield, IL: Charles C. Thomas.

Ivey, A. E., Normington, C. J., Miller, C. D., Morrill, W. H., & Haase, R. (1968). Microcounseling and attending behavior: An approach to prepracticum counseling training. *Journal of Counseling Psychology,* Monograph Supplement, 15(5), Part 2.

J

Jacobs, J. (1969). *The search for help.* New York: Brunner/Mazel.

Johnson, C.A., & Katz, R.C. (1973). Using parents as change agents for their children: A review. *Journal of Clinical Psychology and Psychiatry, 4,* 181– 200.

Johnson, B., & Morse, H.A. (1968). Injured children and their parents. *Children, 15,* 147–152.

Johnson, S.M., & Lobitz, G.K. (1974). The personal and marital adjustment of parents as related to observed child deviance and parenting behaviors. *Journal of Abnormal Child Psychology, 2,* 192–207.

Joyce, K., Singer, M., & Isralowitz, R. (1983). Impact of respite care on parents' perceptions of quality of life. *Mental Retardation, 21,* 153–156.

K

Kammerlohr, B., Henderson, R.A., & Rock, S. (1983). Special education due process hearing in Illinois. *Exceptional Children, 49*(5), 417–422.

Kanner, L. (1949). Problems of nosology and psychodynamica of early infantile autism. *American Journal of Orthopsychiatry, 19,* 416–426.

Kansas Children's Service League. (1984). *Task force on respite care in Kansas.* Unpublished report presented to the Kansas Planning Council on Developmental Disabilities.

Karnes, F.A., & Karnes, M.R. (1982). Parents and schools: Educating gifted and talented children. *The Elementary School Journal, 82*(3), 236–248.

Karnes, M.B., & Teska, J.A. (1980). Toward successful parent involvement in programs for handicapped children. In J.J. Gallagher (Ed.), *New directions for exceptional children: Parents and families of handicapped children,* (Vol. 4, pp. 85–109). San Francisco: Jossey-Bass.

Karnes, M. B., Zehrbach, R. R., & Teska, J. A. (1972). Involving families of handicapped children. *Theory Into Practice, 11,* 150–156.

Kasdorf, J., & Gustafson, K. (1978). Research related to microcounseling. In A. E. Ivey & J. Authier (Eds.), *Microcounseling: Innovations in interviewing, counseling, psychotherapy and psychoeducation* (pp. 323–376). Springfield, IL: Charles C. Thomas.

Katz, J. (1984). Why doctors don't disclose uncertainty. *The Hastings Center Report, 14*(1), 35–44.

Katzen, K. (1980). To the editor: An open letter to CEC. *Exceptional Children, 46*(8), 582.

Kauffman, J.M. (1984). Saving children in the age of big brother: The moral and ethical issue in the identification of deviance. *Behavioral Disorders, 10*(1), 60–70.

Kazak, A.E., & Marvin, R.S. (1984). Differences, difficulties and adaptation: Stress and social networks in families with a handicapped child. *Family Relations, 33,* 67–77.

Kirk, S.A. (1984). Introspection and prophecy. In B. Blatt & R.J. Morris (Eds.), *Perspectives in special education: Personal orientations.* Glenview, IL: Scott, Foresman, and Co.

Klein, S.D. (1972). Brother to sister/Sister to brother. *Exceptional Parent, 3*(2), 24–27.

Klein, S. D. & Schleifer, M. J. (1980). The challenge for the 1980's: Parent-professional collaboration. *The Exceptional Parent, 10* (1), 2–3.

Knapp, L. (1972). *Nonverbal communication in human interaction.* New York: Holt, Rinehart & Winston, Inc.

Knighton, C.E., & Knighton, W.

(1985). The colors of the rainbow. In H.R. Turnbull & A.P. Turnbull (Eds.), *Parents Speak Out: Then and Now* (pp. 271–280). Columbus, OH: Charles E. Merrill Publishing Co.

Koegel, R.L., Schreibman, L., Johnson, J., O'Neill, R.E., & Dunlap, G. (1984). Collateral effects of parent training on families with autistic children. In R.F. Dangel & R.A. Polster (Eds.), *Parent training* (pp. 358–378). New York: The Guilford Press.

Kolstoe, O.P. (1970). *Teaching educable mentally retarded children.* New York: Holt, Rinehart and Winston, Inc.

Kroth, R.L. (1975). *Communication with parents of exceptional children.* Denver: Love Publishing Co.

Kroth, R.L. (1985). *Communicating with parents of exceptional children: Improving parent-teacher relationships* (2nd ed.). Denver, CO: Love Publishing Co.

Kroth, R. L., & Simpson, R. L. (1977). *Parent conference as a teaching strategy.* Denver, CO: Love Publishing Co.

Kupfer, F. (1982). *Before and after Zachariah.* New York: Delacorte Press.

Kushner, H.S. (1981). *When bad things happen to good people.* New York: Avon Books.

L

LaBarbera, J.D., & Lewis, S. (1980). Fathers who undermine children's treatment: A challenge for the clinician. *Journal of Consulting and Clinical Psychology, 9,* 204–206.

Latham, G. (1981). Serving the rural handicapped: Multiple methods. *Rural Educator, 2*(3), 25–30.

Lay, C.A. (1977). Due process in special education. *Dissertation Abstracts International, 37,* 7687A.

Lee, G.R. (1982). *Family structure and interaction: A comparative analysis.* Minneapolis: University of Minnesota Press.

Leslie, G.R. (1979). The nature of the family. In G.R. Leslie (Ed.), *The family in social context* (4th ed., pp. 3–23). New York: Oxford University Press.

Lewis, C.L., Busch, J.P., Proger, B.B., & Juska, P.J. (1981). Parents' perspectives concerning the IEP process. *Education Unlimited, 3*(3), 18–22.

Liebman, R. (1975). *Constructing a workable reality* [training video tape]. Montalva, B. (Ed.). Philadelphia: Philadelphia Child Guidance Clinic.

Lipton, H.L., & Svarstad, B. (1977). Sources of variation in clinicians' communication to parents about mental retardation. *American Journal of Mental Deficiency, 82,* 155–161.

Lombana, J. H. (1983). *Home-school partnerships: Guidelines and strategies for educators.* New York: Grune & Stratton.

Lombana, J.H., & Pratt, P.A. (1978). *Communication skills for career success.* Jacksonville: University of North Florida.

Lonsdale, G. (1978). Family life with a handicapped child: The parents speak. *Child: Care, Health and Development, 4,* 99–120.

Losen, S.M., & Diament, B. (1978). *Parent conference in the schools: Procedures for developing effective partnership.* Boston: Allyn and Bacon, Inc.

Lowell, E.L. (1979). Parent-infant programs for preschool deaf children: The example of John Tracy Clinic. *The Volta Review, 81,*

323–329.

Lucito, L.J. (1963). Gifted children. In L.M. Dunn (Ed.), *Exceptional children in the schools* (pp. 179–238). New York: Holt, Rinehart & Winston, Inc.

Lueger, S.A. (1981). *Respite care: An aid for planning services in Kansas.* Topeka, KS: Kansas Planning Council on Developmental Disabilities.

Lusthaus, C.S., Lusthaus, E.W., & Gibbs, H. (1981). Parents' role in the decision process. *Exceptional Children, 48*(3), 256–257.

Lynch, E.W., & Stein, R. (1982). Perspectives on parent participation in special education. *Exceptional Education Quarterly, 3*(2), 56–63.

M

MacMillan, D.L., & Turnbull, A.P. (1983). Parent involvement with special education: Respecting individual preferences. *Education and Training of the Mentally Retarded, 18*(1), 5–9.

MacMurphy, H. (1916). The relation of feeble mindedness to other social problems. *Journal of Psycho-Asthenics, 21,* 58–63.

Maddux, C.D., & Cummings, R.E. (1983). Parental home tutoring: Aids and cautions. *The Exceptional Parent, 13*(4), 30–33.

Malmberg, P.A. (1984). *Development of field tested special education placement committee parent education materials.* Unpublished doctoral dissertation, Virginia Polytechnic Institute at State University, Blacksburg.

Mann, J.A., & Kreyche, G.F. (1966). *Approaches to morality.* New York: Harcourt, Brace & World, Inc.

Margolin, G., & Christensen, A. (1981). *Treatment of multiproblem families: Specific and general effects of marital and family therapy.* Paper presented at the XIII Banff International Conference on Behavioral Sciences, Banff, Canada.

Marcus, L.M. (1977). Patterns of coping in families of psychotic children. *American Journal of Orthopsychiatry, 47*(3), 388–399.

Marion, R. (1979). Minority parent involvement in the IEP process: A systematic model approach. *Focus on Exceptional Children, 10*(8), 1–16.

Marsh, C. (1985). To the core. *Kansas Alumni Magazine.* Lawrence, KS: Alumni Association of the University of Kansas.

Marshall, N. R., & Goldstein, S.G. (1969). Imparting diagnostic information to mothers: A comparison of methodologies. *Journal of Speech and Hearing Research, 12,* 65–72.

Martino, M.S., & Newman, M.B. (1974). Siblings of retarded children: A population at risk. *Child Psychiatry and Human Development, 4*(3), 168–177.

Masnick, G., & Bane, M.J. (n.d.). *The nation's families: 1960–1990: A summary.* Cambridge, MA: Joint Center for Urban Studies of MIT and Harvard University.

Mattson, B.D. (1977). Involving parents in special education: Did you really teach them? *Education and Training of the Mentally Retarded, 12*(4), 358–360.

McAndrew, I. (1976). Children with a handicap and their families. *Child: Care, Health and Development, 2,* 213–237.

McCullough, M.E. (1981). Parent and sibling definition of situation regarding transgenerational shift in care of a handicapped child. (Doctoral dissertation, University of Minnesota). *Dissertation Abstracts International, 42,* 161B.

McGill, D., & Pearce, J.K. (1982). British families. In M. Goldrick, J.K. Pearce, & J. Giordano (Eds.), *Ethnicity in family therapy* (pp. 457–482). New York: The Guilford Press.

McGoldrick, M. (1982). Ethnicity and family therapy: An overview. In M. McGoldrick, J.K. Pearce, & J. Giordano (Eds.), *Ethnicity in family therapy* (pp. 3–30). New York: The Guilford Press.

McKinney, J.D., & Hocutt, A.M. (1982). Public school involvement of parents of learning-disabled children and average achievers. *Exceptional Education Quarterly, 3*(2), 64–73.

McLoughlin, J.A., Edge, D., Petrosko, J., & Strenecky, B. (1981). PL 94–142 and information dissemination: A step forward. *Journal of Special Education Technology, 4*(4), 50–56.

McMahon, R.J., Forehand, R., Griest, D.L., & Wells, K.C. (1981). Who drops out of treatment during behavioral training? *Behavioral Counseling Quarterly, 1,* 79–85.

Mehrabian, A. (1969). Significance of posture and position in the communication of attitude and status relationships. *Psychological Bulletin, 71,* 359–372.

Meier, J.H., & Sloan, M.P. (1984). The severely handicapped and child abuse. In J. Blacher (Ed.), *Severely handicapped young children and their families* (pp. 247–274). New York: Academic Press.

Mercer, J.R. (1973). *Labeling the mentally retarded child.* Berkeley, CA: University of California Press.

Mesibov, G.B., & LaGreca, A.M. (1981). Ethical issues in parent professional service interaction. In J.L. Paul (Ed.), *Understanding and* working with parents of children with special needs (pp. 154–179). New York: Holt, Rinehart and Winston.

Meyer, D., & Fewell, R. (1985). Supporting extended family members (SEFAM) program: A handbook for fathers. Seattle, WA: University of Washington Press.

Michaelis, C. (1980). Home and school partnerships in exceptional education. Rockville, MD: Aspen Publications.

Michaelis, C. (1980). Mainstreaming: A mother's perspective. Topics in Early Childhood Special Education, 1(1), 11–16.

Midwest Regional Resource Center. (1982, October). Child-Parent-Educator: The link to success. Des Moines, IA: Midwest Regional Resource Center, Drake University.

Miller, J.A., Bigner, J.J., Jacobson, R.B., & Turner, J.G. (1982). The value of children for farm families: A comparison of mothers and fathers. In N. Stinnett, J. DeFrain, K. King, H. Lingren, G. Rowe, S. VanZandt, & R. Williams (Eds.), Family strengths 4: Positive support systems (pp. 33–42). Lincoln, NE: University of Nebraska Press.

Miller, N.B., & Cantwell, D.P. (1976). Siblings as therapists: A behavioral approach. American Journal of Psychiatry, 133(4), 447–450.

Miller, S., Nunnally, E. W., & Wackman, D. B. (1978). Alive and aware: How to improve your relationships through better communication. Minneapolis, MN: Interpersonal Communication Programs, Inc.

Milofsky, C. (1974). Why special education isn't special. Harvard Education Review, 44, 437–458.

Minuchin, S. (1974). Families and family therapy. Cambridge, MA: Harvard University Press.

Mitchell, S. (1976). Parental perceptions of their experiences with due process in special education: A preliminary report. Paper presented at the meeting of the American Educational Research Association, San Francisco, CA.

Mitchell, S. (1976). Parental perceptions of their experiences with due process in special education: A preliminary report. Cambridge, MA: Research Institute for Educational Problems, (ERIC Document Reproduction No. ED 130 482).

Morgan, D.P. (1982). Parental participation in the IEP process: Does it enhance appropriate education? Exceptional Education Quarterly, 3(2), 33–40.

Morton, K. (1985). Identifying the enemy—A parent's complaint. In R.H. Turnbull & A.P. Turnbull (Eds.), Parents speak out: Then and now (pp. 143–148). Columbus, OH: Charles E. Merrill Publishing Co.

Moses, K.L. (1983). The impact of initial diagnosis: Mobilizing family resources. In J.A. Mulick & S.M. Pueschel (Eds.), Parent-professional partnerships in developmental disability services (pp. 11–34). Cambridge, MA: The Ware Press.

Mulick, J.A., & Pueschel, S.M. (Eds.). (1983). Parent-professional participation in developmental disability services: Foundations and prospects. Cambridge, MA: The Ware Press.

Mullins, J.B. (1983). The uses of bibliotherapy in counseling families confronted with handicaps. In M. Seligman (Ed.), The family with a handicapped child: Understanding and treatment (pp. 235–251). New York: Grune and Stratton.

Murphy, A.T. (1982). The family with a handicapped child: A review of the literature. Developmental and Behavioral Pediatrics, 3(2),

73–82.

Murray, M.A. (1959). Needs of parents of mentally retarded children. American Journal of Mental Deficiency, 63, 1078–1088.

N

Nader, R., Petkas, P., & Blackwell, K. (Eds.). (1972). Whistle-blowing. New York: Grossman.

National Association of Parents and Friends of Mentally Retarded Children. (1950, September). Proceeding of the first convention of the National Association of Parents and Friends of Mentally Retarded Children, Minneapolis, MN.

National Association of State Directors of Special Education (NASDSE). (1978). The implementation of due process in Massachusetts. Washington, D.C.: Author.

National Center for Citizen Involvement. (1984). Involving the handicapped as volunteers: A guidebook. Arlington, VA: Volunteer: The National Center for Citizen Involvement.

National Society for Autistic Children, Board of Directors and Professional Advisory Board. (1977). A short definition of autism. Albany, NY: Authors.

Neugarten, B. (1976). Adaptations and the life cycle. The Counseling Psychologist, 6(1), 16–20.

Neulicht, A.T. (1984). Developing residential opportunities for persons with autism. Overland Park, KS: Johnson County Mental Retardation Center.

Nivens, M.K. (1978, January). Parent power: Assertive training as a tool for obtaining services for exceptional children. Paper presented at the state convention of the Alabama Association of Children with Learning Disabilities. Montgomery, AL.

Northern, H. (1982). *Clinical social work*. New York: Columbia University Press.

O

Office of Special Education, U.S. Department of Education (1984). *Sixth Annual Report to Congress on the Implementation of P.L. 94–142*. Washington, D.C.: Author.

O'Hara, D.M., & Levy, S.M. (1984). Family adaptation to learning disability: A framework for understanding and treatment. *Learning Disabilities, 3*(6), 63–77.

Olshansky, S. (1962). Chronic sorrow: A response to having a mentally defective child. *Social Casework, 43,* 191–194.

Olson, D.H., McCubbin, H.I., Barnes, H., Larsen, A., Muxen, M., & Wilson, M. (1982). *Family inventories*. St. Paul, MN: Family Social Science, University of Minnesota.

Olson, D.H., McCubbin, H.I., Barnes, H., Larsen, A., Muxen, M., & Wilson, M. (1983). *Families: What makes them work*. Beverly Hills: Sage Publications.

Olson, D.H., Russell, C.S., & Sprenkle, D.H. (1980). Circumplex model of marital and family systems II: Empirical studies and clinical intervention. In J.P. Vincent (Ed.), *Advances in family intervention assessment and theory* (Vol. 1, pp. 129–179). Greenwich, CT: JAI Press.

Oltmanns, T.F., Broderick, J.E., & O'Leary, K.D. (1977). Marital adjustment and the efficacy of behavior therapy with children. *Journal of Consulting and Clinical Psychology, 45,* 724–729.

O'Neill, K.K. (1978). Parent involvement: A key to the education of gifted children. *The Gifted Child Quarterly, 22*(2), 235–242.

Osterkamp, L., & Press, A.N. (1980). *Stress? Find your balance*. Lawrence, KS: Lynn Osterkamp and Allan N. Press, P.O. Box 763.

P

PACER Center, Inc. (1984). *Parents Helping Parents*. Evaluation Report. Minneapolis, MN.: Author.

Parent Involvement Center, Albuquerque Public Schools, Albuquerque, NM.

Parsons, T., & Bales, R.F. (1955). *Family, socialization and interaction process*. Glencoe, IL: Free Press.

Pasanella, A. L., & Volkmor, C. B. (Eds.). (1981). *Teaching handicapped students in the mainstream: Coming back or never leaving* (2nd ed.). Columbus, OH: Charles E. Merrill Publishing Company.

Pate, J.E. (1963). Emotionally disturbed and socially maladjusted children. In L.M. Dunn (Ed.), *Exceptional children in the schools* (pp. 239–283). New York: Holt, Rinehart, & Winston, Inc.

Patterson, G. R. (1971). Behavioral intervention procedures in the classroom and in the home. In A. E. Bergin & S. L. Garfield (Eds.), *Handbook of psychotherapy and behavior change* (pp. 751–775). New York: John Wiley & Sons.

Paul, J., Turnbull, A., & Cruickshank, W. (1977). *Mainstreaming: A practical guide*. Syracuse, NY: Syracuse University Press.

Pearlin, L.I., Menaghan, E.G., Lieberman, M.A., & Mullan, J.T. (1981). The stress process. *Journal of Health and Social Behavior, 22,* 337–356.

Pearlin, L.I., & Schooler, C. (1978). The structure of coping. *Journal of Health and Social Behavior, 19,* 2–21.

Peck, M. S. (1978). *The road less traveled: A new psychology of love, traditional values and spiritual growth*. New York: Simon & Schuster.

Pepper, F.C. (1976). Teaching the American Indian child in mainstream settings. In R.L. Jones (Ed.), *Mainstreaming and the minority child* (pp. 133–158). Reston, VA: The Council for Exceptional Children.

Perino, S.C., & Perino, J. (1981). *Parenting the gifted: Developing the promise*. NY: R.R. Bowker Co.

Perls, F. S. (1969). *Gestalt therapy verbation*. Lafayette, CA: Real People Press.

Pfeiffer, S.I. (1980). The school-based interprofessional team: Recurring problems and some possible solutions. *Journal of School Psychology, 18*(4), 388–394.

Pfeiffer, S.I., & Tittler, B.I. (1983). Utilizing the multidisciplinary team to facilitate a school-family systems orientation. *School Psychology Review, 12,* 168–173. Staff. (1976). The trend toward more parent/teacher conferences. *Phi Delta Kappan, 57,* 633.

Staff. (1985). *An introduction to Phi Delta Kappa*. Bloomington, IN: Phi Delta Kappa.

Pistono, W.J. (1977). The relationships between certain identified variables and parental participation during the educational planning and placement committee meeting for handicapped students in Michigan. *Dissertation Abstracts International, 38*(5A), 2705.

Powell, T.H., & Ogle, P.A. (1985). *Brothers and sisters—A special part of exceptional families*. Baltimore: Paul H. Brookes Publishing Co.

President's Committee on Mental Retardation. (1977). *Mental retardation: Past and present*. Washington, DC: Government Printing Office.

Price, M., & Goodman, L. (1980). Individualized education programs: A cost study. *Exceptional Children, 46*(6), 446–458.

Prieto-Bayard, M., & Baker, B.L. (in press). Behavioral parent training for Spanish-speaking families with a retarded child. *Journal of Community Psychology.*

R

Reed, E.W., & Reed, S.C. (1965). *Mental retardation: A family study.* Philadelphia: Saunders.

Reynolds, K., & Shanahan, V. (1981). *The parent to parent program: Organizational handbook.* Athens, GA: University Affiliated Facility, University of Georgia.

Roberds-Baxter, S. (1984). The parent connection: Enhancing the affective component of parent conferences. *Teaching Exceptional Children, 17*(1), 55–58.

Rockowitz, R. J., & Davidson, P. W. (1979). Discussing diagnostic findings with parents. *Journal of Learning Disabilities, 12*(1), 11–16.

Rogers, C. (1951). *Client-centered therapy.* Boston: Houghton-Mifflin Co.

Rogers, C. R. (1961). *On becoming a person: A therapist's view of psychotherapy.* Boston: Houghton-Mifflin Co.

Roos, P. (1985). Parents of mentally retarded children—Misunderstood and mistreated. In H.R. Turnbull & A.P. Turnbull (Eds.), *Parents speak out: Then and now* (pp. 245–260). Columbus, OH: Charles E. Merrill Publishing Co.

Rosenberg, H., Tesolowski, D., & Stein, R. (1983). Advocacy: Education responsibility to handicapped children. *Education and Training of*

the Mentally Retarded, 18(4), 266–270.

Rosenberg, M.S., Reppucci, N.D., & Linney, J.A. (1983). Issues in the implementation of human service programs: Examples from a parent training project for high-risk families. *Analysis and Intervention in Developmental Disabilities, 3,* 215–225.

Rosenberg, S.A., & McTate, G.A. (1982). Intellectually handicapped mothers: Problems and prospects. *Children Today, 11,* 24–26.

Rotunno, M., & McGoldrick, M. (1982). Italian families. In M. McGoldrick, J.K. Pearce, & J. Giordano (Eds.), *Ethnicity in family therapy* (pp. 340–363). New York: The Guilford Press.

Rousso, H. (1984). Fostering healthy self esteem. *The Exceptional Parent, 8*(14), 9–14.

Rousso, H. (1985). Fostering self esteem, Part Two. *The Exceptional Parent, 15*(1), 9–12.

Rubin, L.B. (1976). *Worlds of pain: Life in the working-class family.* New York: Basic Books.

Russell, L.M. (1983). *Alternatives: A family guide to legal and financial planning for the disabled.* Evanston, IL: First Publications.

Rutherford, R.G., & Edgar, E. (1979). *Teachers and parents: A guide to interaction and cooperation.* Boston: Allyn & Bacon, Inc.

S

Safer, N.D., Morrissey, P.A., Kaufman, M.J., & Lewis, L. (1978). Implementation of IEPs: New teacher roles and requisite support systems. *Focus on Exceptional Children, 10*(1), 1–20.

Sager, C.J., Brown, H.S., Crohn, H., Engel, T., Rodstein, E., & Walker, L. (1983). *Treating the re-*

married family. New York: Brunner/Mazel.

Sales, T. B., & Fox, C. L. (1982). Exceptional children: Culture, language and the law: A cross-cultural training challenge. *Education, 102*(3), 226–231.

Sandler, A., & Coren, A. (1981). Integrated instruction at home and school: Parents perspective. *Education and Training of the Mentally Retarded, 16*(3), 183–187.

Sarason, S.B., & Doris, J. (1979). *Educational handicap, public policy, and social history.* New York: The Free Press.

Scanlon, C.A., Arick, J., & Phelps, N. (1981). Participation in the development of the IEP: Parents' perspective. *Exceptional Children, 47*(5), 373–374.

Schalock, R.L. (1985). Comprehensive community services: A plea for interagency coordination. In R.H. Bruininks & K.C. Lakin (Eds.), *Living and learning in the least restrictive environment* (pp. 37–63). Baltimore: Paul H. Brookes Publishing Co.

Scheerenberger, R.C. (1983). *A history of mental retardation.* Baltimore: Paul H. Brookes Publishing Co.

Schreibman, L., O'Neill, R.E., & Koegel, R.L. (1983). Behavioral training for siblings of autistic children. *Journal of Applied Behavior Analysis, 16*(2), 129–138.

Schulz, J.B. (1985). Growing up together. In H.R. Turnbull & A.P. Turnbull (Eds.), *Parents Speak Out: Then and Now* (pp. 11–20). Columbus, OH: Charles E. Merrill Publishing Co.

Schulz, J.B. (1985). The parent-professional conflict. In H.R. Turnbull and A.P. Turnbull (Eds.), *Parents speak out: Then and now* (pp. 3–11). Columbus, OH:

Charles E. Merrill Publishing Co.

Schulz, J., & Turnbull, A. P. (1984). *Mainstreaming handicapped students: A guide for the classroom teacher.* Newton, MA: Allyn & Bacon, Inc.

Schumaker, J.B., & Sherman, J.A. (1978). Parent as intervention agent: From birth onward. In R.L. Schiefelbusch (Ed.), *Language intervention strategies* (pp. 237–315). Baltimore: University Park Press.

Scott, S. (1984). *Family systems.* Unpublished manuscript, The University of Kansas, The Research and Training Center on Independent Living, Lawrence.

Seligman, M. (1979). *Strategies for helping parents of exceptional children.* New York: Free Press.

Serf, G.M. (1979). [A conversation with Alice Scrogin, President of ACLD]. *Journal of Learning Disabilities, 12,* 50–61.

Shearer, D.E., & Loftin, C.R. (1984). The portage project: Teaching parents to teach their preschool children in the home. In R.F. Dangel & R.A. Polster (Eds.), *Parent Training* (pp. 93–126). New York: The Guilford Press.

Shearer, M.S., & Shearer, D.E. (1977). Parent involvement. In J.B. Jordan, A.H. Hayden, M.B. Karnes, & M.M. Wood (Eds.), *Early childhood education for exceptional children* (pp. 208–235). Reston, VA: Council for Exceptional Children.

Sheridan, M.D. (1956). The intelligence of 100 neglectful mothers. *British Medical Journal, 1,* 91–93.

Shevin, M., & Klein, N.K. (1984). The importance of choice-making skills for students with severe disabilities. *The Journal of the Association for Persons with Severe Handicaps, 9*(3), 159–166.

Simpson, R.L. (1982). *Conferencing parents of exceptional children.* Rockville, MD.: Aspen Publications.

Singer, J., Bossard, M., & Watkins, M. (1977). Effects of parental presence on attendance and input of interdisciplinary teams in an institutional setting. *Psychological Reports, 41,* 1031–1034.

Sirkis, N. (1970). *One family.* Boston: Little, Brown & Co.

Sirridge, S.T. (1980). Transactional analysis: Promoting OK'ness. In M.J. Fine (Ed.), *Handbook on parent education* (pp. 123–153). New York: Academic Press.

Skrtic, T.M., Summers, J.A., Brotherson, M.J., & Turnbull, A.P. (1984). Severely handicapped children and their brothers and sisters. In J. Blacher (Ed.), *Severely handicapped young children and their families* (pp. 215–246). New York: Academic Press.

Sloop, E.W. (1974). *Problems with parents as behavior modifiers: How to fail and how to succeed.* Paper presented at the meeting of the Southeastern Psychological Association, Hollywood Beach, FL.

Smith, J. M., & Smith, E. P. (1966). *Child management.* Ann Arbor, MI: Ann Arbor Publishers.

Snell, M.E., & Beckman-Brindley, S. (1984). Family involvement in intervention with children having severe handicaps. *Journal of Speech and Hearing, 3,* 213–230.

Sonnenschein, P. (1984). Parents and professionals: An uneasy relationship. In M.L. Henniger & E.M. Nesselroad (Eds.), *Working with parents of handicapped children: A book of readings for school personnel* (pp. 129–139). Lanham, MD: University Press of America.

Spiegel, J., & Machotka, P. (1974). *Messages of the body.* New York: The Free Press.

Spradley, T.S., & Spradley, J.P. (1978). *Deaf like me.* New York: Random House.

Stephens, T.M., & Wolf, J.S. (1980). *Effective skills in parent/teacher conferencing.* Columbus: Ohio State University, National Center for Educational Materials and Media for the Handicapped.

Stewart, C.J. (1986). *Counseling parents of exceptional children.* Columbus, OH: Charles E. Merrill Publishing Co.

Strahan, C., & Zytowski, D. (1976). Impact of visual, vocal, and lexical cues on judgments of counselor qualities. *Journal of Counseling Psychology, 23,* 387–393.

Strain, P.S. (1982). *Social development of exceptional children.* Rockville, MD: Aspen Publications.

Strickland, B. (1982). *Perceptions of parents and school representatives regarding their relationship before, during, and after the due process hearing.* Unpublished doctoral dissertation, The University of North Carolina, Chapel Hill.

Strickland, B. (1983). Legal issues that affect parents. In M. Seligman (Ed.), *The family with a handicapped child: Understanding and treatment* (pp. 27–39). New York: Grune & Stratton.

Suelzle, M., & Keenan, V. (1981). Changes in family support networks over the life cycle of mentally retarded persons. *American Journal of Mental Deficiency, 86,* 267–274.

Summers, J.A. (in press). Family adjustment: Issues in research on families with developmentally disabled children. In V.B. Van Hasselt, P.S. Strain, & M. Hersen (Eds.), *Handbook of developmental disabilities.* New York: Pergamon Press.

Switzer, L. S. (1985). Accepting the

diagnosis: An educational intervention for parents of children with learning disabilities. *Journal of Learning Disabilities, 18*(3), 151–153.

T

Tallman, I. (1965). Spousal role differentiation and the socialization of severely retarded children. *Journal of Marriage and the Family, 27,* 37–42.

Tawney, J.W., Aeschleman, S.R., Deaton, S.L., & Donaldson, R.M. (1979). Using telecommunications technology to instruct rural severely handicapped children. *Exceptional Children, 46,* 118–125.

Taylor, P.W. (1967). *Problems of moral philosophy: An introduction to ethics.* Belmont, CA: Dickenson Publishing Company, Inc.

Terkelson, K.G. (1980). Toward a theory of family life cycle. In E. Carter & M. McGoldrick (Eds.), *The family life cycle: A framework of family therapy* (pp. 21–52). New York: Gardner Press.

Terman, L. (1916). *The measurement of intelligence.* Cambridge, MA: Riverside Press.

Tew, B.J., Payne, E.H., & Lawrence, K.M. (1974). Must a family with a handicapped child be a handicapped family? *Developmental Medicine and Child Neurology, 16,* Suppl. 32, 95–98.

Thomas, C.A. (1977). The effectiveness of two child management training procedures for high and low educational level parents of emotionally disturbed children. *Dissertation Abstracts International, 37,* A12.

Thompson, T.M. (1982). An investigation and comparison of public school personnel's perception and interpretation of P.L. 94–142. *Dissertation Abstracts International,*

43, 2840A.

Tomlinson, J. R., Acker, N., Canter, A., & Lindborg, S. (1977). Minority status, sex, and school psychological services. *Psychology in the Schools, 14*(4), 456–460.

Traux, C. B., & Mitchell, K. M. (1971). Research on certain therapist interpersonal skills in relation to process and outcome. In A. E. Bergin & S. L. Garfield (Eds.), *Handbook of psychotherapy and behavior change* (pp. 299–344). New York: Wiley.

Trevino, F. (1979). Siblings of handicapped children: Identifying those at risk. *Social Casework: The Journal of Contempory Social Work, 60,* 488–492.

Trout, M.D. (1983). Birth of a sick or handicapped infant: Impact on the family. *Child Welfare, 62,* 337–348.

Trungpa, C. (1976). *The myth of freedom.* Berkeley, CA: Shambhala.

Turnbull, A.P. (1983). Parental participation in the IEP process. In J. A. Mulick & S. M. Pueschel (Eds.), *Parent-professional participation in developmental disabilities services: Foundations and prospects* (pp. 107–123). Cambridge, MA: The Ware Press.

Turnbull, A.P. (1985). The dual role of parent and professional. In H.R. Turnbull & A.P. Turnbull (Eds.), *Parents speak out: Then and now* (pp. 137–142). Columbus, OH: Charles E. Merrill Publishing Co.

Turnbull, A.P. (1985). From professional to parent—A startling experience. In H.R. Turnbull & A.P. Turnbull (Eds.), *Parents speak out: Then and now* (pp. 127–135). Columbus, OH: Charles E. Merrill Publishing Co.

Turnbull, A.P., Blue-Banning, M.,

Behr, S., & Kerns, G. (1985, May). *Family research and intervention: A value and ethical examination.* Paper presented at the Symposium "When are Intervention Decisions for Severely Retarded People Ethical? Toward an Ethically Relevant Research Agenda," Vanderbilt University, Nashville, TN.

Turnbull, A.P., Brotherson, M.J., Bronicki, G.J., Benson, H.A., Houghton, J., Roeder–Gordon, C., & Summers, J.A. (1984). *How to plan for my child's adult future: A three–part process to future planning.* Unpublished manuscript, Kansas University Affiliated Facility, Bureau of Child Research, University of Kansas, Lawrence.

Turnbull, A.P., Brotherson, M.J., & Summers, J.A. (1985). The impact of deinstitutionalization on families: A family systems approach. In R.H. Bruininks (Ed.), *Living and learning in the least restrictive environment* (pp. 115–152). Baltimore: Paul H. Brookes Publishing Co.

Turnbull, A.P., & Strickland, B. (1981). Parents and the educational system. In J.L. Paul (Ed.), *Understanding and working with parents of children with special needs* (pp. 231–263). New York: Holt, Rinehart, and Winston.

Turnbull, A.P., Strickland, B., & Brantley, J.C. (1982). *Developing and Implementing Individualized Education Programs.* Columbus, OH: Charles E. Merrill Publishing Co.

Turnbull, A.P., & Summers, J.A. (1985, April). *From parent involvement to family support: Evolution to revolution.* Paper presented at the Down syndrome State-of-the Art Conference, Boston, MA.

Turnbull, A.P., Summers, J.A., & Brotherson, M.J. (1984). *Working with families with disabled members: A family systems approach.*

Lawrence, KS: Kansas University Affiliated Facility, University of Kansas.

Turnbull, A.P., & Turnbull, H.R. (1982). Parent involvement in the education of handicapped children: A critique. *Mental Retardation, 20*(3), 115–122.

Turnbull, A.P., & Turnbull, H.R. (1984). Developing independence in adolescents with disabilities. *Journal of Adolescent Health Care. 6*(2), 108–124.

Turnbull, A.P., & Winton, P.J. (1983). A comparison of specialized and mainstreamed preschools from the perspectives of parents of handicapped children. *Journal of Pediatric Psychology, 8*(1), 57–71.

Turnbull, A.P., & Winton, P.J. (1984). Parent involvement policy and practice: Current research and implications for families of young severely handicapped children. In J. Blacher (Ed.), *Severely handicapped children and their families: Research in review* (pp. 377–397). New York: Academic Press.

Turnbull, A.P., Winton, P.J., Blacher, J.B., & Salkind, N. (1983). Mainstreaming in the kindergarten classroom: Perspectives of parents of handicapped and nonhandicapped children. *Journal of the Division of Early Childhood, 6,* 14–20.

Turnbull, H.R. (Ed.) (1978). *The consent handbook.* Washington, D.C.: American Association on Mental Deficiency.

Turnbull, H.R. (Ed.) (1981). *The least restrictive alternative: Principles and practices.* Washington, D.C.: American Association on Mental Deficiency.

Turnbull, H.R. (1982). Youngberg v. Romeo: An essay. *The Journal of the Association for Persons with Severe Handicaps, 8,* 3–6.

Turnbull, H.R. (1985). Jay's story.

In H.R. Turnbull & A.P. Turnbull (Eds.), *Parents speak out: Then and now* (pp. 109–118). Columbus, OH: Charles E. Merrill Publishing Co.

Turnbull, H.R. (1985). Jay's story—The paradoxes. In H.R. Turnbull & A.P. Turnbull (Eds.), *Parents speak out: Then and now* (pp. 119–124). Columbus, OH: Charles E. Merrill Publishing Co.

Turnbull, H.R. (1986). *Free appropriate public education: Law and interpretation.* Denver, CO: Love Publishing Co.

Turnbull, H.R., & Barber, P. (1984). Perspectives on public policy. In E.L. Meyen (Ed.), *Mental retardation: Topics of today—issues of tomorrow* (pp. 5–24). Reston, VA: Division on Mental Retardation of the Council for Exceptional Children.

Turnbull, H., Brotherson, M., Wheat, M., and Esquith, D. (1982). The least restrictive education of handicapped children: Who really wants it? *Family Law Quarterly, 16* (3), 161–200.

Turnbull, H., Brotherson, M., Cyzewski, M., Esquith, D., Otis, A., Summers, J., Van Reusen, A., and DePazza-Conway, M. (1983). A policy analysis of the "least restrictive" education of handicapped children. *Rutgers Law Journal, 14* (3), 489–540.

Turnbull, H.R., Guess, D., Backus, L., Barber, P., Fiedler, C., Helmstetter, E., & Summers, J.A. (1985). *On the legal, ethical, and moral aspects of aversive therapy.* Unpublished manuscript, University of Kansas, Department of Special Education, Lawrence.

Turnbull, H.R., & Turnbull, A.P. (1978). *Free appropriate public education: Law and implementation.* Denver, CO: Love Publishing Co.

Turnbull, H.R., & Turnbull, A.P.

(1985). *Parents speak out: Then and now.* Columbus, OH: Charles E. Merrill Publishing Co.

Turnbull, H.R., Turnbull, A.P., & Strickland, B. (1979). Due process: The sword the untrained should not unsheath. *Boston University Journal of Education,* Summer, 40–59.

Turnbull, H.R., Turnbull, A.P., & Wheat, M. (1982). Assumptions about parental participation: A legislative history. *Exceptional Education Quarterly, 3*(2), 1–8.

Turnbull, H.R., & Wheat, M. (1983). Legal responses to classification of people as mentally retarded. In J. Mulick & J. Matson (Eds.), *A handbook of mental retardation* (pp. 157–170). New York: Pergamon Press.

Turner, R.M., & Macy, D.J. (1980). Involving parents in special programming. *Journal of School Health, 50,* 281–284.

Tymchuk, A.J. (1976). A perspective on ethics in mental retardation. *Mental Retardation, 14*(6), 44–45.

U

Ulrich, S. (1972). *Elizabeth.* Ann Arbor, MI: The University of Michigan Press.

United Cerebral Palsy Association. (1950). *First Annual Report.* New York: Author.

U.S. Department of Commerce. (1923). *Feebleminded and epileptic in institutions.* Washington, D.C.: U.S. Government Printing Office.

U.S. Department of Commerce. (1934). *Mental defectives and epileptics in state institutions, 1929–1932.* Washington, D.C.: U.S. Government Printing Office.

U.S. Department of Education. (1982). *Fourth annual report to Congress on the implementation of Public Law 94–142: The Education for All Handicapped Children Act.* Washington, D.C.: Author.

U.S. Department of Education. (1983). *Fifth annual report to Congress on the implementation of Public Law 94–142: The Education for All Handicapped Children Act.* Washington, D.C.: Author.

U.S. Department of Education. (1984). *Sixth annual report to Congress on the implementation of Public Law 94–142: The Education for All Handicapped Children Act.* Washington, D.C.: Author.

Upshur, C.C. (1982). An evaluation of home-based respite care. *Mental Retardation, 20,* 58–63.

Utley, C.A., & Marion, P. (1984, May). *Working with black families having mentally retarded members.* Paper presented at the annual meeting of the American Association on Mental Deficiency, Minneapolis, MN.

V

Vadasy, P.F., Fewell, R.R., & Meyer, D.J. (in press). Supporting extended family members' roles: Intergenerational supports provided by grandparents. *Journal of the Division for Early Childhood.*

Vadasy, P.F., Fewell, R.R., Meyer, D.J., & Greenberg, M.T. (1984). *Supporting fathers of handicapped young children: Preliminary findings of program effects.* Unpublished manuscript, University of Washington, Seattle.

Vadasy, P.F., Fewell, R.R., Meyer, D.J., & Schell, G. (1984). Siblings of handicapped children: A developmental perspective on family interactions. *Family Relations, 33,* 155–167.

Van Reusen, A.K. (1984). *A study of the effects of training learning disabled adolescents in self-advocacy procedures for use in the*

IEP conference. Unpublished doctoral dissertation, The University of Kansas, Lawrence.

Vincent, L., Davis, J., Brown, P., Broome, K., Miller, J., & Gruenewald, L. (1983). *Parent inventory of child development in nonschool environments.* Madison Metropolitan School District Early Childhood Program, Active Decision-making by Parents Grant, Madison, WI.

Vincent, L.J., Laten, S., Salisbury, C., Brown, P., & Baumgart, D. (1981). Family involvement in the educational processes of severely handicapped students: State of the art and directions for the future. In B. Wilcox & R. York (Eds.), *Quality educational services for the severely handicapped: The federal perspective* (pp.164–179). Washington, D.C.: Division of Innovation and Development, Department of Education.

Visher, J.S., & Visher, E.B. (1982). Stepfamilies and stepparenting. In F. Walsh (Ed.), *Normal family processes* (pp. 331–353). New York: The Guilford Press.

Vyas, P. (1983a). Getting on with it. In T. Dougan, L. Isbell, & P. Vyas (Eds.), *We have been there* (17–19). Nashville: Abingdon Press.

Vyas, P. (1983b). Just another little kid. In T. Dougan, L. Isbell, & P. Vyas (Eds.), *We have been there* (pp. 50–53). Nashville: Abingdon Press.

W

Wadsworth, H.G., & Wadsworth, J.B. (1971). A problem of involvement with parents of mildly retarded children. *The Family Coordinator, 28,* 141–147.

Wahler, R.G. (1980a). The insular mother: Her problems in parent-child treatment. *Journal of Applied Behavior Analysis, 13,* 207–219.

Wahler, R.G. (1980b). The multiply entrapped parent: Obstacles to change in parent-child problems. In J.P. Vincent (Ed.), *Advances in family intervention, assessment, and theory* (Vol. 1, pp. 29–52). Greenwich, CT: JAI Press.

Waisbren, S.E. (1980). Parents' reactions after the birth of a developmentally disabled child. *American Journal of Mental Deficiency, 84,* 345–351.

Walsh, F. (1982). Conceptualizations of normal family functioning. In F. Walsh (Ed.), *Normal family processes* (pp. 3–42). New York: Guilford Press.

Warren, F. (1985). A society that is going to kill your children. In H.R. Turnbull & A.P. Turnbull (Eds.), *Parents Speak Out: Then and now* (pp. 201–221). Columbus, OH: Charles E. Merrill Publishing Co.

Warschaw, T.A. (1980). *Winning by negotiation.* New York: McGraw-Hill Book Co.

Wasik, B.H. (1983, August). *Teaching parents problem solving skills: A behavioral-ecological perspective.* Paper presented to the American Psychological Association Meeting, Anaheim, CA.

Wasserman, R. (1983). Identifying the counseling needs of the siblings of mentally retarded children. *The Personnel and Guidance Journal, 61*(10), 622–627.

Webster, E. J. (1977). *Counseling with parents of handicapped children: Guidelines for improving communication.* New York: Grune & Stratton, Inc.

Wedel, J.W., & Fowler, S.A.(1984). "Read me a story, mom" A home-tutoring program to teach prereading skills to language-delayed children. *Behavior Modification, 8*(2), 245–266.

Weicker, L. (1985). Sonny and public policy. In H.R. Turnbull & A.P. Turnbull (Eds.), *Parents speak out: Then and now* (pp. 281–287). Columbus, OH: Charles E. Merrill Publishing Co.

Weikart, D. P., & Lambie, D. Z. (1970). Ypsilanti-Carnegie Infant Education Project. In J. Hellmuth (Ed.), *Disadvantaged child 3-compensatory education: A national debate* (pp. 362–404). New York: Bruner/Mazel.

Weinrott, M.R. (1974). A training program in behavior modification for siblings of the retarded. *American Journal of Orthopsychiatry, 44*(3), 362– 375.

Weintraub, F.J., Abeson, A., Ballard, J., & Lavor, M.L. (1976). *Public policy and the education of exceptional children.* Reston, VA: Council for Exceptional Children.

Weintraub, F., & McCaffrey, M. (1976). Professional rights and responsibilities. In F. Weintraub, A. Abeson, J. Ballard, & M. LaVor (Eds.), *Public policy and the education of exceptional children* (pp. 333–343). Reston, VA: Council for Exceptional Children.

Weyhing, M.C. (1983). Parental reactions to handicapped children and familial adjustments to routines of care. In J.A. Mulick & S.M. Pueschel (Eds.), *Parent-professional partnerships in developmental disabilities* (pp. 125–138). Cambridge, MA: The Ware Press.

Wiegel, R.R. (1982). Supporting today's farm family: An opportunity for family life educators. In N. Stinnett, J. DeFrain, K.King, H. Lingren, G. Rowe, S. VanZandt, & R. Williams (Eds.), *Family strengths 4:Positive support systems* (pp. 409–423). Lincoln, NE: University of Nebraska Press.

Wikler, L., Wasow, M., & Hatfield, E. (1981). Chronic sorrow revisited: Attitude of parents and professionals about adjustment to mental retardation. *American Journal of Orthopsychiatry, 51,* 63–70.

Wikler, L., Wasow, M., & Hatfield, E. (1983). Seeking strengths in families of developmentally disabled children. In L. Wikler and M.P. Keenan (Eds.), *Developmental disabilities: No longer a private tragedy* (pp. 111–114). Washington, D.C.: Library of Congress, National Association of Social Workers, Inc.

Wikler, L., Wasow, M., & Hatfield, E. (1983). Seeking strengths in families of developmentally disabled children. *Social Work,* July-August, 313–315.

Willer, B., & Intagliata, J. (1984). *Promises and realities for mentally retarded citizens: Life in the community.* Baltimore: University Park Press.

Williams, J.A., & Stockton, R. (1973). Black family structures and functions: An empirical examination of some suggestions made by Billingsley. *Journal of Marriage and the Family, 1,* 39–49.

Willner, S.K., & Crane, R. (1979). A parental dilemma: The child with a marginal handicap. *Social Casework, 60,* 30–35.

Winer, M.E. (1982). Parental involvement in special education decision-making: Access and alienation. *Dissertation Abstracts International, 43,* 1116A. (University Microfilms No. DA8220975)

Winton, P., & Turnbull, A.P. (1981). Parent involvement as viewed by parents of preschool handicapped children. *Topics in Early Childhood Special Education, 1*(3), 11–19.

Winton, P., Turnbull, A.P., & Blacher, J.B. (1984). *Selecting a preschool: A guide for parents of handicapped children.* Austin, TX: Pro-Ed.

Witt, J.C., Miller, C.D., McIntyre, R.M., & Smith, D. (1984). Effects of variables on parental perceptions of staffings. *Exceptional Children, 51*(1), 27–32.

Wolfensberger, W. (1970). Counseling the parents of the retarded. In A.A. Baumeister (Ed.), *Mental retardation: Appraisal, education, and rehabilitation.* Chicago: Aldine Publishing Co.

Wuerch, B.B., & Voeltz, L.M. (1982). *Longitudinal leisure skills for severely handicapped learners.* Baltimore: Paul H. Brookes Publishing Co.

Y

Yockey, K. (1983). Facing the inquisition. In T. Dougan, L. Isbell, & P. Vyas (Eds.), *We have been there* (pp. 79–86). Nashville: Abingdon Press.

Yoshida, R.K. (1979). *Developing assistance linkages for parents of handicapped children.* Washington, D.C.: Department of Health, Education, and Welfare, Bureau of Education for the Handicapped.

Yoshida, R.K. (1982). Research agenda: Finding ways to create more options for parent involvement. *Exceptional Education Quarterly, 3*(2), 74–80.

Yoshida, R.K., Fenton, K.S., Kaufman, M.J., & Maxwell, J.P. (1978). Parental involvement in the special education pupil planning process: The school's perspective. *Exceptional Children, 44*(7), 531–534.

Ysseldyke, J.E., Albozzine, B., & Mitchell, J. (1982). Special education team decision making: An analysis of current practice. *The Personnel and Guidance Journal, 60*(5), 308–313.

Ysseldyke, J. E., Thurlow, M., Graden, J., Wesson, C., Algozzine, B., & Deno, S. (1983). Generalizations from five years of research on assessment and decision making: The University of Minnesota Institute. *Exceptional Education Quarterly, 4*, 75–93.

Z

Zamarripa, S.J., & Goldstein, F. (1980). *Respite services—Temporary support for people who are mentally retarded and their families.*

Atlanta, GA: Georgia Department of Human Resources.

Zeller, R.W. (1980). Direction service: Collaboration one case at a time. In J.O. Elder & P.R. Magrab (Eds.), *Coordinating services to handicapped children* (pp. 65–91). Baltimore: Paul H. Brookes Publishing Co.

Zimmerman, W. (1982). A professional handles his child's diagnosis. *The Exceptional Parent, 12*(4), 27–29.

Ziskin, L. (1985). The story of Jennie. In H.R. Turnbull & A.P. Turnbull (Eds.), *Parents speak out: Then and now* (pp. 65–73). Columbus, OH: Charles E. Merrill Publishing Co.

Ziskin, L. (1985). Transition—From home to residential care. In H.R. Turnbull & A.P. Turnbull (Eds.), *Parents speak out: Then and now* (pp. 75–78). Columbus, OH: Charles E. Merrill Publishing Co.

Cases

A

Anderson v. Thompson, 658 F. 2d 205 (7th Cir. 1981).

Armstrong v. Klein, 476 F. Supp. 583, *aff'd in part* and *remanded sub nom.*, Battle v. Commonwealth, 629 F. 2d 269 (3d Cir. 1980), *cert. den.*, Scanlon v. Battle, 452 N.S. 968 (1981).

B

Board of Education v. Ambach, 458 N.Y.S. 2d 680 (N.Y. Sup. Ct., App. Div. 1982).

Board v. Rowley, 458 U.S. 176 (1982).

Brookhart v. Illinois State Board of Education, 534 F. Supp. 725 (C.D. Ill. 1982).

Brown v. D.C. Board of Education, No. 78–1646 (D. D.C. 1978).

C

Christine L. v. Milan School District, 4 EHLR 554:435 (Sup. Ct. N.Y. 1983).

Concerned Parents & Citizens for the Continuing Education at Malcolm X (P.S. 79) v. New York City Board of Education, 629 F.2d 751 (2d Cir. 1980), *cert. den.*, 449 U.S. 1078 (1981).

D

Davis v. D.C. Board of Education, 522 F. Supp. 1102, 530 F. Supp. 1209, 530 F. Supp. 1215 (D. D.C. 1982).

Dima v. Macchiavola, No. CV–80–2848 (E.D. N.Y. 1981).

Doe V. Anrig, 692 F. 2d 800 (1st Cir. 1981), *on remand*, 561 F. Supp. 121 (D. Mass. 1983).

F

Fallis v. Ambach, No. 82–7877 (2d Cir. 1983), 5 EHLR 555:116.

Foster v. D.C. Board of Education, 523 F. Supp. 1142 (D. D.C. 1981).

G

Georgia ARC v. McDaniel, 511 F. Supp. 1263, *aff'd.*, 716 F. 2d 1565 (11th Cir. 1983).

K

Kampmeier v. Nyquist, 553 F. 2d 296 (2d Cir. 1977).

L

Larry P. v. Riles, 343 F. Supp. 1036, *aff'd.*, 502 F. 2d 963, further proceedings, 495 F. Supp. 926, *aff'd.* 502 F. 2d 693 (9th Cir. 1984).

LeBanks v. Spears, 60 F.R.D. 135 (E.D. La. 1973).

Levine v. N.J., No. A–55 (Sup. Ct. N.J. 1980).

M

Maryland Association for Retarded Children v. Maryland, Equity No. 100/182/77676 (Cir. Ct. Baltimore Cty., May 4, 1974).

Matthews v. Campbell, Education of the Handicapped Law Report, Section 551, p. 264 (E.D. Va. 1979).

Miener v. State of Missouri, 673 F. 2d 969 (8th Cir. 1982).

Mills v. D.C. Board of Education, 348 F. Supp. 866 (D. D.C. 1972).

P

PASE v. Hannon, 506 F. Supp. 831 (N.D. Ill. 1980).

Pennsylvania Association for Retarded Children v. Commonwealth of Pennsylvania, 334 F. Supp. 1257 (E.D. Pa. 1971) and 343 F. Supp. 279 (E.D. Pa. 1972).

Poole v. Plainfield Board of Education, 490 F. Supp. 948 (D. N.J. 1980).

R

Robert M. v. Benton, 634 F. 2d 1139 (8th Cir. 1980).

S

S–1 v. Turlington, 635 F. 2d 342(5th Cir. 1981), *cert. den.*, 454 U.S.1030 (1981).

Sessions v. Livingston Paris, 501 F. Supp. 251 (M.D. La. 1980).

Silvio v. Commonwealth of Pennsylvania, Comw. Ct. (Jan. 20, 1980).

Smith v. Cumberland School Committee, No. 76–510 (D. R.I. 1979).

T

Tatro v. State of Texas, 104 S. Ct. 3371, 82 L. Ed. 2d 664 (1984).

W

William S. v. Gill, No. 81–C–3045 (D. Mass. 1982).

Index

Ann P. Turnbull is professor of special education and acting associate director of the Bureau of Child Research at the University of Kansas at Lawrence. She received her Ed.D. from the University of Alabama, her M.Ed. from Auburn University, and her B.S.Ed. from the University of Georgia.

Dr. Turnbull is the author of numerous books and articles on the subject of disabilities, with a special focus on families, the integration of people with disabilities into the mainstream of school and community life, and the individualization of their education. Recently she has co-edited *Parents Speak Out: Then and Now,* and has co-authored *Developing and Implementing Individualized Education Programs, Mainstreaming Handicapped Students: A Guide for the Classroom Teacher,* and *Selecting a Preschool: A Guide for Parents with Handicapped Children.*

Dr. Turnbull is a former Vice President of the American Association on Mental Deficiency. She has received awards for outstanding teaching from the North Carolina Association for Retarded Citizens and the University of Kansas, and together with her husband, H. Rutherford Turnbull, III, she received the 1982 "Educator of the Year" award from the Association for Retarded Citizens-United States. Her son, Jay, is mentally retarded.

H. Rutherford Turnbull, III, is professor of special education and law and senior research associate of the Bureau of Child Research at the University of Kansas at Lawrence. He received his Ll.M. from Harvard University, his Ll.B. from the University of Maryland, and his B.A. from Johns Hopkins.

Mr. Turnbull has published widely. He co-edited *Parents Speak Out: Then and Now,* is the author of *Free Appropriate Public Education: Law and Interpretation.* He has written books on consent, the doctrine of the least restrictive alternative, and disability-related issues of law, ethics, policy, and families. He has been legal counsel for the North Carolina legislature for disability matters and was the principal draftsman of that state's special education and limited guardianship laws. He has been an expert witness before committees of the U.S. House of Representatives and U.S. Senate and special counsel on two disability cases in the United States Supreme Court.

Mr. Turnbull is President, American Association on Mental Deficiency; former Secretary, Association for Retarded Citizens-United States; former Director, Foundation for Exceptional Children; former member of the Kansas Developmental Disabilities Planning Council; and father of Jay Turnbull, who has mental retardation.

Jean Ann Summers is acting director of the Kansas University Affiliated Facility at the University of Kansas at Lawrence. She will receive her doctorate from the University of Kansas in 1986; she received her B.G.S. from the University of Kansas.

Ms. Summers edited and also contributed to *The Right to Grow Up: An Introduction to Adults with Developmental Disabilities;* she co-authored *Living with Disability and Chronic Illness: A Decision-Making Guide for Families.* In addition, she has written a number of articles, monographs, and chapters. She serves as a member of the Kansas Developmental Disabilities Planning Council, The American Association on Mental Deficiency, committees of the American Association of University Affiliated Programs, Kansas Society for Autistic Children, The Association for Persons with Severe Handicaps, and Kansas-Paraguay Partners.

Mary Jane Brotherson is assistant professor at the University of Minnesota at Duluth. She received her Ph.D. from the University of Kansas and her B.A. from the University of Nebraska.

Dr. Brotherson is co-author of *Living with Disability and Chronic Illness: A Decision-Making Guide for Families,* and of numerous articles, chapters, monographs, and research reports on disabilities and families. Recently Dr. Brotherson has been the Project Director of a U.S. Department of Education project that helps families plan for their futures and for the futures of their children with severe disabilities. Dr. Ann P. Turnbull and Mr. H. Rutherford Turnbull, III, co-authors of this book, have been co-principal investigators of that project.

Holly Anne Benson is presently a social work intern at the Menninger Foundation in Topeka and a doctoral candidate at the University of Kansas at Lawrence. She expects to receive both the Ph.D. and M.S.W. degrees in 1986. She received both her M.Ed. and B.A. from the University of Vermont.

Ms. Benson co-authored with Ann P. Turnbull a chapter entitled "Approaching families from an individualized perspective," in R.H. Horner, L.M. Voeltz, and H.D. Fredericks, (eds.), *Education of Learners with Severe Handicaps: Exemplary Service Strategies.* She is a member of American Association on Mental Deficiency, The Association for Persons with Severe Handicaps, and Council for Exceptional Children, and has been a classroom teacher of students with severe and profound disabilities and director of a community-based residential program for people who are mentally retarded. In addition, she is a qualified social worker with special training in working with and counseling families of people who are disabled.